Miss Cranston's Omnibus

Miss Cranston's Omnibus

RECOLLECTIONS OF GLASGOW LIFE

Collected and compiled by
ANNA BLAIR

Illustrated by
Bill Taylor

LOMOND BOOKS

© Anna Blair 1985 and 1991
Illustrations © Bill Taylor 1985 and 1991
ISBN 0 947782 44 3

First published in two volumes in 1985 and 1991 by
Shepheard-Walwyn (Publishers) Ltd entitled
Tea at Miss Cranston's and *More Tea at Miss Cranston's*

This omnibus edition published 1998 by
Shepheard-Walwyn (Publishers) Ltd for
LOMOND BOOKS
36 West Shore Road
Granton, Edinburgh EH5 1QD

Typesetting by Alacrity, Banwell Castle, Weston-super-Mare
Printed and bound by Bath Press

Contents

MORE TEA AT MISS CRANSTON'S

TEA AT
MISS CRANSTON'S

Acknowledgements

To all those rememberers who are acknowledged in various chapters of this book alongside quotations from their recorded conversations, and to others who prefer to blush unseen under the *noms de memoire* selected for them, I offer grateful thanks.

I acknowledge also my debt to Bill Taylor for his delightful illustrations of the text, to Elizabeth Dewar and Edith Dykes and to H.G.A. Anderson for patient secretarial work.

A.B.   Giffnock, 1985

To all who have shared with me their recollections. But especially in memory of PATRICIA who at nineteen had not lived long enough to have a great store of memories, but who left glorious ones of herself for her friends to carry into their old age.

Introduction and Historical Note

The days of George III and Robert Burns seem astonishingly close when one hears a man of ninety-five speak with clear memory of a loved grand-father born in 1797.

There are in this book a few of such memories, but for the most part it contains personal recollections of events and life-styles from about 1890 onwards. It tells mainly of the Glasgow of the first half of the twentieth century, spiced by those older memories of one or two who are, as one eighty-eight-year-old put it, 'a kick out of the old century.'

The Glasgow of those days before the turn of the century was enjoying an industrial and social boom in a wide variety of fields. Its wealthy merchants lived in mansions on the outskirts of the city, its middle-classes in spacious stone tenement homes of several apartments and its poor, whose mass employment produced the goods for the prosperous, were herded into homes of one or two apartments without bathrooms and only the share of an outside W.C. These warrens gave children either clean, decent and virtuous backgrounds, or little chance of any worthwhile future, depending almost entirely on the smeddum, health and energy, or lack of them, in their mothers.

After the first year of the new century Queen Victoria was dead and with her a social and moral way of life which had been on its way out for fifteen years. The cheerful and indecorous prime of the Prince of Wales had had its heyday during that tailing-off and Edward was into his own declining years even by the time of his coronation. A more realistic mood was certainly abroad in Glasgow and, although theatres and music-halls were still popular there were other pre-occupations. There was a lively new interest in political matters. The Irish question was a burning issue in a city with large numbers of Irish immigrants; so too were those of Women's Suffrage and the condition of the working man and his family. There was too, the new film craze which swept Glasgow and brought over a hundred cinemas to the city. But the second decade of the century belongs, without question, to the 1914-18 War. Before it, crowds gathered outside newspaper offices to hear news of its approach. After it, a generation of girls was left to contemplate life without marriage. During the war everything was in aid of it, in spite of it, or because of it.

The armistice brought unbelievable relief and the certainty that the ordinary man, as well as his officer comrade, was now surely worth the dignity of a decent standard of living. But the euphoria was short-lived. The 1920s and 1930s brought disillusion and depression to all except a relatively small number who were able to carve out careers and establish businesses, while their ladies chatted in Glasgow's famous tea-rooms, leaving maids to tidy up for them at home. In the years between 1923 and 1938 there was never less than ten per cent of the available workforce of the city unemployed, and silence fell over the great shipyards. The day of the Red Clydesiders had arrived.

The picture was not of unrelieved gloom, even in the General Strike of 1926. The traditional humour of Glasgow may have become wry and pungent but it was never totally lost. Those were the years too of the Charleston and the Black Bottom, the Big Bands and the barely afforded ballroom-dancing lessons at the McEwans' studio.

There were social improvements too, wider suffrage, improved housing, better provision for the needy, with the children who had shivered into the 'thirties barefoot trudging out of them in decent boots or shoes. Other events marked the 'thirties, two to sadden, four to cheer. There were the launching of the 534 as the new Queen Mary, and the celebrations in 1935 to mark King George's Silver Jubilee. There was his death a year later and, after the trauma of the abdication of a King well-known and loved in Glasgow, his quiet brother's coronation. And as a final fling before the next war, the defiantly brave Empire Exhibition of 1938.

As the 'teen years of the century belong to the First War, the 1940s belong to the Second and its calls on the general energy. Employment was full and the clang of hammers heard again on the Clyde. Life on the home front was brisk and busy. This time people set about their war more soberly and better aware of what fighting men were facing, with air-raids overhead and with radio war-correspondents bringing reality into the living-room. Civilians served as Air-raid Wardens, Fire-watchers, Home Guards, and women who had been 'silver-served' a year before in Cranston's or Miss Buick's tearooms now rolled up their own sleeves to serve meals in station canteens and church halls. Indeed, perhaps the most enduring memory of war-time Glasgow to overseas visitors was the huge reputation the city enjoyed for hospitality.

The end of that war saw the beginning of great changes in Glasgow. In spite of continuing rationing and shortage, long-awaited national reforms brought dramatic improvements to the physical well-being of children in a city which had long been a health black-spot. A re-structuring of education opened doors to entirely new strata of society and threw some of the old social groupings into the melting-pot. Massive housing programmes transplanted people from decaying tenements to new homes with modern amenities, although these were often set in soulless wildernesses with none of the old 'heart' in them.

More recently there have been efforts to implant community spirit by providing centres, halls and corner shops, in what should by then have been maturing districts.

But the 'sixties and 'seventies are not really the stuff of this book. the new ways and the soaring beauty of fine bridges, road patterns and cleaned stone belong to an era which will be remembered by the elderly of the future. Besides, in spite of the great swings of mood and economic circumstance there was an underlying unity of outlook and a common acceptance of what constituted the 'right and proper' throughout the century, until the mid-'sixties when new freedoms lessened certainties, and there came to be as many views of life as people to hold them.

Many books have been written about the great men of Glasgow, magnates and merchants. This one tells not of their achievements

TEA AT MISS CRANSTON'S

but of how their night-shirts were washed, the games their children played in the street, how their labourers lived with eight children in single rooms, how their wives bathed such families in kettlesful of water in zinc tubs in front of the kitchen fire. Much of it is told in the words of those very washerwomen, those labourers, those game-playing children who splashed in the zinc tubs, all of whom have delighted in dredging back to mind the days of starched pinafores, top-hatted school-masters, young laughter in tenement closes and even the tender memories of two generations of 'lost boys'.

A long retired academic is not so dessicated if he can recall with a chuckle that ... 'if I was a good boy I got to do the mangling'.

That is what this book is about.

1

Upstairs had a Gasogene

It is nearly two hundred years since tenement Glasgow first began to rise to house the influx of country folk abandoning the quiet plod of life in clachan and hamlet, bent on finding their fortunes in the new manufactories on the banks of the Clyde. These houses supplied a want then, and have done ever since, for even in the 1980s you would be hard put to it to find a Glasgow man or woman over thirty who has never lived 'up a close' in a city tenement. Certainly, of the army of raconteurs for this book, life in so many-rooms-and-kitchen was a mystery to very few.

The house where Mr. James Shaw was born in 1895 had stood for a quarter of a century before that, and he has made his forays into a long life full of variety and interest from one or other of four tenement homes since then . . . the third generation of his family to occupy such a house.

> My grandpa used to point out to me where he'd lived near Glasgow Green, two stairs up, five houses to the landing, one room to a house. I've aye lived in tenements mysel' but no' a single-end like him.

Mr. Jim Lillie, although on the other hand long-since transplanted to the suburbs, remembers his city-centre origins too, and his playing days there.

> I lived as a wee boy up behind Sauchiehall Street, where the Rennie Macintosh Art School is now . . . played moshie there.

Whatever else has often had to be said about them, and however scunnered some of their tenants may at times have been, they were, and are, versatile houses and whether single-end or one, two, three, or more rooms-and-kitchen, they could absorb great spawns of mixed offspring.

1

The eight of us in our family lived in a room-and-kitchen till I was fourteen, and never a day passed but my mother talked about the big house we were to get some day ... maybe a three-apartment!

I The Kitchen of The Single End

The basic unit of the tenement was the Kitchen, the single-end. This 'Solo Studio' of the 19th century was one apartment, with a four-by-six foot recessed sleeping area where much of the family store of worldly goods was stuffed under the bed. The rest of the apartment served as kitchen, dining-room, parlour, playroom; and work-shop for whatever activities any of the tribe might enjoy.

There was mother, faither, mysel', Willie and the wean in our house before we flitted to the room-and-kitchen. Me an' Willie slep' on the wheelie bed you hurled out from under the big bed at night. The wean (that would be our Annie) was in a wooden crib. there was a kitchen table and just the two chairs an' a bench ... there was a dresser wi' a bunker, a press in the corner and a pulley.

Whatever of their possessions were not under the bed were arranged on and under the shelf running along above the dresser ... crockery, ashets, jelly pan, bowls, string-box and tea-caddy.

Then moving round the room, Jack Wilson's memory reached washing and cooking arrangements ...

The cold tap ... just *cold* mind ... was on the jaw-box (that's the sink). We washed at the jaw-box with water out the kettles at the fire. We'd no range, just an open fire, but wi' hobs. For lightin' we'd gas jets and mantles.

Most rememberers though, were brought up with ranges, a luxury in the 1880s but, for perhaps eighty years after that, the heart of home for generations of folk. They were simple at first with a basket-fire and side-ovens heated from the coals.

Later you got them with a water compartment that you drew your hot-water from, by a wee brass tap. And I mind our last one about 1920 had a black iron hob-top that hinged up and down from the wall alongside. That was called a lifter and it had gas burners and a grill on it and a tap-nozzle for the gas-iron.

And back now to Jack Wilson's memories of his single-end home
off Cumberland Street.

> There was no bathroom in that place mind . . . and all the families shared
> the landin' cludgey.

Few houses in the city's working heartland had inside W.C.s and
where there were, they could be primitive and quaint.

> My aunt in Monteith Row had a queer W.C. It flushed when you pulled
> up a lever from the side. Then the handle just sank when you let go.
> There was no wash-basin in that wee closet and no light.

Whether the W.C. was out on the landing or squeezed into some
small dark cubby in a tiny lobby, that, with the kitchen, was the
whole extent of the single-end.

II   The Room and Kitchen

That kitchen of the single-end, with an extra foot or two and some
additional refinements, was common to all tenement homes however many more rooms it boasted. So in the room-and-kitchen . . .

> The kitchen was still the place you really lived in.

The second apartment was the Room, and as well as being a sitting
parlour for Sunday visitors it slept the children, whatever the mix
or age-range.

> Mother and faither slept in the kitchen bed. The three of us girls slept in
> the old brass bed behind the Room door and the three boys in the recess
> bed that was in the big cupboard in that room too.

For its role as parlour, the furnishing about 1910 in most homes was
horse-hair upholstery and Spanish mahogany with maybe a good
table at the window with a chenille cover to save it from sunlight
and hullarackit children.

> I mind yon horse-hair that prickled your bottom, and that you pulled
> out the wee wiry curls from. My auntie had green velvet on hers but it
> was rough and sore, no' like a dress . . . oh aye, and we had an aspidistra
> on a green wally pedestal and veloury curtains hangin' from rings on a
> pole.

In winter at week-ends there was usually a fire lit in the tiled grate with its surround and over-mantel.

No' carved mahogany like in bigger houses, just maybe painted wood wi' a wee bit design. But we'd a brass fender and fire-irons ben the Room. Just for show right enough. It was the black ones from the kitchen that actu'lly got used.

Chairs, settee, table, cake-stand, cupboard bed, with what one lady calls their 'chiffoneer'; and maybe in a high-falutin' parlour, even a piano and stool . . . all of them sat on, or around, a square of carpet over dark-stained floorboards. And that was the Room.

III   The Two-Rooms and Kitchen

Upmarket a little, but perhaps in the same street and at an annual rent of £26.10s. in the late 'twenties, came the seemly two-room-and kitchen houses. They had virtually three apartments and room for gracious living . . . most children of such homes, where the parlour was the holy of holies, remember it best as the scene of their mother's tightly regulated 'At Homes' for her friends.

Talk about the Japanese tea ceremony, I doubt there was any more ritual about that than about afternoon tea parties at our house around 1910. Everything was re-dusted (for never a day passed but it was dusted anyway) the fire and the gasolier-jets got lit and a white lace-edged cloth got thrown over the chenille on the big table. And d'you mind épèrgnes? We'd a ruby glass one that was one of my mother's precious treasures. It went on the table wi' a sprig or two artificial flowers in it.

And there was the best china, the silver tea-pot, cream jug, bowl of sugar lumps and tongs, and perhaps even a spirit-kettle keeping water hot on that 'chiffoneer'. Where the visited and the visiting had aspirations to real refinement there would be a small tray in the lobby for the leaving of the Visiting Cards.

What I thought was real funny was the way the ladies kep' on their hats when they were at their wee bits of shortbread, or their cherry cake out the cake basket.

So such a house made it possible to entertain with a little style, with the children perhaps brought in to play a piece on the piano and, forbye the chamber-music and afternoon teas, maybe with a glass of lime-ade from the gasogene.

> D'you mind gasogenes? Upstairs had one when I was wee and I thought they must be quite rich. It was a syphon kind of thing in a wire-mesh casing and their papa made soda water in it on Sundays (though mind he was a kirk elder). Then he put in Rose's Lime or lemon juice. That was it ready and he used to say, if you were there, 'Come on and get a drink of gasogene, Hen.'

The main delight of the two-room-and-kitchen was having the bedroom ... the *separate* bedroom, with its privacy and its wee gas fire with the fire-clay pretzels, its starched bed-pawns and its substantial furniture. A woman (no, a lady now) could fair fancy herself furnishing a bedroom.

> In our mamma's bedroom there was a wash-stand with the ewer and basin, soap stands, tooth mugs and all ... everything matchin' in all-flowery china ... even the chantie in the cupboard below. She used to do a funny wee thing, mamma, she used to save any feathers that came out the pillows when she was whacking them into place with her walking stick, and she saved the feathers in the toothbrush-rack till she'd a wee bundle to put back into the pillow ticking ... very thrifty mamma was.

That wash-stand was marble with the back-splash inlaid with coloured bird tiles. There were towel-rails at the ends and a small drawer where mamma kept a little store of 'braw' soap hardening, to make it last when it was in use.

> We had a bathroom an' all mind, but when my granny or someone came to stay, they didnae have to join in the stramash for washing in the bathroom. But what I mind best about that big flowery basin was the fruit steepin' in it come July, when the jam got made.

Dorothy Laurie was born in 1899 and from the days around 1906 remembers the honey-coloured walnut of her mother's bedroom furniture, the wardrobe heavily carved and big enough to hide in, the free-standing brass bedstead.

And Mrs. Helen Stewart recalls the trim of *their* brass and lacquer bed ...

> wi' white frilly material and pawns of hand-crochet tied to wee balls along the bed-rail.

Another down-to-earth lady debunks a favourite myth of later years.

> Oh aye, bed pawns. I mind them. You hear folk say nowadays that people in olden times covered up the legs of their furniture for modesty. I never heard such blethers. Half of Glasgow had to strip and dress and maybe bath, boys *and* girls in the one room. The furniture leg-covers wasnae modesty at all. It was just they liked the frills, and forbye crochet was all the rage. My ma would've put wee dabbie-douces of crochet on anything!

IV   More Rooms-and-Kitchen

When a family reached the dizzy heights of tenancy with more than one bedroom, and roamed about in four or more apartments, anything was possible in those airy and spacious houses with their fine plaster cornices and good woodwork. There social life could really ripen. Miss Nancy Reid enjoyed her childhood in a roomy city-centre home in Chisholm Street.

> We'd a great big hall in our house, big enough for two sets of eightsome reels. What lovely parties we had in that place. I lived there until I was married.

Such lobbies are still unbelievably big, certainly to those who live now in 'little boxes made of ticky-tacky'. One young mother recently measured her tenement flat hallway for floor covering and took her gizinties to a carpet store. The salesman shook his head.

> Away home Hen, you've mishured wrong, that's twice the size of my lounge!

By the time you were into this rent-bracket, zinc baths in the kitchen had been left far behind. The name 'bathroom' seems to have had status enough, for in the early days they were scarcely the havens of steam, hot towels and perfume of even thirty years later. Mrs. May Milree was fascinated by one she knew as a child in the 'nineties.

> I had four maiden aunts who lived near Abbotsford Place. The whole

house was pretty old-fashioned and gloomy (though Abbotsford Place was a good address then). But it's the bathroom I mind ... oh my, that bathroom! It was just a black dark cell-place with no light, no gas, no nothing to brighten it except by a wee grille-thing from the close-wall outside. No wash-basin, just a W.C. and a queer old bath, half built into the wall ... just a cold tap and a plug. You'd to carry the water in jugs from the kitchen and you'd to take a candle in with you!

And toast yourself off its flame, after the bath, perhaps.

So from one apartment to seven or eight $\overline{and}$ lobby, that has been the stone, mortar and remembered furbishing of tenement Glasgow for the greater part of a hundred years.

V   The Outdwellers

Not all good folk who brushed out closes, lit wash-house fires and ran down to back-greens with baikies of ashes spent their entire lives in tenement communities. Some came in to them from other kinds of house, and some went out from them, when the new suburban semis began to barnacle the countryside round Glasgow between the wars, and from the later 'fifties. Maggie Anderson was one who lived her young life in one of the city's outskirt villages.

It was right country in Uddingston then. We had a grand garden wi' chrysanthemums and wi' roses growin' up the wall. And we'd a kind of ramblin' fruit orchard for gooseberries and blackcurrants, plums ... aye and strawberries ... and there was an apple-tree by the kitchen door. My mother made a lot of preserves and jam.

I left all that when I got wed to Davie and came to live in a tenement. My, some change! But it was my own wee place and I loved it ... and I knew I was well off by some, at having an outside toilet that was *ours alone*.

And from six miles to the south side of the river another bride left a country girlhood:

My wife's family lived in a white but'n'ben cottage at the Mearns. There was other low white-washed houses there and milk floats came in from the farms to the Mearns Cross. Now it's a big-big shopping-centre and a garage out there.

These came new to tenement life and liked it well enough, but others, to whom it was old, left with little regret.

> When we had our room-and-kitchen it was aye a pipe-dream that we were to get a big house some day . . . maybe a *two* room-and-kitchen. Pie in the sky! When it actually happened we couldnae credit it!

When the day of the move came, young Nellie Edgar, fourteen at the time, went off to her work at the weaving-mill from the old house in Wodrow Street . . .

> My mother didnae let any of us see the new Corporation house at the Wellmeadow until the day of the flitting. It was her big *thing*, so's that when we came home that night from the mill or the school, it was to the new place . . . seeing it for the first time. Well see! I walked in that door and there on the floor were beautiful Congoleum squares . . . pink in the girls' room . . . the *girls'* room! And kind of blue for the boys' room. Printed waxcloth it would be without a border, just a square laid in the middle, the way you'd a carpet later-on.
>
> And of all wonderful things, a *wooden* bed, after years in an old brass thing!

(Ah Nellie! The world would beat a path now to Wodrow Street for that scorned 'brass thing'.)

> . . . and forbye the wooden bed there was a dressing-table and a wardrobe wi' a mirror and a *lovely* new bedspread. My parents' room was the parlour too, so they had their bed in it and a three-piece-suite. Forbye *that* we'd a real living-room, separate from the kitchen, and a bathroom. No more tin tubs. And there was the garden.

So some moved in and some moved out. But some remained faithful and, when they flitted, just moved from close to close round their own hub. James McClelland was one of the aptly-cried 'flitters'.

> I lived in seven houses, all in Bridgeton, between 1918 and 1939. We were aye on the move, sometimes to better houses, sometimes not so good, depending on how we were doing at the time. Mother loved flittin' and she had it down to a fine art. We were in Silvergrove Street, two houses in Muslin Street and four in Greenhead Street. I doubt she would've stopped at that but the war came and she couldnae very well change after that. I mind the landlady arranging about that last house.
> 'I'll put in hot water and maybe make a bathroom in the attic, and put

in the electric an' all, if you'll take it,' says-she. It was £26.10s. the year, the rent there, in 1938.

By two years later there wasn't a *To Let* board to be seen for an unfurnished house in Glasgow, nor has there been since.

Of all the rememberers past their thirties, only two sisters are still part of that tenement world. The rest are surrounded by gardens or landscaped estates.

But the tenements are not empty, for their children and grandchildren have flocked back to redd them up and make their own first homes there ... all part of the tide of Glasgow folk that ebbs and flows to and from the tenements that have always been the city's heart.

2
Daisies Round My Hat

The photographer of the 1880s swoops under his dark velvet cloth and snaps his fingers at the family group. Breaths are held and, as the cliché says, a moment in time is captured for ever, and with it an array of that era's fashion from infants' to grandparents'. Repeat the process every decade and you have a century of change from bonnet to Princess of Wales' feather, button boot to pink sneaker. Well ... You'd have the gamut right enough, as far as the bien-provided were concerned, but for much of that hundred years there was a broad swathe of Glasgow folk a world away from wool and velvet and starched pinafores.

> I was reared up in Eglinton Street in the 'twenties and it was hard-goin' to get claddin' for the five of us weans. Ma went round the toff houses wi' her bundle and if you were lucky she maybe got a pair of boots your size. Other than that, it was barefoot until you got a pair off the parish.

And another glimpse of garb that was a far cry from fancy pin-tucks or feather boas ...

> I mind my mother goin' her shoppin' wi' the wean in her shawl (there was aye a wean) and I mind the way she swep' the end of the shawl round the baby and tucked it in ... She never wore a man's bunnet the way some did, all the same.

So for sure, you didn't run barefoot in Eglinton Street or carry your wean in a shawl and then find yourself in a photographic studio all doodied up for a family group. And for the eighty-year span of our direct recollections here, there are brought to mind not only the changes in family fashion, where clothes were bought new or made-up from materials fresh-scissored from the bolt, but also the make-dos and hand-me-downs that came home in the old-clo'es

11

wife's bundle. To march them all past for inspection would take a
volume in itself and so a chapter can do no more than flicker
through the memories and frame some of the most vivid. In this one
it will be enough to glance at children's clothing.

The very earliest picture then is second-hand, and certainly not
one captured by the camera. It comes through the diary of Mr.
Walter Freer and by word of mouth from him to his grandson.

> When I was a lad going to work at eleven-year-old in the 1860s I had one
> patched suit and one shirt to wash out at night for the next day, and I
> had to mend my own boots with scraps of leather found at a cobbler's
> workshop.

The earliest first-hand memories are those of Maggie Anderson's
childhood days around 1892.

> I went to school in Uddingston and I mind my button-hookin' boots
> and a wee dress down to my ankles. You wore a white pinafore wi' frills
> . . . a peenie you ken . . . you'd always a peenie. And I had a cloth tammy
> wi' a button-up coat. Then of course you were right dressed up on the
> Sunday. 'Every day braw, Sunday a-daw' my mother used to say.

Mrs. May Milree has wistful memories of her pinnies too.

> I used to watch my friend Mary Aitken playin' peever in her lovely
> pinafores and wonder how it was that hers were all crisp and stiff
> compared to mine. Then I found out her father had a laundry.

But the lady who had been little May, of the limp and second-rate
pinnies, did not say whether the beauty of Mary Aitken's pinafores
came from constant laundering or maybe from getting the choice of
the best that came in for treatment.

The button boots of Maggie Anderson's schooldays were not
confined to the pavements of Uddingston and her namesake Mrs.
Cathie Anderson has a recollection of hers that still draws an 'ouch'
in the telling.

> I've still got my button-hook I had when I was a girl, and I can feel yon
> wee tweaky feeling yet, when you nipped your leg getting hold of the
> button.

But, better than the outer garments, others remember the simmits
and chemises that went under the wincey-frocks and peenies. And

the next-to-skin garb most universally loathed was undoubtedly combinations. Miss Nancy Wall speaks for generations of the tormented, buttoned into combies,

> I *hated* them ... all tight and sore between your legs.

And hated they were, for forty years before and after that. But they were only the first of the several layers deemed essential to hap the kidneys and loins.

> We wore drawers ... just the two legs joined with no middle bit and tied at the waist ... then top of that umpteen petti's ... a red flannel one first, with maybe a wee tate black embroidery to it. Then a plain one like-enough, and a red-and-white striped one over that. Then we'd bodices with bones in them to support our wee bosoms. Mother thought we'd go to seed without these corset things.

Cathie McMillan confirms that fellow-sufferer's testimony, and still shudders at an imposition she and her sisters had to bear.

> Mother made us knitted petticoats that we called the *nightmares*. She was great on keeping us warm and she didn't care tuppence that we looked all bumfly in them.

A uni-sex outfit of the early century and before, was the sailor-suit in varying degrees of chic. Around 1905 or 6 most girls had those or kilted fisher-wife costumes, but the boys were thirled to the fashion for over twenty years. Two school-class photographs, fourteen years apart, show eight of sixteen boys in one, and twelve of seventeen boys in the other, wearing sailor-suits in one form or another, and the unworthy thought occurs that the boys were arranged for the photo by Miss Whatever, so that the lower halves of the suits in cheap and wrinkled cotton 'stuff' were hidden by the shoulders of well-put-on wee lads in decent sturdy wool with polished boots and braw-knit stockings. There were accessories too.

> I had a whistle on a cord wi' my first sailor suit, and once, when I was a wee soul, I blew it out loud in the kirk. I got a skelpit leatherin' for that *and* they took the pea out my birll!

Older boys at posh schools in the city favoured the sailing theme too in the summer months, and wore high-buttoning blazers and panama boaters with school hat-bands. But three miles from such academies, in the old 'country' borough of Pollokshaws, the rugged little Willie Stevenson might have spurned the sailor-suit or boater-and-blazer outfits as 'cissy'.

When I went to the school in 1902 I mind of wearin' wide trousers down over my knees, and stockin's ... and you'd yer jaicket. No school cap nor nothing ... just a big bunnet wi' a button.

Sundays went on being 'a-daw' well into the middle of this century and never-a-one of the rememberers but drew a sigh at the recollection of Sunday bests.

We always had on Sabbath clothes and when I was fourteen I got a nice fur set to go with my mixed-tweed coat ... a fur pull-through tie, a muff and a little fur hat with red cherries. I boasted to all my friends in the Bible Class that I had all this new for the next Sabbath, and when I came down that Sunday morning in my squirrels Pa was sitting at one side of the fire and Ma the other. I bounced in, 'My, aren't the girls all just going to be jealous of me!'

Pa looked at me. 'If that's the way of it just you get back up the stairs and change into what you wore last week and see if the girls are jealous of that'.

And the black-burning shame of turning up at the church hall without the new braws is as sore after eighty years as it was that Sunday morning.

They certainly had their specials for Sunday, and Cathie Mc-Millan's 'specials' were hats.

Mother was a wee bit hatty and she got the milliner in Clarkston Road to line our straw hats with pink silk, and put daisies round them. We all sat in a row in the church. Ten of us in the pew, the girls all with our nice hats ... me and Isa and Anne and Minnie. They would all be lovely, but it's my own I mind the best. Isa was pretty. She had wee round rosy cheeks and I used to think it would be lovely to look like Isa. We'd Sunday coats too, but I loved those hats.

All through Edwardian days and beyond, older boys wore Norfolk jackets and knicker-bockers, and untidy teenage slouching was discouraged by stiff collars. The 'big-big wide collars, near out to your shoulders' were common to most quarters in the city, but the west-end lads wore them also over the cut-away silver-buttoned jackets they had with their kilts. And, even without either Eton-collar or kilt, Willie, the lad of the 'big bunnet wi' the button' has to admit,

Oh aye, we were a'-dressed up for the Sabbath ... smart turned-out to go to McAlpine's kirk.

But whether from villa or single-end the boys all had one style in common.

Wir hair was cut to the knuckle.

It was often cropped by fathers, along a line made by the rim of a bowl held with the back of the head firmly into it, although boys from families with money to burn, went to have theirs done professionally.

I remember when I got my hair cut for a penny. I used to get a balloon from the barber in Nithsdale Road.

The boys' clothes, buffed of their Sunday newness, did further service at school, until wrists dangled out of sleeves and suits were passed down the tribal line. But few girls recall turning out on weekdays in the faded glory of Sunday bests.

> They were too fancy for school wi' their cape-shoulders and velvet collars. They just got passed on to your wee sister for the kirk and then when there was no more wee sisters they went to the old-clo'es wife.

May Gilmour agrees,

> No, no, never your Sunday things through the week. I remember summer Sundays the best. There was a terrible lot of gingham dresses and straw hats with flowers when I was young.

There were infant fashions too before the First War, and those babies who boasted nannies in dark dresses, stiff collars and cuffs, sat in high wicker prams like tiny rosebuds, in frothing crumples of lace trimming bonnet, pillow and pram covers. And while the rosebud baby's next-up brother, aged about three or four, was photographed gazing into a goldfish bowl, long hair curling about his neck and shoulders and wearing a white cotton dress with lace inserts, white socks and boots, his small contemporary on innercity streets was toddling barefoot alongside his shawlie mother.

Throughout these years of Eton collars and flower-decked hats the cotton pinny had had a long innings but by the early teenyears of the century it was changing. It wasn't quite out yet though.

> I mind of wearing a nice white peenie wi' a square flap. My mother was awful fond of the crochet and my peenies had nice wee crochet bibs on them.

But it was becoming more of a main garment, first as a pinafore dress and then later as the most enduring garment of the century. The full flowering of the slip-over they wore with jersey or blouse, came when the day of the *gym tunic* dawned. Among the rememberers, the first to mention that ubiquitous and perhaps eternal garment was one who, as young Cathie McMillan, tholed a home-made green one in 1912 when all her classmates were in navy blue.

> My mother made it, so I just kept quiet and suffered it.

May Reid had a tunic at the Big school in 1916, and the Edgar girls

had them around 1919. Nellie Edgar had a vision of their top to toe
silhouettes in not only the gym slips themselves.

> We had hand-knit stockings with our gyms. Mother knitted them for
> the three of us girls. She'd her own pattern eight rows plain ... one row
> purl. That made an inch y'see. She just did so-many patterns for Nellie,
> so-many for Maggie, so-many for Bessie. Didnae need to stop talking to
> look ... just felt the ridges.

The century climbed on into the 'twenties, 'forties, 'sixties and
'seventies and on marched the gym tunic with it. Surely not a
schoolgirl from 1910 to the present day has survived girlhood
without one. Let a 1970s school-leaver have the last word on gyms.

> The one I got when I was in Primary I, did me all my schooldays to
> Secondary IV. It must've been down to my knees when I was five and
> well up my bahoochie and straining at the shoulder buttons when I was
> fifteen.

An investment was that gym.

Other fashions came and went for your average bien wee citizen
during those post-war years.

> Boys in my class were into wee navy jerseys ... genzies we called them ...
> all rough and jaggy wi' collars and no ties, sometimes a wee loop and
> butt'n. You wore them over wide home-made breeks that the wind
> go'ed skimmin' up come the winter. The toffs in the class didnae wear
> genzies mind.

There was no whinge in the tone of that 'home made'. But not
everyone was quite so jokoh about having their seams run up on the
Singer by a less than skeely mother.

> Mother made my clothes till I was well up ... Did I like that? No indeed
> I did not. I used to wonder to myself, 'May, are you *never* to get any-
> thing *bought*?

It wasn't only their clothes that delighted and tormented the
embryo ladies of pre-1914-18 days. Their hair gave them hours of
urgent consideration and care and, where the boys were uniformly
short-backed and sided, the girls were pig-tailed and ringletted, or
even almost clothed in flowing cascades of hair that reached their
bottoms. All of them ... Muriel Wotherspoon was sure, except
herself.

I had thin hair, just in wee straggly skinny pigtails, with ribbons on the ends that kept getting lost. The girl in the pew in front of me at the church made me angry at the way she could toss her thick pleats over her shoulders, and when they came flying back, I used to clamp the ends into my hymn book. Anyway, once that girl let out a yell when she stood up for the hymn and I just didn't know where to put myself . . . my mother knew where to put me though.

And the hats that topped or framed the glory of rag-curls or bunches are well-remembered too . . . not so much the woolly pull-ons for school but the Sunday-best as recalled in the Edgar family.

We had our good Sunday hats, the three of us girls. Just shapes they were, really, that did us for years. Say about June, mother used to take off the velvet band that was for the winter and do them round and round wi' flat silky kind of straw, in and out the brim. Then wi' wee bunches of red cherries or purple grapes and a bit ribbon, that was your braw summer hat for the Secession kirk on a Sunday.

By the 'twenties and 'thirties a kind of blight descends on children's clothes. They may have been more sensible, easier to live in and launder, but they were certainly less memorable, although there are some visions. Babies' clothes were less frilled and goffered by then . . . infants were, rather, cosy bundles of chilprufe and wool.

I mind when our twins, Gracie and Em, were wee, my granda' used to call them Tweedle-dum and Tweedle-dee. Just like clootie dumplings they were, in their woolly coats and pantaloons.

Older children too had cast most of the suffocating layers and flounces of twenty years before, and remember simpler garb.

Skirts were that short that my granny used to tut-tut at seeing wir knees. She'd've been right past hersel' if she'd seen us wi' wir frocks tucked into wir knickers turning wir wilkies in the school sheds.

Underneath that short skirt or gym, girls in the 'thirties were still struggling to peel off the last vestiges of what thirty-odd years before, had been the wee McMillan nightmares.

You had them liberty-bodices, all cotton and fleece and wi' buttons at the hems to hold buttonin'-on suspenders for your long wrinkly stockings . . . though what was 'liberty' about yon I cannae think.

Although the good coats, the liberty bodices and even the

scratchy genzies eventually found their darned and well-worn way
to needier homes, there were still children who not only never had
anything new themselves, but who fell through even the net
provided by decent hand-me-downs. Their plight was met by the
Parish.

When I was teaching around 1933 it was the time of the slump, and
Glasgow was really hit. Lots of the weans were very scanty-clad and off
the school many a day, while the clothes they had were being washed or
maybe pawned. A lot got free clothing but they stood out like sore
thumbs. I just don't know where the Corporation got the shoddy trash
they gave these bairns for clothing ... I just don't. For a time they
would be in green issue and later a kind of gingery yellow. Awful. Rough
and cheap ... The teacher got a flimsy saying 'So-and-so's got one pair
knickers, one dress, one pair boots' and you were s'posed to keep an eye
open to see them being worn. If not ... 'Where's that *beautiful* dress
you got from the school-board?' I had to ask.
    Sometimes it wasnae at the pawn ... 'My ma biled it and now it'll no'
go on me.'

But there was a change brewing; imagination and good sense
were brought to bear and within ten years you couldn't tell a
Corporation-dressed child from any other.
    Simplicity, practicality and the need for plenty of garments for
frequent changing, are the modern principles for children's clothing. Very sensible. But clothes are not cherished as they were, nor
are the memories of them. Certainly not as they were in the Edgars'
home in the 'twenties when economics dictated attitudes. And
perhaps the most vivid picture of all, of the way decent Glasgow
parents turned their children out, on wages like eighteen shillings a
week, is this memory of young Nellie Edgar's.

We didnae have a wardrobe. In the first place the house was too wee,
and then wardrobes were dear things. But there was a big kist in the
corner of the lobby and it had wee flap-lid compartments at the sides,
for faither's bowler and the rest of us' hats. On a Sunday night, after
wearing our braw clo'es, the lid got lifted and faither's suit went down
first, then mother's clo'es, then Willie's and Jim's, then Maggie's,
Nellie's, Bessie's, then George's ... and all the Bibles. In went the moth-
balls and the lot lay there till the next Sunday morning when we all lined
up in our undies to get out our braws for the Kirk. The boys and girls all

got dressed together in the one room and nob'dy thought a thing about it.

After the Sunday School our good shoes got taken from us, all brushed, and polished wi' velvet, then they were put up on a shelf above the lobby door. We'd no slippers, so for the rest of the Sunday evening you wore your school shoes.

Mind that next time you're rummaging in your whole wall of built-in wardrobes for something to wear!

3

No Hoovers nor Nothing

Our maids dusted and polished, cleaned brasses and silver, did mountains of dishwashing, black-leaded grates, answered the door, sat in with the children, attended the family at table when my ma tinkled her wee handbell and generally kept the home-fires burning ...

and they were paid wages varying from eight shillings a month at first mention in 1895, to twenty-five shillings in the early 'thirties, and a breath-catching three-pound fortune in 1939. And forbye that, they were to be grateful for their *keep*.

Some maids were large cogs in the wheels of household management, some small, but whatever part they played their job was either to keep mansion or villa running smoothly in Pollokshields or Milngavie, or to maintain the good ordering of three-storey-and-basement town houses in the likes of Clairmont Terrace. They were paid to bring an atmosphere of calm-sough to the homes of the busy merchant and professional men who kept the city humming. The daughter of one such house remembers.

> Our maids used to come from Islay or other places up north. We usually had a cook, a table and parlour-maid, and a woman to do the rough work ...

and one of the cogs has *her* say of a maid's life in 1928:

> I was put out to service wi' the Honourable Charles Smithson, and I worked as a kitchen-maid wi' them in the town and then at their country place down Dumfries way. I got twenty-two pound a year for that, an' it was drudgery. I got to see Dumfries just the once, all the time I was there.

Other maids were just wee lassies-of-all-work in two-room-and-kitchen tenement houses where there were delusions of grandeur. They changed their garb between morning and afternoon to match the different jobs done by various 'grades' of girl in more pretentious establishments.

> It was a two-room-and-kitchen tenement we lived in — you didnae call them flats then. There were my parents and us three children. I think my mother had big ideas because we had a maid even in that wee house. She wore a blue wrapper-thing, white cap and apron in the morning and maybe a thibbet pinny for the dirty work. Then she was all done-up in the afternoons in her black and whites ... very trim, wi' long streamers dangling from her cap and pinny. That was for opening the door and serving up the tea. She took the baby out too, but-here, the joke was that she'd him in a shawl instead of a pram and that took the tone down a peg or two. So she was a poor folks' nanny as well's everything else. She slept in the kitchen bed recess.

The maids themselves needed no lessons in sorting out the caste of their mistresses.

> Aye, there were the toffs in the fancy houses and the wee folk wi' big notions of theirsel's in tenements.

But between the two extremes were the modest households in the spreading suburbs. Says Lily Timlin...

> By my time in the 'thirties, it was mostly just ordinary nice houses wi' gardens and wi' nice-enough women to work to. You just helped wi' everything, cleanin' and makin' beds and maybe switching the carpets wi' damp tea-leaves. No hoovers nor nothin' then.

These were the middle years of remembered service, but it's not so long since one old survivor of Victorian times used to tell his daughter of his sister's working days as a housemaid.

> He used to talk about her being in service in the 1880s. Once she went on holiday with the family to work in the house they took. It was hard work and after it, her mistress gave her a whole shilling and the week-end off. What a treat!
> 'It was Hallowe'en,' he used to say, 'and I'll never forget the excitement of her coming home and bringing sweets and an apple for every last one of us. It was luxury I can tell you.'

And another glimpse of life from under-stairs.

> It was a big house and I was the kitchen-maid. The housemaids did the rest of the house, and the parlour-maid attended to the family. I helped the cook, swep' the kitchen, washed the black pots wi' scourers, and the copper ones wi' vinegar and salt. I done the dishes wi' washin' sody. Oh and my hands got that raw! I was just a skivvy. Come to think on it, I'm seventy now and I'm still a skivvy. I've aye been that.

and she laughs without malice or resentment.

> The thing I got to do that I liked best was sittin' at the big fire making toast for us in the kitchen. Another time I mind of at that place, was me havin' a nice pair of patent shoes that I saved for, and that were kind of precious to me, and I had them on once when the Honourable Madam sent for me. And did I get lalldy for not having on my right strap-and-button shoes to come into that parlour? I was made to go away and change out them into yon other things.

But there was often an affectionate and long-lasting relationship forged between family and help, that had nothing to do with being set apart, 'them and us'.

> Other people had cooks and kitchen maids. We had Nana. Nana came to us about 1899 when she was fifteen to wheel out my brother James in his pram.

And Nana flits into the speaker's memory at every stage of her life.

> I remember Nana standing ironing all that broderie anglaise with flat
> irons, and all those frills with the goffering iron.
>   Nana used to come with us on holiday to Maidens, just to help with
> the family.
>   There were five of us children, always one being wheeled in the pram.
> Nana seemed to push that pram for years and years.
>   My mother and father died within a short time of each other when we
> were still young girls and Nana just came with us when we moved into a
> flat.

Nana had come to the Wotherspoons in 1899 and, still part of the
family, died in the 1970s, at the home of one of the boys she had
come to wheel out in the big wicker pram around Maxwell Park so
long ago.

Couples who found romance in service at large establishments
and had spent years jointly absorbing gentry customs, often
brought a distinctive style to their own home-lives. Miss Marie
Condie looks back,

> I had this aunt and uncle, she'd been the cook in a big house and she'd
> married the butler ... my Uncle Bill, that was. At Christmas-time
> around 1906 and 1907 all the family used to go to their place in
> Uddingston and I mind the spit over their fire turnin' slowly wi' a bit
> roast or a fowl on it. It was great! Then the gas-lights would go down to
> a wee peep, the door used to open and Uncle Bill walk in wi' a big flamin'
> pudding and the wee sprig of holly on the top.

But the niceties of life in douce homes, with worthy Glasgow
matrons training up maids to be quiet-spoken and lady-like, sometimes had less seemly secrets. And about 1910 a group of alert
citizens began to be aware of one of the hazards of being a young
woman in service in Glasgow ... a young woman who, however
cherished a daughter on a Highland croft or in a mining village
somewhere, could be anonymous and unprotected in the city. They
heard clash of things that went on hidlin's under the attic roofs of
west-end houses.

> You aye got wee-wee attic rooms. But if you came off a big family,
> sharing your kitchen bed wi' maybe three sisters, you thought you were
> in heaven up there wi' a room and a bed to yoursel', three or four empty
> drawers and hooks for your clothes. It was quiet and private.

But Mrs Purvis, now of Eastwoodhill House who joined the
Vigilance Committee set up in 1910 to protect these attic-dwellers,
tells just how 'private' their rooms often were.

> It was quite a thing for the sons of some families to slip up the wee
> narrow stair. The girls would tell us that if these boys didn't get their
> way they would threaten to tell their mistresses that it was the girls
> made the advances. If they held out, the next thing would be they were
> out on the street, no pay, no reference, no ticket home.

And Mrs. Nell Brodie remembers the set-up well.

> There you were, out the door, wi' your wee buckled trunk nowhere to
> go.

The 'where' they often found was, according to Mrs Purvis,
literally the street. With no way at first of getting home, some were
drawn willy-nilly into prostitution and later, when they had their
takings, too ashamed to face the family, or perhaps afraid that their
new-found wealth would dry up when it was found out at home
where it was coming from.

> The Vigilance people took a house in Glasgow and got someone at the
> Church offices in Edinburgh to contact ministers asking them to send
> word to the committee when girls were coming to service in Glasgow.
> Then they helped them to get decent places and set up a centre where
> they could come for help if they needed it.

Not all the girls felt the need of the Vigilance, and one who could
apparently wither a would-be seducer without help remembers . . .

> One or two places I had, when I was young and maybe quite bonnie,
> where the young gent would try you on. As often's not they were just
> wee nyaffs or big gomerils you wouldnae've looked at twice. So you just
> laughed at them and called them 'sonny', but you were best to leave if
> you could, for you couldnae very well tell.

The maids were as great a mixture of personality as the families.
Some were timid and easily brow-beaten, but others were not so
mealy-mouthed in the face of insult. Certainly not by 1928.

> Once when I was gettin' checked for no' doin' behind a sideboard the
> mistress says to me, quite nippy, 'You'd shift that furniture if you'd
> seen a two shill'ny bit there to put in your pocket . . .' Well see! I just
> went to the kitchen-hook, put on my hat and coat and marched out. I

was that angry. But she came to my house after, and put me up from
nine-shillin' a week to ten, just to get me back ...didnae make much
difference to me mind. I only got to keep one-and-six anyway, and my
granny got the rest. It was the principle but.

Even where a maid might be too mim to protest at a rebuke like
that, there were ways for a girl to bide her time and take an
unsuspected revenge ...unsuspected at least, by her mistress.

We had a maid called Effie when I was about twelve. Once when my
parents were away for a week-end and just me and my brother at home I
saw her goin' out to meet her young man and she was wearing a dress of
my mother's. I remember it, clear as clear, a sort of cherry red. My
mother was quite sonsy and the dress was kind of tight on her, and not
very nice. But it was just the very thing on Effie. I looked to see if it was
back in the press the next morning and so it was. I never told my mother
because I thought, well, if it was who it looked right on, the dress was
really Effie's.

Sometimes though, a mistress's clothes became legitimate perks.

One of my ladies wore lovely clothes. I wasnae far off the same size so I
often got a dress or coat off her. So here was me on my afternoon off
trottin' away up the town for high tea wi' a fella, in my Jaeger or my
pricey wee number out Macdonald's.

That maid had obviously another perk in the freedom she enjoyed
on her day out, but there were also mistresses who thought it quite
legitimate to control their girls' off-duty pursuits. Some have the
grace in hindsight to look back at their own effrontery.

In our district in Whitecraigs there was a maids' club in one of the
churches. I didn't encourage our Mollie to go at all. I thought they
would just sit there and drink tea, talk about their ladies, maybe
compare wages and days off and the work they had to do. I thought they
might get ideas. Come to think on it now though, we all sat over our
afternoon teas and discussed the maids and their shortcomings at great
length ... we had a nerve really, sure we had?

Not all the girls came from hungry or bleak backgrounds. One
recalled by Mrs. Margaret Fotheringham came from a river-fishing
family where certain items that were daily diet would have been a
treat to many city employers.

Her home was up in Perthshire somewhere on the Tay, and when she came for an interview my mother asked if she had any food fads, (fikey eaters were a nuisance in busy households.) 'I'm not used to have to take salmon more'n twice in the week.'

In that fad she was no doubt easily accommodated. At least at the outset of her employment that lass did not seem to grovel for her 'place' and there were others who had good enough conceit of themselves not to be trampled on once they were part of the household. Indeed some maids were quite awesome ot the children of homes where they worked.

We sometimes went to the pictures with Sadie our maid. She knew all the film stars, Tyrone Power, Douglas Fairbanks, Bing Crosby. Once she was sent to take me to see Shirley Temple at the pictures. That was at The Waverley Picture House. But at The Elephant just along the street Robert Taylor was showing in 'Camille'. We went to see 'Camille' and Sadie promised me a clout on the lug if I *told*. I didn'nt know what a clout on the lug was, but I had a fair idea. I wouldn't have dared tell my mother anyway about seeing 'Camille', because there was kissing in it.

Free visits to the pictures, Jaeger clothes, private rooms, pleasant women to work for . . . easy to understand long years of service and goodwill there. But ungallant sons, suspicious mistresses, treatment as skivvies, why did they thole those?

I remember our minister getting wind of the bad way some women treated their girls, and him giving them a right good telling-off in a sermon . . . reminded them that their maids were human beings, young girls with feelings and rights of their own.

Maybe they tholed conditions that none would tolerate now, because the alternatives were worse. Being in service in the twenties and thirties was a way of life for the daughters of families in country villages, and in mining areas where wasting diseases were rife. A place in a decent house with a clean warm bed and good food meant not only gain for the girl but, at home, one mouth less and one stretch of bed more. To be a little drudge was a small price to pay for a healthy settling, and peace of mind for hard-pressed parents. One mistress remembers,

Our maid Nettie had three sisters and a brother died of T.B. in the five years she was with us in the thirties.

And young Violet Baker had surely no wish to go back east to the Children's Home where they were trained for domestic service and sent out in the snell days of winter to the shore at Musselburgh to gather sea-coal for stoking the Home's fires, in the teeth of a wind searing in from the Forth.

By the thirties, time was running out for the 'general' who had been such an institution in small households for generations. But if the girls who fetched and carried for the nippy and the nice, the careful and the thowless among mistresses, ever despaired that they were faceless nonentities at their work-places, they might be surprised to know how well-remembered they are, and with what affection and laughter.

There was Mary Ferguson, who smashed everything smashable, but could heeshie-baw the girniest wean; and Bridie Ryan who kissed her boy-friends good-night in full view of the children at their bedroom window; Ruby Tate who liked a wee sherry from the sideboard while setting the dining-room table and was indulged in her 'secret' sin because she was a rare hand with a girdle scone. And there was Wee Lizzie, bow-hurdied and Methody, who ruled the household absolutely on the matter of Sabbath observance. Not even knitting for the soldiers was tolerated, and any such war-work had to be stuffed under the Gardner family cushions when she came ben the room to set 'your teas'.

Lissie had lingered as maid into the war years, one of the very few left. For by the early days of October 1939 the rest were swept away, as if by landslide. They were in factories and the services, on buses or on the land and, for the time being at least, thought they had found El Dorado.

And their mistresses?

I visited a cousin once, who still had a maid long after anyone else, and I found I had forgotten this gracious living; if that's what you call it to have some other woman whisk away your own dirty dishes from under your nose and remove such mundane things from your very consciousness. I decided I didn't miss it a bit.

4

A Penny-Farden for a One Inch Link

At its peak Glasgow was a city of a million people and, since many of them went to their mort-kists before old age or retirement, it followed that, except during periods of serious recession and in spite of all but the poorest women being firmly thirled to scrubbing board and soup-pot or paying afternoon calls, that population went out to a vast range of occupations ... far too many to do much more in a chapter than passingly bring to mind a few of them.

Some of the earliest handed-down recollections belong to young Maggie Anderson's childhood in the 1890s and are of her great-grandfather, born about 1780.

> Fine I knew my great-grandfather, for he lived wi' my granny. Him and my grandpa were estate workers to the Earl of Home at The Hirsel, but then the Homes took over the Bothwell Estate ... early last century that would be, and they both came there to work and took houses just outside of Glasgow. That's where I was reared up.

They were estate-men, that father and son, but most of the childhood memories about grandfathers and great-grandfathers which stretch back into last century are, perhaps not surprisingly, concerned with the basic provisions of life ... clothing, warmth and food. When Mr. Alick Murdoch's grandfather was still a young man around the 1850s, he saw the end of handloom weaving in East Kilbride.

> He was quite shrewd my grandpa, and he could see he'd be just left high and dry if he waited till the last weaving-shop closed down there, so, before all the other out-of-work weavers came pell-mell to Glasgow, he came and tramped the city streets till he got a place at a power-loom mill

in Bridgeton and set up his family in a wee house near the Glasgow
Green. There was a lot of power-mills in Glasgow by then.

But before they could weave their cloth, there was the spinning,
and that was an attic piece-work job done in the workers' own
homes. Another grandfather passed on word of that grim life to
his family:

> Grandpa used to tell me that when he was wee, maybe five-years-old, his
> mother used to tease out the wool on pin boards, then spin the yarn on
> her wheel. It was set up in their single room, all smelly and oosey wi' the
> wool, and his job was to run between his mother and the mill, wi' creels
> of wool and pirns, and wi' a tally card to get marked up wi' the week's
> one-and-sixpenny earnings for her long hours in that attic.

There was the cotton printing too, long ago established at various printfields in Glasgow and employing thousands of workers.

> My faither was a labourer in what they called the 'calico' at Thorney-
> bank. I mind I used to lie in my bed and listen to the voices of the other
> men comin' up the street, on their way to work by six o'clock in the
> morning. They used to shout him and other two workers down for the
> two-mile walk away along the dark road to the printwork for their
> eighteen shillin' a week.
> 'You right Jimmy?'
> 'You right Tam?'
> 'You right Johnny?'
> and the answers used to come ...
> 'Right y'are.'
> 'Comin'.'
> 'Just be there.'

After the spinning and the weaving and maybe the printing,
there were those who made up the stuffs.

> My great-uncle was a master-tailor near Glasgow Cross with a work-
> room in his house there. You went up an outside stair and pulled a bell
> that jangled the whole place. And inside, there was my uncle sitting up
> cross-legged on his big work-bench where he could look out over
> London Road. It always sticks in my mind that he took £3 for a suit.

You might think that child's memory was misted by fairy-tale.
Cross-legged tailors surely belong to Grimm and Andersen and
Beatrix Potter; but no less than four rememberers with tailor-kin,

spoke of that traditional bench-squat. 'My uncle? Oh aye, always.'
'My father never worked any other way.' 'It was just the tailors' way
... my auntie was a dressmaker and she'd just her chair and table.'

So the Glaswegian of last century was clad and bedded, to a great
extent, in the home-spuns and prints worked by fellow citizens.
What about their warmth and nourishment?

Of those whose darg was to keep the home fires burning, many
still have recollections of old-time links with those jobs ... of
walking above-ground near the Giffnock railway bridge and hearing
miners singing at their work below ... of the colliers' rows near
Cardowan and Thornliebank, of coalmen shouting their wares at
2/3 a bag.

And Margaret Henderson's father is remembered as a tradesman
fitting fireplaces for the coal to burn, once it had been gouged out,
bought and bunkered.

> When I was young in the 1890s my father's work was putting in ranges
> to folks' kitchens. Ranges were the latest thing after the Exhibition ...
> must have been the 1888 Exhibition ... anyway it was Bows of High
> Street that sold them ... oh aye, he put in a lot of ranges for the Bows'
> Emporium.

As for food, Glasgow has always provided a fair variety of its
own; from the flour mills out at the Bun House that became the
Kelvin Hall, from the tea-blenders and fruit growers, and even
small city farms.

> When I lived in Wodrow Street there were still wee farms and holdings,
> cheek-by-jowl wi' the tenements and mills.

There were butchers and bakers and black-pudding makers, and it
was certainly not only menfolk who were masters of such crafts.
Mrs. Janet Purvis recalls two black-pudding-maker-persons. Her
mother-in-law and her sister were two young girls orphaned by a
train crash as children.

> The girls began work in a lace factory but Mary was quite pushy and
> they opened their own dairy business with a comfy wee home through
> the back. They were next door to a butcher and he gave them his scraps
> and the blood to make black-puddings that he could sell. They became
> quite experts at it, but they'd one strict rule. They only ever ate the

burst ones for their own teas, for they'd have lost their profits eating a
good one.

The city even had its very early fast-food and Mr. Duncan White
talks about a one-time Glasgow character called Pie Nanny, whose
pitch was at the north end of the Suspension Bridge where she sold
pies and pancakes.

> If you wanted yours hot, you ordered it, then went for a walk while she
> het it by holding it in next to her, inside her bodice under her shawl.

Duncan White doesn't claim to have sampled one of Nanny's long-
ago pies ... but then it was perhaps *belief* that should have been
suspended at the bridge.

So much for the work of turning out basic needs. But of course
much of the daily work in those boom days of last century related to
the heavy throbbing industry that was Glasgow's heart-beat. Miss
Marie Condie was born in 1896 and remembers one of the hazards
of her father's work.

> At that time he was a big-paid man in Colvilles' working with the
> molten metal as it came out the red hot furnace. But he got rosacea of
> the skin with that and he'd to give up and go on to selling and installing
> coal-cutting machines.

And Mrs. Muriel Lillie's father was also in iron and steel.

> He used to hoof it all around the country-blacksmiths, selling horse
> shoes and things like that, from his catalogue. Another thing he was
> into was the rubber cogs for drivers to put over their horses' shoes to
> give them a grip, going up cobbly slopes the like of West Nile Street.
> Goloshes for horses really ... big sales there were for rubber cogs.

Jim Lillie's father too, travelled to all airts and pairts with his
merchandise.

> He was in oilskins, and he'd a big basket of samples to trail about with
> him. So when he got off the train some-place, he used to hire a 'boy' for
> the day to wheel his hamper on a barrow round his calls and stay outside
> to keep an eye on it. They'd quite fair wee businesses these barrow boys.

But not everyone toiled at the serious business of prospering and
sustaining the city. There were those who beautified and entertained.

My auntie that I stayed with, was a hairdresser and done the Marcel wavin' for a shillin' ... you got a re-set at sixpence ... d'you mind the Marcel waving?

My mother was a workin' lassie before she was wed, but she learned herself to play the piano by ear, and she must've been pretty good for she played the music at the pictures. She did it all slow when it was love-scenes and fast when it was maybe a chase, then changed it to cloppin' and galumphin' music when Tom Mix was ridin' in a cowboy bit. And then some nights she sang at the piano in a wee tea-room cafe on the road to Paisley, at Spiersbridge.

A last view of the previous generations' world of work comes from Mr. James Wisner who remembers old days in Thornliebank.

There was a sort of division among the folks down our way. Nearly everyone was in the print-works right-enough, but one lot was just the workers and the other lot was the bosses. They had different houses in different streets. The workers were in the wee rows and the toffs were in Lum Hat Street. And the 'row' weans got chased out Lum Hat Street if they went there to play.

He doesn't add what happened to the small Lum Hat fry when they ventured into the Rows.

After these second hand memories, recollections from the early years of the century are of rememberers' own working days. Some of them are into their eighties and nineties now and can still see themselves as office-boys in bowler hats, apprentices in short trousers, factory girls in overalls and dust-caps, shop girls in black dresses and young typists earning six shillings a week where they stood at desks to work.

Then you understand of course, there were no first names in the office, always Mister and Miss This or That. I even called my best friend Miss Briggs, and for years after we left the office she was still Miss Briggs to me.

One who was an apprentice in those early days before the First War was William Stevenson.

I was apprenticed as a joiner to wee Humphy-backit McWhirter the builder. He was close-fisted even then right-enough, but I was young and didnae notice ... and I was getting on fine. But then the war came before I was done and I was away till I was twenty-four, with the

hospital and that. I went back to Mr. McWhirter and at the end of the
first week he handed me a pound for wages ... a wee apprentice's pay
and there's me been a Sergeant-Major in the army! But then he got a flea
in his lug from the ex-service association and after months of hummin'
and hawin' he gave me the right money ... two-thirds a journeyman pay
for ex-servicemen. When I was finished I set up a wee joinery business
and did quite nice.

Another who started to his trade before that war was Duncan
White.

I was wi' a railway-waggon shop ... 'The Slaughter House' we called it,
for the sweated labour it was. I made couplin' safety-chains. It was piece
work and you got a penny-farden (an *old* penny-farden) for an inch link
and out of that you paid your mate. That was your hammerman like.
You stood sideways to the fire, in front of your anvil, your feet in a
hollow in the ground to keep your exact place. You wore your apron to
the side for the heat of the fire, then you bent and skeffed the wee metal
bars ... after that bang! bang! wi' your hammer to close the links tight.
You kind of swivelled at your hips to get the rhythm, swingin' between
the fire and the anvil ... it was rare practice for the dancing.

By then, young women in most social groups were persuading
their papas that there was more to life than embroidery and making
paper flowers, and that they were not beyond redemption simply
because they took paid employment.

I went to work at fourteen with William Collins the publishers in
Cathedral Street and I was there until I retired. I worked at the costing
of materials, judging the amount of thread and card for making the
good stitched books.

The stores were a happy hunting ground for young ladies who
fancied meeting the public and working with merchandise they
could never have afforded themselves. May Reid was one of those.

I went into Fraser's at about sixteen. It was old Mr. Hugh then, the
second one of the four Hughs, and very nice and polite he was ... came
round every day to say good-morning and ask after everyone. I mind
once I stayed late sorting through a big order of gowns (mantles we
called them then) and hanging them up. The caretaker told Mr. Hugh
and next pay day when he came round with the packets he gave me ten
pounds out of his own pocket. TEN POUNDS, I couldn't credit it.
But after work I hurried away down to Manson's (yon dear sweetie-shop

in St. Enoch Square) and bought my mother a half-pound box of
chocolates ... Manson's chocolates!

Through time young Hugh left school and came in to learn the
business (him that was Lord Fraser after.) He did some of the buying
with me ... nice man, young Mr. Hugh.

Another young lady whose mother made sure she went into lady-
like employment was Miss Helen Edgar.

There were lots of works near us, bleachers and dyers and bakeries but
my mother wanted us all in genteel jobs, floristry, clerkin' an' that, and
one brother was a compositor. Anyway when it was me to leave school
she took me straight away down Cogan Street to the mill. She knew the
boss-man there.

'I've brought you a new weaver ... I don't want her an ordinary
weaver ... she's to be a Madras weaver,' says my mother.

Seven-and-six I got a week while I learned. Then it was piece-work at
six-and-eightpence for forty yards on my broadloom, less on my narrow
one. When you were skilled you had your two looms, you see, with your
web and weft and the punched cards to give you your design.

In the morning you got a mug of tea at your loom but you darenae
stop it for you tried to get six pieces made in the week. You didnae
manage that often mind, because you'd to stop a lot for the coom (that
was the sooty oose that hung about the ceiling) used to fall on your web
and jigger the shuttle so's you got dirty wee tears ... 'scob flaws' they
called them and you'd to stop and mark the place, to mend it when it
came off the loom. Sometimes there was a breakdown and the tenter
had to come and sort it. If he was slow or had a staw at you, and kep' you
waiting, that was all lost money. But it was quite a good pay if you
worked hard and I took home more to my mother than my faither did. I
got one and six a week to myself.

Private nefarious schemes, for raising take-home pay unofficially,
are no doubt as ancient as the first short-change on bartered fig-
leaves, and were as well known in the years just after the First War
as before or since.

I was in a factor's office when I came back from the war and there was an
old twister there who ran his own wee racket; taking key money when
folk were desperate for houses to rent. The boss Willie Ross caught him
and he got his jotters ... mind Willie himself wasnae always the clean
potato. He got drummed out of the army for drinking and fighting!

There was consternation from the other party to the interview, startled at this revelation after seventy years, about a Glasgow business man, of old and respected acquaintance. 'Willie Ross did ... never!' 'Aye he did!' 'Oh my!' says the deflated lady of eighty-seven.

Although many single girls were taking jobs by the outbreak of the First War, those four years confirmed them as a real part of the work force. Some came back to ordinary occupations from munitions, some from the services. One of them confesses to having been a little confused.

> When I came back from the services I used to forget where I was and stand to attention when I was called to see the boss!

There were post-war adjustments for men to make too, when they found their offices full of women doing very nicely thank you, at almost the whole range of jobs. The men weren't always too diplomatic about re-integrating and some began to throw their weight about 'something awful'. Lists of petty rules began to appear in a number of offices.

> I mind some of the silly orders that our men dreamed up. Daft they were. Here's one I mind. 'No exception will be taken to one signet-ring and a watch-bracelet. No more jewellery than that will be permitted.' And this, 'dark clothing only, will be worn at all times under regulation overalls.' Then, because we were 'office', we weren't to hob-nob with 'warehouse'. *You* could call *them* by their first names, by way of work, but they had to call us Mister and Miss. Staff and warehouse were different species of being.

Between the wars there was seasonal work too, and sometimes there were temporary jobs. The Empire Exhibition of 1938 gave work to attendants, clerks, typists, cashiers, building squads, truck drivers and waitresses.

> I worked in the Big Orange. It was a Juice stall and it was like a big split-open orange. That split part was your counter and you served there. After that I worked at a stall where they sold hot crisps wi' salt n'vinegar in wee paper pokes wi' twirly ends.

From the earliest days there has always been a vast army of women who clean up when office, factory and warehouse closed for the night ... or served food to workers while they were there.

I worked at the cleaning and in the canteens at some of the newspaper offices. I liked The Herald best. They used to call me the 'Auld Yin' there. I peeled the veg and tatties and cleaned up the dirty pots and the greasy dishes. Then when the floor got scrubbed you used to get the big-big rolls of newsprint and let it unwind out, right the length of the canteen floor, so's folk could walk on it wi'out slipping. It was quite interesting workin' there, for when the big news came we got it first. Then the canteen would be open all night and we took round hot soup and rolls.

Some of the rememberers loved their work, some hated it, some tholed it. But whatever the talk of job satisfaction or drudgery, the main interest and gauge of status (though not the only one) was the pay packet; and every last one of them could say just exactly what he or she earned at various stages of working life. 'In 1905 ... six shillings a week as a photographer's assistant.' '1912 that would be ... seven shillings as an office typist.' '1920, passing rich on forty pounds, as a bank trainee.' '1930 ... ten shillings a week when I was a boy workin' to a leather merchant.' '1947, I got twenty pounds a month as a newly qualified teacher.'

And of course there was that 'penny-farden for an inch link' in the first years of the century.

They recall, not only what they earned, but what happened to it and the social consequences of how it was handled.

Although women werenae what you'd say liberated, *they* really wore the breeks (I'm speaking about the days when it wasnae so much the done thing for married women to be out workin'.) My faither wouldnae dared to open his pay packet before he got it home. My mother was real strong. When a man interfered wi' his pay to fritter it, or if the woman was feart for him, she'd a bad time wi' money and the family kind of floundered.

A sad fact borne out by one hard-pressed wife who did not handle the money.

I never saw my man's pay poke till he died sudden and I got the one he was owed. When I saw the good wage he'd really earned, I couldnae believe it. I gret. I'd worked at house-cleanin' all my days just to keep things going.

Booms, recessions, head-work and hand-work ... Glasgow folk

have come through them all with a host of vivid pictures of their jobs, and wry comments on tasks and task-masters. And the pawky Glasgow tradition is still alive with young people who are lucky enough to have jobs now; who *know* they are lucky, but still have the spirit to negotiate their perks in 1985.

> My brother's learnin' to be a butcher. He gets to bring home a' the sausages he makes for the first six months till he learns to do it right. I mean, you cannae sell squinty and shapeless sausages over the counter, can you? ... My mother's hopin' he learns to cut the sirloin steaks wrong an' all.

5
Wages for Principle

They've always been a disputatious lot the Scots; since the Middle Ages certainly about their religion, their kings and their land. But later, when working men first discovered how to face up to their 'betters', both sides had whole new worlds for their cantankers. There were a number of centres of unrest all over Scotland, where men chewed the fat about conditions of employment and, even more seriously, about conditions of *un*employment. Nowhere was it chewed more vigorously than in Glasgow, with its concentration of industry and the conflicting interests of master and man.

The reek of revolution was in the Glasgow air of one-hundred-and-sixty years ago. Dissatisfaction had been at the simmer for a long time but when mass production came to the mills and began to throw handloom weavers out of work, it boiled over.

There was a tradition in our family of being in the thick of the demands for reform. My grandfather came of Radical folk, for they were weaver people and he used to tell me what he minded of those days himself and what he'd been told by his father. His own first home was just the single room with his weaving-loom in the middle and what wee bit-else they had, lying round it. The weaving folk had the name of being well-read and booky, for they were self-employed and they could work double time the one day to get reading the Radical weeklies when they came out the next.

This grandfather wrote in his journal of seeing workmen meeting together round the doors of thatched cottages in the east-end, to listen, while one who could read took *The Penny Post* or *The North British Daily Mail* and read aloud to the rest.

'Where there was weavin' there was agitatin' my grandpa used to say. 'The government was afraid of revolt.' (This was about the 1820s and it

wasn't so long after the French Revolution.) 'They used to put spies in
the pubs so's they could listen-in, then go and clype on the trouble
makers. One got vitriol thrown in his face for being found by the
weavers doin' that. Lost both his eyes.' My grandfather used to tell us,
as well, how his father was with John Baird and Andrew Hardie the
Glasgow Radicals when they got executed at Stirling in 1820, and how
he was with Willie Goldie when he got killed in the riot the Scots
Guards came to put down.

But the Reform Acts were passed, real revolution did not come and
nobody else's grandfather had quite such bloodthirsty 'peacetime'
memories. Mr. Alexander Murdock, now ninety-five, remembers,

My grandfather was a great Liberal . . . thought the world of Gladstone.
But he parted company with him over the head of Irish Home Rule . . .
couldnae thole that idea at all. But he couldnae think to join the Tories
either. He was never a Tory. So he took up with the Chamberlains in
the Liberal Unionists. I mind of seeing Gladstone myself a time or two
in Glasgow at meetings. Very, very popular he was . . . crowds everywhere. (They only do that for the Queen now, or singers with guitars.)
Anyway I was a grown lad when Gladstone died about 1898 or 9, and I
mind that day because the Glasgow Herald had thick black borders
round it.

Politicians *were* the popular idols of Victorian times and two
people tell the same hand-me-down tale of the reformer John
Bright.

John Bright was a great one to a lot of folk, but he lost a wee bit of his
popularity when he was so far-ben wi' Abraham Lincoln over the slaves
an' that. And my father told me, 'Abraham Lincoln wasnae that popular
here till after he got shot, then all-of-a-sudden he was a hero.' Glasgow
folk liked a good martyr.

As a Lincoln man then, John Bright was back in favour and had the
prodigal's rousing welcome when he came to Glasgow. That visit is
recorded in the Freer family annals.

My grandfather and his friends that favoured reform wanted to give him
a presentation. They thought on a nice inscribed Bible but they
couldnae get near him . . . not in the street and not into his hotel. So
they strung it on a long bit string across Argyle Street from one-up
houses each side, and lowered it into his carriage when it came along.

But it wasn't only the menfolk among the famous reformers that

came to Glasgow and its surroundings, and the lady who was little
May Gilmour near the turn of the century, remembers an unusual
setting for a nationally-kent figure to be giving her spiel, this time
on Votes for Women.

> It was a funny place right-enough for Sylvia Pankhurst to be speaking.
> We used to go on holiday down the Clyde and up to Whistlefield. I was
> just a wee thing there that year when we heard she was coming to speak.
> Mind there's nothing at Whistlefield, why she ever came there I don't
> know, except maybe they wouldn't give her a hall in the city. It meant
> nothing to me at that age, but it was a holiday ploy and all the visitors
> and the locals sat on the grassy slope and listened to her there. She was
> lovely and I mind all the grown-ups saying she was a rare speaker.

Although the suffragettes roused passionate controversy in
Glasgow, a booking was allowed for a rally at St. Andrew's Halls.
But before the day of the meeting Mrs. Pankhurst had become their
leader ... she was militant and forthright and thought likely to
cause trouble so the manager of the Halls was instructed that on no
account was Mrs. Pankhurst to be allowed to attend that meeting.

> It was my grandpa that was in charge, and mind-you he was quite a
> supporter of the women, but he had his orders. They put a hundred
> policemen in the basement and had them on duty all along the roads
> leading to the Halls. Seems ridiculous now but she really had them in a
> right panic.
>
> Anyway somehow she gave them all the slip and when the rally
> started she suddenly just bobbed up from behind the table.
>
> The police stormed the platform and there was just a donnybrook wi'
> the Pankhurst folk and the bobbies. The police had their batons right-
> enough, but-here so had the women and *they* didnae know who was for
> them and who not. So they all just let fly. One of them was getting
> arrested and in the mayhem she tore my grandfather's coat-tail away,
> but then she swiped at him with her baton and he grabbed it ... fair
> exchange I suppose, the baton for the coat-tail.

Whether the coat-tail has been cherished and handed down in the
Pankhurst family or not, Thomas Clydesdale Watson has no idea,
but the baton, shown with great pride, has been a treasured trophy
in his family since the day Grandpa jouked its swipe.

The heroes who found their land unfit after coming back
hopefully from the First War to the grand promises of politicians,

struggled to improve their own lot and serious unrest brought rashes of protest meetings and strikes. Families sacrificed wages for principle, stood their ground and eked out their housekeeping purses in various ways. Daisy Baker remembers her parents' enterprising side-lines.

> I mind a strike our way early in the twenties. My mother made trays and trays of toffee-apples, plain ones and coconut ones, tuppence-a-piece. And my father split sticks and made up wee bundles of them wi' wire. They sold the apples and the firewood at the door to make a wee bit money. She was a rare hand at the toffee-apples my Ma.

And the Edgar weans put in their ha'pennyworth to the family kitty.

> The pit at Burnfield near Hillpark was out, and us kids were dispatched up there wi' bags to bring back any coals that were lying about. I was just young but even then I could tell coal from slate and just brought home the good stuff.

As the twenties turned on, social castes were re-inforced, and bitter 'them and us' confrontations began to develop. But there were dissensions even *within* the ranks of each side.

> I was a very young and frightened lieutenant at the Somme and I fought alongside better men than I would ever be, who came back to houses and wages that were a disgrace. I sometimes couldn't believe that friends of my own who'd been through the trenches with working chaps could be so sore against them in the strikes.

But the scolding of striking workers was not all from the men who had been their officers in France.

> I mind when we were in a room-and-kitchen ground floor, and my mother used to bake scones; and here this day, she was standing at the open window doin' a batch of her scones and talkin' out to a wee cluster of striking men standing grumbling on the pavement outside. She started argy-bargying wi' them. I can hear her yet... She was a great wee Conservative my mother *and* she could put-by a wee bit of faither's pay-poke every week.
>   'I'm a Conservative,' says-she to the men.
>   'Whit've you got to conserve?' says one.
>   'My bank book.'
>   'How did *you* get a bank book?'

'Hard work!' says-she, and let that sink in while she whisked her scones off the girdle into a towel.

The period's unrest peaked in 1926 with the General Strike, after economics had dictated that miners' wages were to be reduced and hours of work lengthened. Memories of these nine days are vivid to almost all the rememberers. The strike failed to bring workers what they saw as no more than simple justice, largely because there were, by that date, plenty of alternatives to the public transport they tried to paralyse. There was the new wireless too to bring news and entertainment to the public even when the press was silent.

While it was 'on', overlaying the grim determination of the strikers, there was an atmosphere of almost carnival adventure for those who could enjoy the challenge of trying to keep things running with no risk to their own livelihood. Even the weather was bright and sunny.

> We were students in 1926 and my pals and I all drove tramcars. You just turned up at one of the tramway depots and maybe an inspector taught you to drive. It was all quite a spree really.

So says one driver. But a passer-by was less sanguine about the quick-taught drivers.

> It was some sight, I can tell you, to see the trams goin' by like trains in India, full inside and up-top, and wi' folk cheek-by-jowl, jammin' the platform, then maybe another dozen hangin' on to the brass pole and the runnin' board. I wouldnae've got on to one for a' the tea in China, I tell you.

Armies of private cars came out like ants from warm woodwork.

> My late husband had business cars and a few horse-drawn carts for local deliveries. He sent them out in the strike to carry people to work. They took maybe ten folk to a car and sixteen or seventeen on the carts.

There was no formal asking or granting of lifts. Non-strikers, without a by-your-leave, simply jumped on and off passing lorries or carts going in the right direction, and 'lapped' their way to work like that on perhaps six different vehicles.

And an unfamiliar Glasgow was revealed to young Isobel Cameron who was a student at Gilmorehill at the time.

I found all sorts of new ways about the town. I lived in Ibrox and I discovered the ferry. I used to walk along Copland Road on the south side, cross the Clyde and then walk the length of Kelvinhaugh Street at the other end. Great!

For a few days news was posted outside stations and post-offices, an Emergency Press sheet was published and, at the height of the strike, troops were deployed about the city.

I mind of the soldiers in George Square keepin' order, and that made the men right surly and angry.

Then it was all over. Or was it? They had won nothing and lost much more than just a day-or-two's wages.

I was on strike from my work, and after it fell through, everyone at our work wi' under ten years' service got the sack. So I lost my job, for I'd just been working at it since my five years in the Navy in the war. That was seven years I'd worked. They did that to weed out the younger ring-leaders. A whole generation of workers like, got their books. Anyway I decided to take my family and go to Canada.

So while some, like Duncan White, left Glasgow to look for work after 1926, others, like Janey Brown, hit by the strike and its aftermath elsewhere, came to the city to find new employment.

I came to Glasgow when the depression that came on after the big strike was getting bad. My father'd been a tailor in Manchester with his own place. But there was no more work there, the uniforms he'd made not needed any more, so we came to the Gorbals for him to do his tailorin' for someone else. He worked for a tailor at a place in South Portland Street, in what's now Morrison's.

And for those who like their endings happy the climax of these last two tales of going and coming, is that the travellers met and married much later, he driven home by lack of work in Canada, she, by then, having settled and adopted the city as home.

Real protest can thrive only one some glimmer of hope and even that died when the twenties closed in slump, so that people became dejected and dispirited. Even bright, well-qualified young people, the grandparents of the 1980s' young unemployed, found it hard to get work.

I trained as a language secretary and it was nearly a year before I found a job. Even then it wasn't what I'd studied for.

Men who had been lads in the First War and become the angry strikers of 1926, were the disillusioned fathers of families by the early thirties.

My father was minister in Govan and knew his people well in that parish. Most of the men in his congregation were in the shipyards like Lithgows, and Harland and Wolff, and Stevens of Linthouse, and he was heart-sick for those decent working-men with skills going to waste through the slump years.

Sad times, aye. But there's a wee wag to the most glum tales and Mr. Joe Kyle has it in a memory of his, linking 1926 and 1939.

In the General Strike I volunteered as a Special Constable. I was sworn in, very serious, then sent home to wait, all champing at the bit to get into action. And I heard not another word . . . for thirteen years! Never called out once. Then in 1939 I was suddenly sent for a lined up with others to get a Long Service certificate . . . and given my duties as a wartime Special!

It took the second war to set the factory machines turning again, the hammers clanging, the cranes swinging in the yards; a heavy price for men to get back their industrial self-respect. Since then, the forties, fifties and sixties, the years of the never-so-good life, have passed into memory like the fight for votes, and the old slump. Now the new slump has come. The style of unemployment is different, victims are better buffered against bare want, the job-lack cuts a wider social swathe, but the blight to the spirit is just as bitter.

6
Lum Hats and Leg O'Muttons

That photographer who shuttered the family group at the opening of a previous chapter captured not only the clothes of babies and children that we have already remembered, but those of their parents and grandparents as well. So while the young fry skipped and peeried in tammies and sailor-suits how did the bien-dressed elders of earliest memory look?

> My father used to tell me that when he started his apprenticeship in the 1880s the senior men came to work in tall hats, black jackets and striped trousers!

> I suppose my granny would be about fifty in the 1890s when I mind of her in a bonnet wi' ties under her chin and leg o'mutton sleeves to her dress. It had all embroidery down the front and she'd a shawl wi' that. Then sometimes in the house she'd a wee fuss of lace on the top of her head.

By the early century bonnets were left to the very old, and bigger hats were 'in'.

> My granny was in her eighties when I was young around 1905, and I can just see her wearing a tied-on bonnet with a peak down her forehead. She wore a pelisse-thing too and she was all in black, but for a wee touch purple on the bonnet.

> My mother had a big felt hat wi' a bird and feather to it ... very flat ... my brothers used to call it her doo-lander.

That was country-style out in Uddingston village, but across the city on the gracious avenues and gardens of Pollokshields ladies took the air in upmarket versions of Mother Harper's doo-lander.

> I remember my mother in a flat cartwheel hat, very shallow with huge roses on the brim. She wore a lacey dress with a stand-up collar that had stiffeners in it.

Contemporary and probably 'ages' with granny, around 1910, Mr.
Watson of Redhurst at Williamwood, came in his carriage to the
station every morning to take the train into the city. Little May
Reid used to peer through her garden railings into the station yard.

He was *very* stylish in his shammy gloves and his wing collars and with a
silver knob to his walking cane.

There are surely no equivalent watersheds now in young lives that
have boys and girls trembling one day on the brink of adulthood

and taking the plunge right into it the next, such as there were in the teen years of the century ... watersheds like putting up the hair or letting down the trousers.

Edith Wallace remembers her ordeal.

> It was usually at eighteen you put your hair up and I mind after a year as just a wee typist wi' my hair long, being that nervous about going into the office wi' mine's piled up and stuck through wi' a comb. But by the end of the week I really thought I was something and got quite sniffy wi' the junior still in her pleats.

And Joe Kyle his.

> I wore short trousers for nearly a year when I was apprenticed at the bank. It was quite a thing to walk in the first time in your longs.

For vast numbers of young adults in the overshadowed 1914-18 war years, clothing was uniformly drab, the men in khaki or blue, the women keeping them sombre company. The only vivid memory of happier fashion is of May Gilmour's honeymoon outfit in 1918. Out comes the sixty-seven-year-old photograph of an elegant and beautiful young woman in a classic cream wool belted coat with full skirt, worn with a French-priest style shallow bowler, with wide brim tilted slightly and sweeping round the crown in a great halo ... a far cry from the days when she wondered if she would never get anything *bought*.

A far cry too from the style of a remembered governess of the same era.

> You didnae get a lot of governesses in Glasgow, but this one lived near us and she wore wee nipped-in waists and stiff collars. When you went to visit her and her brother, they always used to sing, 'When you and I were young Maggie'. But you couldnae see her young somehow, and fleein' about in a tammy or that!

Perhaps because the great change to the lounge suit was just round the corner, that period of fathers' attire is very well remembered.

> When we used to go for a walk after church just before the First War, father wore a frock-coat and his tile hat. I can see him yet, standing there in the hall on a Sunday morning polishing round the pile of that hat with a velvet pad.

And here's the same gentleman in a family group of the time, sure
enough, in the rounded collar and high-buttoned waistcoat with a
double loop of gold watch chain, aged perhaps sixty, with white
walrus moustache and smoothly parted snow-white hair. Other
fathers of that period are remembered with just as much affection
but differently.

My father was workin' chap and I mind that on Saturdays and holidays he wore a big flat skippit bunnet . . . 'doo-landers' they called them caps.

And a certain Mr. Wilson who, whatever else he may have achieved in a long life, is remembered by one young neighbour for nothing more than the hat he wore in 1912.

Not a tall hat, not as high as that . . . half, maybe . . . and stiff, wi' a curly brim.

The tall hat was subsiding a little, at least for middle-management. Certainly by 1917 the gaffers from Lum Hat Street, Thornliebank, who went out to work now in three-piece suits and spats, had bowlers instead of lums on their heads (only the gaffers, of course, from the local print-work lived in Lum Hat Street).

The best judge of what a Glasgow gent in his prime should have been wearing then, was surely Mr. Hugh Fraser, grandfather of Sir Hugh of-the-Green-Canopies on the Paisley's building.

When I first went to work at Frasers' of Buchanan Street, it was old Mr. Hugh I was under. He was coming on a bit by then . . . he'd just a wee fringe of white hair. His chauffeur, Milligan, brought him to business at exactly 9.20 every morning and he used to wear a navy Melton coat with an astrakan collar, and he would be carrying a wee bag. We used to wonder what was in his bag . . . don't think it would be his piece mind.

And no doo-lander either for the likes of Mr. Hugh Fraser.

As more and more women joined the workforce on the way into the 'twenties, their clothes became more practical. At the end of the war they were still wearing ankle-length skirts and hand-span waists, but by 1920 stays were out and short loose jackets and straight lines were in.

I mind my goin' away clothes in 1923. I had a beigy-colour boxy costume wi' a loose blouse, and I had shoes to match and my first-ever pair of light stockings. I had a pale straw hat wi' flowers to go my honeymoon in too, and a bonny wee cloche hat for wearing when I got there.

Hair was bobbed too and Miss Marie Condie remembers the scissors finally crunching through her twenty-five years' growth, and the sight of it lying round her shoulders and strewn on the floor.

I was a nurse and you werenae allowed to get your hair cut. So I had the cuttings made into a bun and pinned it under my cap for work. But I was always in a cold sweat for fear the wee tuffety bits would show and I would get dismissed.

By the 'twenties and 'thirties, granny too was into the loose-hung look and most men from eighteen to eighty wore lounge suits which, give or take waistcoats, galluses and vents, have little altered in fifty years.

The Second wartime years plunged happier memories of fashion into the gloom of passed-on clothes, make-do-and-mend and clothing coupons. In time, trends revived and there have been a few discernable styles ... the long-skirted romantic New Look of the 'fifties, the cheeky minis of the 'sixties, and the million miles of denim. What look to us like frenzies of short-lived fads may be treasure to fashion archivists of the future. Who knows, for instance what they'll make of the day of the platform sole? And with this perhaps apocryphal tale we'll leave the fashion of the late twentieth century to them.

I knew a girl who had a pair of yon big-big high platforms, and here she's comin' along Argyle Street in them one day, clip-cloppin' past a workman sortin' somethin' down a manhole. His head comes pokin' up and he watches the feet comin' by.

'Haw, how d'you get down off of them, Hen?' says he. She trots on and just calls back disdainfully over her shoulder ... 'I dreep, son.'

7

Do You Mind of Hengler's Circus?

Picnics, sails, fairs, penny-geggies, Saturday 'bursts', recitals, plays, concerts and operas ... it would have been a poor-spirited Glasgow cratur of the past century-and-a-half who couldn't find a treat or night-out to suit his taste and pay-poke.

Most entertainments over the period were regular features of city life, but there were some one-offs, some annuals and there were the big short-term Exhibitions of 1888, 1901, 1911 and 1938.

Memories of the 1888 one with its Oriental theme and its reconstruction of the old Cathedral clergy houses are inevitably second-hand, but its consequences are worth a mention since the money made from it went to the building of the Kelvingrove Art Galleries.

> My father talked to me a lot about that Exhibition for it was the year I was born in 1888. Two things he used to say ... that Joe Lyons had a big tea-room there with waitresses all dressed-up like Mary Queen of Scots, and that it was that Exhibition made Glasgow start to feel proud of itself.

Not many now remember the 1901 Exhibition held in the area of Kelvingrove Park, affectionately called 'The Groveries' for the period, but young Alexander Murdoch was a schoolboy then and a regular patron.

> My father had a business stand there and he gave me a season ticket. My, what a sunny summer it was, sun from morn till night ... I can think back on a wee bridge over the Kelvin with fairy lights ... and the gondola with two gondoliers they called Hokey and Pokey. But it's the bands I mind best. There was Sousa's band and the Zouave bugles and a big, big concert hall. The buildings had all wee kind of onion domes. It was s'posed to be Spanish but I mind it more Chinese ... but aye, it's the

bands I can hear yet ... and I mind the big car competitions between the likes of Wolsleys and Daimlers ... all open cars of course. The Art Galleries was opened the same day as the Exhibition.

The 1911 extravanganza at Kelvingrove is well within living memory and although the replica of Falkland Palace (which was blown down in a storm the night the Exhibition closed) and the replicas of a typical Scottish town and village, are dutifully reported, the recollections that remain most vivid are those of less educational activities.

That was a rare summer. There was a lot of model ships on the river and a wee boat done-up in the McBrayne's colours sailing up and down the Kelvin. There was an overhead railway too and the trucks used to roar right down into the park from Lord Roberts' statue in the Park Circus. I mind seeing a truck gettin' stuck halfway ... and just hingin' there. And I mind the bands that used to play 'Abide with me' every night.

It was the same memory-story in 1938. For all the treasure-store of history and geography, art and science, offered in the great pavilions, and doubtless properly appreciated at the time, most visitors confess to having better mindings of hushed groups watching the Stratosphere Girl risking life and limb with her acrobatics performed high up on a swaying pole, the screaming joy of a hurl on the scenic railway, or a jaunt up Tait's Tower ... and one housemaid of the time admits, with a happy sigh, to having looked for 'fellas' in the Amusement Park on her days off.

The Exhibition was a Mecca for Kings, Queens and Princesses, and other instantly recognisable greats.

Funny the things that come best to mind. All very interesting it was, but to this day what I remember is, when Gracie Fields arrived to visit the Exhibition and she just stood in front of the crowd, and sang. Not a set performance, just a spontaneous turn. I thought she was splendid. The books all say it was a real wet summer, but I always remember it sunny.

The Exhibitions then were Glasgow 'putting on the style', milestones along the routine years. But between times there were the week-in-week-out looked-forward-to treats that relieved the long hours of hard work most folk remembered of their younger days.

Early-on they had what they called Saturday night 'bursts' ... kind of shillin'y concerts where you got your tea and a bag of cakes. They got that name because after you'd ate your buns an' that, you blew up your bag and Bang! you burst it. My father was on the committee to audition the turns and he minded seeing Harry Lauder, and giving him his first chance on the platform at the Bridgeton Town Hall.

About the same time there were more prestigious concerts at the St. Andrew's Halls, where instrumentalists like the Albertini Band of Mandolins and Guitars and 'chantatrices' like Jessie McLachlan and Ada Leigh, regularly charmed the faithful. The City Hall performers had their following too, among them, young Nancy Reid.

My friend at school came of a theatrical family that did turns at the Saturday afternoon concerts. Ginny was tiny and she wore a wee suit of gent's evening clothes and went on as The Pocket Vesta Tilley, I nearly bust with pride that she was my friend.

Drama too had its place at the Penny Concerts in the various Corporation Halls.

They used to show plays on Saturday afternoons (now I'm speakin' about 1906 or 7). There were 'Jeanie Deans' and 'East Lynne', and I mind 'Rob Roy' an' all. You used to could get in for nothin' and a free programme, half-way through, and pester your neighbours to tell you what happened in the first half.

Then there were the Argyle Street waxworks, the Panopticon and the Animatograph, rounds of the booths at the fair on Vinegar Hill with its coconut shies and hurdy-gurdy music. An eighty-six-year-old 'does' Vinegar hill all over again, chuckles and wags a finger at the earnest group pressing for her recollections.

Och your mother and me and Mary Grady had the time of our lives when we were young.

But upmarket to all these and the local artistes of music-hall and 'burst' before the First War, were the real concerts, usually in St. Andrew's Halls. Tickets were no doubt expensive, but there were Open Sesames if you knew how to find them ... one young man heard Caruso sing, by getting the nod from an official towards a ladder leading from a top corridor, and clamping himself to a roof joist.

... that joist fair vibrated when he hit the high notes.

But steeplejacking wasn't the only way to join the audience without paying. You could cling to other things.

My best friend was a rare pianist. She played sheet music in Paterson's for customers swithering between buying this piece or that, and she used to get free tickets-for-two for the celebrity concerts. I stuck like a limpet to that friend and bought myself a nice dress that I wore every time to the St. Andrew's Halls. It was always evening dress at big theatres and concerts then.

With the coming of moving pictures a whole new world of entertainment was opened up. Glimpses of incredible American glamour and romance dazzled your average wee Glasgow chap doing his courting with a poke of sweeties and a tuppenny tram ride, and his girl, waiting for either him or for her 'china' at a draughty close-mouth, in her other dress and her best scent.

When we were wee, we used to get a penny to go to the pictures at the Burgh Hall on a Saturday. Took the whole afternoon that did, because you stood queuing from about one, for the three o'clock showing. Then when I was just started work I got a chum, a china. She was very adventurous and opened big doors to me ... like going to the Savoy picture-house in the town! You'd to queue for about an hour there, under a canopy but we didnae grudge a minute for there was buskers there. An old man used to sing ... oh I cannae mind it all, but it began ...

'Oh if only, oh if only, she would put away her knittin''
Just as well I dinnae mind the rest of that. He did wee dances an' all ... it was just part of Saturdays early in the 1920s ... the jugglers and paper-tearers and the singers.

The pictures enthralled vast numbers every Saturday night for fifty years, and if you had the inclination, and the 2s.3d. in your pocket, you could slip in a visit to the repertory theatre mid-week as well. Throughout the 'thirties and 'forties the Brandon Thomas Company, or the Wilson Barrett, played to faithful audiences enjoying a weekly dollop of drama.

Some outings didn't involve performances at all, tea at Miss Buick's or Miss Cranston's, or at James Craig's (slightly more stodgy in scone-texture and decor but with interesting exhibitions of pictures). For the West-end or South-side ladies there were afternoons to be dawdled away in the elegance of Rennie Macintosh's Willow Tea-room, or Copland and Lye's with its trio or quartet of Palm Court musicians.

And there were the kind of shopping trips remembered by Miss Marie Condie from her childhood around 1902.

I went with my grandma to Anderson's Polytechnic for shopping, for clothes and household things an' that. Then we always went to Ferguson's for a pot of tea and a cake ... I loved that.

Other bairns had grander destinations.

I used to go with my father to see the pictures at Reid and Lefevre the
art dealers, at their gallery. Alexander Reid was a friend of his and it was
him advised Sir William Burrell about paintings and put him in the way
of collecting some of them you see now at the Burrell. He lived with
Van Gogh in Paris when they were young and Van Gogh painted yon
famous portrait of him. Talked a lot to my father about his days in
Paris.

These were the any-day, any-week outings of long ago, but there were other seasonal or annual junketings that you had to wait for, ticking off your calendar week by week till the great day came or the summer sun shone again, for the Sunday School trip, the paddle-steamer down the Clyde; and perhaps best of all, the arrival of Hengler's Circus. They all recall it but Davie Marriott's is the earliest memory.

I'm goin' back mind, to about 1901, but it came year after year for a long time. There was this big arena wi' clowns and jugglers, acrobats an' that. But the last turn was what you really waited for. Before it started they put up a big high splash-screen all round, with scenery of woods and waterfalls, except at the entrance. Then someway or other the floor sank down and water gushed in, then Indians in canoes came scooshing through, like they were shootin' rapids.

A quiet man interrupts suddenly from a corner of the Eventide-home lounge.

... and d'you mind the horses an' all? Like cowboy films? There was maybe just about six injuns on horses but they seemed like a hunner-an-six because they didnae come up again through the water, they went out some underwater way, then round and back up to do the plungin' again and again.

And his friend gave one of Glasgow's winking, sideways nods of sheer pleasure in shared experience.

Och aye ... Hengler's ... aye, aye.

There were the simplest of all pleasures too, picnics in nearby fields on summer days ... no cars, no pâté, no chicken, no chilled wine.

We'd picnics down Jack's orchard. You'd get your big jug of skim milk to go wi' your piece'n'jam and teeter away down the field tryin' no' to slop it afore you got sat down under a special big apple-tree. Sometimes we played daisy-chains, and sometimes it was shops, wi' stones and leaves and wee windfall apples. Big stones was for tatties.

That was in the 1890s. Picnics weren't new and have never been out of fashion since. Through wars and catastrophes weans have been skipping into city parks or along outskirt burn-paths ... even into graveyards, with their baskets and unbreakable cups, searching for best places to set them down.

We used to go over the kirk hill at Eastwood, two families of us wi' our baskets. I mind one day we met old Lawyer Robertson that lived up Mansewood. We were all rosy and puffed from cavorting about at the picnic, the eight Morrisons and the six of us Edgars, wi' the two mothers.

'My what bonnie bairns!' says-he. 'They're all that alike, how d'you tell the one lot from the other to get them home?'

'Oh,' says my mother, 'we just coont them an' hauf them.'

Some special picnics were further afield, and part of a bigger gathering, Sunday School or Woman's Guild outings, or some like the one where Captain Peter Laurie has a sharp picture of himself as a small boy in the 1930s.

I had an uncle who was a Pipe Major and he once took me down the Clyde to hear his pipe-band at the Cowal Games, in Dunoon. There was me, just a wee chap in this great huge field with my picnic and I remember getting this big busby plumped down over my head and it coming right down to my chin.

In the winter, of course, for the halflin' generation, there was 'the dancin'', not to be confused with 'going to dances' or balls, which was altogether more formal and convention-ridden, with long dresses, dinner or tail coats, with cards, wee pencils, white gloves, Mother's blessing, and a quarter at McEwans' Ballroom Dancin' lessons behind you. 'The dancin'' was not even to be confused with tennis-club hops, Bible Class socials or doing the Charleston at twenty-first birthday parties at the Plaza. 'The Dancin'' was ongoing every-night-of-the-week, a public pay-your-money and take-the-floor activity, and it was the big time to thousands.

For a while I went to the dancin' at the Dennistoun Palais every Friday and then for a wee while it was Barrowland . . . just by the Barras . . . But Green's wi' the different big bands like Joe Loss and Geraldo was the really classy place.

But first of course they had to learn the chassés and the quick-quick-slows, and it wasn't everyone who tripped along Sauchiehall Street with their patent pumps to the select McEwans' studio.

I just went to Thomsons' in Cumberland Street around the time of the First War where they learned you quadrilles and lancers, and when you were comin' on a bit and gettin' good at it, they put you to fox-trots and so on.

Duncan White took his dancin' seriously with almost missionary zeal.

I mind much later, maybe twenty-five years after, we were living in a house that had a long stretch of grass to the front and I showed a friend how to do that fox-trot I'd learned at Thomsons' ... a walk first, then seven wee trots and a long scooshy glide ... that was a long time after. I used to go jiggin' at the Dixon Hall too. I was a keen dancer so I was.

And a short demonstration follows from a man who served all through the First War seventy-five years ago.

Another who didn't go in for the white gloves and programme-card was Rose Baker.

Did you ever hear of the Spookies at Gorbals Cross?

We hazard a guess ... ghost films, or some dark maze of back-courts and dunnies? ... back-street waxworks?

Naw! The Spookies was the Spiritualists. We used to go there just for devilment. I went wi' my pal and they used to have you holdin' hands and feelin' for vibrations or some such. Anyway after the meetin' was done you used to hang about and have a wee dance to the piano in the corner that someone could tinkle a bit. But-here one night the hall got raided by the police and we got caught.
'Yer name?' the polis wanted to know.
I had to appear at Craigie Street station.
'What were you doin' there?' says the man.
I was scared to tell about the Spookies so I says, 'Was there for the dancin',' but that was daft of me, for the place wasnae licensed for dancin' and I got fined two bob.

Glasgow was dancing-daft for the first half of this century and while there was something of the mating ritual about it, many a foxtrotter paid his money for sheer love of the dancing.

I loved all kinds, and I didnae care if there wasnae enough men. I just done it wi' my china. We went to the Sequin Dancin' (sic) at a hall in Govanhill. It was that popular that I mind of a friend tellin' me about the long waiting list to join. She says a woman went to put her name down and the girl at the desk says, 'There's sixty-odd names doon to start next week a'ready Hen.'

So this woman just nods at the baby she's got in her arms, 'Aweel,' she says, 'if your list's that long and you'll no' take my name, just put her'n doon instead.'

Och your mother and me an' Mary Grady had the time of their lives when we were young. And so did you and your pals ...

And so will your grand-daughter and my grand-daughter and some other Mary Grady ... if the yen for music and movement, picnics and entertainers still remains the Glasgow characteristic it's been for generations past.

8

There was a Slitter in Every Close

Weans who lived up closes in the days when they expected a clout for misbehaviour did not much notice whose hand it came from. The close was a tight-knit community and neighbour-mothers doled out their cuffs evenhandedly to their own and other villains; whatever mother was witness delivered the slap or scolding to whatever culprit was caught.

> I had a pal that lived in a house wi' a garden, and I mind once he came to our close to play at dropping wee bags of builder's sand from the top landing into the dunny. Mistress Waddell down-the-stair (her that we called Ducky-toddle) came out and took her hand off the side of my head. My pal was mesmerised.
> 'Are you no' goin' to tell yer Ma on *her*?' says-he.
> 'An' get another fae *her*? No fears,' says-I, 'not on yer Nellie!'

Always a common entry for the inhabitants of the block of houses, until the Second War the close was also a thoroughfare for delivery and other traffic. Postmen brought letters that all the neighbours knew about, even before they fell through the right letter-box. Message-boys puffed up the stairs with great baskets of groceries on their heads, carrying dawds of butter spaded-out from big slabs behind shop counters, steeping-peas for soup, sugar and soaps and sodas, Belfast ham, lorne sausage and mouse-trap cheese. Tinkers came, selling clothes-pegs and looking for pieces for the peely-wally offspring happed in their shawls. Milk-boys clattered and whistled, up and down, carrying maybe a dozen long-handled milk-cans over each arm. In hoity-toity closes even newspapers were delivered.

As well as the communal rearing of bairns and the general traipsing in and out of dwellers and those who called on them, pride

in the close was common to all (or almost all) ... the tiled walls of
the upmarket wally entries kept washed and shining, the plain
plastered ones well-scrubbed and white-washed.

The sedate colours of the tiles in 'good' closes were ornament
enough, but the hoi-poloi kept upsides with the bien by decorating
the floors of their entries at the wall-edges with pipeclay scrolls
carefully and precisely applied in designs peculiar to each close ...
and on the matter of the white-clay handiwork, woe betide the
slattern who let the others down! As William Stevenson remembers ...

There was a slitter in every close didnae do her pipe-clayin' right, and
splashed the walls when it was her turn to wash the entry and the stair.
We'd one like that and there was a right bit of aggravation over her, I
can tell you. The rest didnae get on with her at all. And it wasnae just
the untidy whitenin', she left Brasso smudges round the wee knobs
down the banister an' all.

Another who risked the rough edge of maybe eighteen tongues was the coalman who tramped dirty boots all the way to a three or four-up bunker, leaving a trail of black dust behind him. Of course there were some who forestalled that calamity with a sheet of newspaper on every step of the stair.

A quick shifty up your average Glasgow close now, suggests mutual tolerance, to the point of coma, of dull brasses, unbrushed floors, wind-swept litter and grimy landing windows. And out beyond the dunny, back-courts are silent waste-lands (except where they are expensively grant-landscaped) and empty of all but a woman here and there, on her day off, hanging out clothes on her neat new whirly.

But in earlier days back-courts were colourful arenas of adventure, entertainment and the search for treasure. Weans played there, and wash-house roofs and coal-cellars, fences and barred windows were of the very stuff of tigs and hets and hide-'n-seeks.

> Wherever you were going or whatever you were doin' when you were young, you met your pals there, but what I liked best was the back-green singers. There was a partic'lar kind of back-court voice as if the singers were half throttled and they used to kind of slide up'n down the notes,

and no Glaswegian over fifty, who hears it said of a singer that he has a back-court voice, needs to have it further analysed.

> They sang under the windows, maybe a man or woman alone, maybe a couple. It was usually Irish songs, like the Rose of Tralee or Danny Boy. If your ma thought they were really down in their luck she used to throw over a penny or two in a poke. If she thought they'd make straight for the pub wi' that, then it would just be a jammy piece.

Two entertainers remembered by Mr. James McClelland were the envy and delight of the weans in Silvergrove Street in the 'twenties.

> One had a windy-up gramophone he hurled round in a pram, and he sang and danced to that. Another one I mind had a dressed-up monkey and a hurdy-gurdy.

Then there were the troupes of unwitting entertainers who came after dark and rummaged in the bins.

We used to stand at the window and watch the midgey-men wi' their torches or their candles, late at night, rakin' through the rubbish tryin' to find somethin' worth takin'. I cannae think *what* though, for never a thing went out of most houses that was worth a brass bawbee.

Perhaps the only one likely to throw away carelessly would be the shiftless outsider-woman who slittered the stairs and was lax with her chalk-squiggles. There must have *been* prodigal wasters though or the midden-rake wouldn't have been worth the candle.

Nancy Wall remembers her first encounter with a midgey-man when she was about twelve, in the 1920s.

We'd just flitted to this house from a cottage outside Glasgow. It was the winter and dark, and I was sent down the back one night to put the wringer in the wash-house, for the morning. I did that, and then just when I was goin' to lock the door there was this awful loud bash an' bangin' right beside me and I could see a man at the bins wi' a light. I dropped the key and ran for dear life up the stair and I got a right good flytin' for leavin' the wringer there for the man to take or, worse even, give him a shelter for the night. But flytin' or no, I wouldnae go back down there for nob'dy, and my faither had to go and lock the wringer in safe.

So the tenement precincts had their drifting population of performers and errand-boys, scaffies and hawkers; and in biener areas where they spurned the pipe-clay as 'common', there were paid stair-wash ladies like poor Woodbine Annie who roamed the Pollokshields closes forty years ago with her bucket and was said to be skuddy-naked under the long coat she wore to her ankles.

But the best-loved caller of all was surely the lamplighter.

In the winter when you came home from the school and it was gettin' dark, you used to dawdle in the street for fear the close was all ghoulie and dark. Then you used to see the learie goin' into the close and run to watch him pokelin' up his flame-stick to the gas mantle and yon sort of greenish light comin' sputterin' and floodin' the close and chasin' away the shadows. And then it was safe to go up the stair.

Nightfall still brings its own distinctive feel to the tenement world and where day has held the cheerful bustle of pram-manoeuvring and doorstep clash, children at play and the traffic of daily work, all less now but to be found here and there even yet; only the earnest whispering of courting couples, quick passing shadows and echoing footsteps, people the closes and dunnies after dark.

9
Looking for a Click

When I was going out with my young man in the 1950s he took me to visit an old man he knew, a Mr. Draper.

'So you're winching at last are you Erchie?' says-he and he looks me up-and-down with never even a how d'you do. I was black-affronted I can tell you, and if I'd thought for a minute that what my attentive and romantic Archie was doing was anything so vulgar as 'winching' it would have been all off, there and then.

So says Margaret Pollok of Riddrie. Maybe she had an early, liberated distaste for the idea that it was all his doing and she was just a hapless victim.

I thought we were just modestly getting to know each other and if we both liked what we found, we'd take one another.

Well, maybe some did it old Mr. Draper's 'rough wooing' way and others Margaret Pollok's genteel exploration way, but whatever was the truth about Erchie's attitude, there's always been plenty of *it* going on.

I was in service (och, this would be round about the 1930s) early on ... it was a big house in Jordanhill. They had a cook an' all, a Mistress Good, and I had to help a bit in the kitchen as well's being the housemaid.

The milkman used to come in every morning wi' the milk and the rolls and the pat of fresh butter for their high teas. I was always put to gettin' the milkman a cuppa tea. I was just about sixteen and he never looked the road I was on ... just sat there, right gallus, tellin' his funnies to Mistress Good.

Then after maybe eighteen month, here-I'm washin' the back step one day when he comes out and he says to me,

'This yer hauf-day Hen?'

'Aye.'

'D'you fancy the pictures ... Laurel and Hardy?'

'Y'askin' me?'

'Three o'clock then, the park gate,' says-he and away he goes to his cart.

Well he slep' all through that picture, 'Fraternally Yours' I always mind it was called. I didnae know what 'fraternally' meant or I would have thought it was just like the thing that day ... me sittin' eatin' the sweeties and him gruntin' away beside me.

Anyway I think it would be just maybe the twice more we goes to the pictures, and then he comes in one mornin', puts the bottles on the table, while Mrs. Good was in the pantry at the back.

'D'you tell her we're gettin' wed? says-he, quite jokoh.

Says-I, 'Dod Clark I hardly know you.'

'You're a blether. I'm sure I've been in an' oot here since-ever you came. D'you think I fancied her?'

'No, I think you fancy yoursel' ' says I.

Anyway Mrs Good thought a lot of him for bein' a steady and reliable sort of chap, and I took him.

Courtship wasn't always so direct, and sometimes there were real obstacles in the way. Mr. A.B. Murdoch remembers hearing of his father's problems over the lady he called Miss Right. When the young James Murdoch went for a week-end down the Clyde to Hunter's Quay in the 1870s, two things happened. He met Miss Alice Brown and he heard the Free Kirk minister preach at Dunoon. He came back home to Glasgow saying, as a serious-minded man should, that he had been very taken with the Free Kirk minister.

But the funny thing was, it was the charms of Miss Alice that lingered longer in his memory. She was the daughter of the wealthy Mr. Brown, business man and power in the community at Hunter's Quay. So James's problem was that as a young man starting out in a small way of trade himself, and living in a modest cottage at Tollcross, he felt he was in no position to pay his respects to the bonnie Miss Brown. She had won his heart, but not his head or his pride.

My father couldnae bring himself to court her and thought, how could the likes of him think to win the likes of her? But-here a year or so later the thing that was calamity for half of Glasgow was his *chance*. The City Bank collapsed and my father heard talk that Mr. Brown had lost about everything in that crash. Well ... after that he was up and down to Hunter's Quay every chance he had, and by the spring of the next year,

before her father's affairs had picked up again, Miss Alice was Mistress
Murdoch, quite happy and content in the cottage at Tollcross.

Fathers loomed quite large in courtships of earlier days. They were
jealous of their daughters' welfare, and not so helpless to ensure it
as they are now. They had authority and they asserted their rights.
Mrs. Margaret Henderson was married in 1916, but she recalls a
much earlier romance ... with another dairyman-Romeo.

> The soor-dook man was courting me. D'you mind the soor-dook carts?
> Soor dook was the left-overs when the dairy-wife was done makin' the
> butter ... buttermilk it was really. Anyway I liked yon chap and he liked
> me, and we used to go into the town for our high teas sometimes. I mind
> too that he bought me the first pair of fur-back gloves I ever had. He
> wanted me to marry him and go off wi' him to Canada.
> 'You're no' gaun near Canada,' says my father. And that was that.
> You obeyed your father in those days. So I didnae get to marry the man
> wi' the soor dook cart. I just thought to mysel', 'Well it's no to be,
> Maggie-girl, it's no' to be.' But I liked him fine mind.

Another pursuit that hadn't a hope of ending in marriage was that
by a kilted soldier of the girl in the fishmonger's shop around the
time of the First War. He was stationed in Glasgow and his duties,
or his inclinations, took him past where she worked every day. 'It's
a fishy tale this,' says her granddaughter Norma Smith.

> This soldier took a notion to my granny. She was a lassie workin' in a
> fresh-fish shop near the market and every mornin' when she was
> standin' there guttin' the fish he would come by and plague the life out
> of her to go out with him. And he used to lean over where she was
> slittin' and cleanin' the fish, him thinkin' himself a fine catch in his kilt
> and that. She used to get that mad, my granny, when he came swingin'
> along and turned in to pester her. So one day when he was at his usual,
> standin' there keepin' her off her work, she just wheeched up his kilt and
> slapped him on the buttocks wi' a cod!

That codswallop was delivered within fifteen years of the deco-
rous Victorian days, when only the heedless broke the rules of
decent behaviour between man and maid. There were other signs
too of fresh winds blowing, although parents were still strict, and
certainly to be overtly obeyed.
For instance there was a kind of street-walking enjoyed by
streams of youths and girls, who became the quite awesomely

responsible Glasgow citizens of later years. But in their greenstick days they paraded along certain areas of the city most notably on Great Western Road and around Kelvingrove Art Galleries on the north side of the river, and Victoria Road on the south.

That paradin' up and down Vicky Road on a Saturday, arm-in-arm wi' your china, lookin' for fellas ... and them lookin' for us ... was as reg'lar in its way as goin' to the kirk the next morning.

It's hard to believe that the dawner along that pavement, which went on from early in the century for thirty years, and is so universally remembered by the young of these decades, could possibly have escaped the notice of sharp-eared-and-eyed parents.

> It would be about 1910 that we walked up and down Victoria Road from the Queen's Park Gate to Calder Street and back ... always the same side, the east side ... looking for clicks ...

and the lady who was one of the strollers, when she was young May Gilmour, adds to that ...

> Mother would've been wild at the thought of us looking over the boys and sizing them up, in Victoria Road. Boy-o-boy ...

says the ninety-year-old, with seventy years of church musicianship, marriage and motherhood behind her ...

> Boy-o-boy ... would she had been wild?

When a single parader sits alone remembering those Saturdays she may tell of her part in it, with restraint, but when two sisters remember them together the cat is almost out of the bag.

> Mother didnae approve of the Victoria Road thing, sure she didn't?
>
> No, she did not, and if she happened along herself you'd to jink into a close till she was past.
>
> She caught me. I got into trouble for going to Victoria Road wi' Louise Parrish.
>
> Louise Parrish got into trouble without going to Victoria Road.
>
> So she did ... twice!
>
> I was a bad girl. I used to look for clicks with Frances McGhee ... och here I'm giving away my past. You too sister ... wheesht!

The Cathcart Circle train service had its devotees too.

> We used to go round and round the circle, chatting up the girls on the train. In the winter that was better than Victoria Road or Great Western Road.

Sometimes a pair escaped from the town to romance in outlying villages.

> I once went out with the boy next door to Barrhead for a day out. The new buses there had red lights at the back and he told me they used red oil in Barrhead. I believed him.

A surprising part of the douce life-style of the first years of the century was playing Postman's Knock at parties. When Maggie Anderson's sad little romance with the soor-dook man was long past, her real courting days began.

We werenae really introduced, we just were both playin' Postman's Knock at this friend's party and that's the way we met.

And so the serious business of walking out began.

We used to walk round the lanes in Uddingston or maybe go for high tea at Miss Cranston's, and then get a one-and-sixpenny ticket for the King's Theatre. I liked the plays but I couldnae be doin' wi' panto-mimes or music-halls. We liked the Sabbath concerts in the park fine too, right-enough.

The path of that true love ran quite smoothly into marriage, but there were less happy outcomes, even among your gentry-folk that should have known better.

I mind the Works jilting. The boss's daughter was let down by this fella she was to 've married, and her brother went to have it out with him.

They'd a right set-to and no matter the wrongs and right of it, the boss's son ended up arrested and put in the jail. The day he came out, all the men in his father's works downed tools and set off to carry him home on their shoulders like some big hero. My brother was one of them. Always had a great word of that chap, even though he was an Honorable.

If there had been a dour nub of pride in his father's reluctance to woo the rich Miss Brown from Hunter's Quay, there was a quieter old-world charm about Alick Murdoch's own courtship in 1919... and nothing haphazard in the preparation for the setting of the proposal when it came, after months of walking his lady home after Sunday evening church.

I did my courting around Tollcross. My young lady was Miss Katie McPhee. She was a Sabbath school teacher along with me. We kept company around things in the church and we went walking along-of the banks of the Clyde at Carmyle by the river paths there. Anyway says-I to myself, 'I'm going to try to make it more definite to become allied to Katie.'

So we went on a train trip together on the 31st of May 1919 to Aberfoyle and had our lunch at the Bailie Nicol Jarvie. Then we walked the mile to Loch Ard and hired a wee boat to row away up to the island in the middle. I took it up to the shore and we got out and sat on a nice green sward. Some of my nephews laugh at the way I say 'I plighted my troth' that day. But that's what I did ... and Katie said 'Yes.'

I mind she had a soft pink kind of flimsy scarf and on the way back down the loch a wee wind snatched it off and we watched it drifting away on the water. We didnae care but we always minded that.

And at ninety-five an old man sits back and remembers it all again.

She was a bonnie, nice, wee girl, Katie ... a nice wee girl.

After the first war and through the 'twenties there was a gradual relaxing of convention so that young people met, and arranged their outings without introductions to their elders. Indeed there was a new feeling that for parents to meet boy and girl-friend too soon, put a serious cast on a friendship that might be no more than fleeting.

Your parents liked to know right-enough, who you were seeing and where you were going, but there was no asking permission. You'd've laughed at that. You just met up at the kirk or the school-gate or going to work on the train, and he might ask you to the pictures or for a walk wi' a poke of sweeties. When I was in love with James Henderson at about fifteen, we went walks wi' sweeties.

Sometimes parties were got up for a bit of matchmaking that took the wrong turning.

I went to a party that was thrown to get Rob Gibson to click with Chrissie Hendry the butcher's daughter. But-here it was *me* he phoned after, and Mistress Hendry never spoke to my mother again. When we were courting Rob and I, if we were too long in the close at night my big brother Henry would come out to the one-up landing, and lean over the banister shouting me up ... too big for his boots him!

There was no great hurry in that romance.

Six years we went steady before we got married. Went walks and dancing at the Plaza, and the pictures of course. *The* Picture House in Sauchiehall Street was lovely. It had a palm-court and gold-fish and there were cages of singing birds. It was nice going there with your boy-friend.

Over the decade they met at parties and kirks, there were chance introductions and engineered co-incidences. But by the late 'twenties, holidays, no longer just a whim of the toffs, opened up a whole new field of possible 'clicks'. Meeting on piers and promenades at the Glasgow Fair were generally held to be a chancy foundation for serious romance ... but there were those which survived the holidays.

I met my Jack on the Irish boat. I was goin' my holidays wi' my sister. She was kind of flirty and she was away somewhere on the boat gettin' off wi' a bunch of campers while I was bein' sea-sick. I was just sittin' in a corner wearin' my blue hat wi' the pink rose on it, wishin' I was dead. He came over, this chap, all concerned to ask if I was all right and he took me a walk round the deck. He was in a boardin' house in Coleraine and I was across the water at Greencastle and two days later he came over in a wee boat and walked along the shore lookin' for the wee sick lassie in the blue hat. It was very romantic ... I had a most romantic life.

Back home this romance thrived, with Sunday walks and wee cups of tea or McCallum ice-creams at Muirend. And then came the introductions to the family.

He was very early invited home was Jack. You didn't just take them in right away mind. But Jack was that respectable. He had a gold watch you see. My mother thought he was *very* nice and that I had landed lucky. It was the gold watch I think really. But I did have a very quiet genteel lad there for my intended. A real nice person.

Family involvements were not always of the kind where a dignified father eyed a young man from hair-shed to best boots to judge whether he was fit mate for a beloved daughter. Rose Baker remembers the very different role played by her Aunt Kate.

My Aunt Kate was one that liked a wee refreshment, and she used to go The Snaffles pub in Howard Street. She met a chap there she thought would just do me fine, so she took me there and introduced me. Then we all had a wee drink and went for our high tea at the Queen Anne Rest'urant, and we just clicked, him and me . . . got on like a house-on-fire. I mind his first present to me was a manicuring-set. That was a laugh for I was never done bitin' my nails!

Flowers, manicure sets, sweeties, fur-backed gloves and letters were all aids to courtship over the years, and by the 'thirties and 'forties the telephone was a new boon to shy and very young suitors.

I was thirteen when I first went out with a boy in about 1941,

recalls Maisie Dean of Hyndland.

It was mostly on the phone that chaps made dates and he phoned me, then after a bit of hummin' and hawing, he asked me to go to a Scout dance. I mind thinkin' my mother wouldnae let me. But she did for she ken't his mother. I wore a flowery crepy de chine dress down to below my knees. It had a Peter Pan collar too and tassels. He was about the same age's me and he walked me home and gave me a wee cheeper in the close. Then he came in and waited, all red-faced, till his father came for him, because it was nearly half-past-ten. I didnae tell my friends about that bit because they all did real kissing wi' real fellas. I think.

If you believe all you hear, the shy manoevres of meeting, courting and holding hands, that used to be the way of it, are dead as mutton and the whole caboodle a thing of the past. But no doubt there are still lassies who giggle and plot, and gauche lads who agonise over an opening gambit, and whether they call it 'winching' or just 'going out' find it every whit as romantic as their young grandfathers.

10
Wee Man Round the Corner

There was aye a time for peever and a time for scraps and hunch-cuddy. You never kent who di'tated that ... the seasons just came roon.

Take marbles now. Since the 1890s marbles have been variously big plunkers, steelies, brown claiy dawds, white jauries; and glassies with their mysterious twists of colour inside, sometimes winkled out of lemonade bottles, sometimes bought in packets by plutocrat weans. Whatever the name, stuff or size, they were all bools, and games of marbles clicked and bounced on, and mothers made wee bags to jingle them in, through three wars, depression and boom. The best remembered game of bools was the one they called Moshie. It had interpretations enough to merit a handbook by itself, but it was played in young days around 1912 in Pollokshaws, with each player putting two or three bools into a chalked ring or a dirt circle on the ground.

There was a lot of argy-bargying and counting-out for first shot at trying to skech out as many's you could. You kep' what you skeched out. If it was goin' too easy the boss-man used to toughen it up and make it 'wee man round the corner' for the next game. Then you'd to shoot your bool round past your crook't knee and ankle.

But long before these versions there was a kind of moshie in the 1850s described by Walter Freer in his memoirs.

You needed your bunnet for moshie, and a ball. You laid your bunnet against a tenement wall and you all took turns to roll the ball into the cap from the kerb. When you got it in you'd to breenge across the street and touch the other wall before him that's bunnet it was, took the ball out of your cap and creeshed you wi' it.

There were a hundred-and-one things to do with balls of course.

Many a wee lassie who played ball-beds in the 1890s lived to be great-granny to one still bouncing the ball around chalk grids in the 1960s.

> I mind yet the dunt it gave you when you touched a line and had to sit out until the next time round.
> And d'you mind a-leerie? You could play it on your lone. How did it go again ...? Oh aye ...
>> One, Two, Three a-leerie
>> Four, Five, Six a-leerie
>> Seven, Eight, Nine a-leerie
>> Ten a-leerie Post-man.
> And you stotted your ball off of the pavement on to the wall a lot of different ways, under your leg and birling round and clapping between bounces. You just went on and on till you missed ... oh aye I liked a-leerie.

They all liked a-leerie and they all liked jinkers and other ball, catch and chase games. But, as the present-day granny who was Betty

WEE MAN ROUND THE CORNER

Laurie with ringlets and big bows in the First War years, says,

> I didn't like being het.

'Het' ... nobody fancied being 'het', whatever the game. But if there was one thing worse than being het it was to be called 'It' instead. 'It' was if you were cissy or English (which was much the same thing) or Edinburgh, which was worse than either.

> You always had your het for hiding-seek. You'd to count-out to get who was het.

But apart from counting rhymes to find the chaser, there was a wee two-liner scold for the miserable class of het who lurked around the den instead of going out fearlessly searching.

> You're moochin' the den
> You big fat hen'

That was a right sore insult, near as bad as when you'd cliped on someone and got your come-uppance for that.

> 'Tell-tale-tit, your Granny cannae knit'

The counting-out jingles were legion and better remembered than lots of games,

> 'Azeenti-Teenti-Figary Fell
> Ell Dell Dom-in-ell
> Urky Purky Taury Rope
> An Tan Toosie Joke
> You are HET'

or, and this time with the line of players holding out two fists in front to be cuffed one at a time by the boss-man doing the counting-out,

> One potottie, Two potottie, Three potottie, Four
> Five potottie, Six potottie, Seven potottie, More.

and at More! the last fist to be hit was put behind the back and the whole rigmarole went on again ... and again. Last fist left was 'het'.

> It took that long sometimes that you got shouted in before you were done wi' the pototties, and that was the ball-on-the-slates for your tig or whatever.

Azeentie Teentie was dying by the 1940s, but the fists were still potottied and the new Tic-Tac sorting out first shots at things. Tossing a penny lacked the ritual of any of them, and anyway the penny had usually disappeared into Ogo-Pogo eyes or chocolate-chewing-nuts before the game was planned.

Then there was jumping-ropes! Skipping is remembered with joy across all the years from the 1880s to times present. A solitary wean could just wind her rope round her hands to shorten it and get on with the job alone, but it was the eruption of small girls in a fankle of ropes into the playground when the bell clanged ... and the cry going up 'No ender!', that most remember.

> You done your jumpin'-ropes in the street or the playground or maybe the backgreen. I was a rare wee skipper ... that would be about 1899 ... two an' out was two jumps in a cawin' rope and out the other side ... And d'you mind of 'keep the pot boilin'? That was when the next lassie didnae wait on you finishing, but came in the same caw you went out.

Through the 1920s and 1930s they skipped, backwards and forwards, arms crossed, two turns to a jump, two jumps to a turn, red-faced, breathless, and gasping out their rhyming chants like metro-gnomes.

> Matthew, Mark, Luke, John
> Aks the Ro-mans where they're gaun
> If they say they're gaun to Rome
> Hit them wi' a tattie scone.

And in a Glasgow always beset by 'feeling' between Billys and Dans there had to be a counterblast.

> Matthew, Mark, Luke, John
> Aks the Proddies where they're gaun
> If they say they're gaun to Kirk
> Whack them wi' a great big stick.

Those who neither knew, nor cared, a bawbee about Romans or Proddies had other immortal 'poentry' for their skips,

> A hunner and ninety-nine
> My faither fell in a byne
> My mither came oot wi' the washin' cloot
> And skelped his big behind.

That was in the thirties. By the fifties they had ...

> High, low, slow, mejum,
> Dolly-rocky, pepper, wishy.

The first four were just what you'd think, dolly-rocky was jumpin' side to side, pepper was quick, and wishy your own special trick. You shouted to the enders what you were going to do and they did the rope right for that.

Indeed the skinny-ma-linky wee lassie of any decade that could twinkle her feet like magic in the ropes was more of a queen to the others than the one that could rattle off her tables or get ten out of ten for her spellings, or *even* the one who could sit on her hair. The lady who was skipping as wee Maggie Anderson in 1896 puts it ...

> You were no use if you couldnae skip or peever.

Ah peevers! Peevers were edged from chalk-bed to chalk-bed by the toe, as the player hoppetied her way along in the correct order without the peever coming to rest on a line. It was played in the gaiters and button boots of the turn of the century, the bar-and-button shoes of the 'teens and the canvas sannies of the twenties.

> And *we* played it in the forties

protests one of the four elegant and accomplished Gibson sisters who were hopscotching throughout these ten years, in Croftfoot.

> We had *beautiful* peevers, with our initials on them ... personalised! We played outside, but we played on the blue-square-patterned carpet in the living room as well. Just the thing that carpet!

Some remember singing-games as street-play. But they were the children of the very early years. After that singing-games belonged to indoor parties or the Brownies. For Mrs. Margaret Henderson they were out-of-door games and she can still sing clear and softly the songs she shouted as a lusty five-year-old ninety years ago,

> In and out the windows,
> In and out the windows,
> In and out the windows,
> As you have done before.

And her old hands did the dance that once her feet had done as a follow-my-leader ring game long ago, when Uddingston was countryside, outside the city.

Around 1910 young girls like Cathie Anderson were still singing in the open air and gathering flowers as they went.

> I mind, clear as clear, the smell of wild garlic when we used to go up round Cathcart Castle yonder, every May Day, to gather celandines. And we sang going up that hill ...
> 'You must wake and call me early,
> Call me early Mother dear,
> For I'm to be Queen of the May, Mother
> I'm to be Queen of the May.'

Summer days were always long and to be filled by more than singing-games and skipping. There were the young adaptations of adult sports, played with whatever make-do implements lay at hand. Mr. William Stevenson remembers playing golf.

> Aye we played at golf on the field behind Harriet Street. You dug a wee hole first. Then you bent a bit wire off a fence into a kind of club shape. After that you collected yon washer-rings off of ginger bottles and put them on for the handle. You were a'ready then to hit a bit cork to the hole from so-far away. Sometimes you could do it in two shots or three. Other times it took about a dozen. You didnae have toys or that bought to you. You just invented them.

But he's gone over to the Establishment since those days.

> I've been a member of Cowglen Golf Club and Barassie, these past thirty or so years,

and it's 'bowls' at an expensive club now where once it was moshie in a dirt ring. He considers ...

> but I'm no' sure I enjoy all that better than yonder at Harriet Street wi' the bit fencin' and the ginger-washers.

There were other rule-books games for other boys to copy.

> 'Where are you goin' Alick?' ... Mother out the kitchen window.
> 'Goin' to the cricket Mother,' ... me wi' my best bat all ready to play in the farmer's field.
> 'You see that stretch of garden you were to weed last week Alick?'
> 'Aye Mother.'
> 'There'll be no cricket the day till you've all that done.'
> I knew there would be no cricket that afternoon ... I think the iron entered my soul that day and I've never been that keen on gardening ever since.

Footb'll and cricket were the main things we played at in Tollcross
ninety year ago. That's where you got your discipline

or maybe just from the lady at the kitchen window.

Even some girls endured the discipline of football. Nellie Edgar
played around 1919.

You all played. You ca'ed it seven-a-side, no matter you'd six to play or
twenty-five ... seven-a-side it was. I always bagsed to be the goalie
because I didnae like it rough. The goalie was in the game right-enough
but no' in the stramash.

Sometimes the goal posts in street football were stones or jackets,
or just chalk marks on walls and then, as in street cricket, only a puff
of chalk dust was evidence that a goal had been missed or a wicket
taken.

But it's a panting, peching business, all that skipping, stotting,
tigging and footb'll, and there's another chapter ahead for more
playing. Meantime tomorrow is the Sabbath and that day and its
rituals leave memories that are just as indelible in their way as
moshie or jinkers.

11
Slotted into Pews

You'd think to hear some folk now that in the old days it was 'No, no, no!' that you didnae do this and you didnae do that on the Sabbath ... that you just went about all douce and glunchy. Well right-enough you didnae play in the street or do dice and card games in the house. But Sunday was for a lot of things you did do ... things that made it different from other days.

So it was. It was for kirk and Sabbath School, for Sunday dinners and walks and visiting. And fortifying the tribe for the rigours of the day was the *cooked* breakfast.

It was porridge through the week but, oh aye, we always started Sundays wi' a cooked breakfast. That was one of the high-lights of the week, the eight of us sitting there at our cooked breakfasts. Mother couldnae have done it very easy on a labourin' man's wage, but we'd always our sausage or maybe very occasionally a wee bit scrambled egg, on a Sunday.

Breakfast down and the dishes washed, the next item on the Sunday agenda was the walk to the kirk. For some it was close to home.

We were just marched a wee bit along the street to our kirk for it was part of the same block as our tenement.

For others, like young Joe and Willie Kyle around 1910, there was a fair old hike.

We walked the three miles to the kirk on a Sunday morning, then home for dinner and back again to the Sunday School in the afternoon. There were kirks nearer home mind you, but that was the one where my father was and where we were baptised.

For yet others the walk to the church was a modest flaunting of the Sunday braws.

My friend's family and mine always walked together to church, with the children in front so we didn't get up to mischief. That would be about 1912. Margaret and I usually craiked at our mothers to get us clothes the same. I remember one summer we'd coats alike, but for colour ... mine was gold satin with a hat to match, and she was the exact same but blue. Oh very dressy we were on Sundays! It wouldn't've done to get the satin coats splashed with rain so if it was wet we took the white tram.

Having reached their various kirks, well-nigh the whole citizenry of Glasgow was slotted into pews for the next hour or more ... sometimes much more.

We'd get there and *in* we used to troop to our pew. There was Bill, the eldest, first; then me, then Elizabeth, then Jim and Meg and George, and then mother and faither.

I mind when Bill got away to the far end he used to sit down and hunch up his shoulders, turning towards the wall a wee bit. He was s'posed to be kind of pious and he used to take down the sermon in shorthand so's he could give the gist to the Sunday School in the afternoon. Anyway he always looked like he was taking down the whole service, but I knew fine he was readin' his Dixon Hawke till the time of the preachin' came on. Then he *had* to listen to get his notes right.

Other children spent a fair bit of the service puzzling over strange statements in hymns and psalms about 'throwing weary pilgrimages' and suchlike.

When I was just wee I couldnae understand why a green hill should've had a city wall, so what did it matter that it was without one. The hymn I liked best was The Lord my Shepherd ... but again in *it* there was that head that I thought was messy with all the 'oil and oint' on it ... Every time I sing them even now in the kirk, at eighty-eight, the same ideas I had then, come to mind. And there's me standing there, old and crabby-lookin' and inside I'm smilin' away and just wee again.

Sometimes, of course, there was a baptism. Families were big and all but the youngest (the poke-shakin's) were well-acquaint with Christenings.

I mind when you went to the kirk wi' a Christenin' party and then came out after, your Mother or your Pa had a wee piece or a bit cake wi' them and the thing to do was, that if your wean was a lassie you gie'd the chuck to the first man you met and if your wean was a boy, you gie'd it to the first woman.

That was your own kirk, but occasionally there was a visit to a service in another church, perhaps a parent's childhood congregation. Young Anne Gardner went sometimes as a treat, taking the red tram out Cathedral Street.

> I used to go sometimes with my father to the Barony Church. He used to *be* Barony when he was a young man at the turn of the century. Anyway it was a long tram ride away and there weren't too many trams ran on Sundays, so after church, while we were waiting for a 'car' home, we used to go into the Tallie's shop for a McCallum. Mother would've been horrified ... but I don't suppose we rushed home to tell her.

That tram ride was their lull before Sunday dinner but other fathers took the weans for walks to whet their appetites. Father Fotheringham took his brood to the flagpole at Bellahouston Park after the kirk, or to the Maxwell Park. The Guthrie crocodile was led by their father round Victoria Park and the Fossil Grove.

The Edgars went to Pollok.

> Sometimes between kirks, morning and afternoon, father took us to the Policies, or out the Cowglen for a walk, and I mind sometimes of seeing Sir John Stirling-Maxwell out walking or driving. He would be coming home from kirk too, for he sat under the minister at Eastwood up the hill. Mother didnae go on the walks. She was at home makin' dinner.

These were the stepping-out walks for those who lived on the outskirts of the city. But there were other less energetic after-church strolls nearer to the up-market heartlands of the city, and Great Western Road and the Crescents of the west-end were thronged at noon on Sundays with families making their leisurely way home from morning service. Some socialised with each other in chatting groups, some made stately progress along the pavement, the ladies nodding under the bonnets of the nineties, the cabbage-rose cart-wheels of Edwardian summers, and the twenties' cloches. Their menfolk lifted hats (from lum to bowler in their fashion) and swaggered, ever-so-slightly, their silver-knobbed walking canes and rou'ed up gamps.

Survivors of that Sunday parade admit that there was a showing-off of well-put-on families in their Sunday bests, but point out piously too, that they would no more have gone into God's house

in unseemly claddings than they would have insulted a hostess so, in *her* home.

Then it was back to Sunday dinner. The family home from its walk, hungry and expectant, Mother emerged with ashet and tureen, Father said grace, and they were off!

My mother wouldn't have thought Sunday was Sunday without a joint of meat ... beef or a gigot of lamb with roast potatoes. Soup first usually, and then the likes of a steam pudding or a jam rolly.

Across the city it was the same ritual but a different menu.

Roast beef ... never! Roast beef was just in stories. But my ma made a rare meat-loaf and we'd that wi' champit tatties that had onions through them, and for afters, a suet puddin' in a big bowl. My pa was reared up in the country and he said what he called his bethankit when we were done eatin'. That was Sunday dinner.

Except during a few weeks in the summer there was afternoon Sunday School. Two old ladies drink their tea at a winter fire and forget their angina and rheumatics in quiet laughter over remembered lessons.

I loved the Sunday School Dorothy, did you? D'you mind learning the Bible Stories and getting yon wee tickets from the teacher with golden texts and pictures on them?

Yes, and rhyming off the books of the Bible and the Beatitudes and bits of the Psalms.

Right-enough yes ... and the Catechism. I hated the Catechism.

We sat there and giggled or poked each other. But we must've listened to something, sure we must?

Ah but I didn't always know what the texts an' that meant, and definitely *not* the Catechism. But now it's funny, they come easy to me and I think maybe I know what they mean after carrying them in my head all these years.

Not everyone was so keen.

I didnae like it much. I just tholed it because I was sent. I was the age for Sunday School before the First War and I don't mind that I learned much. I would be well-enough behaved but I never took up with the Kirk when I'd just myself to please.

On the other hand Jack Bute's camsteerie ongoings and verdicts on the Kirk Session, when his Sunday School class observed the Communion Service from the gallery, didn't have a lasting blight on his commitment since he has been devoted elder and session clerk himself for many a long year.

We used to lean over and pass cheeky whispers along the pew about the elders as they filed in, all like black and white penguins. We used to bring feathers to drop over, then we watched them floatin' down to settle on some lady's best hat or a man's good suit.

Another less-than-righteous lad remembers offering more than the coin-of-the-realm to the collection.

> The Superintendent used to tell us at the end of the Sunday School how much the offering was, and where it would go, and I always remember him standing up there looking all stern, without a smile on his face. 'Today's collection came to One Pound Three Shillings and Sixpence, a nice black button and an Irish ha'penny ... and it goes to the Tent Hall Mission and the Leprosy Society.'

Then June came and the Flower Service, when they all brought lupins and fruit for the sick, and got their prizes for good attendance or high marks in the Bible Exam. After that it was the summer holidays. That didn't mean out to play, of course, but the start of the really long walks that were a feature of Glasgow Sabbaths, until car runs and sprawling at the television flabbied walking muscles.

On these summer Sundays the Fotheringham treks went far beyond Bellahouston flag-pole.

> Sometimes we walked from Dumbreck to Queen's Park and took a tram to Eastwood Toll. This was before the First War. Then we walked the four miles to Newton Mearns village. There was a nice tea-room there ... just a house really with a verandah and pillars. I can still taste the scones we got there, but the thing I liked the best was the wee pot of jam you got to yourself. After that if it was a nice day you walked all the way home, maybe eight or nine miles, down by Spiersbridge and through the Pollok estate.

Others walked to Eaglesham or Cathkin Braes ... or northwards to Chapelton Loch or out over the Switchback to Milngavie, and the only refuelling for the long walk home was often a cup of tea or an ice-cream cone — and if your pa was strict about the Sabbath, maybe neither.

Next on the day's timetable, to nail the lie that old-time Sundays were long deserts of boredom and inactivity, was the Visiting ... *from* or *to* the clans of aunties and uncles most folk had before families shrank to two-point-five. It was always for high tea.

Goin' was much better'n *havin'* them, for you could eat what you liked and there was no F.H.B. (d'you mind being told 'family hold back'?)

If there was evening church, friends often came back after the service. Young Maggie Anderson loved that, ninety years ago, and enjoys resurrecting the old scene now.

Father used to bring home Doctor Smith and Mr. Turnbull the organist, after the kirk, and we all sang hymns and sacred songs round the piano with the candles lit on the sconces. We all got to choose our favourites and folk used to stop on the street outside to listen. My, that was lovely on a Sunday night. Then *we* went to bed and the grown-ups had their suppers.

Mrs. Nancy Watt, though, squirms at memories of the tail-end to similar Sunday evenings in her home a few years later.

All the young folk came to our house after church to sing round the piano with my sister playing hymns and suitable Sunday songs ... that was nice. But-here my grandpa stayed with us and at ten o'clock sharp he used to come in and tell them it was time to go home.

Even that wasn't so bad, but then he used to stand at the door and, as they went out, he shook hands with each one and said, 'Joy be with you ... joy be with you.' He was an old saint really, but I was so embarrassed.'

That then was the shape and programme of the Sabbath itself from breakfast to evening blessing. It was regular, planned, obligatory. The almost universal practice of church-going from Victorian times throughout the first third of this century suggests a bland obedience to sameness in religious matters which was far from the truth. They all went to kirk certainly but, in over forty conversations, eleven or more denominations were claimed, from Wee Free to Roman Catholic.

My father was Wee Free, so he didn't hold with Christmas.

I was converted to the Brethren when I was a girl.

We went to the Methody in Cathcart.

A lot of Highland folk like myself took to the Congregationals ...

We were Episcopals, when I was a girl in the nineties and after. I think that was because my folks had been estate workers and they all attended the estate chapel. Anyway, when I got wed I went wi' my man to the Presbyterian Kirk, but after the Piskies it was a wee bit dull no' to take your part in the service. So sometimes at Easter, just to mind me of old times, I used to slip away to the Anglican Church at Polmadie.

The youthful Marie Condie out at Uddingston, didn't sit like Buddha waiting for enlightenment to strike her in her own kirk, she went out seeking for it.

When I got to be about fourteen I used to go to the Hallelujah Hall to see if I could get converted. I wasnae really sure what that meant ... but I knew when it happened right-enough. It was good there. We sang songs and choruses, sometimes solo, sometimes all joinin' together, rousin' and loud. Then cups of tea came round.

Another who went out after more nourishment at night, when duty

had been rendered at her own church and Sunday School, was May
Gilmour, just after the turn of the century.

> When we were about fourteen or fifteen my friend and I used to take a
> ha'penny one in the tram to go to the Congregational Church near St.
> Andrew's Halls to hear Ambrose Shepherd preaching. He was gettin'
> on by then but oh my, could he preach? The place was packed every time
> and people sat on the pulpit steps and stood all round the back. I used to
> grit my teeth all the way home in the tramcar ... 'I'll be good, oh I'll be
> good!'

Eighty-year-old memories of gritted teeth and vows of righteous-
ness are surely a fair tribute to powerful preaching.

Scots have never easily knuckled under to the heresies of those
who disagreed with them. Most especially not in matters of
religion. Having seen the light, offered it to their brethren and been
rejected, rather than sit on, quibbling and chawnering, they have
preferred to take their truth with them and set up new denominations round the corner.

> Our wee Original Secession kirk was quite bien, because a lot of the first
> elders in it, had been kind of thinkin' folk that had come out the
> ordinary kirk over their beliefs. It was a well-run wee place wi' a decent
> building and a paid minister ... and it didnae be that on the six pennies
> Willie and me, an' Bessie and Maggie an' James an' George put in the
> plate, or even mother and faither's wee thrupennies, there were lawyers
> and doctors an' teachers wi' a wee bit more behind them to help things
> along.
>
> That was the Original Seceders,* the Auld Lichts, then another wee
> breakaway of folk that thought they were an improvement were called
> the New Lichts. Later they came together again, the Auld and the New,
> to make the United Presbyterians.

But however marked the differences were among these, they were
all splinters of the Reformed Church. The truly great Glasgow
divide has always been the Grand Canyon between Protestant and

---

* (The reasons for the breakaway in the 18th century of certain churchmen from the
old Kirk were complex ... a skirlie of objections to the placing of ministers by the
laird's patronage and also an alarmed conviction that the idea of reasoned inter-
pretation of Scripture was a do-it-yourself blasphemy, fudging belief in 'Saving' by
God's grace alone.)

Catholic. For over three hundred years Proddy-folk of whatever caste have been making their way along one street to their building while their Catholic neighbours have made theirs to chapel on the next street. Not many like Lily Timlin had the ecumenical experience of being both.

My mother lost her man in the First War and after a while she married again, so we went away to live wi' my stepfather and I didnae see anything of my own father's lot for a long while. My stepfather was very strict and I was at the kirk and Sunday School every week. There was no playin' or workin' on Sundays and I mind that if a button came off of your shoe, like, you didnae get to sew it on so you couldnae even go a walk. Anyway, then my mother died and when I was about fourteen I came back to live wi' my own father's Ma. I mind the day I arrived alone at her house, and sittin' there talkin to this granny that I hardly knew. There was me eyein' up all the holy pictures in the room and just wonderin' to myself . . . then when we were at our tea my granny came away wi' her bombshell.

'You ken Lily, that you're a Catholic?' says-she.

'You're kiddin'!' says-I, for if there was one thing I knew I wisnae . . . it was a Catholic. After all these years in the Sunday School! I couldnae be. So I told her. Well she didnae say any more then, but on the Sunday she took me to St. Mary's and after the service, sure enough, the priest brought out the Baptism register and there was me, 'Lily Timlin, born 31st January 1914 baptised 4th February by the Reverend Father Reilly.' Well, murder-polis, whit a thing! It was like I was two people. Then to make up for the wicked years at the Sunday School I went for about six weeks instruction at the Helpers of the Holy Soul. I took a great notion there to Mother Agatha. She was nice. She talked to me and took me to sales of work and fêtes and suchlike. So you see I've aye been a bit of both really, . . . never felt sore about the one or the other.

And that's maybe a sensible place to leave the Sunday doings of the good citizens of Glasgow, reconciled in the two people who were Lily Timlin.

12
Tam Tunnock did the Purvey

I can trace our family back ten generations and I found out a funny thing about that. I had over five hundred great-great-great-great-great-great-great-great grandparents. Fancy that! But there was really only two I knew about, out of all of them. They were up before the Kirk Session and made to get married. So weddings have been goin' a long time in our family. That one was in 1602.

Others too can pin down two or more of the army of ancestors whose lines finally converged on Glasgow to produce them. Mrs. Margaret Kent has a tangible little item to bring an old family romance to life.

My grannie gave me a ring that was given to my great-great-great grandmother at her betrothal in 1703.

It lies gleaming on her hand as bright and fresh as the day it was slipped on to Bethia Hall's finger when Queen Anne was on the throne. The date 1703 is engraved inside and, beside it, the initials B.H. Neither shank nor setting is crudely cut as in many old rings, but expertly worked and set with amethyst and garnet. With the ring has come down just enough of the family's history to tantalise and intrigue.

Bethia's father Nicholas Deschamp was a Huguenot refugee who came from France in the 1690s, started to collect rags round the doors and then set up his own small paper-making place near the Snuff Mill bridge at Cathcart. There, it's said, he made the paper for the Darien Scheme documents ... and presumably enough money to dower Bethia well-enough to match her fine ring.

The earliest mention of celebrations after a marriage ceremony is from the mid-1800s and is therefore once-removed from direct memory. Mrs. Janet Purvis of Eastwoodhill House describes the occasion as it was told to her. The bride and groom seem to have been young Victorian moderns, well ahead of their time by being wed in church after the English custom, rare in Glasgow.

After the service they went to Hughes' and Pinkertons', a high class restaurant at Bridgeton Cross, for the reception. My aunt was the bridesmaid and so she met the best man that day, on leave from India, and they got married on his next leave.

Then there was a gentry wedding in the 1890s, of a much-loved local laird who displayed a hapless choice of words to present his bride to the local tenantry.

My mother was brought up on the laird's estate. Her father, you see, was a labourer to Sir George. Mother could talk about the tenantry balls and suchlike that she got to, but she liked best to remember the day Sir George got wed. She just loved the laird, did my mother. Anyway when he brought his bride home, a year or so before the turn of the century, the estate carters met the newly-weds at the old station. They loused the horses from their yokes, went into the shafts themselves and pulled the carriage home to the Big House. At the entrance the laird called for all the workers to toast his new wife. 'This is my lady' he says 'and she's better than she's bonnie.' I suppose he meant *even* better, but though she was nice, right enough, she was an unbraw woman so she was. So the men were never quite sure.

Maybe Sir George was a wee frog in a big puddle compared to his future King, but the laird's reputation was above the kind of reproach that that popular but roving monarch had to put up with. But Edward had apparently sterner marriage principles for those who served him than for himself.

I once worked under a Duke and Ladyship when I was about seventeen in wartime when their home was a military hospital. The Duke had been a gentleman-in-waiting to Edward VII but because there had been a divorce before their marriage he was dismissed his place at court. I thought that was kind of funny of Edward VII, sure it was?

There were great lairds like that in Scotland who owned large properties and there were wee lairds who owned small properties. But there was another category too, who were lairds of no more than their own hearthsides.

I can mind of a friend of my mother's that came from one of Glasgow's old boroughs. I used to visit her room-and-kitchen house sometimes and I heard her call her man, not Jamie that was his right name, but 'laird'. 'Put the kettle on the hob for the lassie's tea, laird' she used to say, and he answered her, 'Aye, right y'are then Mistress.'

Plain work-folk they may have been to the gaffers in Lum Hat Street but they were laird and mistress to each other. And a related quirk of Scottish life is brought out by other reminiscences and stabs of memory. More perhaps then elsewhere, women have retained a kind of par-status with their menfolk in the use of their maiden names, in conversation, in newspaper reports and in documents. Even in the end on their gravestones. There a woman may have been that bleak-sounding left-over, somebody's 'relict' but at least she's been a relict with her own name.

Laird and mistress then, in their two rooms, James Macewan and Jessie Storr, and none prouder. The tea was duly masked and served in the wedding-present china of many years before.

Other wedding treasures have survived in the rememberers' homes to be used with pride and footnote still, even among the present day's suffocating amount of gear.

See that teaspoon you're stirring your tea with, well that set came to my mother over eighty years ago as a wedding present from her bachelor brother in New Zealand. They always minded her of him. He was a doctor away in the outback and went on his rounds with his horse, and with the district nurse riding back-saddle behind him.

And there was maybe a tradition of pleasure in good cutlery, for when May Reid herself was married she added to her mother's solid silver teaspoons a present from another noteworthy source.

I was in charge of buying gowns in Fraser's in the twenties when young Hugh came in to learn the ropes, so I knew him pretty well when he was a laddie. By the time I was getting married he was a man though, and he took me to his family's jewellers above the Grosvenor and bought us a lovely canteen of cutlery. Nice he was, Hugh Fraser.

Money may have been tight and food short in the throes of the First War but 'there was none of your silly wee savouries' at Maggie Anderson's wedding in 1916.

We'd our reception in the Public Hall and Tam Tunnock did the purvey (him from the baker's shop), steak pie and potatoes and all that, and a wedding cake. It was the war mind, so there wasnae sugar for icing, just a cardboard cover all decorated wi' plaster. It looked the same's icing and the same cover went over all Tam's wedding cakes, that wartime. It was quite nice and the cake under it was lovely. We just drank juice ... no wine or that carry-on. Couldnae afford that nonsense anyway.

Just as clear in the ninety-five-year-old's memory were her wedding clothes.

My rig-out was yon shot-silk taffeta in all different shadings, and I had a bokay of flowers off a friend that was a gardener at a big house. And I mind having Leghorn straw hat wi' big-big roses round it. My man's knees were gey wobbly that day, for the wedding was in the Episcopal church and *he* was Kirk ... didnae know all the wee ways at our service.

There must have been many a catch to the heart and in the 'I do's' of wartime marriages.

I was married on Sandy's leave in 1917 and we'd a nice week-end at Largs for our honeymoon. Then he went away back to France ... Just his watch came back and two-three letters. I suppose it was a bit of the Somme fighting. I never right knew where. I was that numb sittin' there

wi' the telegram in my hand in the nice room and kitchen I was gettin'
ready for him.

Others had happier reunions, Mrs. Milree ...

I was married six months before the Armistice and then my husband
went back to France. He spoke several languages so he was a liaison
officer with the Seaforths there. I was one of the lucky ones that he came
back. Anyway I wore navy-blue taffeta at my wedding. It was in the
parlour and it was Dr. Cooper of Strathbungo married us. My father
was a kirk elder there.

Through many generations it's been the marriage-right of
Scottish brides, rich or poor, to take up house well-tochered with
presents from neighbours, friends and kin. And few new houses are
short of linen, kitchen-ware, crockery, or little bits of silver for
'best'. But among the recollections are those of one girl whose
hanselling was very sparse.

I'd no family behind me by the time I was fourteen and into service out
Great Western Road. In a few years I was walkin' out wi' this chap on
my afternoons off, when my mistress died. My chap Joe was on his own
too, so we just got wed quiet. The only present I had, bar a new coat
from him, was a tea-set that the mistress's niece gie'd me out the house.
Many's the time I had washed them cups after an afternoon tea, and now
here they were mine's. They were my proudest possession they dishes,
for many a long year. Forbye them, we started off wi' just a few poke-
shakin's he had of his mother's, a bit cutlery, a few towels a pot an' that
... and a stick or two furniture we picked up at a sale.

A mixed marriage in Glasgow has traditionally meant the
coupling of Catholic and Protestant and many a family has been
thrown into confusion at the prospect. But there are, and were,
other graftings and other ways of handling such matters.

I was a member of the Brethren when I married Mr. Purvis and my
father was very firm and wise.
'There must be no divided house. You'll go to the Glasgow Cathedral
with your husband and be in the Kirk there.'
    That was in 1920 when Dr. MacAdam Muir was minister, and I've
been a member there ever since.

Most of the menfolk recall their courting days but not many can
describe their own wedding attire or their bride's.

Mine's was tight at the collar but other than that I couldnae say. Jenny was in pink, was it? Or maybe pale blue. She was aye nice in blue. I mind my honeymoon better . . . just a day or two at Saltcoats. It was that cold we'd to wear jerseys in bed. No' very romantic? Oh aye, bar that, it was quite romantic.

By the early twenties weddings were beginning to come out of parlours and into hotels; and other fashion changes were on the way among post-war brides.

I had my hair cut for the first time, the day of my wedding. It had aye been long, down to my waist then 'up' from I was eighteen. I was early to have short hair and my very first silk stockings were for my honeymoon.

Mrs. Helen Stewart remembers her wedding-day in 1930. By then the day of the hotel wedding was in full swing for both ceremony and reception. Church marriages too were coming in, for some to highlight the earnest of their vows, for some as a braw setting for the great day, for others a thoroughly human mixture of both.

But *we* werenae married in church nor yet at a hotel. Nobody got wed in the Secession Church (that was the Auld Lichts Kirk mind). So it was our parlour at the Wellmeadow.

And she recalls the day of her nuptials with pride, pleasure and unsentimental good humour. The wedding season, of course, began the day before.

Aye, aye, the day before when I left work at the mill, (you didnae go back once you were married) . . . anyway, there was a right carry-on. I was very sedate myself and I didnae think they would do these things to me. But they did. They decked me out with old lace curtains and I had to carry a chantie along the street from the mill to home. I was that mortified! I wasnae that kind at all, but they did it to me. Aye, did they no' just.

Next day the minister came in his lum hat to perform the ceremony in the fine front room with the congoleum floor. Now Nellie and her chap are man and wife and it's reception time. Her mother had the afters organised weeks before.

'It'll no' be big Nellie, but we'll do the whole thing right and have a nice Co-operative Purvey.' And so we did. We'd steak pie and potatoes and peas.

And her rig-out for the day?

> I wore a blue dress at 19s. 11d. out of the C & A ... stiff Taffeta. I got a
> real nice coat too. The first really good thing I ever had. And I had a
> straw hat forbye.
>
> We called that my going-away coat, but-here we werenae goin'
> anywhere. We didnae have a honeymoon but I had a right good setting-
> down in a two-room-and-kitchen with all the wedding-presents. Nice
> presents ... cream jugs and wee biscuit plates and suchlike. The biggest
> was from a brother-in-law in the London Police. He sent a Sheffield
> carving set. I just looked at it and laughed.
>
> 'What do I do wi' that?' says-I, for it was mostly mince we had.
> Anyway it was my man's pride and joy that carving set.

A wedding at the same period of the early thirties *was* in the church,
the fine Trinity (now Glencairn) in Pollokshields. Photographs
show a beautiful bride in a simple white gown surrounded by black
and white morning dress and bonnie chapleted bridesmaids in
dresses that were slender and close-fitting from shoulder to knee,
then flaring out in frothing lace and lover's knots. The lady guests
in the arch of the doorway are in ankle-length coats with huge fur
collars and snug cloche hats. No Co-op purvey at that reception in
Gordon Street's Grosvenor Function Suite, but a fitting menu to
follow an elegant Glasgow wedding of between the wars.

Where there was no mother there were hazards to arranging a
wedding, especially two years into the Second War with all its
regulations and restrictions.

> When Jimmy and I were to get married, we'd each to get our papers for
> the Registry. He got his when he was off and I got mine's when I was off.
> I was on the buses y'see ... shifts. Well all the purvey was laid out at my
> granny's and him and me were to meet our witnesses at the Registry. My
> papers were for the Registry right enough, but I suppose *he* thought you
> went on somewhere else for the actual ceremony, because the papers he
> had were for a church. So they wouldnae do us at the Registry. Oh my,
> what a carry-on! An' the purvey all ready at my granny's! Anyway they
> 'phoned a minister and we just went round to his manse and got married
> there.

So, high-spired church with Lohengrin, or scramble in the
Registry with purvey at granny's, each was the climax to the
winching and the catch, the hopeful prelude to happy married life.

But not everyone found bliss in marriage delivered as promised, and some indeed wondered if it had all been worthwhile. Polly Strang tells of her teaching days in the 1940s.

> I remember a Mrs. Ritchie comin' up to the school to have it out that her girl was being unfairly got at. The family had all been right wee handfuls for the staff and soon the mother and this teacher were having a confidential chat about her difficult man and her hullarackit children. She was ready to go away quite calmed down, and then she turned back
> ...
> 'Mind I sometimes think yous old maids has the best of it ... after yous gets over the affront of not bein' asked'.

Should we let her have the last word on marriage? Why not? She was a realistic wee woman and she must have come to terms with Mr. Ritchie, or else herself been 'got at' because before Polly Strang's teaching time was out at that school there were several more infant Ritchies either in the school or at various stages on the way.

13

Three Miles was Nothing wi' your Gird

So, Sundays over, the week's work and play began again and there's another batch of outdoor playing fads and fancies to be prised out of elderly memory banks. When winter's football, skating and ice-slides were past, when finger and ear-chaps were healed and the Snowfire ointment away at the back of the bathroom press, then all the joys of the long warmer days came and they took up again the round of things they had done last summer.

That was when the call of the yonder came to bairns, from single-ends to Jordanhill mansions, and *wheels* . . . any kind of wheels were the thing.

> We made bogies. You got a plank and a pair of old pram wheels, wi' a swivel bar and a bit of clo'es line for steering. We lived up Rotten Row way and we used to start wi' the bogie up the top of John Street and go breengin' down across George Street. It was a miracle we didnae crash a van or a cart. We never killed nobody either.

They were no more effete in fancier suburbs and the boy that was Ian Fotheringham of the 1912-13-band of bogie-ists was, if not guilty of manslaughter, at least skeely with the swivel-bar, and lucky at that.

> We used to go pelting down the slope into Pollokshields station and out the other side. Once when I was doing that I went right into the crowd disgorging from my father's train, and-here I scattered all these City gents in their bowlers. There they were all scuttling clear of my bogie. I suppose it was funny but I got the worst skelping I ever had in my life.

Some girls too tucked up their petticoats and let their hair stream out behind them as they hurtled down the hills on the boys' bogies.

But an indulgent brother might make a more 'suitable' vehicle for a quiet sister.

I had a beautiful china-headed doll called Daisy and the boys made me a sort of barrow box-on-wheels. We called that the Daisy Express.

That wee sister was not a tomboy, but maybe Daisy was. For she, and her companion doll Ida, had a real doll's pram forbye the cart. But tomboy or no she was part of a two-pram two-doll family in bien Nithsdale Road.

There were bicycles, too, over all the eras remembered, in various forms from bone-shaker to Raleigh magnificence, but those who

didn't actually have bikes or bogies were philosophical. Who
wanted a bike anyway? Bikes were posh and cissy. Wheels whatever
the form, were transport.

Nobody round us had bikes and weans didnae have prams for to get
bogie wheels, (it was just shawls they got taken out in). But we did have
girds and cleeks and we thought they took us just as fast. You would
girn at a half-mile walk to go a message for your Ma, but three miles
planned-out wi' your gird was nothing ... maybe five times round the
public library or two or three blocks of Alexandra Parade ... that was
nothin' wi' your gir' and cleek. The flat iron yins ran quite sweet, but
the lassies had mostly wooden ones that bounced and wobbled ... nae
use! But well, a lassie couldnae expect ...

What a lassie couldnae expect was mercifully left unsaid. and we
passed thirty-five years on, to the 1940s. The last recollection of
real hoop running was from those war years, but girds were going
out by then, and the cleeker of that memory found few to travel
with. Her hoop mouldered for twenty years in a cellar until she
passed it on to children with shiny pedal-cars who didn't know
what to do with it.

D'you mind biff-bats? Wee rubber balls on an elastic pinned to a bat like
a ping-pong bat, and you kep' up twenty or thirty hits, or maybe fifty if
you were good at it.

But they were 'hi-li' bats when they came back in the 'fifties,

says one of the delightful and humorous ladies (of the personalised
peevers) and, as if conducted by Sir Hugh Roberton, their precision
so immaculate, three of them standing in the gleaming kitchen of
the youngest burst out chanting, and with actions, (hi-li-ing across
three throats) ...

Mary Queen of Scots had her head chopped off
Her head chopped off, her head chopped off
Mary Queen of Scots had her head chopped off
HEAD!   CHOPPED!   OFF!

Girds, tigs and hets and high-low water ... organised, strict-ruled
and innocent ... ah innocent! Even city-core weans were innocent
in the days before the 'fifties ... sure they were?

Box-beds, bogies and statues. I played the whole jing-bang in the 'twenties. But playing in the street was more interesting. Quite a lot of nasty wee tricks we played there ... like chap doors and run.

Mrs. Helen Stewart, as lively now in her Kirk Care flat as she was sixty-five years ago in the school-shed two miles away, remembers planning the nasty wee tricks that sent the giggles echoing down the closes of her childhood. Ah yes, for all their being mim and respectful to their elders (virtues much claimed by those who were the children of long ago) they played a mischief or two that would bring howls of 'hooligan' from them now, about similar delinquents of the 1980s.

Some swopped around the doormats outside various tenement homes, and that door-chapping was a simple version of the long-time favourite of bell-ringing. Glasgow doorbells have been mischievously pushed, pulled and jangled for certainly ninety years.

I think I pulled every bell in Stevenson Drive in the summer of 1897. I mind that because it was the old Queen's jubilee and I lost my medal up one close and was feart to go back. There was just ordinary ring-and-run, but if it was a quiet close and you didnae like the woman, you sometimes tied the pull-bell of one house to the door handle across the landing. Then you rang that second bell and skedaddled. You just left the woman to open her door and it pulled the string to the opposite bell ... many's the time I've wondered what they two women said to each other.

And Duncan White remembers another crime.

There was 'clockwork' too. Easy enough on a ground-floor windie. That was nothing. But we used to fasten the washer wi' the button or the wee screw dangling below it, to tap the pane of a one-up windie. You'd to climb up a pipe to do that. Then you sklimmed back down carrying the long thread and sat behind the wash-hoose to tap-tap the glass. Quite brave mind-you, for if you got caught the woman would hand you a skelp worse'n your own Ma, and you neednae bother complain at home for fear of another one.

So for sure, it wasn't all the gathering of rosebuds and cradling dollies folk think of in the childhood of eighty years ago. Bricks in paper bags or under old hats to stub passing toes, string across back courts, squibs in wash-houses. They weren't nice. But maybe that skelp from the clock-worked woman was the answer. Retribution was swifter, less debated and more readily understood, than more careful punishments.

No doubt there were worse villainies but, if there were, the rememberers were loyal to the reputation of their generation, and smiling secret smiles over old devilments, went back to tell of more innocent pleasures.

These were the conkers and rounders and cricket common to most areas, and more local occupations where terrain and landmark called for particular inventions; where the marsh-pond skating of winter gave way to jam jars and tadpoles, where building and demolition sites were littered with see-saw planks and all the other stuffs of adventure playgrounds. There were idling pools on Cart, Clyde and Camlachie Burn, for swimming and fishing. And there were fields in the old days which seemed to belong to no one but the children who wanted to play there.

> We used to make fires in our field and cook tatties in the embers. D'you mind that tingly black crust you'd to crunch through to get at the white? . . . and we used to cook sausages, and kippers at tuppence a pair (that was about 1937). And then you lay back like old men, puffin' away at your share of a five packet of cigarettes.

But more than anything, then as now, water drew weans, like magnets drew filings.

> I mind the day I fell in the duckpond at Carolside farm. I was leaning over for taddies and I just toppled in . . . came out all green and slimy. My what a mess, and what a reek there was off me. Didnae half get a skelpit leatherin'. Oh dear aye!

That's Mr. Noble Boyd's memory of First War years but when there's an added sin to the draw of water it's irresistible.

> There was a sluice on the river Cart and about September the water was low and we could get over to Lammie's field and scrumpie the apples in his orchard. Usually got our feet all plashing wet as well.

Glasgow children seem always to have been vigorous in their play and street language, and young incomers over the century from Ireland and Italy, Belgium and Poland, and from Jewish communities all over Europe have been quickly absorbed into the mysteries of hets and leave-o. There's always the fear that weans here, as elsewhere, will lose the art of simple play without gear or little miracles of wire and bleep. But it was heartening to hear recently of a gang of youngsters scuffling in a game of tig on a Gorbals street and a skinny red-head shouting to one of his mates from the multi-storey,

Haw Mahomet ... you're *het*!

14
Chores and No Chores

I   Mothers and Daughters

Scrubbing, polishing, burnishing, clawting out clinkers from coal fires ... no doubt they're all still done in small endurable doses in Glasgow homes here and there, but surely not often enough to demand of your average 1980s weans the regular commitment to them that youngsters of even thirty years ago, knew as their Friday night duty, come what may.

> We'd all wir own chores (just the girls mind). The one week you'd get the manglin', the next the ironin', next help wi' the washing or the brasses or sweep and pipe-clay the front step. Never two weeks the same job. My mother was a wee thin-thin cratur but she took no snash off of us and had us all choopered up to wir jobs.

Of all the tasks doled out to the family, those centred round the fire are the ones best remembered after eighty or more years. Since the first fire-slab was laid under the first lum-hole in a turf roof, the hearth has been the heart of home. It's not surprising that the two words have a common root, for the fire and its tending have been a core memory of every childhood, and living memories of the hearth go back to the days even before ranges were commonplace.

> My most vivid memory of my granny was seein' her bend over the open fire in her cottage swingin' a swee over the coals and turning scones on a girdle. I didnae think then on the hard, dirty work it was, I just liked the smell!

William Stevenson's mother cooked the meals of his childhood over the fire too.

We'd no range mind, a range was a kind of luxury, but there was hobs, one each side the hearth, that swung in over the fire.

But for the rest, it was the range, all the way to the 1940s, that was comfort, bane and chore.

We all congregated, the thirteen of us, in the back kitchen at nights for our high tea. That was from the 1890s. The range was there, and the

black kettle on it was never off the simmer. There was a big-big pot of
soup aye spitterin' away on the hob too.

And a glowing range with a hissing kettle was a cheerful background
to studies, from the days of the 'Tupenny' to the college finals.

We all used to do our lessons, and later on our studying, in the kitchen.
It was warm and cheery and if your Ma was baking you got a treckle
scone or that, off the girdle.

But there was a price to be paid for the comfort.

I mind black-leadin' night. Forbye the range itself to polish, there was a
clawt, a shovel, a brush-handle and your open-work fender to be
blacked.

Thon range was the scunner of my life. You'd to blacklead it and emery
round the steel trims ... scoor it like daft! My mother wouldnae thole
anything less than perfect ... or maybe less than Mistress Purdie's down
the stair ... but I liked making the toast after, on the end of a fork at the
bars.

There were at least the compensations of warmth and toast for
the drudgery of burnishing the range but, unless a wean was old
before her time there was precious little in polishing the brasses.
Certainly not for Helen Stewart, just one of over thirty who
claimed Brasso-ing as a major thrall of childhood.

These brasses, outside and inside, were the bane of my life on a Friday
night. My sister got out of that because she had a right genteel job with a
florist and she often went out to big posh do's on Friday evenings.

Of course, needs and chores changed with the times and circumstances.

In the time of the Second War when I was young it was my job to *mix*
the margarine and butter rations, you beat them together to give the
margarine a wee bit of the butter flavour. Spoiled the butter mind, but
made the marg better tasted.

Little of the cleaning done in Glasgow at the turn of the century
was by short cut or miracle dust-dissolver and spray. But there were
aids. Throw a 'do you remember?' into a Sunset Home lounge and
you get almost a Greek chorus ... 'D'you mind Lysol?', 'D'you
mind Zebo?', 'D'you mind fly-papers?' or Monkey Brand, or

Babbit's Powder or Brooke's Soap? As well as the Lysol and the Monkey Brand for the fierce cleaning of the house itself, there was always the struggle for personal freshness. Unlike the view taken in 1790, by 1890 'clarty' was no longer considered 'cosy'.

Those who had hot water taps at the turn of the century were not merely keeping up with the Joneses. They *were* the Joneses. And their bathing facilities were the wonder and envy of the majority whose arrangements were more primitive.

This would've been about 1916-17 and in our room'n' kitchen we had the 'cold' but no' the 'hot'. So there was a special bath-night . . . Friday night was the *big* night.

But it was Thursday night the whole caper began. All the clinkers and big cinders from the fire got laid aside and the rest riddled through to the ash-can for throwin' out. It was that dusty too, the whole place! Then the cinders went back wi' new sticks and coal for to start the fire up again. When it was goin' nice it got banked up wi' dross and let burn low till the next night under the big kettles and pots so there was lots of hot water for the bath. First though, we'd all our hair unpleated and washed, and Mother got out the small-tooth comb and paraffin in case of lice or nits. Then the zinc tub came out from under the kitchen bed and one after the other we all got our bath.

More explicitly than 'one after the other' Mrs. Helen Stewart describes the ritual in their house.

I had *my* wash first, in the zinc tub in front of the fire. Then more water was added for Bessie, then Maggie, then John . . . *added* mind. Last one got the rinsings off the rest. By that time around 1916 my bigger brothers had graduated to the tuppeny bath-house in McDougall Street, but we were still in the tin bath. What a job it was, when I think back, to tim the water out that tub.

In another more conservationist house it wasn't always jawed out the minute the last back was scrubbed.

Your Ma sometimes used to take the chance to wash through a few clo'es.

But of course it wasn't only weans who steeped themselves at the fire, and the steeping wasn't always private to the family. The daughter-of-the-manse, who was the shy young Sunday School teacher Isobel Cameron, was paying a parish call once in the 1930s.

I was taking a wee prize to a laddie in the Sunday School. He lived in one of the miners' rows for the Cardowan Colliery ... the Rows were a place apart, unique, with names like Heathery Knowe and Maryston. It was my first visit, and I chapped the door.

'Come awa' in, come awa' in,' says the mother, very hospitable, ushering me in. And there was her man sitting black as night and quite jokoh, in a big zinc bath in front of a fire that would've roasted an ox, soaping himself ready for her to scrub him. The whole place was festooned with washing and a chair was swept clear of clutter — and the cat, for me to sit down. I ducked the hangings and sat myself there. I was *manse* mind you, and a bit prim, but they weren't a hate put-out and we just sat there chatting as if it had been my mother's parlour; me and the wife and the tubbing miner.

It was certainly cleanliness that was next to godliness, but not far down the seedings were the other tasks demanded of youngsters in big families if the knit of life was not to fall apart. Eking-out and making-do were prime concerns that give rise to a plethora of chores.

Mr. James Ross had a memory of his frugal childhood which he repeated more than once to his daughter Margaret.

When my father was a boy he used to get sent to the fish shop on a Saturday just before it closed when there were bargain prices. He got five pounds of whiting for a shilling and that fish was their Saturday tea and their Sunday breakfast.

And for the Laurie family there was another pet economy.

We used to get sent to Scotland Street, maybe two miles away, to get broken biscuits from Gray Dunn's factory . . . not for visitors mind, just for the family.

The Browns had a recipe for fuel saving . . .

I lived in the Gorbals in the 'twenties. My mother used to just half-bake her bread then send us with it like that to the bakery. You got putting it in the big ovens there when the baker was finished his own batches and yet there was still heat in the ovens. Even better, you could take your own flour an' that, and mix your sponges and tea-breads in his big mixers. You used yon big paddles to put things in and take them out the ovens.

Then there was the endless shopping, carrying of rubbish to the midden, chopping sticks and the minding of the *wean*.

My job was, every day after the school, to take my wee sister, happed in a shawl, out for a bit fresh air in the street. We'd no pram you see . . . no' many had prams in our street, and that was the way she got taken for her walk.

That was William Stevenson's recollection of his place in the scheme of things. But it has to be said that, if the women who look back are to be believed, he must have been almost unique in doing any household duties. There are not many ardent feminists among octogenarian ladies but, almost without exception, their asides about their girlhood chores show how long ago the seeds of protest were planted.

The five of us girls had all our set jobs. One sister did the hall and stair, one the bathroom and two did all the beds. That was before you went to school or work ... the brothers did *nothing*. They got waited on hand and foot.

That was no gripe-voice in the wilderness. There were plenty more. 'My father *do* anything in the house? Never ever!', 'My father or brothers work in the house? You're kidding!' What an inelegant cry from an eighty-eight year old gentlewoman! But it was wrung from her by wry memories of long ago injustice. And there's a memory of a health conscious grandfather, born probably around the start of Queen Victoria's reign.

Our grandfather always stayed in bed on Sundays, in the concealed bed in the kitchen ... thought he needed that once a week to keep himself fit. We used to visit every Sunday and see him lying in bed. He got his meals and everything served to him there.

And the twinkling ladies who recalled that scene added, 'He was in provisions ... cured hams', his own included, presumably, after a hard week's work on his feet.

Another husbandly view of his wife's implicit marriage vows to 'love, honour, and run after me' is remembered nevertheless affectionately by a son of the union.

My father was devoted to his clay pipes, used to break off the stems short so's they would sit comfy in the corner of his mouth, even while he was speaking. Had it in his bed at night too for a last wee puff before sleeping. He smoked an ounce-a-day easy. But he would never buy his own tobacco. That wasnae a man's job. He used to pass the shop every night and then send my mother out to buy it for him.

And the prize for making all such arrangements possible, goes to the lady who could say,

Our brother was waited on hand and foot. We'd to clean his shoes and get up early to cook his breakfast. We'd all left school at fourteen and we worked at outside jobs all our lives. But I still think it's a woman's right place to serve the man.

II Fathers and Brethren

Well that's the way the women remember it all, but the menfolk have a few rankles too, about what was expected of them by way of carrying coal, emptying ash-baikies, splitting firewood, humphing shopping, and lighting boiler fires on perishing, dark, raw mornings. And Duncan White never knew whether to enjoy his chore when he reached the steamie or die of embarrassment on the way.

> Us boys had to march along the street to the steamie carryin' the dirty washing bundle in the tin tub on our heads. Took turn about on the road there. Then after, we'd get to trample the sheets or blankets in the steamie stall.

Whatever the truth about the household efforts of the menfolk, mothers, grannies, and aunts tend to come across the years as uniformly clever-handed domestic providers, dinning manners and morals, cleanliness and economy, into their children. Fathers, grandpas and uncles, on the contrary, are remembered in fifty different guises of personality, affectionately but, dare it be said, on the whole with marginally less respect. Some were stern disciplinarians of course, but they're credited mostly with telling stories, drawing sweets out of baggy pockets, bestowing pennies and sneaking saucers of creamed butter and sugar to coughing weans, with winking behind the heads of scolding mothers ... and even sometimes with misbehaving themselves. On occasion there was good reason for Ma's tight lips.

> My father used to come home sometimes quite late from his work, after a wee refreshment. My mother was angry then. Sometimes he used to hide his whisky-bottle behind the gas meter in the bathroom. She didnae like that either.

The tenement Saturday night, unlike the Cotter's, was something else mothers often had to bear, and Mrs. Edith Dykes feels for hers after nearly fifty years.

> Every Saturday night at tea-time when my father and my brother and my Uncle Willie had all been to the same football match, you'd have thought from the argy-bargying of them that they'd all been to different games ... the rows! It was just a right rammy every week ... terrible!

And the father who was one of the long-ago arguers is still there to agree and add his pennyworth.

> I could still near tell you the Third Lanark team about that time, there

was Brownlie, McCormack, Fairfull ... I cannae mind the next one ... but then Fergus, Main, Reid, Sterowski, the Walker brothers and Hillhouse ... that's no' bad is it?

Fathers, then, came in a wide range. Some, of course, were step-fathers and this one was hardly run-of-the-mill in domestic matters.

> He'd been a cook in the navy in the First War. He was English and my mother was Scottish. He used to make rare steak pies and when there was a family 'do' he put a pastry thistle at the one end of the crust and a rose at the other.

Grandpas too had their share of characters.

> I mind of Grandpa Gibson. He kept cough candy unwrapped in a drawer and he used to hand out oosey chunks of it. He was like a wee elf wi' sunk rosy cheeks and bright eyes and he used to take out his teeth to frighten us ... all gumsy!

Other grandfathers have lived long in the memory, but at ninety-five years old herself, Mrs. Henderson recalls not only her grand-parents but her great-grandfather who must have been born around 1790.

> My great-grandpa lived wi' my granny in Uddingston. There's nothin' new, you know, ... them wi' the granny-flats! He'd that in 1894, his wee kitchen and his own room. But then you just called it 'your grandpa stayin' wi' you'. Anyway, he kept a big whip in the corner of his room and if he was angry wi' you for something he used to crack it and threaten you. He'd a staw at m'Uncle Jake and *his* lot ... no' so much at us ... but just now and then, aye.

Few remembered fathers came in the Wimpole Street mould. Certainly that whip's crack must have been worse than its lash, for none of the family seems to have been much fashed when it was produced. No word, though, of what Uncle Jake had done to deserve that staw.

15
Their Weans Would Never Be

I   A Gallus Adventure

1914-18, 1939-45, the two great watersheds in the lives of over-sixties everywhere. They were not more traumatic in Glasgow than elsewhere but there were some experiences that were peculiar to the city. Birmingham's wars were Birmingham's wars, Glasgow's were Glasgow's.

But echoes of other wars before 1914 still linger in minds that were young in what we call the First War.

I mind my grandfather telling me that he remembered the Crimean War of 1854 and the way they said it was General 'Winter' that was the real enemy and no' just the Russians. He said the sufferin' was that horrible folk thought there could never be another one. Then the Boer War comes along and all the flag-wavin' starts up again. And when he was an old man in 1914 people were singin' and cheerin' theirsel's silly again.

I got taken to see Lord Roberts when he came to Glasgow in 1893 after he was famous in the Indian Wars and the big trek from Kabul to Khandahar. I expected a big giant of a man and-here he was just a wee toty man.

There was an uncle in our family that had been on yon terrible march from Kabul to Khandahar about 1880 when nearly the whole army died.

My brother was born the day of the Relief of Ladysmith in 1900 so they called him George White Henderson after General George White. It was just at the same time too that one of our neighbours got killed in that Boer War.

Then came memories of 1914.

I remember fine the beginning of the First War. I was about nine years

121

old and there were two things I've never forgotten. It was the end of July and we were away our holidays up at Nigg and there was a German brass band in the village. I can just see them standing playing outside our cottage and collecting money. About two days after that they were rounded up and it was all round Nigg that the police had found maps and charts of the Cromarty Firth stuffed down their instruments.

And the Fotheringham holiday was cut short a few days later when Father was recalled to Glasgow. The family travelled south by train.

I can see this yet too. There was a big Scots Guardsman in the compartment in his scarlet tunic and his kilt. He was away south to join his regiment for going off to France.

A toy-box soldier to a goggle-eyed small boy.

Whether it was true or not that that German band was a group of spies, the north was certainly a sensitive area in wartime. Mr. Harry Anderson recalls,

My parents were from Golspie and we always went there on holiday. I remember that in the war my mother had to show a special pass to soldiers at Inverness for us to get any further north.

The Andersons had been in Golspie when war was declared.

I was there at my granny's. The Seaforths came to Golspie to muster and I remember that one of the jam or marmalade companies, maybe Robertson's, very quickly brought out wee cardboard diced Glengarry caps for the children and I remember marching and bobbing along to the recruiting band trying to keep step. All the wee Golspie boys were there wearing their paper Glengarries.

Mr Duncan White has a more sinister memory of the period just before the war, in Glasgow.

My father worked for a German company near the Suspension Bridge and earlier that year they built a big high new buildin' and I mind the way he used to shake his head. 'The Jerries can see right away-way doon the Clyde from that place. It's no' right. They can see the whole jing-bang of ships and yards on the river.'

But whatever the Germans spied from the Suspension Bridge or from the charts in their trombones, by August it was all 'on' and the enlisting began.

I had taken the shillin' to be a Territorial when I was sixteen ... joined at the hall on Howie's farm-road wi' all my pals in the Auldhoose Thistle footb'll team. We went to Terrier camp at Macrahanish the summer of 1914, came home on a Saturday and were away to the real army come the Monday. I was in the Argylls and I went to France in the April when I was seventeen.

Others joined the Navy.

I joined the Navy in 1914 and was sent to a coast-guard station at Cape Wrath. But I had been an apprentice blacksmith so I was sent to sea at my own trade, and I was the whole war after that, out east on the cruiser H.M.S. Blenheim. It wasnae such a bad life the navy. We'd good times and I liked sleepin' in the hammock well enough. Five years of it I had. Came out in 1919.

It seemed romantic enough for the girls at home to see their boy friends ready for glory.

I was nineteen in 1914, right in that war generation. All the chaps I knew mustered in the local schools and our lot got locked into Cuthbertson Street playground. We used to go round and talk to them through the railings. They were all laugh and chaff then. 'Och we'll be home by Christmas.' Everybody said that.

Those were the very early days when it all seemed a gallus adventure, but by the turn of the year with news of the real war starting to trickle through, it began to turn sour.

It became the thing to go and see off your friends and relations in the forces leaving the Central Station. The trains were jam-packed as they moved off, the boys leaning out and waving, the wives and mothers standing there singing with tears running down their faces, 'Will ye no' come back again?' I was forever at that station waving off cousins and friends.

Although there was now an awareness at home of the slaughter, only those who were there can suggest the feel and smell and horror of trench war. Mr. William Stevenson is one.

I was a machine gunner and the first time I got wounded was in the foot ... that was the month after I got to France ... on the Somme. When I was better I was straight back up the line.
     After that I think I was in a' the big battles except Loos (it was Kitchener's lot at Loos) but I was at the Somme and 'Wypres' and at

Passchendaele ... what a dirty hole that was, a' glaur and squelchin'
mud. I was a private at first, but there were that many gettin' killed that
I was a corporal for just five days, then a sergeant at nineteen and a
sergeant-major at twenty.

I got bad wounded at Amiens when the Germans were tryin' for a
breakthrough. I was wounded right through the buttocks ... no feelin'
in my legs and just collapsed ... lost the use of my legs for a long time
and after that I was three-and-a-half year in the hospital.

And Mr. Roxburgh remembers his part in the army's attempt to
take the Menin road.

The place was all pitted wi' shell holes and laid wi' mines. We'd to try
and follow a tape to guide us through the minefield. But then a shell
burst beside me and I got a 'blighty', wounded in the head and neck.
The war was over before I was fit again.

But I was lucky by my brothers! The three of them were all killed, two
of them under age ... and my mother was a widow, mind. One of my
brothers wasnae found till ten years after the war when workmen on the
Menin road found his body buried shallow there, just the week I got
married.

For a long time there was little comfort either for those who were
having a break from the fighting.

> If you'd a few days back from the line there was no canteen nor nothin', no proper beds. You came out maybe in winter in the snow and just put your waterproof sheet on the ground. That was your bed.

But perhaps they did have time during the break for one of the more laborious chores of the kilted troops.

> I mind of just sittin' there in perishin' cold behind the lines goin' up and down the pleats of my kilt wi' a match or a lighter to kill the lice that got in there and drove you daft.

Then it was back to the trenches.

At least when it was not seeing action the Navy seems to have been more comfortable for greater stretches of time. And more entertaining.

> We'd a monkey on our ship, and we used to make it drunk ... used to pour rum on the table and the monkey used to lick it up. Then when it got lively and tried to swing from place to place it used to miss its grip. A shame? Naw, it wasnae a shame, and it wasnae cruel. The monkey thought the rum was lovely.
>
> A lot of the sailors were right keen dancers too, so we just danced wi' each other ... thought nothin' of it. Then we'd concerts, sailors doin' all sorts of turns, singin' and dancin' and conjurin', and kiddin'-on they were winchin' couples in funny sketches.

No doubt there were less happy times for the concert-party tars, as there were for the soldiers. Even at home the authorities were slow to provide even the barest comfort for servicemen in transit.

> I mind of twice comin' into Glasgow late at night. The first time was early in the war and I'd just to sleep on my greatcoat on the station floor. But by the second time, a year later, they'd canvas beds laced up to scaffolding in the station basement, and you got a pillow and a blanket.

So things were moving on the home front and when the first forlorn results of the stunning German advance arrived in Glasgow, the city was prepared to meet them. Twelve hundred Belgian refugees came, first of all to temporary billets made ready in the corporation halls. They came with nothing but what they had worn as they streamed out of their villages, and perhaps a parcel or handbag. Some of them were almost as afraid of the wild mountain people they expected to find living in rough stone dwellings in savage

Scotland, as they had been of the Germans. The organiser of the Belgian operation left a diary.

> 1915 Had big two-hundred gallon tanks of cold water at the station to serve in tin mugs from fifty tea-pots, to give them a fresh drink before sending them off to the various halls where settled and fed. Glasgow woman in thibet skirt and peenie brought huge barrel of apples to one hall and went round handing them out. One woman refugee had to be rushed to the Maternity to have her baby. Went to London to find small box of belongings she left there. There was much work getting them all settled and billeted into houses and fixed up with clothes and necessities ...

> 1919 The King of the Belgians presented me with the King Albert medal.

There was no keeping this kind of war at arm's length in distant places. Information came with brutal starkness.

> The thing folk dreaded the most was the casualty lists ... just sheets and sheets with hundreds and hundreds of names listed in the newspapers.

> I was at the Boys' High School and every morning at Assembly the names of the latest Old Boys killed were read out, names for the Roll of Honour.

Apart from the droves of women going into munitions, more and more war work was taken on at home. Marie Condie took up nursing.

> I joined the V.A.D. I was young and shy and real shocked when I'd to empty urinals and such, but I got over that when the wounded began to arrive and I'd maybe to work on a laddie with no legs or one with half his face blown away. Later on near the end of the war I went to Bangour hospital when what they called the Big Push was on, and oh my, the terrible wounded that came in on the railway that ran right into the hospital grounds ... truckloads and truckloads of human wrecks, boys just!

> I joined the Woman's Volunteer Reserve under Lady Cargill. We drilled like soldiers in the drill hall at Butterbiggins Road and after the drill and maybe a pep talk, got detailed to go on different duty rosters. You'd canteens for a week or two and then maybe collecting wastepaper.

There were other less worthy activities.

A lot of nasty things went on, profiteerin' an' that, but the worst was when silly women seen you in the street in your civvy clo'es, maybe just on leave, maybe no' in the army for some reason, and handed you a white feather for a coward.

There's a rag-bag of recollections too, of taking part in fund-raising concerts, selling war bonds from tanks in George Square, the rounding up of Lord Derby scheme recruits by officials with brown armbands, marathons of knitting, endless queues.

There was a real shortage of a lot of things before they brought in the rationing. You'd to stand in line for tea and sugar and bread and meat. One particular day, for some reason, stands out in my mind. I'd be about ten and I stood for two solid hours outside Kate Young's fruit and veg shop for two *pounds* of potatoes. Then I remember that we used to get extra sugar so that the rhubarb we grew wouldn't go to waste.

Tobacco and drink were short too and men complained that their beer was watered down. The rueful complaint going the rounds was that the dire lack of liquor could be clearly detected at normal peak drinking times ...

It's Saturday nicht and there's nobody drunk on the tram.

Another fleeting recollection of 1915 was the swift passage through wartime Glasgow in a bleak week of smirring drizzle and gloom, of an exotic party of Canadian Indian troops commanded by Chief Clear Sky. They were on their way to the war and sampled Glasgow hospitality enjoying a first, and no doubt last, taste of black pudding.

But they left one young Indian behind. His name was Gay Flier. He was very very ill with 'flu and he died in Govan Military Hospital. My grandpa had been seeing to Chief Clear Sky's men when they were in Glasgow and so's not to let the boy get buried in an unmarked grave he claimed the body and saw to it that there was a right funeral in Glasgow with magistrates there, a gun carriage and a party to fire a salute at the grave. It wasnae among his own open-air folk but it was better than being not heeded at all.

Comments and memories about wartime politicians and leaders are few but the two big Ks were passingly mentioned.

Everyone knew Kitchener's face fae yon pointing poster and it was a terrible thing when he got drowned. It would've been like Churchill gettin' killed in the next war.

The Kaiser was never such an ogre or wicked bogeyman as Hitler. There was a kind of sneakin' disappointment that one of the old Queen's grandweans had turned out so bad and been against Britain, just a dozen years after she died.

Mrs. Nancy Watt has a memory of an odd little dispensation granted, even encouraged, at her church in Govanhill.

I remember sitting in the pew during the war at Sunday services knitting white balaclavas for troops fighting where there was snow.

Eventually it was over and not a soul among the rememberers but recalls precisely where he or she was at the moment of Armistice, from mixed infant to veteran soldier.

I was just a wee lassie at the school and the Room 2 door got chapped. Miss Craig went and spoke to another teacher and came back in, greetin'. I never saw a grown-up greetin' before ... but-here she was just happy! After, we went on a Peace outing and got Armistice medals.

I was at the High School then and we'd got word to listen for the kirk bells. We were all hanging out the windows in Elmbank Street and when the bells rang out we just rushed out the school and away up Sauchiehall Street, swept along in the crowd.

Another boy remembers school boaters and caps spinning across the heads of stampeding people and getting trampled to nothing under running feet.

Office girls went mad too.

It was indescribable ... amazing ...hoardes of douce wee Glasgow folk singing and dancing, shouting, kissing and hugging total strangers. It was quite late when I walked home across the bridge to the south side and there were still folk careering about with wee Union Jacks stuck in their hats. Don't know who thought on having the wee flags ready.

But as the saying goes 'there's aye someb'dy isn't there?' That was at home. For the serviceman it was all more sober ... well, perhaps not 'sober', but at least less euphoric. Duncan White was aboard the Blenheim ...

On Armistice day I was sailing up the Dardenelles. We celebrated by splicing the mainbrace. That was getting an extra tot of rum. The

monkey? I suppose he got the lickin's too. And that was it ... wi' a wee
bit cheerin' and the flags up.

William Stevenson of the Argylls:

I was in the hospital on crutches at that time. I'd gone into the town wi'
a friend from the Coldstream Guards. Everyone was going daft huggin'
and kissin' in the street and makin' a fuss of the likes of us in our blues.
But it was all that *much*, we just got on the tram and went back to the
hospital. It was quiet there.

Two post-scripts sum up the forlorn waste of that decimating
war.

It was horrible, but you didnae realise the awfulness until you came back
looking for your friends again and more'n half of them just werenae
there; and their weans would never be.

In 1914 we'd been eight in our house. By 1918 my three brothers were
killed and my father and grandmother had died. Now there were just
the womenfolk left at home, me, my ma and my wee sister just turned
eight.

There's also a third post-script that tells of the tempering of boys
into warriors over the years when they should have been learning
their trades, playing carefree games and wooing their girls. This
post-script is left almost to the end because that's how the old man
spoke of it, as an afterthought when the reminiscing was done and it
was time to go home. He pointed to a shelf in his room.

That's my things there. That's my D.C.M. (There's a wee pension wi'
that) and that's my Military Medal and my Bronze Star. Aye ... read
them if you want.
   'I wish to congratulate Sergeant W. Stevenson on the gallantry
displayed by him on 31st July and 1st August 1917.'
   'I wish to congratulate Sergeant-Major W. Stevenson on the gallantry displayed by him on 21st March 1918.'

He puts the medals back, and the next person to handle them will
be the chirpy lass in Eastwoodhill House who keeps them polished
for him.

II This and Other Rough Ways

All these memories still haunt those who speak of them after seventy years and perhaps some are blurred a little in hindsight. But among the rest were the recollections of one who was part of a band of bonnie fechters whom no one else had even mentioned, the Servicewomen of the 1914-18 war. Extracts from her diary deserve their own space, for its entries are not blurred by tricking memory. They are not spoiled by what she *should* have said, or *wished* she'd said. Young, fresh and immediate, lit with unconscious humour and irony they tell of her first days as a recruit, aged eighteen.

There was me, with two brothers and a nice boyfriend having a terrible time in France, so I decided to join the W.A.A.C.S. It certainly wasn't for the glamour of the uniform I can tell you, because we'd just a shapeless coat dress and a wee pork-pie hat that pulled down to your eye-brows.

Later she moved from posting to posting, mainly in transport administration in the Royal Flying Corps, and ended the war in the much smarter outfit of the newly formed W.A.A.F. But it was in the very first weeks of her training that Nancy Reid kept her little journal. She recalls, first, the basic rules.

Members (of the W.A.A.C.) must not alter shape of hat. Any girl who disregards this, will be required to purchase a new one at her own expense.

Members must discard all jewelled haircombs and ribbons and all jewellery except signet or wedding rings, and address all administrators as 'Ma'am'.

Members must behave in an orderly manner at all times.

In spite of the holocaust in France, the filth and lice attending the nice boy-friend and brothers in the trenches, she writes.

One fact which shocks us is that there is no cover on the dining-table here. Had some of the girls known about this and other rough ways I guess the number of recruits here would not be so many.

After Roll-call we reported for our first lessons in forming fours . . . two deep etc.

For dinner we had a small piece of boiled mutton, one potato and a little rice without milk. One of my room-mates, a rather fragile affair, hasn't got into the way of eating in the army. She is very particular about her food and a girl of that sort is *absolutely no use here*. We can only leave her alone until she eats what is put to her, dainty or otherwise.

And an item that in a later age might have been headed, 'Don't let's be beastly to the administrators'.

> When an administrator enters, everyone is silent and stands to attention. This is really very nice to see because all the officers are extremely nice and deserve a little appreciation. So it is good to have such rules because some would never dream of having any esteem for those in higher rank. The least we can do is lessen their burden by being well-behaved and orderly.

> I had a letter from mamma today and brightened up wonderfully. I seem to see a fire in my bedroom in Chisholm Street and a table set with everything good for eating.

> Salt is very scarce here and when we were in a fish restaurant in town Sally pinched a little to save it for a rainy day.

> Supper ... good old soup, alias hot water!

16

Shrivelled Livers and Live Worms

We were always teetotallers in our house so we got sent to the Band of Hope. I signed the pledge, och as many times!

That was in the 1890s and the Band of Hope was just as popular twenty years later in the time that James McLachlan's was a regular pledger.

It was a great thing on a Friday night, the Band of Hope. They showed you shrivelled up livers and live worms curlin' up, demented and suffering, in jars of alcohol.

Of all the people remembering for this book, who were young from the 1880s to the early 1930s, only one solitary soul was not a member of the Band of Hope, in some Glasgow church hall or backroom somewhere. Its aim was simple ... to bolster youngsters against the temptations of liquor-abuse in a city scourged and sick with drunkenness. For most secure bairns it represented no more than a worthy activity encouraged by sensible parents; like Sunday School, cleaning the brasses and practising the piano from Hemy's Tutor ... but one that, for the most part, was fun.

The baldie truth was, you went to get entertained, to have a good night-out wi' friends.

admits James Shaw of Cardonald.

The earliest first-hand memories of the Band of Hope are Margaret Henderson's of the 1890s, when the young world of Uddingston flocked to its meetings in the church hall.

You got talks and lanterns and a bag wi' a cookie-bun and a cake, and maybe an orange at the swarry. Everybody came to the Band of Hope in our church hall. And we signed the pledge ... as many times ... aye dozens of times.

132

And the same pattern of nourishment for body and soul was repeated on the fringes and in the heartlands of the city, alike.

> I was in the Band of Hope before the First War. You sang temperance songs on ordinary nights and got buns and tea at the swarries in the Mission Hall near Cumberland Street; and you used to slosh your tea on the floor so's to make slides. We liked the swarries and the magic lantern and we liked Big Dick, the man in charge. I signed the pledge, we a' signed the pledge ... many's the time.

A real good night-out for most youngsters, but for others the Band of Hope was the start of a lifelong commitment to temperance.

> I chanted wi' the rest ... this would be 1913 or so .... 'Wine is a mocker, strong drink raging. Whoever is deceived thereby is not wise ...' and I just signed up wi' all the others. It was nothin' to me then really, bar a rare night-out. I liked the Sunday School, but I liked the Band of Hope better wi' the lantern and the swarries and throwin' your sweeties at the girls. D'you mind them sweeties you used to could buy ... readin'-sweeties wi' words on them ... 'Be my rosebud' or 'Can I walk you home?' But all the same somethin' must've got across, for there's still a wee voice inside minds me of the Band of Hope and I never took to drinkin' wine or beer or that. And I'm no' sorry.

For yet others the Band of Hope had a very different appeal, street waifs who counted the days between meetings, with longing.

> For a few hours' warmth and comfort inside a decent building ... just that once in the week.

That's what one grandfather told his grandson of his very young days in the 1850s.

> He told me that he minded standing as a wee laddie outside a pub on a cold night with his bare feet in his bunnet to keep them warm, while he waited on his father to come out and give him a penny to get him a bed for the night in a common doss-house.

It was small wonder that bunnet-boy hankered to join the Band of Hope, and he hung about the meeting place wishing he had the penny needed to be a real, pledge-carrying member. His grandson goes on ...

> Then his widower-father married again. He set up in a bare tenement room and young Wattie thought life had taken a turn for the better. But-here the new stepmother was a bit drouthy too.

The night the boy came home at last to show off his pledge-card that some kindly man had bought for him, the woman was sitting half-tipsy in the kitchen. She laughed at him for his pledge, tossed his card in the fire, and when he protested threw a plate at his head.

> He jouked it then he ran out the house to a brother's place and he never set foot in his father's home again ... he must have been about nine-year-old then, my grandpa.

But now that young man was in the Band of Hope, pledged and set on course. He learned his texts at the meetings, won a book, taught himself to read and, over the years of self-discipline and improvement, left bunnet and doss-house far behind: but not so far that they were ever forgotten, and during the First War when he was discussing with Andrew Bonar Law the possibility of urging the troops to sign similar pledge-cards (at least for the duration of the war) he had a wry smile at the memory of the barefoot laddie warming his feet in that bunnet half a century earlier.

Not everyone was as alert to what he was doing in the Band of Hope as that earnest member. Eighty years after *his* pledge, little Nellie Edgar made hers.

> I just loved the Band of Hope. You started off each meeting chantin' the pledge. I was just wee but I chimed in as clear as a lintie wi' the rest. I didnae quite understand how Provost Gray of our wee burgh came into it, *or* the girl in my class that was called Isa Beveridge but I fair enjoyed saying that pledge and it gave a right rousin' start to the night ... 'I agree, with the help of Provost Gray, to abstain from all intoxicating liquors, Isa Beveridge.' Why *she* signed off I really didn't know till I learned the right pledge when I was a little bigger. 'I agree, wi' the help of promised grace, to abstain from all intoxicating liquor, as a beverage.'

That principle and the pledge, were the bones and stomach of the Band of Hope, but there were all the extra-mural delights as well.

> We got rare lantern shows wi' stories about strong drink and drunken fathers and poor wee Nellie sittin' bein' hungry in the corner. But the swarry was the great thing. You got your poke wi' a bun an' a cake an' your biscuit.

Sometimes there was a concert as part of the soirée and those youngsters with talent, or just nerve, did 'turns', reciting heart-rending story-poems, old Scots songs and innocent, romantic

ballads. There must have been shy weans at the meetings but the
rest jostled for places on the programme, parts in a play maybe or
solo spots. And the Band of Hope in its heyday was well-known to
be a breeding ground for popular performers who grew up to
entertain Glasgow in concert parties in the city's public halls. But in
young days the church hall was glory enough.

> It was faither always got us ready for the swarry, specially us girls. He
> used to pleat our hair after its wash-night and leave it tight-screwed-up
> for a week to get a' ripply for the concert. Sometimes after the week we
> were more like Zulus than th'angels we were s'posed to be. But we
> thought we were just the last word when we stepped out on to that
> platform. After, my mother learned to do rag curls and they were a *lot*
> more flattering. Faither missed doing the pleats just the same.

Most young people who attended the Band of Hope were happy
enough to humour their leaders by obligingly signing the pledge as
often as the forms were produced. But not everyone did. From
around 1910 Miss Jean Thomson remembers ...

> We all signed the pledge-card ... all but David Kirk. He wouldnae sign,
> and that was funny really, because he was right serious David Kirk ...
> thought about it a lot. Maybe he had the second sight or something, for,
> even though he was a very abstemious man when he was up, the queer
> thing was, he went to work for Johnnie Walker's.

There's a patronising twinkle about most memories of the Band
of Hope and it's easy to mock at the ongoings there with the
shrivelled-up livers, the readin' sweeties and the concerts. But there
was a fair bit of laughter at the time, at the meetings themselves,
and maybe the worthy men and women who gave up their time to
run them, unconsciously knew a thing or two about psychology and
had the right way of it.

> They were a bit kind of psychy I think ... knew how to put it over, so's
> that you minded things as were rousin' and funny, better'n long-faced
> teaching.

And from his own memories James McLachlan agrees ...

> You dinnae easy forget the way they used to could put a wee pinch iron
> filin's on a saucer of burnin' alcohol and show you them goin' red-hot
> and sparkin' up ... it was s'posed to be a dreadful warnin' all that, about
> what went on inside of you, if you drank.

17

Boiler, Steamie and
Green Soft Soap

Mary MacKenzie came to Glasgow as a child from the clear light of the Highlands in the summer of 1898. At home in fair weather they had still taken their clothes in boynes to the peat burn for soaping, slapping and syning in the running water. Before she came to Glasgow one of the tales told her was that the women there still lit fires on the Glasgow Green and heated water in baikies to tub their washing, and that all over the green on winter afternoons there would be the dying lights of fires flickering low in the gloaming.

> I didn't believe that any more'n I believed that the streets were littered with gold. But I did think there might be pumps and wells and a lot of carrying of water up the close-stair to do the washing in the houses.

Glasgow was grey and dreich to Mary MacKenzie but she came to love the wee warm stone-built wash-houses she found in the back-greens of the tenements.

Glasgow wasn't all tenements, but even the inner-city cottages and rows, as well as the bien villas on the outskirts, had their washing-houses attached beyond the kitchen. But whether the wash-tubs were in the back-courts or butted onto the houses they were all much-of-a-muchness for fittings and had all the banes and bonuses of wash-day in common.

In the early days of living memory, two round, iron-hooped wooden tubs with handles sat on a long low table in most wash-houses. There was a safety-plank nailed to front and back, because a tub of hot suds on a table slittered with soft soap could be lethal. A cold water tap was set into the wall and an iron boiler, built round with brick or stone, sat over a fire-place. There was a 'dolly' and

dolly-barrel for dumping out the grime and sometimes a big mangle in the corner.

The ritual began early, winter and summer, with someone going down to fill the boiler and kindle the fire under it. Most of the family took a turn at that chore. Most of them, but not all.

> My mother sometimes, or maybe me or yin of my brothers, we a' took wir turn ... except of course my faither. It wasnae his place to do things like that.

Mary Hardy remembers the next part of the time-table.

> When the water was hot and there was a good steam-up in the wash-house, whoever was to do the washin' (mostly the washerwoman) went away down the stair and disappeared for the whole morning. Some of the hot water was jawed into one of the tubs and some left for boilin' the whites that had been steepin' all night to loosen the dirt ... Then everything boilable was boiled.

The rest was pummelled by the dolly and if there was a spare child in the back-court it was conscripted for the mangling. Eventually the washer, with a face red as a winter sun, emerged to hang up the clothes on the green or upstairs on the kitchen pulley, or perhaps set them up in front of the fire on a winter-dyke.

> But it wasnae aye just your clo'es that came out clean fae the wash-hoose, for many's the time, after the washin' was done, there was still a good boilerful of water that had taken a bonnie penny to heat, and your ma couldnae think to waste. So she kep' an eye on it till the boilin' heat was off it then she used to get us in fae our peevers or peeries, strip us and gie's a good latherin' in the suds. After that her week's shot of the wash-hoose was done.

When the high tea was over and the dishes washed, the wise and far-seeing of the grown members of the family had pressing engagements elsewhere, while the foolish virgins found themselves caught up in the ironing. The flat irons lay on the kitchen range, two or more of them to keep the work going.

> You could get quite a heat up on them mind and you used to lick your pinkie and just tip the iron and if there was a wee sizzle, it was ready. Ma's rough sheets that she got for her weddin' (that was 1882) were the worst. Too dry and you couldnae get them smooth, too wet and your iron just stuck, and crumpled them as bad's ever again.

Well-ironed clothes were a matter of pride, not only for the ironer, but for the wearer.

> Oh you got your orders right-enough, from them all. 'See and get they cuffs right Annie. You cannae be slip-shod about the cuffs.

A dead metaphor, odder than the simple reminder ...

> Mind my sash for the swarry ma.

or a dapper father's requirement.

> My father was a right wee toff ... used to want his bootlaces ironed.

By the early 1900s the tubs in the washing-houses were plumbed in, and there were wooden sinks with sloping fronts for comfortable standing and a good rasping angle for the wash-board. Fifteen years later in newer buildings and the kitchens of genteel villas, the tubs were white wally. But the coal-fired boiler was still to the fore.

Even in areas of congested living there was pride in the job well done and old, trusted and faithful aids to the decent line of suds were carted downstairs every wash-day.

> There were eighteen families to our block, six houses to a landing ... a room-and-kitchen and two single-ends at each side ... three storeys, eighteen families. When it was mother's wash-day and the water was steamin' in the boiler, she'd get away down there wi' her board and her packet of Co-operative A.I. washin' powder (none of your fancy biological this-or-that, mind). And aye, she always had her windsor soap for scrubbin' and dolly-blues for the table-covers and pillow-cases.

By about 1915 the ironing was done with a bolt iron, its red-hot slab inserted from a cleek through a slot in the back of the iron. And a year or two later in houses with gas-rings at the range, there were gas-irons. The job was done on the kitchen table, the jets inside the iron fed through a tube from a tap at the range.

The names of first teachers, favourite concert turns, family doctors and local characters trip off the tongues of eighty and ninety-year-olds so readily that when many of them remember, just as easily, various washerwomen of their childhood it must surely have been that they were women of unforgettable personality. They were also, of course, of prime importance to the decent survival of the family ... Cathie McMillan's family anyway.

I mind Molly Stevenson, she came to wash. It was a great day . . . wash-day. I can smell the suds yet. I used to like that smell . . . washing-soda it would be, likely. My mother didn't think Molly Stevenson was very good at the washing, but she put up with her for fear of having to do it herself.

I mind of Bridie Traynor. It was the way she spoke! We had a friend called Miss Connell when I was wee, and once when I heard Bridie ask ma for a caun'le to light the wash-house, I must've rankled that round in my mind for a while, then I asked ma. 'Is Miss Connell's right name Beatrice *Candle?*'

It was hard work, but there were perks for the washerwomen too.

We'd an Irish one, Mrs. Monaghy. She came every week. The hot water and the green soft soap would be ready for her and she got a tot of whisky before she started. Then she got her dinner and another tot afore she went home.

Some preferred a longer drink.

Our Daisy Watson aye started wash-day wi' a Wee Murray out the kitchen press.

The washerwomen had their side to it all too, of course, and they had sometimes to come to terms with their ladies. There was a general belief among those 'ladies' that it kept the 'women' on their toes, to have to re-do work occasionally, just on principle. Violet Tomkin's grandmother was one such 'woman'.

My granny used to go out washing. One of her 'places' was a posh-house in Jordanhill. She got half-a-crown for a day's work (this would be about 1922). She was a real worker my granny, and a rare washer, and so she was awful insulted when the mistress came out one day and looked at the washin' on one of the lines.

'I think that stretch could do with another wash and dolly-blue, Teenie.'

Now my granny wasnae a young woman. She'd a hard life, lost a son an' a grown-up daughter and now she was rearin' *me* up. She looks at the washin' . . . 'It was a lovely washing Hen, so it was,' she told me when she came home.

But she needed the work and so she just nodded to that Mistress Eadie.

'I'll just hang out this pile first,' says my granny. The mistress comes back later from her afternoon at some tea-party. The washin's done and there's my granny synin' round the sink, and the clo'es all out blowing an' billying on the line just as clean's the madam had left them.

'That's better Teenie. What a difference with the extra run-through and the dolly,' says-she.

And my granny just says, 'Aye'.

Although that granny did her scrubbing in the back wash-house, the days of wash-houses were numbered. But there's just a last minding of their hey-day when one wean could still say, with venom, to another, as an even deadlier insult to its mother than impugning her morals.

Your mammy *smokes* in the wash-hoose!

Whether the taunt suggested that only a slattern would breathe tobacco or spill dog-ends among the new-washed clothes or that the very act of lighting-up in secret, tokened a woman who was no better than she should be, the rememberer would not tell, and the answer is buried in the rubble of the derelict back-court washie.

The days of solitary rub-a-dubbing were nearly over since by then Glasgow had built its chain of Public Baths and wash-houses, and brought revolution to wash-day. Revolution and a new social divide. The Steamie had arrived.

Ladies did not go to the steamie, but those who did, found that it had its own culture and chaff, from which the toffs were never missed. The steamie was divided into stalls, each with its small iron boiler and sink, let out at a shilling an hour.

If we werenae there to help her carry the wash-bundle to the steamie, ma used to put it in a zinc bath and tie it to an old pram, then push it there hersel'. But many a time I was there wi' her, to tramp the sheets or blankets or just help her to manhandle the clo'es. I mind there was an iron dryin' rack called a horse. It was a long thing and you pulled it out, put your clo'es on it and then pushed the whole lot back into a kind of quick-drying chamber. And there was another thing forbye that, a sort-of hand-cawed drier. There was a man there did that. You draped your washin' on a frame, he birled it round wi' the handle and all the wet came spinnin' out the clo'es.

It was during that break when you were getting your tuppence-worth of the drying that there was time for a bit of clash with neighbours and friends. There at the steamie, women whose homes

were too small to entertain visitors enjoyed an alternative social life
... in winter it was warmer and brighter than the street, where they
hobnobbed and heard the bruit of the district in spring and
summer.

Oh aye, the steamie was warm, and on cold days it drew you like a
poultice.

I was twenty-one when I got married and went away to live, over three
hundred yards from my mother, the other end of the village. I was
terrible hame-sick because I didnae know the neighbours. Besides,
though I had a nice house (red sandstone wi' a wally close) there was no
hot water. At first I went to my mother's to do my washing, but then I
heard women talking abut the steamie and all the jokin' and gossip that
went on. 'Nellie,' says I to myself, 'you're missin' a lot of fun, no' goin'
to the steamie.'

So I booked a stall and in I went, I was that green and stupid I didnae
know I had it for just the one hour. I thought it was mine till my washin'
was done, so I didnae hurry up. Here was me, thinkin' it was nice to be a
grown-up married woman washin' at the steamie, when two big *irate*
women descended on me and gave me lalldy for goin' over my time.
Well, here's me wi' my wee iron boiler boilin' away good-o, and I didnae
know how to get my things out quick. So I yanked it out best as I could
and slittered it trailing away, to get dried off a bit for takin' home. I
never had the nerve to go to the steamie again.

The next change in washing arrangements came with the rash of
new housing schemes ... those marvel-homes with four rooms
forbye the kitchen and bathroom, and set in small enclosed gardens.
The steamie was left to the tenement dwellers.

There was a double wally sink, a shallow side and a deep. And there was
a grand galvanised gas-boiler in the kitchen that stood on wee bowley
legs and had a gas ring under it. I'd never seen anything so labour-saving
in my life. You could do your washing in your own two tubs wi' the
boiler lid plopping and shushing there in your own kitchen ... *and*, any
day of the week. That was a real treat after the wee cafuffles you used to
have, up the close, over the head of the wash-house.

And something even more labour-saving than the magic boiler was
on its way, to the Watt household, anyway, very early in the
gadget's history.

My husband won a money prize from his employers and decided to instal a washing-*machine*. It was the wonder of Clarkston for it must've been one of the very first in the neighbourhood. It had a rotary action and friends used to come in and watch the things birling round, and even bring wee bundles of their clothes to get them done for them ... very sociable really.

Just like the steamie in fact. But private, and in Clarkston.

The novelty of gawping at someone else's washing-machine soon wore off. Indeed the greatest boom it was offering before long, was that you didn't have to watch it at all, and you could do six jobs on wash-day instead of just one. What started the mid-century years as a decadent indulgence soon became as necessary to a young working bride as her wedding ring. Built-in spinners and driers even threatened to kill off pulleys ... although many a sensible household has since re-discovered the usefulness of the old 'pole'.

With that mention of the pulley, let the chapter end as it began, with another Highlands lass come south. She went into service in Pollokshields, intelligent, but new to the sophistications of city life. During the girl's first week the mistress of the house went into the kitchen to find her new maid perched on top of the step-ladder carefully draping the washing over the pulley, quite unaware that the contraption could be let down.

And if you like a happy ending ... that girl learned quickly, and about more than pulleys. She occupied her walking-out time to good purpose and subsequently married a Pollokshields gentleman. In time she was, no doubt, able to put some other naive girl wise to the ways of her own kitchen equipment.

18
Rothesay was the Big-Time

Until the turn of the century a day off work in July was as much as most ordinary folk could expect for their annual holiday. They might make a round of the Fair on the Glasgow Green, take a walk to either the Queen's Park Flagpole or the high point of the Necropolis to see the strange sight of their city, smokeless, while its factory chimneys were at rest. Some with a little money put by took a 'shillin'y' evening cruise from the Broomielaw, listened to the German band on the paddle-steamer and saw the villages beading the edges of the Firth of Clyde. Perhaps that was what started them dreaming, or gave them big ideas.

Actually, as always, it was the top-drawer folk who started the drift to the Clyde coast for holidays, by building second homes with vistas up the sea-lochs and across the scattering of hilly islands.

One who saw himself at his sea-side mansion as a host of real distinction and flair was Mr. Tom Watson's grandfather, Walter Freer (noted elsewhere as the blaefoot laddie warming his chapped feet in his bunnet). By the years of the fine coast-house he was a man of wealth and consequence, known to many as 'Mister Glasgow' himself.

My grandpa bought a big place at Saltcoats and he used to have week-end parties there. He'd horses in his stables for his guests and all-his-orders, but it's the invitations he sent out that I mind as well as anything. There used to be a note at the bottom of each card ...
'Train with special saloon carriage attached, leaves St. Enoch Station Glasgow at 2p.m. for South Beach Station.'

The fashion was now set by the likes of Walter Freer. Bien folk began to copy biener, in this fancy for real holidays, sleeping in other people's homes: and your ordinary wage-earners took to the

147

whole idea like ducks to water ... literally water, for the Clyde in all
its glory was on their doorstep, with small towns and clachans set in
sandy bays, ready made for every taste and pay-poke. The coast and
island folk themselves discovered that the sea could bring them
more than fish and seaweed, and they began to cater for their city
neighbours' new whim.

> My grandfather was piermaster at Kirn at the time the big houses were
> being built down the Firth of Clyde. He could see that wealthy folk
> were beginning to rent out these houses for holidays when their owners
> werenae using them. So grandpa says to himself that why should
> ordinary folk no' come their holiday as well, if they could get wee places
> to stay. Well, he'd a good bit money put by, so he built a nice tenement
> block at Kirn and began to let out the houses for a week or a fortnight to
> just plain folk from Glasgow. Then he put up a row of shops for them
> too. Kirn thought itself a cut above Dunoon mind, and the Kirn folk
> were angry at grandfather to start with. But they soon got used to the
> idea and were letting out their own rooms. Later he built a whole lot of
> wee summer houses for letting on the ground behind his own cottage.
> His name was Brown, so they called his place Broon's Back.

Glasgow in these heady days was boom city and the boats were
coming down the river packed with summer visitors, the menfolk
often commuting morning and evening.

> I mind Kirn pier when it was black wi' jerry hats night and mornin'.
> Jerry hats were kind of high bowlers like chamber pots.

That was Broon and those were the visitors he provided accommodation for, ninety-odd years ago. Other hosts, with only their
homes to rent out, squeezed themselves into their back kitchens
and let every other inch to ma, faither and the weans from Glasgow.
The Edgars from Pollokshaws were ahead of their neighbours
when it came to getting away for more than just a day trip.

> We were one of the first families round our way to have regular
> holidays. Oh my, but you should just have seen the washing and ironing
> and packing to get the eight of us ready for off! We used to take our
> Japanese hamper ... yon soft kind of woven straw like potato baskets. It
> started off flat when it was empty, then, when you piled in the coats and
> towels and sheets, the sides came up higher and higher. The lid was deep
> as well so that packing could go away above the rim of the bottom part.
> the very first holiday we had was at Saltcoats. My mother took a house

for a fortnight and I mind the other kids standin' at the close-mouth
and chantin' when we were going away ...
'Gooo — d ridd — ance tae baaa — d rubb — ish!
Gooo — d ridd — ance tae baaa — d rubb — ish'

In the earliest years of holidays, the Clyde coast resorts remained
mainly the quiet communities they had always been, but as the
seasons came and went, each one acquired the personality and
characteristics of the clientele which came back year after year.
Largs, Saltcoats, Dunoon, Rothesay and Helensburgh were the
big-time, with dancing, entertainers, pubs, cafés and souvenir
shops, while in the quiet hamlets round the Gareloch and Strone,
Skelmorlie and West Kilbride, you found your own amusement.
Memories of one style are as much cherished as those of the other.

But before enjoying the charms of the chosen venue you had to
get there. Part of the excitement was the journey itself, whether by
train, sailing all the way, or a combination of steamer and rail to
add to the adventure and confusion.

It was 'train' for the young Wotherspoons.

When we went to Maidens seven summers in a row, before the First
War, we went by train with three or four hampers and hat-boxes and the
high wicker pram in the guard's van.

It was 'sailing' for the Whites. On the paddle-steamers the crew
seem to have been pretty eechy-ochy about the amount of the fare,
depending on the whim of the man who collected the money.

We used to go to Ro'say and I mind one time we were all sittin' (the
eight of us) in a row on one of them long slatted seats. Along comes the
man in the cap and looks at us all. He jerks his head to my father.
'They a' yours?' says-he.
'Aye,' says my father, gettin' out his money.
'I'll just take it for the hauf of them.'

There was real competition among the private companies that
sailed their paddle-steamers all the way down from the city's
Broomielaw, but many folks preferred to take the train to Gourock, Wemyss Bay, Largs or Ardrossan and then the shorter sail to
the holiday place. The Big Three railway companies, The Glasgow
and South-West, the Caledonian, and the North British all had
their own steamers meeting the trains, and competition among

these three was notorious. Although one steamer could have taken
all the passengers on a particular trip, there would be three sailings
perhaps no more than fifteen minutes apart.

The holiday-let was by now usually for a month ... a month's
holiday for mother and the younger weans, with father and the
older ones taking their week or fortnight and joining them for the
week-ends.

> Mother used to take this wee house at Ro'say. there was Willie, myself,
> Rachel, James, Robert and Emma; the young ones went wi' her, but
> father and them that were workin' or goin' wi' milk or papers dinae get
> down till the week-ends.

That was the pattern, and for some, holiday time off at all was a
generous perk of the job, for others it was a sacrifice.

> When we'd our holiday it was just a wee-wee house we took and faither
> came for a week ... a week mind ... wi' no pay.

Meeting father was one of the holiday highlights.

> We used to go down the Clyde and up to a wee clachan near Inveraray
> for a month. Father came at the week-ends by horse charabanc over the
> Rest-and-be-Thankful from Helensburgh.

> Father used to take the train to Craigendoran, then up the West
> Highland line to Garelochhead at a shilling for the whole journey. We
> used to go and meet him at tea-time on Saturdays.

So now they're all settled in their cottages, rooms and farm-
houses up the Kyles of Bute, or along the Clyde coast and its sea-
lochs: and the roaming and explorations begin that are to be
fondled in the memory for ninety years.

These were the laid-on excitements that were revelation to little
girls like young Miss Janet Macleod, from douce homes with strict
fathers ... fathers for the moment safely at home making the family
pennies.

> We were usually Whiting Bay people, quiet sedate Whiting Bay ...
> but-here this year it was Rooms-with-Attendance at Largs, and Largs
> was a milestone for me, for that was the year I discovered the *enter-
> tainers*. I had never in all my born days seen anything like them ... the
> Alvin Sawyers Troupe, with their dancing and singing, their comic cuts
> and their chorus. We used to sit in the open air, *behind* the rows of

benches that you paid for, and watch them. They wore white sailor caps and reefer-kind jackets in the day and monkey mess-jackets in the evenings. This was all about 1910, about the time of Alexander's Ragtime band. I'm sure they played that. I used to sit there with my sisters in the mornings, carried away by Miss Sylvia Watt's singing. Then we couldn't get our dinners down fast enough to get back for the afternoon show, and the same at tea-time.

'What's the good of "attendance",' ma used to complain, 'if you don't stay long enough to eat what the landlady makes?'

And there were the pleasures of the pier.

I used to like the machines at Ro'say pier. I never-ever had much money for the footballers and the palm-reading machine wi' the wee metal buttons, so I always ended up at yon crane that lifted prizes from a pile of jelly beans. You used to see a watch or somethin' gettin' into its claws and then just when it began to swing over to the chute that sent it out to you, everything except a coupla jelly beans dribbled back down among the rest. But once I got a silver cake-fork that I have yet.

Apart from the entertainers idolised by young holiday-makers, there were sometimes other notable people to be seen at the Clyde resorts.

When I was staying in Rothesay in 1907 I can remember we used to see the Bute bairns, the Marquis of Bute's wee ones, coming along the shore carried in two creel-pannier things slung over a donkey. That's a picture I always have in my mind about Rothesay.

Even in quieter spots there were characters worth seeing, and better adventures in finding them.

We used to take a wee boat across Loch Long and beach it on the shore near a cottage where there was an old man lived. He would've been maybe ninety-eight years old the first year we went, then up to a hundred-and-one in the next three. It was quite the thing for holiday-makers to go and just *look* at this old chap, sitting outside his cottage selling post cards of himself as souvenirs.

'How are you the day?' you used to ask.

'Och I'm fine . . . fine,' says-he. Same thing every time. He just made a living out of being a hundred. He was there for *viewing* beside his wee house on the shore.

Another quaint house, another yearly visitation by the young Gilmours.

We used to scramble along the shore to visit an upturned boat that was made into a home, a proper wee dwelling-house. The locals used to call it Susie's Castle, and Susie lived there with her man. It was an old Para Handy kind of coal-boat that used to sail the Clyde and they lived there, those, two, like Pegotty, summer and winter with their wee bit garden round them and a path running up behind it to the Garelochhead road. If we hadn't been afraid to go too near we'd maybe have got to see the inside. But it was just enough to go and look at them from a safe distance ... at the boat with its tin chimney and wee bits of curtain at the port-hole windows and at them sitting outside chawnering and quarrelling all the time, Susie smoking her short clay pipe ('cutty cleys' they used to call those).

Of course it wasn't all as idyllic as that picture suggests ... it never is.

I mind the local folk used to tell us that they took a terrible lot of drink the two of them, and when they came back from the pub taking the width of the road, they'd just stop at the top of the path, lie down, and roll home to the bottom.

It's difficult for modern folk with gardens, or their cars to whisk them to coast or country in half an hour, to sense the exhilaration of pavement-and-cobble weans, in the openness of sea-shore or green field. In those days, both of these were too many hours, and too much money, away from the city for anything but that once-a-year visit for the holidays ... it's difficult to understand the love and loyalty a few summers could arouse in such bairns for a holiday place.

I loved Clynder, we went every year and I knew every chuckie on the Clynder beach.

Ah Whistlefield! We went for years to Whistlefield. When we stayed at the croft there we knew everyone. We rambled in the hills and up the burns and we helped with the three cows and the hens ... and then at the haymaking.

We went to a cousin's cottage near Inveraray. He'd a small boat that we used to sail and when we were old enough we used to take it over to St. Catherine's for the village hops and then sail home by moonlight. It was very romantic.

Holidays were never holidays without paddling and bathing, and

recollections of costumes stretch from bloomer suits and rubber mob caps, to clinging two-tone cottons with thigh-hugging legs, and on, in the march of fashion, to the man-made nylon ruches and svelte tricels. (There the recorded memories of swimsuits end, except for comments from eavesdropping grandweans who sport bikinis and less, scarcely worth the manufacturer's effort of knotting the thread to stitch.)

Not all the paddlers went down to the water's edge. The sea was brought up to some, sitting Mahomet-like on the prom.

My aunt always took her family to Rothesay. She was very stout and like to sit on a bench above the shore. There she used to dispatch her daughters down to the jetty with a bucket for sea water for her feet. Down went the girls and spoke to the boatman, very polite.

'Please may we have a bucket of water for mother?'

'Help yoursel's lassies. It's a' free.'

But total immersion was better.

We went paddlin' and bathing. We'd no costumes or that, and I mind once seein' the boys goin' in, just in their wee breeks and wantin' to do the same. So I just sat down on the sand and wriggled off everythin' but my knickers and went wadin' away in like that. I didnae half get a leatherin' after, for wettin' my knickers.

Then it was time for the last picnic, the last washing of sand from between the toes, the last visit to the entertainers, the last buying of sea-side rock, and souvenir hankies with Bonnie Scotland embroidered on them ...

But there are souvenirs and souvenirs, and not many found one like Mr. Alick Murdoch's.

When I was a laddie I spent all my holidays at Kirn, helping on the pier. And I got to know the steamers and the different wee things about them all ... every detail ... I just loved those steamers. Then when I was a man and they were breaking up the old 'Iona' paddle-steamer in 1936 I bought the bridge and deck-house. Had it for a summer-house in my garden for over forty years. When we moved house it had to be lifted by crane over the garden wall to a lorry and taken to the new place. Yon was a grand summer-house.

So while most folk were content to enjoy the Clyde, recreate themselves at its beauty spots and then leave those joys behind, and come home with no more than their sticks of rock, a handful of shells and their memories, Alick Murdoch brought back his bit of the river's life to the city. He was sitting in that deck-house on fine days still, at ninety-four, seeing himself as a paddle-struck laddie on Kirn pier, signalling in the steamers to disgorge the streams of his fellow Glaswegians come 'doon the watter' for their holidays.

19
Doin' Business with our Scraps

What do Samantha's computer toy and Jasper's Action Man of the 1980s have in common with Mary's post-card album or Davy's diabolo of long ago. Not much you might think.

And yet for the hundred-odd years this book concerns itself with, children's indoor toys and games have been more or less simple answers to seven needs: to collect or compete, to read or to cuddle, to perfect skills, to invent or to revel in games of chance.

Take collecting. Children have ever been magpies. Roman bairns stationed with fathers guarding Antonine's Wall at Milngavie, probablyn amo-amassed legion buttons or helmet feathers; young Mungo may have decorated his cell with chuckies from the Molendinar, and no doubt wee Burrell hoarded broken plate chips before getting into the big league with his first teen-age purchase of a painting.

Perhaps the items most persistently collected by the young over the years have been their *scraps* ... flowers, baskets of fruit, beautiful ladies, soldiers, little brides and grooms, funny bauchly wee men and babies have all gone in and out of scrap fashion over the years, but throughout all the decades remembered by elderly Glasgow ladies, who once haggled over their exchanges, best cherished and valued have been their beloved Angels.

Around 1906 Dorothy Laurie was a far-ben scrap dealer and collector, who kept hers in a Gold Flake box.

The second best things were Hands ... two hands clasped across a map of the world. You got that picture in all different sizes. But the very favourite were your Angels. You got a lot of Angels ... all like fat cherubs really. You used to sit at the close-mouth to change them with your friend. 'An Angel for a Hand' you used to offer, and if it was wee

155

Angels you'd to fit three or four of them to a big Hand ... or four-five teenie-wee Hands to a big Angel ... to make it fair you see.

They went through the decades cutting up crisp new sheets of Angels, Hands, Lucy Atwells, Mickeys and Minnies. They hoarded them, scarce and thinning, through two wars, then swapping new ones and pasted them into scrap books through the 'forties and 'fifties ... All too innocent a pleasure surely for the 'eighties, you say to a lady who loved her scraps at the turn of the century.

That's no' true. I was in the shop this past week just, and there was this wee lassie rummaging through a box of scraps. And you know I could just see mysel' sittin' on the school wall wi' my pal, me wi' my legs through the railings one way and hers the opposite, doin' business wi' our scraps.

An exploratory slip round to the same shop reveals the 'eighties' taste in scraps, Top Cat, Mister Men, Space-folk ... and still holding their holy own, sonsy dimpled angels with damp curls and blue wings, swathed in soft clouds.

Scraps were not the only barter-currency, there was silver-paper too and the stamps the brainy boys swopped.

> But wi' us it was mostly ciggy-cards. You got them off of some man you seen lightin' up. 'Gaunie gie's yer cigarette-photie, Mister?' you used to say.

And Mister usually obliged without a word.

Collecting post-cards to put in albums wasn't an extravagant pastime either, when you could buy them at twelve for fourpence-ha'penny.

> I remember being on holiday at Largs about 1908 or 1907 and buying them at fourpence ha'penny a dozen. The stamps were a ha'penny each so you could send cards to twelve friends for tenpence ha'penny.

There were novelty shapes in post cards too.

> My very best were the ones that you got in the shape of letters, and people sent you the right ones so's that on the front page of your book you had them arranged in your own name. So I had eleven cards making up ...

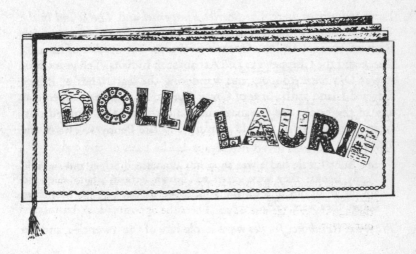

There have always been true originals who hoard the odd things that intrigue and pleasure them particularly, bobbins, thimbles, bottle-tops, butterflies, but the post-cards, the scraps, the stamps, the ciggy-cards and the autographs belong to mainstream collecting and are true fashions of the past century.

When you tired for the time being of your precious albums and shoe-boxes of treasure, and were ready to pit your wits against a rival, there were games and competitions galore, dominoes, charades, happy famiies and ping-pong. Shorter-lived crazes were pegotty, lexicon and the 'fifties obsession with canasta and Chinese chequers. And for Mr. Noble Boyd in his young years around 1912 there was ... the dreaded cribbage.

> My oh my! Was there no' just cribbage in our house? My father deaved us about cribbage when I was young. We spent hours and hours, days and days, months and months ... *years* playin' cribbage. My father kept a league table all totted up in notebooks. Oh my, that cribbage!

When there was no one else to play with, there was always something to read.

> I liked *The Basket of Flowers* and *Helpful Nellie* when I was about nine. Then a bit older, *John Halifax – Gentleman*. But best of all I liked *The Channings* and I used to nearly cry at the bit where young Charley gets his head shaved in the fever. You see I mind it all after seventy years.

Later favourites were *The Scarlet Pimpernel* and *The Wind in the Willows*, but by the 'twenties the craze was for adventure with Richard Hannay and the Gorbals Diehards. *The Settlers of Karossa Creek* and the Chippewaya and Athabascan Indians. Ten years later it was *Out with Romany* and wandering the leafy lanes of Prince Edward Island with *Anne of Green Gables*. As well-remembered as any of the books are the magazines and comics that poured out, from *The Quiver* of the old century and the Penny stories of the 1900s.

> My Aunt Lizzie had a wee shop in Cumberland Street and she sold Penny books; they were green wi' brown letterin'; fairy tales and adventure stories, and when my hands were clean I got to read them before they were sold.

Playbox, Rainbow, Jingles were staple fare of the 'twenties, and ten years later *Little Dots*, *Mickey Mouse*, *Film Fun* and the *Dandy* and *Beano*. And there's no generation gap even now, between grannies and their grandweans over Oor Willie and the Broons, intimates of all for surely fifty years. Big boys had *Rover*, *Wizard*, *Hotspur*, and *Adventure*, and Frank Richards, who gave them Harry Wharton and Billy Bunter, became *Hilda* Richards to bring Barbara Redfern and Bessie Bunter to their sisters. Mrs. Colinette Allan remembers them.

> I loved a Friday. I got the *Girl's Crystal* at lunchtime and read it during Silent Reading while the teacher did the register. D'you remember Silent Reading? I don't suppose it was for the *Girl's Crystal* really, though.

And Kate Thomas ...

> But you couldnae aye be readin' books or playing tiddlywinks. There were times, when you were wee, that it was just your teddy or your doll that you wanted ... when someb'dy'd stolen your scone or give you a cuff on the ear.

Teddies were perhaps more comforting, but give or take an eye or a chewed ear they have been much of a muchness for general appearance and style since they first appeared. They rejoice in no other names; no other adjective than 'my' was used by any rememberer to describe them; and they were, without exception *he*. The 'I' of the 'my', of course, could be either boy or girl.

Dolls on the other hand ran the whole gamut of styles, came in *he*s and *she*s and had as many different names as their owners who were, until the birth of Action Man, always girls. Mary Hardy remembers her Rosy.

> She had a china face and real hair and she had jointed arms and legs and dainty wee toty fingers. She was dressed in helio satin with lovely petticoats and knickers and she had a hat with a feather. Mind I only got to sit with her when visitors came. She wasn't for what you might call *playing*. I kept her to give to my own wee lassie, but when I took her out, the elastic in her joints was perished and she all fell apart. I was as sad as if I'd been seven.

And the daughter who didn't get the ornamental doll remembers getting another.

My father won a huge dolly at the Empire Exhibition in 1938, so there was no other name for her but Bella Houston. She'd long, long dangly legs and woolly pigtails, and she'd a tartan tammy and skirt. I loved her till she burst and all the sawdust came out.

Twenty years before that, Betty Laurie had another beloved doll.

He was a boy-doll and I called him Gordon. He had a blue-ish green furry body and a lovely face, not china but smooth and made of some hardwearing stuff because he lived to be an old man did Gordon. One time I changed him to be a girl right-enough (away ahead of the doctors I was, doing that about 1917). But *I* just did it by sticking on some of my own curls that had got cut off when I had sore eyes.

Girl-dolls, boy-dolls ... and of course baby-dolls, to be petted and crooned over and cradled. Muriel and Margaret of the 1910-14 batch of little mothers remember a holiday house with lace curtains that they could tie-up into loops that made perfect, draped cribs.

There were other homes of course where it would have been unthinkable to buy a child a doll at all ... make one of wood, or knit, aye ... but money to burn at a shop — never.

In our house you didnae get anything you didnae actu'lly *need*. And sure you didnae need dollies. In our day 'needin'' meant soup and tatties, or your boots gettin' sorted.

Few children, though, went quite without something to cuddle. They didn't have much in the Edgar home but Nellie remembers her dolls.

I don't mind of havin' toys at all ... except our cloth dolls of course ... not bought mind, but because faither worked in the calico print works and they printed doll-face there. He used to bring home wee torn-off bits for dusters or sweat rags and my mother washed them and sorted out the bits wi' faces and sewed them up into dollies for us. Oh aye, we'd always our cloth dolls.

Boys cuddled their teddies when they were small of course, but the men remembering now recall better their skeely ways with diabolo or yo-yo. Diabolo ruled okay until the 'twenties, but from then forward the yo-yo was the thing.

You could do a lot of funny wee tricks wi' your yo-yo. Just plain 'upsy-down' was easy, or 'out'n'in' and 'ower yer heidie' or 'cradley'. But the best was 'get along little doggie' when you kind of spun the yo-yo at the end of the string and walked it along the floor. Well *I* couldnae right enough, but Jimmy Gilchrist could. *He* could do them all.

If you were really stuck for something to do in the house when it was raining outside, there was always something at hand for inventing games.

My granny had a sore back and there was a table-leaf kep' under the mattress on her kitchen bed. It was polished and shiny and when she was out we used to prop it from the bed and jam it against the fender. You got a rare slide down that.

Others raided the hall-stand and drawers.

We'd a big lobby in our house and we used to get walking sticks and rolled-up socks to play a kind of hockey between the front door and the lobby press.

Board and chance games seem almost as old as memory.

I play Ludo and Snakes 'n' Ladders wi' my grandweans and I mind playin' them wi' my granny, and I wouldnae wonder but she played them wi' hers. That would be what ... seven generations? Fancy that!

But then, when you visit the Border abbeys they'll show you a scratched slab where, they say, King David I's abbey builders of eight centuries ago played their games of chance. So stakes on the throw of a dice are not new.

Nothing is ... under the sun. Mary Hardy, at eighty-four, looks round at today's bairns building with Lego, cutting up their grubby pastry and heeshie-bawing their dolls.

Oh aye, I see the weans doin' their jumpin'-ropes funny, and playin' wi' clever dollies that greet and wet their hippin's ... but they're really no' doin' anything much different from what we were doin' in the 1900s or my own lassies in the 'thirties ... [She pauses ...] I'm no' sure about them computers all the same.

20
I Got Ecclefechan Right

Schools in Glasgow of the past hundred years have come in all shapes, sizes and materials, from large ancient stone-built academies with centuries of tradition behind them, to the modern comprehensives sprawling over landscaped campuses. Between these two, in both type and period, there have been a variety of others. In the biener urban districts, with their tree-lined avenues, there were the little seminaries for young ladies, carried on mostly in gardened private villas. Then, each area of the inner-city had its board school which set out, late last century, to give a decent grounding to the tribes of children from teeming tenements, and to riddle out the lads and lasses o' pairts clearly destined for higher things. In the suburbs too, fast creeping out round the city in the inter-war years, authorities hastily threw up temporary wooden or corrugated schoolrooms to accommodate the new breed of semi-detached weans there. But whatever the style of the alma mater, all of them have been rich in plain talent and personality, and with teachers remembered with pain, pleasure and hindsight amusement.

There were all sorts of reasons for choice of school in the days before it was simply the local place or else pay fees at an old-established town grammar school. Mr. Alexander Murdoch knows why *he* went to Bridgeton Secondary in 1898.

> The reason I went there from the old dominie at Tollcross, with his white beard and big red face was that, as a nipper my father kept rabbits with a boy called Robert Paterson, in a back-court at Greenhead Street, and now that same Robert Paterson was heidie at Bridgeton Secondary. Mind he'd a lot of respect for Paterson forbye the rabbits, and thought any school wi' him in charge had to be good.

162

That school was a substantial building with real classrooms and echoing corridors, purpose-built in its time. Mrs. Tait's early lessons, on the contrary, were in make-do and certainly cosier premises, but with an equally memorable teacher.

Our school was just the room of a house really, and I had a tiny bird of a teacher there. She was a bloodless-looking wee thing but she was a rare teacher, and a stickler for good writing. D'you remember Vere Foster copy books? Well she was a great one for them, with their proverbs in joined-up writing along the top of each page and maybe five blank lines below to make better and better copies of it. I loved my Vere Fosters and got to be quite good at them ... and quick ... because when you were finished your page you got making toast at the schoolroom fire. But it wasn't just the writing she dinned in, it was other lessons and when I left her after a few years and went to a big academy I was well up with the others there.

And well enough grounded for a good classics degree by the end of the first war ... happily married too to the only Heidie who ever palmied the compiler of this book.

Out in the budding suburbs, by the turn of the century, houses were built before schools, and lessons took place in any suitable accommodation.

There was no proper school our way when I was wee about 1904, but the classes were held in the two small rooms up the Orchardhill Church tower, square rooms they were, with a coal fire in each and rare views across the hills round Glasgow. You went up the windy stair to the two teachers ... Miss Johnson was one ... but I can't just think on the other. Then, after that, the Tin Academy was put up nearer the main road and we all went down there with Miss Johnson. You stayed there till you sat your Qually.

Apart from the fact that there were no fees, going locally to school had other homely advantages, and Miss Nan Gardner has a vision of one of those that would bring joy to the heart of an observant advertiser.

I was a bit lost and tearful when I went to school at first, so every morning at playtime my mother came to the school railings and passed a Chocolate Vienna biscuit through to me. After sixty years I never see a Chocolate Vienna but I think of my mother at that railing.

But there were perks in being at the posh schools too. With

travelling money to manage, you could practise economies that were surprising in view of the substantial fees willingly handed over by your father. But perhaps it was just that the seeds of thrift and business acumen were being sowed.

> I was at Glasgow Academy in the 'thirties and I remember I used to walk from Kelvinbridge to the town to save the penny tram fare and get it to spend.

Some schools had airy assembly halls with elegant arches, pillars topped by classical mouldings and dux medallists listed in gold leaf. Some had little more of a hall than a tiled central corridor. Yet others had dunny-halls in deep wells below several storeys and surrounded by open stairways. In these last, some musician-teacher would start morning and afternoon school by thumping out marching music on the school piano while the 'lines' clumped upstairs to the classrooms and the janny prepared to take his first lot for drill in the hall. Classrooms, big or small, once reached, were much of a muchness everywhere, with blackboards, chalkdust, rows of desks in pairs, satchels at the feet and foreign bodies, various, stuffed down wally inkwells.

Just before we leave the architecture and fabric of schools to look at the memories of the pedagoguery that went on inside, it's worth perhaps taking a glance at certain of its important precincts. And, as every schoolboy knows, whether the school was gracious and spacious, or simply your functional Corporation pile, it was sure to have notable lavvies for a variety of the kind of undouce shennanigans remembered by one dainty old lady after seventy-five years.

> D'you mind when you were going to the toilets and you always asked your best friend of the moment to come and 'hold the door', just to stand outside holding it shut. You were maybe shy of the other girls but more likely the locks were broken and the boys threatened to lean over the top from their side to swing open the doors and *look at you*!

And the devil-may-care among the older pupils, boys and girls alike, indulged from time to time of course in the playtime 'puff'

What of the classroom itself?

Ask any liberal-minded modern what schools were like fifty years ago and he'll no doubt assure you in almost Dickensian terms that they were nasty, brutish and dull.

But ask anyone who was actually a victim of those days and you get surprising answers. Of our rememberers certainly, not a single one but had mainly happy memories of schools and teachers. Such bad days as there were, were wryly recalled it's true, but only as black spots in otherwise interesting and purposeful years. Sure they stood in lines, did multiplication tables and regimented exercises to the teacher's counting, sat in rows, had Friday tests, gold stars and cleaning the board for good work ... palmies for bad ... (and not one but laughed at the word 'beating' used modernly for what they knew, and accepted with only small griping, as 'the belt'). The psychology may have been all wrong, but the educational errors of those old days are on the whole remembered philosophically. And recollections explode the myth that heads were constantly held down over sums and spellings and loathsome reading books, from nine till four without diversion.

> I mind of havin' wee honey-comb frame-things in a square box, maybe the size of a half-a-pound chocolates, and you got tiny coloured cubes, red and yellow, green and blue, white and black, and you put them into the wee spaces. You used it for counting and when you'd done your sums, you got making designs wi' the cubes.

That was around 1929 and from two or three years earlier there are those who remember knitting and plasticine, and an even more splendidly messy craft ...

> You used to get treats on Friday afternoons after the Register. I mind of takin' old newspapers to soak for makin' paper-mashy bowls and things. Then you painted them, put on a wee scrap and varnished over that.

They made d'oyleys and raffia bags for mothers' Christmases, compiled drawing books with works of crayon art; and Keating-copied Old Masters. In season they grew cabbages at the back of the school and bought them for a few coppers to take home. They rehearsed concerts, held Cake 'n' Candies for the 'poor' and organised bulb-growing competitions. Sometimes the ploys were approved-curriculum, sometimes simply the whims of inspired teachers.

> We had a schoolmaster called David Horne. He'd been in the army and he was a rigid stickler for discipline. But he was fair right-enough, and

we liked him. He'd a way of getting a notion suddenly and on a nice day he used to just stop the work suddenly and take the whole class off to Sir John Maxwell's estate at Pollok, right across the road from the school. He showed us all the different plants and trees and birds ... even squirrels. And I once saw a beautiful kingfisher there.

Another who remembers a remarkable nature 'lesson', this time on the way back to school after lunch, was the lady who was once young Janet Macleod. Her home was just outside the city.

I was with my brother going along a road with drystane dyking each side. He was playing his mouth-organ and we'd just passed a stretch of dyke when I happened to look back and saw ... like a grey wave ... a mass of weasels, as if they were rising and falling like sea, but on the road. We'd heard from the teacher about flitting of weasels, and we thought this was it. But father said 'no', it was the sound of the mouth-organ that brought them out the wall.

Apart from handwork and wild-life outings there were other welcome breaks from lessons, even before the days of school milk.

We got wee mugs of Horlicks every mornin' at our school for a ha'penny. I liked it when it was my turn to go for the rack wi' the mugs in it. Then you got to collect the ha'pennies and take them back wi' the empties to the Horlicks lady.

There seem to be few embittered memories or twisted personalities among the rememberers, left over from these days of unsound teaching practice, when pupils expressing themselves uninvited, merited a passing clout; but even the rosiest blinkers cannot deny injustice or shame, and there's a punishment or two that still rankles after sixty ... seventy ... even eighty years.

I got the belt at school for writing a letter in the class to a boy called Peter Johnson. I don't know whyever to him because I didn't even like him. Another time I had to stand under the hall clock for talking in the line. That was worse than the strap because the Heidie might see you and ask what you'd done.

I never smoked in the school sheds like some, nor nothing like that ... but I mind of gettin' into trouble once. I was in a Home and all the others in my class were just in their own famiies wi' mothers and fathers. They'd gardens too, and they brought flowers to the teacher. So when I saw that, I pinched some from a garden on my way to school. I got caught and dinae get to the Qually party. The teacher offered to pay my ticket but the Heidie wouldnae let her.

The Mr. Harry Anderson of 1984 doesn't seem like one who would ever have threatened the peace of Albert Road Academy, but ...

I once got the belt for pretending to fight with my desk neighbour ... maybe a wee bit of horse play. But anyway the Headmaster looked over the partition and saw us. He kept us sitting in his room for about two hours and then walloped us. He was a big tumphie really, him with his tile hat and frock-coat and dangling his gold watch chain.

Nor does Mrs. Janet Purvis seem a natural villain, self-confessed prim wee teacher's-helper that she was, at Lochfield school in the early century.

I was put to the bottom of the class for talking to my friend about the Alvin Sawyer entertainers I'd seen on my holidays at Largs. Oh the shame of that ... *me* at the bottom of the class! But there was worse to come. The Inspector. He began to ask spellings and I was the only one that got Ecclefechan right ... *and* five more words. But I got served right when he asked what such a good speller was going at the bottom of the class and the teacher said I'd misbehaved ... I would've been better to keep 'Ecclefechan' to myself.

And that was school ... from the days of slates and sponges, penny-plain and tuppence-coloured books, and of brief sulks over scoldings, to the dawn of present enlightenment and teacher-pupil harmony ... both a far cry from the long yonder schooldays of Mr. Tom Watson's grandfather in the 1850s.

He used to tell me that all his schooling, before he went to work at a printer's, was three months at a penny-school in a dark close off Argyle Street, a cold bare room with rough benches. Every Monday the 'master' collected their pennies and went off with them to get drunk ... just left the boys to do as they pleased. He learned nothing there, my grandpa, and when he left at nine-years-old, to work at feeding paper into a ruling machine, he couldn't write at all, and could just read but a word or two. He taught himself to read after that, from a book he got as a Bible prize, and to write from bits of the copy books they printed at his work.

Marching to music and the chanting of tables and lists of towns and dates with perjinkety teachers doesn't seem like gross hardships to thole in the face of that dour fight for education.

21
Cadgers and Hurlie-men

They'll chuckle with mirth for sure in sixty years, at the memory of each other's wee round yirdfast bottoms in blue jeans, that they were ever the height of youthful fashion. They'll organise nostalgic societies to sigh over cars that crawl along at 80 m.p.h. with exhausts that puff out smoke, and they'll protest at the pulling down of quaint old concrete-and-glass office towers.

But look at your average stirring street of long since, and of now, and you can be certain that, if humanity has not destroyed itself, the same three elements will make up the city streets of 2050 A.D., give or take trace-horse boy or traffic warden; penny-farthing or Fiesta hatch-back; multi-block or jenny a'thing.

Streets are People, Wheels and Buildings, whatever their appearance and purpose.

Ordinary people, adults and weans, doing ordinary things, walk and dance through other pages in this book; the peeverers and moshie-boys, kirk-goers and soldiers, shawlie-women and nurse-maids, hearse-followers and Royal visitors. But *they* have all been bound for the places where they really belong, the rooms'n'kitchens, the pews, the trenches, the grave. Those who belong to street-scenes may have lives apart, beds where they sleep, firesides where they sit, but for rememberers their place was the *street*, policemen and penny-jo's, buskers and hawkers and, perhaps most popular of them all, the lamplighters.

I mind the leeries lightin' the street lamps. They carried wee cutty ladders to get up to clean the glass or change the mantles. D'you mind the pole wi' the light in it that never went out? And the tinkly click when the pole went up and poked the glass flap open, and then the pool of grey-green light that came down?

I mind sklimmin' up the lamp-posts to swing on the cross-bar, then dreepin' doon and runnin' away when the polis came.

Flower-sellers, hawkers and beggars had their pitches and every morning down Jamaica, Union and Argyle Streets came files of billboard men setting out from agencies to advertise hairdressers, cut-price bargains, restaurants and hell-fire.

Like Punch and Judy they were, wi' their heads pokin' up between their boards.

These were unconscious entertainers in their way, but real street buskers and musicians were as much part of the evening in town as the hall turns you paid to see ... and whatever their particular skill, masters, most of them, of pavement patter as well.

You'll no' mind of Old Malabar. I saw him when I was wee, and heard him at his bawdy stories and street chaff, but his real thing was that he used to throw up a heavy ball and catch it in a leather cup strapped to his forehead. Mind his nose was all over his face wi' the times he'd missed, but he was a great turn.

Some hall-entertainers let passers-by taste their talent on the street in the hope of luring them inside for a full performance.

My grandfather knew one like that, this Jimmy Taylor that was around last century. Seems he had a right good conceit of himself and once when the owners of two different halls each wanted him, he auctioned himself in the open market-place at St. Enoch Square. A big-big crowd gathered and my grandpa watched him get knocked down by the auctioneer to the highest bidder, for a huge pay of a hundred pound for the week.

But most of the buskers were outdoor-only performers.

D' you mind the way we used to gawp at the buskers outside of the picture-halls in Argyle Street. There was yon wee Egyptian that put down his board and clapper-danced on it. That would be in the 'twenties. Then there was an organ-grinder wi' a monkey ... you must mind of him in Union Street.

... and the paper-tearer, the tin whistler, the one-man band, the juggler ... and a dozen others. Nancy Wall remembers one striking city-centre figure of the 'thirties and 'forties.

... a right kenspeckle figure of a man that played the fiddle. He'd an interesting, worn sort of face and a shock of iron grey hair ... used to play outside the Georgic tea-room. D' you mind the Georgic?

He is recalled by others too as having been more tangibly recorded than in mere memory.

We used to see a painting of yon violinist in the Art Galleries. It was a good portrait that.

But ask any group of over-seventies, who was the best-known Glasgow street character of the century, and they come out in unison with one name, 'The Clincher'.

Mr. Duncan White remembers him well.

The Clincher oh aye. A tall-tall man he was, in a lum-hat and frockcoat or tails. He got his nick-name from puttin' out a news-sheet that was called *The Clincher*. It was aye gettin' at the town council and the officials ... takin' them down a peg. I mind him standing outside of Lewis's selling his sheet.'

Another memory sees him on the move.

I mind seeing The Clincher one Christmas when he walked back and forward between Glasgow Cross and Jamaica Street with a sprig of mistletoe on his tail-coat. To kiss the lassies, I suppose.

But whether he lifted the coat-tail overhead to bestow his cheepers, the memory couldn't tell.

Och, he was a thorn in the breeks to a lot of folk was The Clincher, and there was once he got taken away to one of the asylums. Well, he was no more daft than the next chap and they had to let him out. But he wouldnae go, not without a certificate that he was right in the head, and after that he used to say that he was the only sane man in Glasgow wi' a certificate to prove it.

Before the First War such characters had their beats or pitches in the city centre, and the rest of pedestrian Glasgow, including wandering tykes and moggies, wove its way round and past them, jay-walking in its own whichever way. So too did much of the traffic. The earliest living memories of traffic are of carts, bicycles and cabs and, since many homes were still in the town, horse-drawn vans delivering milk, fish and bread. Wheels rumbled on the cobbles, steam-flanked horses snorted, and tossed great curls of

mane and tail. Public transport added to the general stir and young
Alick Murdock caught the end of one era.

> I just remember the last of the horse-buses. They ran for about two
> years after I started to go into the town to school about 1897. They
> were three-horse buses that were stabled at Spittal's yard in Tollcross. I
> mind gangs of wee boys went after the horses with buckets and shovels
> to collect the manure to sell to folks with gardens.

And a very few years later, about 1900 horses that had pulled the old
horse-trams were also finally put out to grass. By 1902 electric
trams were on the go.

> The trams were the same both ends. They'd outside stairs that curved
> up to open tops, where you sat wi' your gamp up when it rained.

Those trams provided interesting diversion for street-smart boys
who seized adventure wherever it was carelessly offered.

> You used to could go from one place to another on the trams for
> nothing. When you saw the conductor goin' away up the stair, you
> jumped on the running-board and got a hurl, hangin' on to the pole till
> he came down again. Then you got chased off that car and just waited
> for the next. Sometimes you were goin' somewhere, but mostly it was
> just for the ride. We used to hang on to the back of carts too and cadge a
> wee hurl from them.

Changes came in the design of trams over the years. They acquired
roofs and upholstery and inside stairs.

> They got to be quite comfy. I mind when we were young we used to take
> a pennyworth and go right to the terminus to see the driver swingin'
> back the overhead trolley and then changin' ends wi' the conductor.
> The driver used to close himself in wi' a gate-thing so's nob'dy could get
> on at his end. There was the bundy clocks too, where they stopped to
> get their time-cards punched.

For nearly forty years the real characteristic of the Glasgow tramcar
was that the broad band of colour across the top-half . . . green, red,
blue or white . . . indicated its route direction . . . north, south, east,
west. But in 1938, the new fleet of Coronation trams took to the
rails, uniformly green and yellow, streamlined and modern. The
'red caurs' and the white or blue 'caurs' lingered on until they were
worn out, but it was the end of an era and for the thirty-odd
remaining years of its service the Glasgow tram was 'Coronation'.

The new cars looked quite nice but the older ones had wee compartments upstairs, front and back, and you used to get closed in there wi' your friends comin' home from the school and giggle and talk boys . . . and if your added-up tram ticket number could be divid' by seven, then the boy you fancied, fancied you!

It was fortunate that at least the trams ran in their appointed channels, for any old Glasgow street photograph tells that precious little of the other traffic kept strictly to lane. Cadgers and hurlie-men took their own short-cuts and weavings, and a one-time Buyer in Macdonalds of Buchanan Street remembers them from sixty years ago.

The suppliers used to send travellers with samples for buyers to look at. They'd come by train to Queen Street station and there was a rank of barrow men lined up there waiting on the train coming in. The travellers used to hire them to hurl their samples round the various stores.

One of the travellers too recalls the hazards of that.

The hurlie-men jouked in and out the traffic and you'd a rare old time of it keeping them in sight. We'd a lot of moneysworth in them barras. So you'd to watch out.

Trace-boys in West Nile Street, working up until the Second War, also caused a fair bit of congestion although, when they did set out with a load, they led the horses in between two smooth hollowed tracks, for the easy rolling of cart-wheels.

The trace-lads used to sit in shop doorways watching their horses at the kerb and waiting for single-horse carts that were too heavy-laden to take the hill. Then they hired out their horses to haul them up the tracks. When I was wee I used to watch the Clydesdale horses feeding from their nose-bags and the pigeons all flutterin' around yon big shaggy feet to peck up the corn that fell on the ground. Oh aye, and when the horses moved off you used to could see sparks where their shoes struck against the cobbles.

D' you mind when they tried havin' wooden cobbles up the top of Buchanan Street, and then the rubber ones?

Cabs and carriages wheeled and changed course with little heed to other traffic and while their high-sitting drivers may have had a clear enough overall sight of the street, those at a lower level had their view dangerously blocked, and there are those who will tell you that it was no light undertaking to cross Argyle Street in the early century. But carriages remain in most memories as characteristic of a more gracious, or perhaps haughtier, age.

> When I left school at fourteen in 1912 I went to work at Laing and Prentice, the ladies' outfitters in Sauchiehall Street. Next door was another very elegant dress shop called Grieve's. I can remember, at that time that ladies coming to be measured and fitted, arrived in carriages and left their footmen outside to wait for them. The men often stood there kicking their heels for long enough until their ladies came sweeping out in long skirts and into the carriages, sometimes with never a word to the men.

No doubt such ladies were born into the carriage 'set' but one of Glasgow's richest and most admired sons certainly was not.

> Thomas Lipton was a close friend of my grandfather from when they were boys. Grandpa used to tell me that it was Lipton's ambition to see his parents in their own carriage and pair. My grandfather went with him the day he met the old people off the train from the country and handed them up to the new carriage drawn by two beautiful grey horses. My grandpa said Lipton stood there with tears in his eyes watching the driver moving off with them in their grand new turn-out.

Buildings of the Glasgow of eighty-odd years ago, apart from slums mercifully flattened, or fine blocks and churches less mercifully mown down by planners, are still there to be seen and enjoyed in their refurnished glory . . . the hotels, circuses, crescents, colleges, shops and well-ordered sweeps of tenements. And if the eye can blot out the more recent additions (and enjoy the best of them another time) Glasgow, as the rememberers knew it, is still there.

We've looked at tenements and churches in other chapters so let a few of the shops serve to give a glimpse of the buildings on the street scene. As well as those high-class establishments where carriages disgorged the clientele at Charing Cross, there were many other well-known names that made Sauchiehall Street, Buchanan Street and the rest, famous and fashionable in their heyday; and made one lady grue, at the query of a new-met Edinburgh acquaintance. 'D' you never come shopping to Edinburgh?' What!

with Coplands, Gardners, Wyllie & Lochhead's at the end of a tram
ride!

> Sauchiehall Street was lovely. (Did you know that sauchs are willows
> and that long ago the haughs of the Clyde were covered with willows,
> like the Broomielaw was with broom?) Anyway there were fine shops
> there when I was young. Copland & Lye, Treron, Daly's ... all good
> expensive stuff ... I'm talking of Colonel Daly's time mind. Then in
> Pettigrew and Stephen's you could sit at your tea and listen to the
> orchestra.

Those were the streets in the heart of the town, but there were
more village-like aspect in the side-streets and on the outskirts.

> In my earliest mindings of the streets round Ibrox in 1892 there was no
> cars yet, just a few gigs and pony-traps. The doctor had one and drove
> around his calls sitting up there in his lum hat and frock coat.

And he would have to steer his way among carts and barrows,
scooters, girds, bicycles, old clo'es women and the ubiquitous
Glasgow shawlies.

> Och I mind my mother could pass a nice afternoon airing the wean in
> her shawl and meeting her friends for a chat ... Now, what else was
> there in the street? ... Oh aye, the Co-op coal-cart and d' you remember
> yon narrow carts they could back right in the butchers' doorways with
> whole carcases in them, so's they didnae have to carry them from the
> street. More the shape of coffins? Then there was the chap we called
> Late-and-Early, with his milk float, that you didnae know whether you
> were gettin' last night's milk late or the next day's early. And there was
> the soor-dook cairt wi' the buttermilk.

One who went out with the soor dook in another district was
young Jimmy Wisner.

> I was just a laddie then and I got to ride with the soor dook man and
> shout for him.
> 'Soor Dook, Thruppence-a-jug, Soor Dook!'
> No, we never took it over your way ... too toffy-nosed there for soor
> dook.

He went on to greater things though, than promoting soor dook,
for he grew up to have streets named after him for dedicated service
to the community. Another lad who did a hawker's street cries for
him, was Duncan White.

I went wi' the fishmonger's cart, and shouted, 'Tripe, best tripe . . . tripe-bags!'

Telling you that, it brings back the street to me, clear as clear, wi' the boys taking steppies on the carts till the carter chased them, and me delivering fresh and skim milk twice-a-day for two shillin'-a-week. Did I get keepin' it? Did I hang? Your mother was aye waiting on it when you got home.

All day long provision carts trundled the streets and then when it began to get dusky of a winter evening . . .

The horse-vans used to have wee lights flickering front and back. I liked that for I kent our teas would be ready on the table.

The shops of these side-streets too were a little different from the Dalys' and Grieves' and the high-class Italian warehousemen of the town. Mrs. Milree remembers the Queen's Park area.

When I was wee the fishmongers used to have water running down their windows and we used to pretend to lick it as it came scooshing down, and feel the window cold on your tongue.

Few streets within a radius of six miles of Glasgow's centre were outwith earshot of a clanging tram trolley, but in the elite residential suburbs there were also grander versions of town carriages and Mrs. Muriel Lillie remembers their stately progress along Nithsdale Road with an occasional interesting mishap.

Sometimes on a frosty day when the cobbles were slippery, you used to see a horse stumble and go down. Then the men seemed to have to sit on the horse's head to calm it down and put a hood over its face to get it to its feet again.

But for that same young lady carriage travel was not only spectator-sport.

My family used to hire a landau sometimes, to take my grandmother for a drive and I used to get to go with her. So, there was me in my wee best coat driving like a lady with my granny all round Maxwell Park. The landau had a hood that came up snug when it was wet or windy, and went down if it was sunshine.

Mr. Harry Anderson, too, has a street memory of long-ago Pollokshields:

When I was a wee lad about 1907, sometimes on Sundays when we came out of Albert Drive Church on to Darnley Street, we used to see four-horse charabancs coming along, full of bad people going on Sunday trips. These charas were very noisy and the horses set up clouds of dust with their hooves ... no tarmac you see.

Although horse-traffic in haulage and delivery-service in city and suburb didn't entirely die out between the wars, the arrival of more lethal vehicles demanded new disciplines of lane, speed and signal. Street scenes became less of a circus and more of a purring progress towards destinations with only changes in the shape and colour of cars and vans to mark the years. The Second War drew a final curtain over what was left of that cheerful wayward bustle in Glasgow streets. Black-out and austerity brought sudden change instead of the slow evolution they had known before ... the neon Elephant tossing his trunk above Pickard's cinema, the other lighted cartoon adverts, the great *Capstan* banner across the Hielan'man's umbrella, all snuffed out. Almost the last of the horses (except those pulling the Black and White Whiskey drays) turned finally into city stables before retirement. Hooded lamps, tramcars with painted windows and dim-blue lights inside, dun coloured vehicles, sandbagged buildings, made a dismal scene.

No doubt there will be nostalgia someday for what emerged of people, buildings and wheels, on the Glasgow street-scene after the war, even for the bleak demolishing years before graceful fly-overs louped the waste-lands and the stone-work began to come up smiling again. But not yet.

22
Don't Call Me Wonderful

They say that death, not sex, is the taboo-subject of our time. Is it? Is it not perhaps that not so many meet it intimately in their young lives and there seems no need to get het-up about it until nearer the three-score and ten, or the time for sheltered housing. Of course there are tragedies that caw the feet from us and stop us in our tracks, but it's their very unthinkableness that stuns.

> You know fine death's comin', but it's no' so much part-parcel of your day-by-day life the way it was when we were young and there was a lot more killin' diseases. There's that much to think about just livin', you cannae forever be harpin' on about somethin' that's comin' anyway. Maybe it'll no' be that long right-enough but you just try and live right and get ready wi' God ... but no' to go out lookin' for death.

A patronising murmur to the ninety-five-year-old philosopher that she's wonderful, brings a richly merited rebuke.

> Don't call me wonderful. I hate folk to say I'm wonderful. I'm just *here*.

Bereavement was certainly part-and-parcel of everyday life at all levels until around the middle 1940s. Apart from the grim casualty lists of both wars, all those who can recall their own experiences in the previous six decades and one or two handed-down tales from their elders, paint vivid memory pictures of death and illness.

> My grandfather used to tell me that his grandmother and most of her generation were pock-marked, some of them so badly that a lot of bairns were feart to look at them. But among the older people it was just an accepted thing. He told me too about his mother dying of cholera when he was about six in the 1850s. She'd had it before but this time he minded seeing her lying fighting for breath on the kitchen floor and his older brothers trying to rub away her dreadful cramps. That was the way the cholera took you. She died though, for all the rubbing.

There was an echo of death too in this eerie tale-of-a-grandfather from the 1870s.

> My grandpa told me that he was once sent by his catering employer to look over the old Wellington Church in Waterloo Street to see if it would do for function premises. It was a Saturday afternoon and he was alone in the basement when the wind slammed the door shut. His candle snuffed out too and he fell into a kind of big long hole. When he got used to the near dark he found he'd tumbled into one of the graves in the old kirk crypt and there were all these other ones round him as well.

There was no explanation of how Grandpa was rescued from this gloomy predicament but he certainly didn't moulder there for ever, because the place did become The Waterloo Rooms for functions, when the bodies had been moved to the Glasgow Necropolis to lie peacefully beside John Knox and Wee Willie Winkie.

There are grim memories too of the fate of the flotsam souls of Glasgow's archways and dunnies, whose cravings denied them even the meanest comfort at the end of their days. Drink and drugs still take their toll but there can't be many living now who ever saw the 'drunk barra's' of the city. Mr. Tom Watson's father told him about those.

> The police would go round at night with a flat barrow, picking up drunks from pavements or gutters, then tip them out somewhere more sheltered, to sleep off their dwam. Then, come the morning, the barra's went round again to gather up the ones that hadn't survived the night and take them to the morgue.

Recollections of illness and death after that are within living memory. In 1901 there was a serious outbreak of smallpox and, on 5th April of that year, eleven new cases were admitted to Belvidere Hospital to join the two hundred-and-fifty already taken in during the epidemic. That was more than eighty years ago, but the legacy lingers in more than that statistic of long ago.

> There was this big-big outbreak of the smallpock in the year the old Queen died. Two weans in my class took it and everyone got inoculated. My friend's wee sister, Lucy, was just a baby at the time but she got done and she come deaf and a wee bit coofy after that and she's been like that all her days since.

Fevers were a scourge of past days too. Mrs. Mary Milree still shudders at the memory of the Fever Van.

> Scarlet fever and Typhoid and the Measles were very-very common and you got the colly-wobbles when you saw the Van coming down your street to take away whoever had the fever to Belvidere Hospital. It was all hush-hush and mysterious because the Van windows were smokey blue and you couldn't see through. If Scarlet or Typhoid or even the Measles was in your house you were kept off the school for so-many weeks till the infection was gone. They burned your school books as well. Everyone dreaded those fevers and the Diphtheria too of course.

Very occasionally a milder case was nursed at home and sometimes one disease was complicated by another.

> When we lived in a tenement it was a bottom flat wi' no bathroom and just the outside toilet. But we didnae share it wi' anyone. Just as well, for when one of my girls had the 'Dip' there was Scarlet going as well and the doctor said we were lucky that no one else used the toilet or my lassie would've got the fever along wi' the diphtheria and there was no sayin' ...

and after sixty years Mrs. Margaret Henderson still shakes her head over that unfinished sentence.

If the victim was left at home there were strict rules of sanitation.

> Your Ma had to put up a blanket over the room door, wrung-out of disafectan', and then after that the fumigatin' man came and burned sulphur or some-such on a shovel to make the place safe again. Mostly folk got over whatever it was and came back to school, but they were often gey peely-wally an' wi' their hair cut off. But sometimes they died and then you stood behind your curtain and watched their funeral, feart that it could easy be you, next time.

There were other hazards too before a youngster could properly be claimed to have survived childhood and be ready to face the risk of teenage tuberculosis.

> My mother lost two babies at different times from the whooping-cough, both of them called William. When a third boy arrived she couldn't bring herself to have another William. So he was John.

Another wheezy crickle that sounded alarm-bells was the croup.

> In our family there was me and my half-sisters Betty and Frances. I mind when Betty had the croup. They boiled up kettles of water for the steam

to break the croup and try to get her breathin' again, for she was just gaspin'. I can see her yet. She was a right bonnie wean wi' black curls and rosy cheeks. But she died of that croup.

The funeral of a child taken away in its small white kist was, and is, heart-rending, but any funeral in olden days was more sombre and spectacular than today's stream of limousines purring swiftly and silently among the rest of the traffic to the crematorium.

I mind of the big Clydesdales wi' the black plumes and gear, that used to rumble the funeral carriages over the cobbles to the graveyard, when I was young.

A more personal tragedy and the funeral after it has lived a long time in Mrs. Rose Lindsay's memory of the early 1920s.

My mother had nice long hair that was piled up and I used to like to stand on a wee stool and take the hair-pins out, so's it fell all round her shoulders. Well, this night, I can just see mysel' doin' that. It was Hogmanay. My mother said she smelled smoke and right-enough the house down the stair was on fire. My father couldnae get the door open for to get down so he opened the window, threw down a rope and told us to get out. My sister went first, then me, the both of *us* dropped safe-enough into a blanket. But at my mother's turn, a corner of the blanket was let go and she fell and hit her head. She was expectin' too and she had the baby right-enough but she was never hersel' after, and a wee while later, when she was ill in her bed, I mind her sayin' ... 'It's awfu' cold, come in beside me Rose, girl.' So I went in under the clo'es and she just died there beside me. I was about twelve.

And the picture of the funeral three days later, is still etched in the memory after sixty years.

I mind when she was to be buried, the big black horses standin' outside, frothin' at the mouth, and me just standin' there at the close watchin' them takin' my wee mother away in a black coffin. It was horrible.

Girlhood snapped shut for Rose Lindsay that day. She didn't go to the graveside. That part of the proceedings belonged to the menfolk at any funeral. Even small boys were not exempt. Most of them walked in their first procession at the burying of a grand-parent.

When my grandpa died I was comin' up twelve, and me and my wee brothers, (they would be maybe ten and seven) we a' wore wee dark suits and bowler hats to walk to the graveyard. It was all walkin' funerals then.

I was at my grandpa's funeral a long time before the First War. It was a horse-drawn hearse and we followed it on from Camden Street to Caledonia Road. There was nothin' fancy about it, nothin' dressed-up. We'd just black ties like, and wee bowlers. It was only the men and boys followed the coffin, the women just stayed at home and got ready the steak-pie. Mind I don't think we'd steak pie that day . . . too dear . . . just be a cup of tea and maybe bridies.

There's not a lot of light relief in clash about death and funerals, but if a child wasn't taken up personally with a death and lived near a funeral undertaker there was endless interest and drama to be had from stranger funerals.

We stayed near the undertaker's in Pollokshaws. He was a *very* popular undertaker . . . easy the best for funerals around that part of Glasgow . . .

and the innocent query to that rememberer, 'Was it Wyllie and Lochhead's?' she laughs at your folly.

Och dearie me, no! Wyllie and Lochhead's was for when you died in Newlands . . . no' Pollokshaws!

Long after the parlour blinds were up again, the clock re-started from the time of death and the funeral flowers withered, there were other continuing death rituals in the early days of the 1900s.

I don't know about other places, but round us when a woman died in childbed leavin' her baby, the wee soul had bits of black ribbon in its bonnet and sometimes in its pram pillow!

and even after death at the other end of life . . .

When I was six in 1905 my granny died and I got two black outfits at the dressmakers, one for the school and one for Sundays.

These conventions were still flourishing ten and more years later. Mrs. Hilda Gibson remembers her father's death in 1915.

I was eight and I was dressed in black from hair-bow to boots.

Her sister was seven years older and ready to leave school.

I was all in black. It was quite the usual thing to have two or three in the class in mournings for some kin or other. I mind Mr. Watson, my teacher at Queen's Park school, stopping me in the playground and asking quite kindly ... I mind his very words, 'Dear me, Dorothy, and who have you been losing?'

The return to ordinary clothes was in stages.

Near the end of mourning-time for Papa I went to a party in a white broderie-anglaise dress wi' black ribbons threaded through it and black trims.

Smallpox, Measles, Typhoid, T.B., and by the late teens of the century there was a new toll. There had always been accidents with wheel and horse, but now there were fast-moving cars, and in the early days weans were not so schooled in traffic-codes as they are now, bunnets and school-bags carried no rhymes or fluorescent bands and lollipop persons were unknown.

I mind my cousin's wean dyin'. He was just a toddler and-here he dropped his dummy-teat on the edge of the street. He leaned over to get it and a motor car came by and struck him. Killed him.

There was a wake for that wee chap.

Wakes could be roistering affairs, enjoyed in the earnest notion that it was doing old Tom or Joe an honour and giving him the very kind of send-off he would have favoured and savoured himself ... just the way he would have wanted it ... a pious certainty many have, of the wishes of dead friends ...

Many's the wake I've been to, oh aye. A wake's just sittin' up a' night, in the same room's the coffin. Some call it a lich-wake and it's just keepin' the dead company between the dyin' and the buryin'. You say the Rosary and sometimes you play cards and drink tea ... aye and stronger than tea, forbye. It's all to keep you from goin' to sleep. A right wake can sometimes get a wee bit out-hand ... but that wee thing's wake wasnae like that, poor bairn.

I mind the wee white coffin open in the middle of the room and the tiny waxy boy lyin' in it wi' his baby hands claspin' on a bunch of snowdrops. There were candles all round and everyone sayin' the Rosary at the right times through the night. I've aye had that sad wee white picture in my mind.

There's scarcely a one over seventy-years old, talking of young days, who doesn't speak of the 'flu epidemic that ravaged Europe just after the Armistice of 1918 and of friends who died in it. Men and women who had survived the most fearful war in history, even some who were still in military hospitals recovering from wounds, fell to the killer 'flu.

> I was nursing in a military hospital when the big 'flu came. Patients and nurses died like flies and the staff nurses' home had to be turned into a ward. A lot of the girls died as well as the men, and some of them that did survive were left wi' things like sleepy-sickness and fits. It was a wicked 'flu that.

But healthier days were coming, and year by year the fevers and the rickets, the smits of single-end and shared cludgy, and the risks of childbirth, dwindled as medical skills and health care increased.

> I taught in Glasgow schools for forty years and the change in the health of children was astonishing over the years. The evacuation alerted tolk to a lot of hardship and lack of care among the weans. Afterwards teachers watched for everything, and sent every rash, sniffle and itch to the school-clinic. Eyes, teeth, feet and heads were examined and all sorts of things were nipped in the bud.

That was Miss Isobel Cameron's experience between the twenties and the seventies, and a fellow-teacher bears her out.

> It was a lot more work for the schools, mind you, but I never yet met a teacher that objected to Teenie having her jags or what d'you McCallum getting his verrucas seen to.

A teacher of more recent years adds her observations.

> In my mother's day there were families in her school raddled with T.B. so that maybe two or three in the same house died or were years in hospital. I started teaching in 1947 and I never once in thirty years had a child in a class that died of T.B. or any of the fevers . . . a few cancers, aye, and accidents, but the other things, no. And not many children had to face the death of parents.

So maybe it's not surprising that people, meeting less frequently with untimely death, don't talk so often about it, or brood so much on the prospect, as bairns who had the chitters every time they saw the Fever Van or heard that a classmate had the 'Dip'.

23
Medals Dinnae Compensate

In many a douce wee sitting-room in Glasgow, the kind called 'little boxes', by foolish folk who judge that rows of like-houses contain rows of like-minds and life experience, there are mementoes and echoes of wartime adventure, tragedy, humour and endurance which along with life's other pummellings and small triumphs, make ordinary people into uniquely moulded, one-off individuals.

We've already captured a few of the memories of the First War which erupted into such a stark and bitter shock to those who had waved their flags at the beginning. The Second War came to more reluctant but better-prepared people who had watched its approach with dread, not bunting.

> Hitler was a kind of brooding monster, a dark shadow out there when I was wee. I was feart for him for all the things my faither said. He used to say he wouldnae trust that man an inch and he didnae like him comin' to be the leader in Germany.

> When we began to see the war gettin' closer all I could think on was my own time in the trenches and the green kind of mist that was the poison gas of 1915 comin' across No Man's Land. And now I had three grown sons that were age for soldiers.

There were plenty of signs of the coming war, fed by tales from European holiday-makers in the 1930s, and by word of the kind of brief adventure had by John Kent, a young Glasgow minister in the summer of 1939. His wife tells of the incident.

> John always travelled on the continent during his month's holiday and that particular year he had been asked by the Armenian mission in this country to collect money belonging to the mission, that was lying in a German bank. It was August and his contact was a man called Minker.

They met. Minker was friendly and warned him not even to try to get the money because the authorities would never let it go, but to get himself out the country as fast as possible. John was travelling by car and this Minker offered to come and guide him towards the border. He hid in the back of the car and while they were driving down the road they passed swarms of German troops doing some exercise or other. At a bend when the road was clear Minker shouted to John to drive fast to the border and he jumped out of the car himself and scrambled down a bank into the cover of trees. John was only across the border two or three days, when the Germans marched down that same road into Poland.

On September 3rd, war came.

I mind of that day like it was last week. We were at the kirk and the beadle came in and handed up a note to the pulpit, and the minister read out what Chamberlain had said on the wireless. We'd just a short service that day and I sat there terrified, and sure that before we got home the bombs would be droppin', like in the newsreels about Spain and Abyssinia. They were nightmares to me these news pictures when I was wee.

To another child, of twelve, it was the end of a chapter.

That day was like a kind of terminus to my childhood because we'd three much younger cousins came evacuated to us from nearer the middle of the town. The maid had opted to be 'bombed' with her own family so now there were shoes to clean, dishes to wash and the wee cousins to look after. I was likely-enough growing out of it but I don't mind of even really 'playing', again.

If war is ever tidy this 1939 war was tidier than the 1914 one. Call-up was organised from the start, air-raid precautions ready, and evacuation planned. Glasgow prickled with Lord High Everythings in arm-bands, and conscripted servicemen quietly catching trains for initial training centres. No rush-muster or recruiting hullabaloo this time. Call-up lasted throughout the war and long after, but it always took the same form.

I remember the day Jim was called-up. The postman rang the bell. 'There's your man's call-up papers. I've delivered that many I know them whenever I see them.'

Jim Lillie went to the army. Joe Kyle went to the navy.

I was called up at thirty-eight years old. I was a banker, married with a young baby and at first I went on to the lower deck of a destroyer and slept in a hammock. It was a big change, I can tell you, from the bank and the comfortable home in the suburbs.

The girls were in the call-up too this time. Janey Brown was one of them.

I was called to the air-force ... to the W.A.A.F. You'd your bad times and your good but afterwards you forgot the weary miserable times and just minded the fun. I got stationed at Norfolk and was the whole war as a cook.

The home-front was mobilised quite quickly too. In Glasgow the first big concern was to get young children away from the city centre to areas reckoned safe. The evacuation was planned in detail beforehand, but, even so, there was inevitable stramash when the real thing came. Isobel Cameron was a teacher directed away with a batch of fearful city weans.

Our instructions were that if the war came we'd to gather at the school right away. It was a terrible feeling packing your bags for off, without knowing where you were going or when you'd be back. We felt like the trails of refugees you saw on the Pathescope News.

We'd no idea where we were bound until after the train left Parkhead Cross, and then we were told 'Perth'. What a journey! Hundreds of mothers, weans and bawling infants packed like herring, and no toilet on the train! Things were that dire by the time we got to Auchterarder we'd to get the train stopped. But just think on yon wee platform at Auchterarder with its *one* toilet and dozens of weans dancing desperate on that train. What could you do?

'Everybody out! Boys ... all go and perform down that side of the train. Girls ... come on now ... down the other side!'

Then back to the train for the last lap.

At Perth we were herded into the ice-rink all labelled. It was like a slave-market, us all lined up in rows and a wee man with a bellowing voice and two lists in his hand, one of hosts and one of Glasgow children. Oh what an uproar of greetin' and girnin' from frightened tired weans, away from home ... maybe forever for all they knew!

One of the evacuating mothers who went in the opposite direction was Helen Stewart.

I was to be evacuated with my girls and we'd to meet at the school on the Sunday morning, the minute the news came over the wireless if it was war. So there was me, leavin' my man behind, and standin' wi' my three wee lassies in their covert coats wi' labels tied to their button-holes and makin' sure my money was safe.

'*You* just sew a wee pooch into your stays, Nellie,' my mother had insisted. She thought nothing could go amiss if I'd that wee pocket in my stays. It was midnight when we got the length of Dumfries and I was wabbit and near weepin'. The billeting man put us in a nice-enough house, but along with other Glasgow folk that I thought were that rough and coarse.

It was my fault, I was too upset to give them a right chance, for they would be good-hearted people just as upset as I was. I made up my mind to come home, although the officers tried to persuade me to stay. But I was thrawn and next day I trailed my wee lassies all back to Glasgow, and we just plowtered on through the war at home after that.

Within a few weeks, people settled into the first phase of wartime routine with very few folk, over the age of twelve, playing no part at all in the war effort.

I was an Air Raid warden round our way. You went about checking stirrup-pumps and buckets of sand and water. That was alright, but you didnae half get cold shoulder when you went to a door to tell them there was a chink of light showing through their curtains in the black-out. I often think on Dave Willis and his 'air-raid-warden' song:

'In my wee gas-mask I'm workin' out a plan.
Tho' all the kids imagine that I'm just a bogey man
The girls all smile, and bring their friends to see
The nicest-lookin' warden in the A.R.P.
Whenever there's a raid on, listen to my cry
'An airy-plane, an airy-plane away-way up-a-kye.
Then I run helter-skelter, but don't run-after-me
You'll no' get in my shelter for it's *far too wee*'.

Mrs. Jean Tait remembers her war work as being a model of preparation for disaster.

I was attached to the first-aid post. Doctor Anderson gave us a good grounding in emergency treatment and we all had shifts, so the post was manned day and night.

Others maintained a constant after-dark vigil . . . with companions.

My father was a squaddie fire-watcher, and funny-enough he worked with three Browns in his roster. There was Aluminium Brown who was in that line of business, Salmon Brown that was a rare angler, and, Poison Brown the pharmacist. They watched out for even wee fires that could help the German bombers. D'you mind the slogan 'Fires help Hitler'? That was on a lot of posters. So was 'Careless Talk Costs Lives', that was for fear of spies.

For many years it had been traditional for country folk and travelling people to harvest the acres of soft fruit in Perthshire, but many of them were called up or placed in essential work, and so it fell to school children to do the berry-picking.

We went every summer for about four years to the berry-picking at Blairgowrie. We got paid a penny-a-pound for rasps, and some got quite quick at it, but not like some of the tinks that were the real pickers. They could fill two or three luggies for every one of ours. They were interesting people and they used to sing and play fiddle music in the bothy-place at night.

Glasgow won a good name among British cities for its service to troops passing through or stationed nearby.

I worked in two different canteens. We did four hour stints and maybe three shifts a week. There was the Y.M.C.A. in Buchanan Street and the Churches' Canteen. It was heavy work when maybe a troop train came in with droves of hungry men and women. There were other canteens all over the city too.

Mr. William Stevenson, as stalwart a citizen in this war as he had been soldier in the First, used his building expertise in his voluntary service.

I was leader of a wee emergency team set up to go digging or shifting rubble if there was bombing and for a long while it looked as if we wouldnae ever be needed, but we were, later.

Elderly ladies had work-groups to make oiled-wool sea-boot stockings, hospital slippers, or balaclavas for search-light units ... even for Home Guards.

I was in the Home Guard ... Was it like Dad's Army? ... no, no, it was better'n Dad's Army. It's true enough we drilled wi' broom handles at first, but we really trained quite well and did our watching up at Corkerhill. We'd some right pompous wee officers right-enough, that didnae know much about drill, and I mind going up early one night and here's two of them sittin' hearkenin' each other out the wee drill book.

And there was nursing.

I did voluntary nursing at the Royal Infirmary when they were short, and had a lot of valuable experience for the time when the bombing came.

The air-raid precaution work, the canteens, the first aid, the Home Guard and even the little knitting and sewing work-parties, were all voluntary activities, but other people were directed into work vacancies left by the young called up to the services.

I was made to be a clippie in the war. If you werenae in the forces you got sent to what they called essential work, munitions or that. Wi' me it was the buses. It was quite cold in the winter and it was difficult at night in the black-out because you'd only a kind of dim blue light inside the bus for takin' fares and countin' your change.

Some found new purpose in their own daily work and even a perfectly legitimate by-product-boost to business.

By 1939 I ran a wee cobbler's business alongside my joinery and when the Rouken Glen was turned to a big-big army camp with trucks and lorries and thousands of troops I got the job of doing their shoe and boot repairs.

School teaching too widened in variety and challenge in some respects, and narrowed itself down to essentials in others.

I was teaching in Bridgeton and the Fire Service took over the bottom floor of the school. Classes were on shifts and you'd fifty to teach in the mornings and fifty in the afternoons. There was just time for the three Rs and no frills. After one bombing when the upstairs was damaged I taught for long enough downstairs with the weans sitting on mattresses among stirrup-pumps. When the radiators got hot the smell of heated rubber was suffocating. I used to think to myself. 'Oh my, imagine that perished rubber going out to a fire sometime.'

Alongside all these public preparations and precautions against bombing and invasion these were the pinpricks and vexations of daily wartime life ... remembering to carry gas-masks, coping with ration books, running with potato-peelings and left-overs to the neighbourhood swill bin, sticking unsightly anti-splinter netting on window panes for fear of air-raids. But that was all small thole while young men and women were facing the waste of real war.

My most vivid memory of the navy wasn't a battle, it was a terrible storm when we were off the Irish coast at one stage. The sea was like grey walls heaving up and crashing down over you again and again. That day I was really afraid. Later we went minesweeping off Grimsby and we convoyed and escorted the big Mulberry harbours down the east coast.

That was Joe Kyle's memory, and here is Elizabeth Dewar's of her father ...

My father was involved in the famous 'Laconia' incident, when the survivors in the lifeboats were taken in tow by the German U-boat which had sunk the ship. But it had to cut them adrift and crash dive when it was bombed itself by an American aircraft from the Azores. The survivors were left hundreds of miles from the West African coast, and a lot of them like my father died from exposure.

And there were those who operated from nearer home but just as dangerously.

Three of us, me and the two Jimmys, went to the R.A.F. We were just eighteen, all air-crew. In June 1940 I got taken prisoner and I was five dreich years a prisoner. Then I came home, but the two Jimmys didnae.

Except for the sound and fury of ack-ack guns, signifying not very much, Glasgow itself was far behind the battle-lines, until 1941 brought the noise and smell and sight of actual war to Clydeside with the blitz. People opened their homes to bombed-out and bereaved victims.

The day after the Greenock blitz we'd a young boy sent to us as an evacuee. He was in a real state of shock. He'd run up the hill behind Greenock when the bombing started, carrying his baby sister and lain over her all night to protect her with his body.

And Mr. William Stevenson's little unit of tradesmen-rescuers, in business at last, was sent to Clydebank during the devastating air-raids there. They found the main part of the town utterly destroyed and it was reckoned later that in three nights of bombing only twelve houses in the whole of Clydebank were undamaged. They dug out the dead and injured, with bombs still exploding around them.

I mind one house that was just a heap of rubble except for a bit of stairway you could just see, away-way deep in. They thought there was someone trapped there, so says-I, 'Cut out a coupla risers and treads and make a way in there.' Under all the sandstone and plaster and roofin' we found an old woman and a wee lad both sittin' on the stair, dead, the old body clutchin' on to a handbag wi' four hundred pound in it.

Mrs. Janet Purvis recalls her work during the same week at Clydebank.

Thousands were bombed out their houses and ever so many people lying injured. But the queer funny wee thing that I remember so vividly was the sight of all the folks' budgies bombed out their cages and fluttering about in a frenzy ... green and blue and yellow. It was bizarre really in all that devastation, and I can see those budgies yet. But the real job was to see to the injured and set up canteens to feed people in whatever bits of building were still standing until other arrangements were made for them.

Stray sticks of bombs landed too in areas in and around Glasgow that were patently not targets.

A lot of funny things happened the night our road got bombed. My uncle ran with his stirrup pump and bucket to put out a fire, but-here he forgot to take water in his pail. He took a lot of snash afterwards from his friends for that.

And then next-door's greenhouse light flashed on by itself (maybe with the thudding of the bombs) and everyone was screaming for somebody to smash the lamp before the Germans saw our street and bombed us to pulp.

In the morning we'd a thirty-foot crater in our garden and six others in a line down into the next road. Even a clothes pole, with a big concrete blob on the bottom, had sailed over a roof from a back garden and landed on the road.

As they cleared away the debris and called in the emergency builders for makeshift repairs there was a lot of dark muttering over that maverick stick of bombs.

We blamed it all on our local spy. He was a Mr. Brown that had worked in Germany before the war and had a German mistress living with him in our road. Everybody remembers how he'd thought Hitler was a great chap early on, and when he came back from wherever he'd been that night nob'dy spoke much to him for years, even though you knew fine that it couldnae be true that he'd had our wee suburb singled-out for attacking. But-mind he shaved his head just like you saw Germans at the time.

Sense of humour creams up again though, when shock is past, and Mrs. Margaret Kent recalls an incident after a raid which sent three hundred people to be bedded down in their church hall emergency centre.

One man told me he was a baker and could I waken him at 3 o'clock in the morning to go and see the state of his bakery whether he could turn out his usual batches. I went to the hall with these rows and rows of sleeping people to waken him at three, and then realised I didn't know which of the three hundred he was.

There was selfless and faithful work done in Glasgow during the six years of the war but the highlight and glory was reserved for one local farmer and his wife, the Eaglesham Dad's Army and the Giffnock Police.

I was about fourteen and I was walking home in the black-out one night and you could hear a plane quite clear. Then the engine cut out. It was awful funny ... suddenly just nothing and no airfield near. Next day all the rumours were fleein' about that there'd been a crash on the moor, a farmer'd taken in a German spy and got the Home Guard, and that now he was in our Scout Hall or maybe the cell at the police-station. Then the next far-fetched tale was that Rudolf Hess had landed somewhere in Scotland and it didnae take long for folk our way to put two and two together and guess that the rumours were about the same thing.

All the boys cycled out to the farm to see this crashed 'plane. My brother took home two wee bits of it for souvenirs; before he even knew it was Hess's right-enough.

William Stevenson gives his account of that same strange incident.

Tom Hyslop, the Police Inspector, was a friend of mine and came to my house early hours one morning. 'There's a plane come down, up-by, Willie. I want you to come wi' me and see it.'

And away we goes to where the crash-land was, at a farm field. They still didnae know then for sure who the pilot was. It was that hard to believe his claim that he was Hess. Anyway the Home Guards had taken him to the Giffnock jail. We went into the 'plane and Tom handed me a metal label that had got torn off in the crash. I have it here yet, that wee minding off of Hess's plane.

It's over forty years now since Hess lost his aircraft and Willie Stevenson went out with his inspector friend to find it. Both surely remember that night in their different ways. But the one has filled half-a-lifetime since then, with other memories, and lives his latter years in the freedom and companionship of home, while the other, of much the same age, has paced out forty empty years in loneliness and captivity.

After the Clydeside blitz local people could feel more keenly for the battered folk of the south, but its own worst days were over. War work went on, belts were tightened yet again, and then at last it was finished.

I mind the Armistice in 1918 and the kind of two-stage one in 1945, and they were quite different. It was quieter in 1945. Nobody went mad the way they did before.

Perhaps that was because the euphoria of 1918 had so quickly given way to the sober reality of recession gloom and the incredible horror of seeing the fore-shadow of that Second War.

The only bit of celebration was an odd Victory ball or dance, and the flags put out at windows or gate-posts when a boy or girl came home for good.

Like other big exhausted cities and ageing villages, Glasgow took a long time to pick up its steady, prosperous heart-beat again.

We werenae wed until 1952, seven years after the war and we'd still Ration Books. I mind specially because you'd to hand them in, in your pre-wedding names, at your honeymoon boarding-house and so everyone knew you were honeymooning ... or maybe wondered *if*.

And then, you see, our tenement house was furnished with the standard Utility furniture and sheets an' that. I've got some still. Most cups and saucers were plain white wally and if you got a wee bit decoration on your weddin' china, you treated it like best Crown Derby.

Anyone who lived through the darg and destruction of war, either at the beginning or the middle of the century, can surely only yearn to see it end without another one.

Medals dinnae compe'sate you, for seventy year of your lungs still pechin' from the gas, or shufflin' along wi' gammy legs.

Nor for seeing the poppies blow among endless rows of crosses where the friends of your green years lie buried.

24
All Flags and Bunting

Ask your average Glasgow eighty-eight year old who calls himself the man in the street what he thinks of the royal family and he'll be quick enough to tell you 'no' much', and that an hour spent in a drizzle or jooking behind somebody else's head to catch a glimpse of a royal is an hour wasted. But press him and he can tell you the exact hour and very spot he was standing on, the day he saw the King or the Queen, any one of six monarchs, or their kin.

When an old man of ninety-five tells you the tales of his grandfather, who was even older when he died, and whom he knew as a boy and young man, you get a distinct sniff of the lang-syne middle ages! There must be many octogenarians who just remember Queen Victoria, but Alick Murdock's grandfather gave him a second-hand glimpse of an even earlier day than hers.

My grandfather was coachman to the Marquis of Bute, sometime about the 1830s. That was at Rothesay and most of the time he'd to drive the family about the island yonder. But sometimes they took the carriage by ferry across the Firth of Clyde and up the old road to Glasgow. Then, come the 'season', they used to go up to London, changin' the horses right-enough, at post-houses or coachin' inns on the way. Many's the tale I had off my grandfather when I was young and I mind him comin' away wi' a story about one time when they were in London for the Season.

He took Miss Stuart (that was the Marquis's sister) to this society revel at a house someway out at Richmond. He halted the carriage in the driveway and handed Miss Stuart down the step and saw she was escorted into the big house.

'Then,' says Grandpa, 'I was standin' wi' the carriage chattin' among all the other coachmen in their liveries, when a braw carriage arrives and a couple gets out.' The gent peers at the Bute coat-of-arms on the side of

Grandfather's machine and looks up. 'Afternoon Sir,' says Grandpa. 'Afternoon,' says the gent. 'You in charge of this carriage?'

and the ninety-five year old grandson draws himself up in his chair and speaks, all haughty and clipped, as he sees and hears the gentryman addressing the Clyde-born coachman a hundred-and-fifty years ago.

'Aye Sir.'
'Lord Bute's I see. I take it then that Bute has already gone inside?'
'No Sir, His Lordship's sister Miss Stuart ...'
Then, my grandfather said, they spoke a wee while about the road down from Glasgow, and the gent asks if the Butes are goin' on well ... so on an' so forth. Then he turns to his wife.
'Well, there you are my dear, you can chat with Miss Stuart inside ... thank you, coachman.'

And again Mr. Alick Murdoch draws himself up, every inch the lordship.

The couple goes up the steps and Grandpa turns back to his friends. 'What did he say to you?' they want to know.
'Just asked gin it was the Bute coach and after the health of the family,' says Grandfather.
'That was the King you were talking to, you know!'
    I knew my grandfather well. I'm ninety-five and he lived to ninety-six and he told me to mind and tell my grandweans that he'd spoken wi' King William the Fourth.

Alexander Brown wasn't a gentleman's coachman all his life. Not at all. From the island of Bute he took a shrewd look at what was happening on the Clyde and saw the trickle of wealthy Glasgow merchants, who had begun to tak' tent of the bonnie clachans on the Firth, grow to a steady stream, followed by boatloads of lesser citizens taking up the new fashion of installing their families in rented accommodation for holidays. Alexander counted his bawbees, took a lease on Kirn pier and bought a pair of cottages at the pierhead. Mansions and villas had to be heated and they had to be let from time to time. He set up as coal-merchant and factor and soon he himself was quite the up-and-coming businessman in Kirn. But that was not all ...

Grandpa wasnae done yet. He began to charter yachts for the merchant 'lairds' and their visitors and he started a wee yacht club. Nothin' very grand. But then he thought that considerin' he'd once met the Queen's uncle at Richmond he and his friands had some sort of nodding acquaintance wi' her son the Prince of Wales, and so they might could ask him to come and sail on the Clyde . . . give it his Royal patronage . . . They werenae blate, mind, were they? Anyway, maybe the Prince was a wee bit amused at the quaint invitation. Well, he came and he enjoyed the Firth . . . it's a bonnie place, mind you. So you see yachting on the Clyde became quite the thing for the Prince's friends and hangers-on. And what had been my grandpa's wee club, began to run the famous Royal Yacht Races, and we got to see the Prince of Wales quite often on the Clyde.

Another haunt of Royals has always been the north-east of Scotland and the same Prince, from time to time, found himself there to refresh himself for the rigours of his London social life or his yachting on the Clyde.

Glasgow has been home to Mr. Harry Anderson for many years but his roots are in Golspie and so too are some of his inherited memories.

Queen Victoria was often a guest at Dunrobin Castle with the Duchess of Sutherland and the Prince of Wales used to come sometimes too. My grandfather was a tailor in Golspie so he used to get orders to make clothes for the Prince, country-gentleman sort of clothes for wearing about the estates there.

All that was still in the mid-years of the century before Edward came into his inheritance and long before his mother's Diamond Jubilee in 1897 ... an occasion never forgotten by the lady who was five-year-old Maggie Anderson in Uddingston that year.

> I mind of Queen Victoria. I saw her once. She came in her carriage when I was just young. It was at her Jubilee time and we were all in the park wi' our wee flags to wave. She was a dumpy wee body, very proud I thought she was, for she just bowed a wee bit from her head. A' in black she was, and wearing a bonnet tied wi' ribbons in a black bow under her chin. She was very very old ...

But nearly twenty years younger than the little flag-waving Maggie of those days, is now.

Others had more official roles on that Jubilee visit. An old lady produces a spiked helmet. Her father, she explains, was in the Queen's cavalry escort through the city and she has kept his helmet for eighty-seven of her ninety-six years.

> He'd a grey horse, I think, and I was taken into the town to watch them passing. I was so busy looking at my father that I near didnae see Her. I mind thinkin' she wasnae much to look at anyway, compared wi' him and his glitterin' helmet. She'd no crown or jewels or anythin'. She was just wee and pudgy and dressed in black. At home they were cross wi' me and said she was a Great Lady, a Queen and an Empress and suchlike. Maybe she was, but I still thought she was wee and pudgy.

Many remember that 1897 visit to Glasgow, but fewer recall in detail the old Queen's death four years later, perhaps because it happened far away in Osborne House and word of it came to children only in wae echoes of the grown-ups' hushed voices. That's how Miss Marie Condie remembers it.

> My memory of Queen Victoria's death is just shadowy. I was a wee lassie at Merry Street school and the teachers were talkin' yon way in low voices about someone that had died. Then it was all explained to me at home that it was the Queen that had died, that's picture was up on the parlour wall ... When I think back I'm sure they were all wonderin' how it was to be, with Victoria no' there, and just the Prince of Wales.

On the other hand there was much more to remember about Edward's coronation, and there are souvenirs a-plenty to show for it.

I have this perfect clear memory of a picnic we had at the time of Edward and Alexandra's coronation. I've got this picture in my mind of a big big brown Clydesdale horse wi' its bushy feet, standin' hitched up to just an ordinary cart that had seats across it wi' a safety-board thing round the sides ... and it full of us weans. I had a tin mug on a blue ribbon round my neck, and what I mind, clear as clear, was us all squealin' and laughin' when we moved away. That's all I can think-on about that coronation, except we got medals as well.

And Kate Thomas's memory of the same event.

I mind Edward the Seventh's crownin' was delayed because he'd the appendicitis, but when it did come off, it was all flags and bunting and we got mugs wi' the King and Queen on them. There's mine's there in the display cabinet.

There were coronation visits too, up and down the country, for Edward and Alexandra to show themselves off to their people as King and Queen at long last, after what had seemed an interminable apprenticeship. Some visits they made together, some separately. Mrs. Jean Tait remembers one of them.

My father was a kind of big shot in the gardening world and he was asked to organise the floral decorations for Queen Alexandra's visit and I distinctly remember that he did them mainly in pink.

There was a red carpet too and my mother got it afterwards and made it into a real nice cover for the dining room table. But even better I remembered what happened to me. Because of my father, we got a seat at an open window above the street and I was all dressed up in my good dress and best beads to watch the Queen and the procession going by. Well, a band was playing, and there was me, beating time to the music and twirling my string of beads round my finger. Then just as the Queen's carriage passed under the window, the string broke. The beads bounced off the window sill and mercy me! ... there was the Queen's hat right below. I heard my mother calling it a 'toque' but I just remember that it seemed to be made up entirely of violets. No brim, of course. The Royal ladies never wore brims. Anyway if the beads were in among the violets *that* would be a wee surprise for Queen Alexandra when she took her hat off.

To mark Edward's death, eight short years later, most Glasgow children, like their parents, attended memorial services. Tokens of mourning too were worn by the general public for months afterwards, even by children like young Dorothy Laurie.

Everyone wore some wee bit of mourning, black armbands or small black diamonds sewn on to your coat sleeves. I was ten years old and I mind of having a white coat at the time and a nice white boater-hat to go with it, but I had to wear a black band round the hat when the King died and I wasn't very pleased.

The black bands and mourning diamonds were scarcely unpicked from the 1910 braws, when it was time for the coronation of the quiet George the Fifth and his Queen. The wally mugs, the medallions, the streamers and the cart-horse ribbons were ready in Glasgow and its surrounding cluster of boroughs. Picnics and parties were organised, concerts and pageants rehearsed in a hundred church halls and classrooms.

When the new King came to Glasgow I went to Scotland Street to see him going past. I was that small I could hardly see him. I just got a glimpse of a man with a brown beard, but I waved my wee Union Jack like mad.

Young May Reid too had good reason to remember that coronation for the regal part she played in the celebrations.

We'd a concert in the school with a tableau at the end ... and-here *I* was Britannia! Now my mother wasn't really a very dressy person but oh my, she was proud of me over the pageant! 'You're going to be just right, May. None of your old sheets and silver paper.'

She took me to Josephine Smith's the theatrical costumière. *She'd* likely enough laid in a few dozen Britannia sets that spring. Anyway I got the whole jing-bang that was on the new penny, helmet, trident, shield and all. I always had lovely long hair away-way past my waist and it was usually in pig-tails. But for the concert it was all combed out and rippling over my shoulders. I had to sit high and prominent, and all the children representing other countries had to come in from the sides and bow to *me*. I was up on a step-ladder draped with cloth ... purple I think ... and there was me up top.

I was the centre-piece and I thought I was great. Mind nowadays I'd like to believe all yon bowing was just because it was *our* coronation, and if it had been, say, the King of Spain, *we* would've been bowing to *him*. But I don't think so ... I mean to say, we did have all the pink bits on the map in 1911, sure we had?

George V was a sober monarch, after his galravaitching father, and not much noted for his bonhomie, but one Glasgow man did

remember at least a chuckle from the king and passed on word of
the incident to his family.

> It was my grandfather came home this day and told us about being with
> George V when he was getting the Freedom of the city ... a right big
> Glasgow celebration that was. Anyway it was my Grandpa's job that
> day to be in attendance with the king in an ante-room. He wrote all this
> down mind as well, so I can tell you pretty exact what happened.
> Here's what Grandpa says.
> 'I was alone with the king for quite a while and we had a wee bit
> conversation. He was quite easy and chatty and I told him that when my
> uncle was a worker at Loch Katrine water-works he'd got the job of
> giving Queen Victoria a cup of tea the day of the opening in 1852. My
> uncle always made his brew-up special by putting in a wee tate baking
> soda (maybe he didnae trust the new water). Anyway, George V had to
> smile at the idea of his granny drinking the bicarby tea on a public
> occasion. After that George V was quite jovial that day.'

But life wasn't all flags and bunting for King George and Queen
Mary, not in their private lives at least. Their ailing youngest son,
John, is not much remembered now but there are those who do
passingly recall that he lived through childhood into adolescence.

> I always mind of comin' out the pictures one night, maybe a year or so
> after the First War, and hearin' the newsboys shout ...
> 'Times, News, Cit — iz — en Prince John dies!
> Times, News, Cit — iz — en Death of King's son!'

The eldest son, on the other hand, was very much alive, and like
enough to his grandfather to give twinges of unease to his strict
father. The Prince was charming and immensely popular, and
people waited with affectionate but disapproving interest, to see
which of the string of ladies in his life would become the Princess of
Wales. Miss Marie Condie felt that she was getting a more personal
keek at some of the action than most people.

> I went to America in the 'twenties to do a bit nursing there and see
> what-like it was. I sailed from The Broomielaw with my wee letter of
> introduction to the Chief Steward that I'd got from a friend of a friend.
> Anyway I got to know him quite well and we got to see round the boat.
> At the time the Prince of Wales was friendly with the actress, June, and
> they had dances and parties on board. So-here, this steward said he
> would give me a present of something Edward had used. He offered me
> a choice of coffee-cups, sweet-dishes or a cushion. I don't know if he'd

any right to do the likes of that, but I wasnae goin' to turn down the chance. It was maybe funny, but I chose the cushion for I knew it wouldnae break ... the cushion-cover's done long ago, but what you might call the Prince of Wales's feathers are there in the very pillow I still use.

Others saw him in his young-god heyday.

I seen the Prince of Wales once in the 1930s when he was comin' along Pollokshaws Road standin' in an open car. I couldnae mind ever seeing even a picture of a king before wi' no beard or whiskers (and he was near-enough king). He was handsome, this blond chap, a lot younger-lookin' than he really was, and awful shy and embarrassed lookin'. Mind I don't think he was all that shy!

But there were a few years left to George and Mary before the dashing, clean-shaven Prince became King. There were two royal weddings and the new interest of seeing the two little princesses, Elizabeth and Margaret Rose beginning to emerge on occasion into the public eye. But the climax to the reign was the celebration of the Silver Jubilee. There may have been different souvenirs but Glasgow did its weans proud by giving each a silver-coloured tin of toffees with pictures of the King and Queen on the lid, and putting on firework displays.

Another year brought the end of the reign.

I've never forgot hearin' on the wireless about 'the King's life drawin' slowly to its close.' I was just nine then, and I was a Brownie. We'd to wear a thin black braid like an armband on our wee cotton uniforms. I thought it was all awful sad wi' the black edges to *The Bulletin* and the slow dreich music on the wireless. I mind of seeing the funeral at the pictures and yon horses bobbin' along wi' the black plumes, and I mind seein' the new King, and his three brothers followin' the coffin.

The general public knew nothing then about the storm to come and, respectful sadness for George V over, it looked forward to having a modern king genuinely interested in the lives of his people. When Edward VIII came to Glasgow on a private visit about that time and drove through the city to stay with his friends the Weir family at Eastwood Park, people looked at his pale, set face and hoped they saw high purpose in it.

I saw him arriving at the Park. I mind him sitting in the back of a great big car. He was good-lookin' but his face was awful white and kind of glum. All the same he gave a wee stiff smile and waved to the handful of folk standin' there at the lodge gate.

There were other reasons of course for the serious face and, as 1936 wore on, people began to talk, and the young couldn't help but overhear.

I was nine years old then and and I loved Edward. I collected pictures of him and read all about him. But I was right miserable when I heard the grown-ups talk and knew he was in some kind of disgrace (though I had an uncle that thought it was everyone else that was the disgrace). I've still got the newspaper picture of him sittin' at the microphone talkin' on the wireless, all sad and tired, about 'the woman I love'. Fifty years old, it is, that picture, and a bit yellow, but I'll no part with it ... I've got a kind of non-memento too ... an Edward VIII coronation mug.

But loyalty is fickle and sadness put away with photographs. The Duke of York was the new hero, the new King with his comprehensible life-style and his family.

I saw the King and Queen when they came to Glasgow not long after their coronation. I stood in Argyle Street and they came by in a high car, or maybe it was a carriage. They were lovely!

Of all the Glasgow folk between the ages of fifty and sixty-five who have cast their minds back for this book to the coronation of 1937, when they were school-bairns, at least half still keep dominoes, buttons or other trinkets in the square blue assorted toffees tin handed out to them by some genial councillor, as they filed past him in their school hall.

It was a century since a child had been heir to the British throne and the sensibly rare public appearances of Princess Elizabeth and her sister were the better remembered for their rarity. Glasgow caught one such glimpse when they came to the Empire Exhibition in 1938.

I mind I saw the Princesses there. I can just see them yet, looking as if they didnae know what it was all about, and wished they were back home wi' Crawfie. Maybe they were enjoyin' it all fine right-enough but they didnae look like it, sittin' up prim in their wee pink coats and hats and other weans screamin' wi' fun on the helter-skelter. I mind seein' Princess Marina and the Duke of Kent at the Exhibition too; they said he'd make-up on his face but I thought he was very handsome.

Royal memories of the war years are sparse. Recollections are of other matters than public appearances and junketings. There must *be* veteran servicemen and women who cherish a word spoken by a King who was tiring too young or a sighting of his sparkling Queen in her brave wartime braws, but none have reminisced for this book. But Mrs. Janet Purvis has one memory of the days just after the war.

> I was awarded the City of Glasgow medal for the nursing I did in the war and the presentation was at the City Chambers. I remember we drank tea from real Crown Derby china. Then the Queen gave me my medal. The invitation said to dress simply because, you see, clothes were still on coupons. But our gloves had to be *pristine* white.

And the rememberer in her high-backed chair enunciated the word like a royal curtsey, and repeated it.

> *Pristine*! I had a very nice ensemble, black, with grey fox fur round the hem and cuffs, and I had a black polished-straw hat from Daly's, with two marguerites at one side and a wee drift of veiling.

Simple? Perhaps not. But used no doubt for a long time and kept in memory, for ever.

Since those days royal personages have become more visible and more approachable. Encounters are more frequent and delight most ordinary mortals, apart from those whose teeth are set on edge by their mere existence. But recollections about the present royals are no great test of memory and we can leave such reminiscences to mature until they are the stuff of nostalgia and ready to be told to some collector of tales a hundred years from now.

MORE TEA AT
MISS CRANSTON'S

Acknowledgements

I should like to record my gratitude to all the rememberers for these pages who trustingly welcomed me and my inquisitive questions. I hope I have not let them down. I acknowledge my debt too to Bill Taylor whose sensitive illustrations make a fine contribution to the book. Warm thanks are due also to Mrs. Elizabeth Dewar for invaluable help, to Jean Matheson of Kilmartin for access to taped material, to Shepheard-Walwyn Ltd. for advice at every stage and finally, as always, to my good-humoured and encouraging husband.

To Margaret and John for long
friendship and, in the year of her
ninety-fifth birthday, to CONNIE,
who first called me a 'writer'.

Introduction

There are some periods which attract to them the name of a feature, a movement or person dominant during its timespan ... the Churchill Era, the Iron Age, the Thatcher Years, the Enlightenment. On a more domestic scale when one speaks of the days of the Glasgow tearoom the name of Kate Cranston is the one that springs to mind, presiding, as it were, over the civic tea-pot and cakes. It conjures up a vision of part of the city's lifestyle from the 1880s to the mid-twentieth century ... the Miss Cranston Years.

This book is not *about* Kate Cranston, but the writer was called to account after *Tea at Miss Cranston's* by a cheated reader who had expected to find in its pages a biography of that good lady. The title of that book, as of this, was meant simply to evoke a picture of those years in Glasgow when tearooms were in their heyday, when tramcars clanged and shipyards' hooters sounded, when some children ran barefoot and others walked the west-end parks with nursemaids, when music-halls were popular and pavements checkered with peever beds. In short what the books contain are the recollections of elderly Glasgow men and women, of many aspects of their lives, at home, at school, at play, and on occasion (just one memory among a host of others) being taken as a treat for tea at Miss Cranston's.

Nevertheless, to appease that disappointed reader, let's set the scene with a word or two about that doyenne of the city's tea-shops, where she catered for grandmothers in bonnets with bows at the side, for little girls in trubenised collars, wearing Leghorn hats over rag-ringlets, and for small boys in velvet suits and crocheted collars (a confession from one who can look back

215

nearly eighty years to such humiliation). And ...

> When I went for tea at Miss Cranston's my mother would be wearing
> a long dress with a nipped-in waist and brush-braid round the hem to
> stop it getting all tattered. It was always long dresses. Y'know when I
> was a wee thing I could only see my mother's toes. I only knew she
> wore 'directoire' knickers because I saw them on the kitchen pulley.

Kate Cranston's lifetime spanned all those changing fashions.
She was born in 1849, the daughter of the owners of the Crow
Hotel in George Square. Little is recorded of her young life but by
the 1870s, seeing her tea-merchant brother Stuart offering tastes
of his different blends to his lady customers at his Argyle Street
premises she was inspired to go a step further and open her own
place below Arthur's Hotel at 114 Argyle Street, providing not
only the tea but dainty snacks and cakes, and a pleasant room in
which to linger over them. The enterprise prospered and expanded
when, as a wedding present in 1892, she was given the whole
building of Arthur's Hotel to develop, the Argyle Street area at
that time being the main shopping area of the city with Daly's still
an elegant store there.

At forty-three Kate had married John Cochrane, a Barrhead
man of thirty-five with the wealth to allow them to move in
musical and artistic circles where they met Alexander Reid, who
had lodged for a time with Van Gogh and been painted by him, the
artist brothers Walton and the young architect-designer Charles
Rennie Mackintosh. Kate was also now in a position to indulge her
ideas for the fine furbishing of her home and her tearooms.

The couple settled first at 'Eastpark' in Carlibar Road, Barrhead,
a roomy semi-detached house which Kate invited George Walton's
company to decorate. After a century, the hand of his associate,
Mackintosh, is still to be seen in the elegant and gracious drawing-
room, which generations of occupiers have appreciated sufficiently
to keep almost exactly as it was originally, with slender white
columns, trellis-work and stained-glass featured in the oriel
window area, with seating still upholstered in Art Nouveau fabric,
with a fine fireplace and overmantel and handsome plaster-work
on ceiling and frieze.

Kate was into her stride now. She opened a chain of tearooms

and, having found the style of Rennie Mackintosh in total sympathy
with her own discerning taste, commissioned him to design the
interiors of other strategically placed establishments like The
Willow in Sauchiehall Street and those in Ingram Street, Buchanan
Street and Renfield Street. Glasgow was in its great tearoom period
and Cranston's egalitarian doors were open alike to suburban
ladies, working-class sweethearts and maids on half-days off, all
enjoying favourite rooms in the different restaurants, the White,
the Green, the Dutch etc.

By now Kate and John Cochrane had taken the more imposing
mansion of 'Househill' on the bank of the Levern, where they
employed a large indoor and outdoor staff and also, once again,
the talents of their protégé Rennie Mackintosh. 'Hoozel', as the local
people called the place, became a prime example of the designer's
unique spacial, slender-lined and light-filled style.

There are still those in Barrhead who carry pictures of Kate,
living and entertaining as the 'lady of the Big House', and setting-
off for Glasgow of a morning with her husband in carriage and
pair. Somewhere on the journey, it's said she shed the persona of
Mrs. Cochrane and became Kate Cranston.

> Quite a wee madam she was s'posed to be at the tearooms . . . strict
> but fair they said she was . . . went round all her places every day and
> made all her staff hold out their hands for her to inspect. People said
> she had her kitchens white-washed every week.

It wasn't always easy to ensure total hygiene even with the nail
inspection and the white-wash brush. Miss Jenny Logan once
came on a Cranston rebuke to a habit which had obviously
affronted Kate in the early days.

> I remember a notice in the Ladies' Room.
>   'Would ladies please refrain from combing out their hair, as there
>   have been complaints of hair being carried away on people's
>   skirts.'
> That must have been quite an operation to take down long hair, comb
> it out and put it back up again.

Tea at Miss Cranston's in Mackintosh surroundings was the

great treat for upwards of half a century in the city. John Cochrane, whose circumstances had allowed this social flowering and artistic patronage to take off, died in 1917. Kate herself lived to be eighty-five and died in 1934, the very year that fire swept through and destroyed the Mackintosh masterpiece at 'Househill'. Her grave is in Neilston Cemetery.

Present generations can be grateful not only that they can eat in the restored version of The Willow tearoom, but to Kate Cranston for encouraging the genius of Rennie Mackintosh, letting it emerge as part of the distinctive Glasgow Style, which looks like being an enduring part of European artistic history.

Having done justice (if perhaps a little scant) to Miss Cranston, we can turn our attention in succeeding pages to the many and varied facets of the vibrant life that throbbed elsewhere in the city during her reign as Queen of the Tearooms.

1

Mixed Infants

It's a startling, if self-evident, truth when it first dawns that one is not just the next-one down in a vertical line of forebears, but the product of thirty-two great-great grandparents and sixty-four thrice-greats . . . and consequently a queer mixture of genes, personality and talent. Your 'ordinary' Glasgow man or woman is like that . . . with a dash of teuchter and teuton, latin and slav, hebrew and hibernian, anglo and asian, to spice the basic lowlander stock rooted here since the Clyde was shallow and the Tobacco Lords a scarlet novelty.

So the rememberers for this book gather-in many strands to weave the picture of Glasgow life since the turn of the century, not only from all airts of the city, but from north, south, east and west, of the world beyond.

In this opening chapter there's a kind of thumbnail index of the cheerful band who offer here their tales of life as children of Glasgow, nearly always struggling with a budget and the grime of an industrial city . . . a life sometimes hard, sometimes joyful, but always realistic. Let's name them and root them, so that in later recollections we can meet them as acquaintances already made. For those who prefer to remain anonymous a 'nom de réminiscence' has been used so that we can enjoy the memories of the bashful without making them wish they had kept themselves to themselves.

Perhaps no one has better right to first mention than Mrs. Peggy Carson, now of Ibrox.

> You couldn't get more Glasgow than my grandpa because he was born on a Fair Monday, in 1836, up the High Street. That was before Victoria was Queen, mind. My grandma was Argyle Street. Mysel' I was born and reared in Govan, at school and lived all my life there.

Since then she has spent all the years of her marriage and widowhood in a solid Ibrox tenement. So if birth beside the Tolbooth bell, and life in earshot of a shipyard hooter, equates to Bow Bells in London as a measure of the true native, then Peggy Carson is surely a child of St. Mungo.

Gallowgate must also lay claim to being at the core of Glasgow, and Mrs. Agnes Grove had her early days close by.

> I stayed, first, up off the Gallowgate as a child . . . in Cubie Street on the way to Camlachie, near Macfarlane's bakery. My father was a tailor and cutter and worked from the house. After Gallowgate we flitted up to Duke Street, near the school, and the church at Sidney Place and the Tennant's Brewery. My father used to say our district was Salvation, Education and Damnation, because of the church, the school and the brewery.
>
> My grandparents lived up there too and I had a great-grandmother who worked as a caretaker at some mission, Portland Street way. My husband and his father were both tenters in the silk weaving.

Further east, Miss Jenny Logan was born at the tail of last century in bien Dennistoun where her early memories are of the 'Parade' school . . . and the tragedy of her doll's pram, on the day they left that area.

> It was one of the ones with two handles instead of a bar across, two big wheels at the front and two small ones at the back. The small ones were bashed out of place at the flitting and I was heartbroken, Moving to the southside was a big change for the family but it's the broken pram that I remember. My father was a school teacher so Giffnock was just as convenient.

Another who recalls Alexandra Parade school is Mr. Struan Yule, but we have to take the tram or the three-horse 'bus (stabled in Spittal's yard) to find his birthplace at Tollcross.

> Yes, I was born there, but it was quite a long way into Dobbies Loan where my father had a cabinet-making and joinery business. (My grandfather had been a cabinet-maker too.) So when I was still quite young we moved into a tenement flat in Mackinfaulds Mansions, Dennistoun . . . a lot of rooms off a big hall with a high, fancy ceiling and a huge cupboard. I remember it was cold except in the kitchen with the big black range. It was there I went to school.

So he was brought up in Dennistoun from the time he was a Mixed Infant at the Parade school, and it was there that he watched his father build his castle in the air.

My father always had this dream of building his own home. Every week-end he used to take out his drawing-board, his double-edged and chisel-pointed pencils and work on designing this ideal house he was to put up. He never did. He eventually bought one in Burnside. But he always had that dream.

Dennistoun claims many a well-doing son and daughter, but none sturdier-spirited than Miss Janet Kay.

Dennistoun, yes. That was my part of the world, though for a time we lived near Rutherglen. I was an only child, born well before the First War and I was considered a bit delicate so I was wrapped in cotton wool. But here's me now, still going strong. My mother's family further back were handloom weavers south-west of Glasgow but the more immediate family were mill-workers come right into the city when the weaving died out. My father worked in Singer's at Clydebank.

To the south-west of the dreaming cabinet-maker and the coddled Janet was born Mr. Jack Roche in Bridgeton.

I think I would've been born in Muslin Street. But we kept flitting . . two houses in Greenhead Street, others in James Street and Main Street. If my Pa was bringin' in a good wage my mother took a two-room- and-kitchen, if things were rough it would be a room-and-kitchen or maybe just a single-end wi' a landin' cludgie . . . and a wee black iron jawbox. It was always my Ma arranged the flits. One place I mind of, you looked out on to the Umbrella at the Cross, and from another it was the Wills's tobacco place. My father was in different jobs loading vans for warehouses. I was the only boy and my Ma was determined that when I grew up I would get a good job and go dressed to my work. That was the big thing folk boasted about, 'goin' dressed to your work'. Meant a suit an' a collar'n'tie. Status.

Born to a clay-pipe-making father, Alex Donnelly was a child of the same area though he prefers 'Calton' to Bridgeton.

They're near, but no' the same. No, no. Kent Street I was born, in 1901 near Wills's and Mitchell's tobacco places. Then I stayed in King Street close by Annie Lavery's fish shop. Everyb'dy knew Annie Lavery.

Over to the north-east of the Cathedral the ghost of a small, pinafored girl dances over Garngad Hill. Now she is Mrs. Mysie Kyle but early in the century she was the youngest of the Morton family and, unlike all the other Glasgow-born rememberers, lived in a villa rather than a tenement.

I was born in Garngad. My father had an aerated water factory there . . . lemonade and so on. It was a big cottage with cam-ceiled rooms. I was the baby of the five of us . . . two brothers and three sisters. One of my grandfathers was the lock-keeper at the canal so my father was brought up beside that. My other grandfather worked at Dalmeny House with the Earl of Rosebery . . . the race-horse people y'know. So my mother was brought up there on the estate. That would all be away back into the last century. My mother's family moved into Glasgow when she was young.

The west-end, where Miss Alison Dow lived, was a different, more rarefied kind of Glasgow than we've seen so far.

We lived off Great Western Road. My father was a lawyer in the city and we lived in a big maindoor flat. It's quite sad really but I remember my nursemaid almost better than my mother, at least when I was small. Later I was with her more, but we were never very close. Nana slept with us and gave us our meals, took us to school and out walking . . . and if you fell or got into trouble it was always Nana you went to. Except Sundays. Then my mother and father took us to my grandmother's after church. Sometimes in the afternoon she sent for a carriage and we went for what she called 'an airing. I suppose I don't know much about real Glasgow life . . .

Then the ninety-year-old head cocks to the side . . .

. . . unless, of course, my kind of life was just a different slice of Glasgow.

Perhaps she's right, for another whose memories are of the west-end and its wide crescents and avenues, its social cachet and gracious social round, is Mrs. Millicent Davis . . . yet her background family-profession was Glasgow, root and branch.

Both my parents were Glasgow, born in the 1870s . . . and my paternal grandparents before that. There's been a long family connection with Fairfield's Yard. My husband was with the company, my father was chief engine designer and my grandfather was works manager. Our life was all to the west of the city. I was born in Marlborough Avenue, then we went to Old Kilpatrick for a while and later came back into the west-end.

Mr. James Dewar was born in King's Park . . .

. . . at my granny's house because my father was away. He was a trader along the West African coast in the early years of the century . . . very little at home. Then for about four years I went to Rothesay. So I was a wee Ro'say boy at first, watching the electric trams and putting down farthings on the rails to make ha'pennies. But I really began to be Glasgow when we came back to a tenement in Cartvale Road. Mother was a midwife there. She always wanted a garden so eventually we moved to Auldburn Road in Pollokshaws. It was 'country' then, and she loved the country. I remember the rasp of the corncrakes there, the open fields and roaming away up the burn.

Long before young Jimmy was wandering there, Ann Hutchison was born in the older, central part of Pollokshaws, and passes a sad little judgement on her arrival.

I was born at 45, Pleasance Street near the shirt factory and the kippering store. I was the baby . . . the one that wasnae wanted. Th'was two that died in infancy and other ten, George, Sam, Davy and Thomas . . . and five girls, Mary, Lizzie, Meg, then Jeanie-that-brought-me-up, and myself. We'd what you call a main-door, not a close . . . th'was only two of these in the street. We'd a front door with a back door and a back close. And we'd *lovely* windows, curtains an' that. It was a room and kitchen, with a coal fire in the room and the range in the kitchen. My Daddy kept the range lovely. That was his job in the house. His right work though, was going round with his horse and cart selling logs, fire sticks and coal briquettes.

In the first decade of the century there began to be migration to the suburbs of people who could manage to buy rather than rent, and Miss Isobel Horn's family was part of that.

I was born in a tenement in Shawlands, but my brother was ill at one point and the doctor advised living somewhere higher. So we went to Giffnock three miles away. My grandmother lived in the same road.

The First War was then blighting the prospects of marriage for the young women of that generation . . .

My mother was one of ten, and the only girl to get married. There were four young unmarried aunts over in my grandmother's and she was very much the head of that house. My family was in whisky broking.

From the same district come recollectios of another war . . . of Mr. Hamish Thomson's R.A.F. days as a 'teenager and years as a prisoner-of-war. And his wife Mrs. Helen Thomson speaks of the watershed in her suburban life brought to it by active service in the A.T.S.

Perhaps the most intriguing nest for Glasgow-born-and-bred fledgings to fly, was that in McLean Street, Govan, where the Rodgers sisters, Christina and Mary, were born in the first decade of the century. Chrissie, now Mrs. Ronnie, speaks first.

We were a big family . . . twelve of us (with the two that died young)
. . . five boys and five girls left. It was a two-room-and-kitchen tenement
house and my mother had a farm through the back.

Then Mary, now Mrs. Brisbane . . .

There was a close through to the back court, th'was stables there and a
dung midden and our three/four cows. And we'd chickens. My mother
had come from Greenock and I think she'd worked on a farm there. The
farm at the back and the dairy she ran on the front street was her work.
My father driv the big Finnieston cran.

There's a fading photograph on a table, of a young woman in that
back-court, fine-featured, with lively intelligent eyes, carrying a
milking stool and a wooden bucket, standing beside a cow with
curling horns. She wears a plain round-necked shirt, sleeves
rolled up, with a long coarse skirt and apron . . . and she is
quite beautiful.

That's Mother going to milk the cows.

But my . . . ect . . . sure-as-death, Clyde-built Glasgow bodies . . .
. never with a gene or two from a far forebear come
Mount . . . n. But over this present century the city has
. . . tides of incomers who have greatly enriched the
. . . nging style and talent, exotic tastes and customs,
. . . rgy and culture to colour life in every corner of the city.
. . . ne made quite short journeys to settle here . . . Mr. Robert Ford
from no further than Portpatrick.

I was born in Portpatrick in 1905. My father worked on a farm
there and had his own wee croft as well. I left school at twelve.
(You could do that in the First War when they were hard-up
for farm workers). It was hard-hard work, five in the morning
to seven or eight at night. Too hard. So I learned my trade
as a joiner and later came to Glasgow. I've been here ever
since.

Portpatrick is the place where the saint once left his footprint
after crossing the Irish Sea in a single stride. Less miraculously,
Mrs. Eileen Reilly's parents made their journey by boat, to be
Glasgow immigrants around the time of the First War.

Both my parents came over from Ireland. Separately. My father came from Armagh, to improve his prospects and because of what seemed, even then, like never-ending Irish troubles. He became a passenger-guard on the railway here. His sister came too, with a friend. The friend became my mother because when there was some talk of her going on to North America my father got a move on and proposed.

The two immigrants began the task of house-hunting.

In those days you needed 'key money' (that was just a back-hander to the factor). So until they'd saved that up they went into digs . . . the attic of a big house in West Street, and that's where I was born. My mother took me back to see it later. Not much of a place, but I think if you've come from a background where your parents have had it hard and made sacrifices for you, you should be proud to talk about that.

Mrs. Bunty Angles had a sadder start to life.

I was born in the Isle of Man then my parents went off to a job in Africa and left me with my granny in Glasgow. They were to colle me on their first trip home when I was a wee bit bigger. mother died out there and I just stayed on with my granny . . knew my mother. My granny stayed in a room-and-kitchen in Street.

Then things looked up . . . by one vital apartment.

We moved to a room-and-kitchen with *an inside toilet*.

. . . and progressed to having a proper bedroom.

Yes, the next move was to a two-room-and-kitchen and we lived with my aunt and her new husband. My granny used to go out as a midwife.

Such were the transplants from adjacent towns and islands, some of them no doubt traumatic enough. But other incomers had more daunting decisions to make before they threw in their lot with the 'dear green place', with its different climate and language and utterly strange lifestyles. Pogroms and poverty were powerful springboards for Mrs. Lily Joseph's family, although at first it was a build-up of unhappy circumstances that propelled her mother at least, into a foreign future.

My mother's father in Russia was very very comf'table . . . a big house and their own horse and trap. He went round farms buying up oats. But his wife died at my mother's birth and it was a housekeeper brought her up. My mother liked the housekeeper and she loved her father, but then he married again and she never settled with her stepmother. So she married the first man that came along just to get away . . . married beneath her, that's what they said. I don't know. Anyway they'd two baby boys there, and then because of the pogrom in 1897 they set out for America. They'd to come third class, below decks, but that didn't hinder them. When they arrived at Liverpool they thought it was America. But they just stayed, and later came to Glasgow and my father got work in the cigarette factory close to where they lived in the Gorbals. That was in Adelphi Street. I was the eighth to be born there . . . right at the tail end. By that time they were well into being Glasgow from head to toe.

Head to toe maybe, but not to tongue.

Mind you, my parents always conversed in Yiddish and while they were alive we were bi-lingual, but then it dropped off. All their folks were still in Russia but they lost touch in the next generation. I'm just Glasgow. All my life Glasgow's been good to me.

East European rumblings were in the background of another who knew Yiddish as her home tongue, Mrs. Lily Balarsky.

My mother and father were both immigrants from Vilna in Lithuania. It was a college town . . . 'Vilnius' they call it on the B.B.C. When my father was a boy at the end of last century, young men were being forced into the army and Jews in the army had a bad time . . . anti-semitism y'know. So quite a lot decided to come west. America was the Mecca. But my parents just got on a boat, came first into Scotland and stayed here . . . settled in Glasgow. 'Getting on a boat' was a sort of jargon for going away as emigrants or refugees . . . they really didn't know where. It was a big adventure I suppose. They spoke Yiddish so there was the language thing to cope with too. It's not much used now, Yiddish, but I belong to a group called the Friends of Yiddish and on a Sunday afternoon we have readings from the Jewish classics, Sholem Aleichem or Sholem Asch. It's nostalgic and it's very expressive . . . some German, Slav, Romany and Hebrew in it. It was common to Latvia, Estonia and Lithuania so it kind of bound the immigrants together in those old days.

Lily's father bought small goods and a suitcase, set himself up as a travelling salesman and did the rounds of country villages with his wares.

> My mother came from Vilna too. Things in Lithuania had been bad for every one, especially Jews. My grandmother was a widow and could hardly support her family. So my mother and her sister 'got on a boat' too, and landed in Glasgow. They got lodgings in a part of the Saltmarket where a lot of Jewish people lived when they first came . . . d'you know Skipka Pass?

Both girls met their husbands in the city.

> There were social meeting-places for the immigrants. My mother and father met there.

On his peddling travels the Jewish salesman had taken a notion to the country town of Cumnock and after they married the young couple stayed there with the suitcase for a year or two until Lily was born. But life was strange without a Jewish community . . .

> . . . so we came back and settled up a close in Stockwell Street

Unrest and poverty further south in Europe, in Italy, perhaps as a legacy from the Garibaldi period, brought another enriching influx to towns all over Britain, with waves of Italians coming to seek their fortunes, or at least a modest competence, here. Glasgow may have been a little suspicious at first, but has never had cause to regret their arrival. It's a poor row of shops that doesn't have its café or chippie, and a fair bet that if it has, it's run by Glasgow Italians of the second or third generation of a dynasty . . . like Mr. Angelo Lamarra.

> One side of the family was originally from Tuscany. My mother's people. It's a lovely part in the north.

And this most genial of Glasgow-Italians has a photograph of his mother's home village among the folding mountains of North Italy, beside the cash-desk of his Glasgow restaurant.

> Beautiful . . . but there wasn't much work there so they moved south at the turn of the century to farm work there. My father lived in the south at that time, near Monte Cassino. My parents met there and got

married. They were of big families . . . too big to give a living to all
the sons, so my mother and father came to Scotland and all the family
was born here. They settled first at Stenhousemuir (and y'know it's
a funny thing . . . all my life, though I've never seen them play, I've
always supported Stenh'smuir football club . . . the first result I look
for every Saturday). Anyway we'd a fish-and-chip shop there, so I've
been in the same trade all my days.

But now Angelo presides over the spacious and popular city-centre
Trees Restaurant in Union Street.

My father died when I was still young and things came to be very hard
so my mother brought us to Steven Street at St. George's Cross. That
was us into Glasgow and I've been happy here ever since. There was
the war and internment of course. That was a wee bit difficult. But it
passed.

Other arts and skills arrived with the Italian community.
Mr. Mario Servadei's background story is similar to that of
Angelo Lamarro's . . . even to the Tuscany mother. But his craft
is different.

My father came from near Rimini on the Adriatic side. The farm
holdings were small . . . not big enough for a lot of sons. So one
young fellow would come here, get started and then send for another
. . . and another. My father had been a shoemaker over there, then
learned the hairdressing in Genoa. My grandfather made barrels for
the wine trade, so there were a few skills in the family. My mother's
brothers came and opened a small café on the south side, and when
they went into the army in the First War she came from Italy to keep
the café going. So that was her here. My father'd come to work for an
uncle who was a hairdresser in Clydebank. Later he opened a place of
his own. He met my mother with some Italian friends. They married,
settled in Glasgow and I was born in a tenement in Daisy Street So I
was real Italian-Glasgow from birth.

That then is the cast of this book. There are others who have
thrown in their tuppence-worth to a chapter here and there, just
eaves-dropping in an eventide home lounge, dropping remarks at
parties, or in casual 'bus encounters; but since their appearances
are as 'extras' only and not as stars, we can simply meet them as
they cross our paths.

2

I Couldn't Sing for Toffee

A gazateer of 1881 gives a certain Edinburgh school a pat on the back for innovation recording that 'the changing from room to room is effected to music five minutes before each hour . . . showing a model of organisation'. It's a second-hand memory of that same institution, founded in 1695, that is the earliest in this chapter.

> My granny stayed with her grandparents in Edinburgh and went to the Merchant Maidens' school there. That was because her father had been a cooper in Leith, but he'd died when she was young, so she was considered to be an orphan and the school was for the daughters of deceased tradesmen.

That sad little tale of the 'other' city may not seem to hold much place among Glasgow memories but it does deserve the passing observation that that guardian great-great-grandmother of Miss Isobel Horn's must have had her own education, however much or little, in the time of George III or at least in that of one of Queen Victoria's wicked uncles, George IV or William IV.

But let's leave the Edinburgh Maidens and sift through the school memories of Isobel's own Glasgow contemporaries.

It may not be the three Rs that are recalled with the greatest affection when the elderly talk of their classroom days, but since these Rs were dinned into them as thoroughly as the Shorter Catechism perhaps we should begin with them. Little Eileen Duffy's school at Tollcross might have been purpose planned to daunt a timid 'only'.

I'd no brothers or sister to tell me what school would be like . . . to *warn* me. I went to St. Marks at first. It was traditional . . . very old-fashioned methods . . . chanting the alphabet and saying 'Cee-Ai-Tee spells cat' instead of sounding it out. And the teacher pointed out letters on the board. We did everything to numbers. On 1! you stood up. On 2! you moved into the passage. On 3! you lowered your hinged seat. On 4! you stood up on the seat. Then you chanted the letters to her pointer and you got it across the legs if you were wrong.

Eileen was not going to knuckle under to that without showing a little spirit.

I tried to run away and the teacher put a boy each side of me to make me stay put. Then I tried putting my hand up to get out, the way I saw others doing for the toilet . . . and that was another chase.

But there was a more enlightened regime at her next school where the Montessori System of teaching had arrived.

As far as the reading was concerned, I soon got the hang of sounding out the words (although at five I thought the new teacher just didn't know any better). But I stayed a kind of poor speller for a while with the mixture of the Cee-Ai-Tee and the phonetics.

And the later English graduate produces a childhood scribble in one of her old books C.R.O.C.A.D.L.E., written beside a tale of adventure on the Nile.

One who could have done with the improvement Eileen Duffy later showed, was the labourer remembered by surveyor Tom Marchant.

This chap was sent out to a building site to check amounts of materials stored. He scribbled the amount on a scrap of paper . . . 100 wat son. And came back. 'What's this?' says I. 'A hunnerweight san" (1 cwt sand) says-he, as if it was me that was daft. Another time we got 'joist' spelt J.O.Y.C.E.

Mario Servadei was never as bad as that, but confesses that *he* wasn't great at the spelling either.

Italian was what I heard at home and you just spell it the way it sounds. Well, you can't very well do that with English. But y'see *I* tried. And got a bit confused. I got kept back for my spelling. So was another boy and he wasn't Italian. Funny enough though, he became a reporter on

The Glasgow Herald and I used to ask him, 'Who does your spelling for
you now, Charlie?'

One of an assortment of rememberers who attended the 'Parade'
School between the late 1890s and the First War was little Jenny
Logan.

> When I first went to school in Alexandra Parade, I was in a great big
> room with the Infant Mistress Miss Towers in the middle, and a pupil
> teacher at each end. (They were maybe from the Normal School. That
> was the teacher-training college at that time).

In Struan Yule's time at Alexandra Parade school, Miss Hunter
was the first teacher.

> She was a terror, but she could teach. And there was a Miss Walker
> who played the piano for us all to march like troops in the door
> and up the stairs. I remember her playing 'Blaze Away'. The piano
> was down in the corner of the stair-well, really what passed for a
> hall.

'Blaze Away' was recalled by another Parade infant.

> Oh yes, fine. But there was a Sousa march as well and the big boys
> used to march in singing their own words to that . . . under their
> breath mind.
>   'All of a sudden a big mealie pudden'
>   Came flying through the air' . . .

I never knew the rest of it, if there *was* any more. Struan Yule
remembers learning to write and, in common with every other
who ever wielded slate and slate-pencil, still grues at the scree-
eeech of pencil on surface, and remembers the special stone sill in
the playground where they sharpened the points of their 'pinsels'.

They had a quieter way of learning their letters in Jimmy
Dewar's school at Battlefield.

> We'd Miss Burns at first, followed by Miss Carlyle, a small diminutive
> figure in black button boots. When we were very wee we formed
> our letters in trays of sand . . . made a mess with the sand mind
> you, but it must've been quite economical. You just rubbed it
> smooth again after the teacher came round and saw you'd done it
> right.

Counting methods were neither so ingenious nor so progressive.

> First you sat with your back bolt-upright, then you recited the tables
> . . . up to twelve times. If anyone doubts that was an ideal way to learn
> to multiply they've just to ask you thirteen times this or that, and you
> cannae do it. I'm always foozled after the twelve times. It was maybe
> old-fashioned, but it worked.

They didn't use the sand for written sums though.

> We'd slates for that, and the usual wee smelly rag in a tin, that you spat
> on to wipe the slate.

Mysie Kyle at Rosemount School had her sums from Miss
Clenaghan . . .

> . . . you'd to do your sums on boards all round the walls and the
> teacher stood behind you with the belt.

Another octogenarian still smarts at the thought of that belt.

> Nothin'to dae wi' you were good or bad behaved. Just you maybe
> couldnae dae your seven-times. Diabolical liberty it was to get hit for
> that!

Pointers seem to have been as much weapons as teaching
implements. Bunty Angles remembers fidgets and chattering
that merited a wee rap from one of her first teachers. She recalls
the grim rule of the janitor too, although *he* wasn't armed except
by a large pair of hands.

> It was the jannie ruled the playground and chased you into your lines.
> He could just about lift some of the big boys with one hand.

As well as sand-trays and screaming slates, there were pot-
hooks and jotters, with urgings to take your pencil 'up light
and down heavy', and then all the blotty intricacies of joined-up
writing in ink with a nib. But there was one teaching aid that
did a double turn by offering a grounding in proverb as well as
copperplate. Vere Foster copy-books, of the Art Nouveau-covers
and age-old wisdom, are recalled with respect, if not affection.

> Vere Foster . . . some of us quite liked our Vere Fosters but some
> couldnae be bothered. 'A Rolling Stone Gathers No Moss' or

'Discretion is the Better Part of Valour'. You'd maybe get that on the top line of a page and you'd to copy it better and better on the lines below that.

Not all remembered schools were your School Board Elementaries.

My school was a wee bit different. It was a room in the Langside Halls at the Queen's Park in Shawlands. I'm going back now to about 1907. I'd be about five when I started. Well, there was just the one class and Miss Sharpe took it . . . all ages up to big school age, about ten. We'd little desks and she taught us in groups . . . one lot getting on with work by themselves while she gave a lesson to another. None of this playing yourself with bricks, and calling it 'learning'. None of that nonsense. It was a private school, about twenty children but, for all it was wee, we were well up in everything. The older ones even had the beginnings of French. She was strict was Miss Sharpe, but she was nice . . . Once she cuddled me into her when I fell, and when I held my breath she thought I was in shock. But-here it was only because of the moth-balls in her clothes. I remember my two years at that wee school better than the eight I had at big school.

Isobel Horn was at another Dame School.

At first I was at the local school, but just for two weeks, because I got the belt from the Infant Mistress for swooping about like an aeroplane. So I got my wee palmy. My parents weren't very pleased, so they sent me instead to Miss Gardner's wee private school at Ingleneuk. It was just a cottage really with a kind of big shed at the back where the school was. We all sat at a big round table . . . all ages, and Miss Gardner taught us. She wore a long grey skirt and a high-necked blouse with stiff cuffs.

Miss Gardner had no strap. She had worthier, more personal sanctions at her disposal . . . She had Presence. She was neither cosy nor lovable but she could teach and she could quell a miscreant with a word or glance, and total order reigned at Ingleneuk.

We sat at this table doing set work, and were kind of divided into stages . . . maybe three or four in each. When your 'class' was called you trooped over to stand round Miss Gardner in her chair in a corner. We all learned quite well there, but I never mastered 'notation'. Do you remember notation . . . putting the commas in for tens and hundreds and thousands? She was strong on manners too, Miss Gardner.

Perhaps the most unlikely location for schooling was a church tower used before there was a local public school building in the area.

There were two small rooms with fires. If you were good you got to put on the coals. There was a toilet and wash-hand basin outside the door of each room. I left there eighty-six years ago but I remember it fine, quite different from the big Dennistoun school I'd been at before that.

For a few more years pinafores, button-boots and Norfolk jackets went up that spiral stair for lessons and played in the kirk yard, before the whole complement of two teachers and perhaps two dozen children was moved to a temporary but purpose-built, corrugated school quarter of a mile away.

That was the Tin Academy. I got a prize at the Tin Academy . . . for tidiness. That was well over eighty years ago.

Miss Mabel Logan has lived with little Jenny's tidiness for a long time.

She's still tidy. The only tidy one in the family.

Neat, she may have been . . .

But I wasn't very academic . . . diligent maybe . . . but not academic.

That's a self-calumny for she was academic enough later to take a double Maths degree as one of Glasgow University's very early women students.

As well as the rote learning (some of it enjoyed in a way perhaps incomprehensible now when the education process has to be not only relevant and self-expressive but 'fun' as well) there were also domestic skills, social and artistic graces imparted long ago. Mrs. Lily Joseph was introduced to the first at her Gorbals schools.

In our family it was Buchan Street and Adelphi Street school we went to. I learned to darn at school, along with everything else.

Her teacher killed two birds with one stone when she discovered young Lily's skill with bodkin.

I was the darner in our class and the teacher brought in all her darning for me to do. I was daft enough to be honoured. We learned to knit too.

But properly honoured she must have been half-a-century or more later, by her family.

D'you know I've knitted *eight* shawls in two-ply Shetland for the babies in our family.

To the cognoscenti the knitting of *one* two-ply shawl is an achievement of high plain-and-purling order. *Eight* is cottage industry.

Mrs. Agnes Grove learned to knit too . . . at Tureen Street school.

The first thing you knitted were your own garters . . . twelve stitches wide . . . you knitted that up and measured it round your leg until it was long enough.

Perhaps an early step in learning to sew were the cards handed out at the little Ingleneuk dame school.

These cards had had holes punched in them and you'd to lace threads in and out. The stitches made texts and I think they got sent to a mission.

Pious little workers loved the cards, the rest tholed them as they tholed the redoubtable lady who ran the school.

For the boys, an advance on pulling wool through cards were the raffia shopping-bags the boys in Mario Servadei's class made and took home to their mothers. For the girls, as soon as small female fingers were supple enough, there came the dreaded 'specimens', the shoe-bags edged with cross-stitch and the lap-bags that portended gloomy years of school 'seams' ahead. But the shoe-bag, at least, was a symbol of the better-loved 'drill'.

You were in lines according to your height for drill. We'd the smallest boy I'd ever seen in my life in our class, Harold Brett. He was always

at the front . . . two rows of boys, two of girls . . . then all the orders
. . . Hips . . . firm! Arms . . . bend! Head . . . up!

Sometimes it was just the jannie who presided over the drill,
reckoned to be well up in that sort of thing after his years
in the army. Even if there was no hall, or much other space,
for the jannie to hark back to his military days, all was not
lost.

In our single room school at Langside Halls, at some stage every day
the teacher would stop us all from our work and get us to stand up and
do drill just at our seats. We'd head and arm exercises, moving and
bending and turning our trunks left and right. Just cleared our heads
and suppled us up.

Those were the physical jerks of school life but there was also
the gentler art of dancing where that was possible . . . even at
Ingleneuk cottage . . .

. . . what Miss Gardner taught us was probably just singing games
with hopping-about bits.

But it was a preparation for greater things, and certainly by the
1930s older boys and girls were galumphing about getting ready
for school Christmas parties . . . Military two-stepping, Dashing
the White Sergeant and Waltzing the Valeta.

I was a bit stooky, more of a clod-hopper . . . didnae *sway* enough. But
I clumped my way through and, mind you, it's been useful ever since.
D'you mind all the twirlin' in the Pride of Erin and hooching when you
were at the far end fae the teacher. She could never find who hooched.

There came a less innocent day when the early disco-dancing
young thought nothing of a quiet canoodle behind the sheds.
And yet one teacher of those days recalls the protest when she
lined up a class for their first dancing-lesson.

Aw naw, Miss. No' that! yon haudin'-on-to-each-other kinda dancin'.
Naw, naw!

In spite of such rebellion many a wedding, even yet, is the livelier
for the learning of hauding-on-to-each-other dancing in reluctant
youth.

The other arts had their place too even in the early days of
compulsory schooling. Apples, books and drapes were set up as
'still life' and tongues licked lips in the effort to get them right.

> Oh aye. You fair agonised to get the two sides of some ugly vase the
> same. And if you done them right they got pinned up on the wall . . .
> and there was yon wee kinda stick figures you did, like . . . what was
> his name . . . Lowry? That was because you couldnae help it . . . no'
> like him that *meant* it!.

Perhaps for most rememberers it is the school musical efforts
that stick in the mind.

> We'd little songs at Langside eighty-odd years ago.
>> How many miles to fairyland?
>> Anyone call tell,
>> Up one flight, to the right,
>> Please to ring the bell.
> . . . a nonsense rhyme, but I thought it was lovely and I sang it lustly.

And Mrs. Agnes Grove found her gift for singing a happy and
profitable little talent at Cubie Street school.

> D'you mind how you used to sing in the class at Christmastime, in
> wee concerts? You got a sweetie for doing it. Well, my grandma was
> a great one for teaching me songs and I once sang one of hers. Part of
> it went like this . . .
>> She wouldnae leave her Mammy
>> And she wouldnae leave her Daddy
>> But noo she's left the both of them
>> For a hurdy-gurdy laddie.
> That's all I can mind now but I must've been good because I got taken
> to the class next door to sing it there. So that was *two* sweeties!

One who was less accomplished but just as enthusiastic, was
young Eileen Duffy.

> I couldn't sing for toffee, but all the kind of well-doing children (of
> whom I may say I was one) got into the school choir. So I just went
> along and mouthed the words without singing: One day when the
> teacher came round to listen she came to me. 'Eileen Duffy, you're
> opening your mouth but there's not a word coming out.' So I was sent
> back to my own teacher as red's a beetroot, and-here the next practice I
> wasn't going to go, but the teacher just sent me along to enjoy myself

and I went and did my goldfish thing, opening and shutting my mouth
at the right time.

For those who could't sing for toffee, or were only clod-
hopping dancers, there was always 'poentry' . . . mostly taken
after Silent Reading on a Friday afternoon. There can't be many
who went through school without thrilling to the courage of
Barbara Frietchie in the American Civil War.

> Up from the meadows rich with corn
> Into the cool September morn
> The clustered spires of Frederick stand
> Green-walled by the hills of Maryland

. . . or who doesn't recall the tearing and shooting down of the
Union flags and poles, and the old woman leaning out of her
window waving the last one herself and challenging the enemy
leader, General 'Stonewall' Jackson?

> 'Shoot if you must, this old grey head
> But spare your country's flag,' she said.
> A shade of sadness, a blush of shame
> Over the face of the leader came . . .
> 'Who touches a hair of yon grey head
> Dies like a dog. March on!' He said.

And many a one who met Barbara Frietchie eighty years ago,
can still rattle off whole verses of her story. Fine visual
stuff!

A haunting poem of schooldays that appealed to Mrs. Eileen
Reilly in her Duffy days, perhaps more than to others who didn't
have her fey Irish background was an old cradle song. It called for
quietness for a sleeping child, and protection from the peaty fumes
of a winter night.

> O men from the fields come gently within
> Tread softly, softly, men coming in . . .
> From the reek of the smoke and the cold of the floor
> And the peering of things across the half-door
> O men from the fields, softly, softly come through
> Mary puts round her mantle of blue.

You see I used to go to my great-grandmother's cottage in Ireland for the holidays and there was the cold floor and peat-reek there, *and* the half-door, and when you'd been brought up like me on ghoulie stories . . . you could just see 'the peering of things' across that half-door, and the trees with their dark outlines changing in the dusk.

It was a long day at school from nine until four, making letters, doing your gizinties and spouting poetry. But there were breathers . . . interludes of one kind or another that leavened the hours. There was *resting*. Peggy Carson did that in style.

D'you mind of putting your hands behind your head with your elbows out like wings, to rest your head. Or another way was to put your head on the desk. Once when I was wee I fell asleep like that.

Another welcome interruption to routine was for the class photograph, to be immortalised in sepia with your tie-knot under one ear, your Kirby grip or your ringlets over your eyes. There may have been neat well-groomed little pussies . . . but they were never you.

In the early days of the century there was a German photographer went round the schools. His name was Volgemuth but we called him 'Wiggly-mooth'.

'Wiggly-mooth' ducked under his black cloth in Miss Jenny Logan's day until the First War when he prudently packed his tripod and disappeared from the scene. For a long time afterwards it was Mr. Prophet's photographs that were carried home. Then sadly the day of the class photo was done, in came the studio-type individual portrait and one of the nostalgic joys of putting names to wee bun faces in future middle-age was lost.

There was another break in routine which could be had for the asking, and not even the most awesome teacher could gainsay the need.

One of the things I mind about our school was the toilets . . . just a row of dry closets under a wooden board with holes in it . . . and how you used to sit there and lean sidieways and skelp the bottom coming through the next hole.

In a more sophisticated establishment the W.C.s flushed and had

doors to them, though seldom with satisfactory bolts . . . so that
when there was a rush at playtime . . .

    . . . your best pal 'held the door'.

'Holding the door' was as much a duty of best-friendship as
sharing your play-piece or being your partner in the lines. With
regard to the toilet of course shrewder operators timed their 'calls'
to come during lessons and did not waste good playing time.

    Little Mary Rodger had a kind of dispensation for being a
minute or two late each morning for these marching-in lines. She
was from the dairy-farm in McLean Street.

    I used to take the teachers' milk for their tea with me to the school. I got
    their key and took it into their room. I got paid for it on a Friday.

That was in the days long before there was school milk for pupils.

After that there were spare third-pints a-plenty for the staffroom and even an odd one for home, so that wags could claim to recognise your average teacher anywhere on the street . . .
    . . . wi' a soor face, a bashed case and a wee bottle of milk!

No chapter on Glasgow schools can close without passing reference to the fact that Roman Catholic children are educated separately from the others. There has been the odd fracas from time to time between the two camps, but on the whole there has been give-and-take.

The children from the Catholic school in Govan opposite the Protestant church used to watch for funerals to the kirkyard then go later and take flowers from the graves to put them at their own altar . . .

Give-and-take . . . or maybe take-and-give.

We'll let Mary Rodger, the milk bearer, draw the curtain on early school years with a glimpse of her sister Effie, who seems to have had the kind of rapport not many claim to have had with the teachers of their day.

One of the teachers was very fond of Effie, and when she left the school that Miss Kay gave her *two shillings*. That was a lot of money then. She was nice, Miss Kay, and y'know our Effie kept that florin till the day she died.

3

Three in the Hurlie Bed

In the years before half the city sprawled outwards into suburbia, the near million souls who seethed all day on Glasgow streets disappeared like ants into anthills by night, and life transferred itself just as vibrantly into one, two, three or more rooms-and-kitchen and umpteen single ends. Great spawns of children vanished into the maws of tenement closes and numbers lodged there far exceeded the old legal limits.

> When I was wee it was a single-end we had. Th'was two of these to each landing and two houses with two rooms . . . th'was four landings altogether. That's twenty-four rooms if I coont up, and there must've been three dozen weans in the close . . . for a' th'was a wee brass token at the doors that marked the number th'was s'posed to have been. Nob'dy paid any heed. You'd your inshot bed and a hurlie underneath and one of yon kitchen chairs that folded down. Th'was three of us in that hurlie. No bathroom mind.

Ann Hutchison too remembers the single end.

> When my sister Jeanie got married they rented a house, just a single room. The people in these houses had toilets out on the green. No bathrooms.

Life was a little more gracious with two apartments. There was the extra press-bed of course for the overspill of sleepers, but there was also the pleasant sense that visitors could be welcomed without a blush. The kitchen was still the heart though.

> It was a grand warm room that, with the fire on all night. We kept the dross and the briquettes in there too, handy. My father and mother had the kitchen bed. Th'was a toty-wee scullery too and the zinc bath hung on the wall there.

245

The amazing thing about the room-and-kitchen was that you really lived in the *kitchen* . . . hardly used the Room. It was for best. Kitchens weren't poky mind. You'd have scrubbed table and chairs and an armchair at the range. But the Room was special and nob'dy thought it was funny that you didn't make use of your space just for living instead of showing off. Mind you, it taught you that hospitality was important, and taking care of your nice things. Prepared you for the day, if it ever came, when you might have a big house, a three-apartment maybe. P'raps even wi' a bathroom and toilet.

For the present there were kettles and the jaw-box for washing.

We'd swan-neck taps at the sink in our room-and-kitchen in Cubie Street. Brass they were, and you could hinge them down and put a board over the sink for a kind of working top.

Niceties like keeping the Room *good* were not possible when the family was nine or ten.

We'd two big iron beds in the Room, forbye the one in the press. The girls were in the press and the boys were in the Room. I don't mind how we all got dressed, but there was certainly no jinkin' about and hidin' fae each other.

When the family had flown the coop, or if Grandma lived next door and could take some in as 'sleepers', the bed-recess could take on a whole new life of its own . . . as Mrs. Grove's father used it.

He was a tailor. He worked in the house and stored his things in the bed-press. My sister and I slept with my Grandma next door . . . for years. *Lived* in our own place but slept at hers.

Mrs. Agnes Grove remembers the move to their two-rooms-and-kitchen.

Big-big rooms they were. Th'was the kitchen bed of course, and the kind of more private press-bed with the door in the parlour. In the bedroom (oh but my mother was proud of that bedroom!) there was a brass bedstead, but you could easy have had two beds in there. There was no bathroom. We'd just to take the tin bath and put it on the toilet floor and carry hot water to it, then tim the water down the toilet. People kept themselves very clean like that. But what a skiddle. All the same you had to. As the saying goes 'maun dae's a guid master'! That house belonged to the publican at the close-mouth . . .

Eventually, after the owner put in a hot water system there was no
more fetching and carrying of water in the black kettles.

A sink with two taps . . . my, that was luxury!

For Jean Paterson, another of the two-room-and-kitchen gentry,
to be able to walk into a room that existed only for sleeping was
fairy-tale stuff. Not that there was much 'walking into' theirs . . .
certainly not by the children.

I don't remember *ever* just walking into my parents' room with its gas
fire and its bed po'nds and the marble-top wash-stand. That wash-stand
was the pride of my Ma's heart, with its ewer and basin in a yellow rose
pattern. I might go in to help turn the mattress and so on, but apart from
that it was special and you kep' out. It was a lovely room.

Two-rooms-and-kitchen were considered good houses and represented a certain social standing, especially if the family was small.

My mother had a maid in our two-room-and-kitchen. There was just
me and my sister. We had the Room bed and my parents the bedroom
so the maid was quite snug in the kitchen inshot.

Even so, not all such houses had mod-cons. Ann Hutchison recalls
theirs in Pleasance Street.

We'd a beautiful toilet . . . nicer than lots . . . all painted on the floor,
and we'd a paraffin lamp hanging and a toilet roll on the back of the
door. We done it out twice't a week, put in a new toilet-roll an' that. But
we'd no bath in the house. You just had the tin tub at the fire. There was
a wee bath-house in Macdougall Street with just a few baths in cubicles.
It was an old neighbour of ours ran it . . . that was all he could do for
he'd a wooden leg from the war. You got red soap, but their towels
were rough and scratchy. Nice folk took their own towels.

Here and there, there were bathrooms. But being posh had its own
dangers. Mrs. Lily Joseph recalls an incident in theirs.

Ours was a small, dark bathroom in Adelphi Street with a gas geyser.
You lit that with a match or a taper. One day, though, there was a
terrible to-do. My sister had been gassed. They did get her out in time
but they never used that geyser again. We went to the public baths in
Gorbals after that.

Another of those afterthought, cupboard-sized bathrooms in the same area, with only a tiny grille on to the close, was also the scene of an accident.

> It was that dark and you couldnae see. You'd just a candle in wi' you and if there was a draught through the grille the flame got wheeched out. Anyway this day my mother skited on the soap and broke her arm. Mind, it gave her a rest for a wee while for she was never still.

That bather too, found her way to the public baths after that, for the weekly scrub . . . a delight found earlier by Lily Balarsky and her mother.

> We didn't have a bathroom in Stockwell Street. My mother and I went to the Gorbals baths once a week . . . as much hot water as you wanted. Great!

If you were young and learning to swim you could have a bath, of a kind, after your dip.

> You went into the wee row of foot-tubs and you and your pal took three of them. You sat in tubs facing each other wi' the extra bath in between, and you both put your feet in it. You sat there slipping the carbolic soap down under your costume and slid it about . . . squirted it out at the top and down your back. You got a rare bath that way for there was no right bath at home. My mother was kinda torn between bein' feart I would get fleas or lice and pleased I was gettin' a good soapin'.

A quite different service recalled by Mrs. Mysie Kyle answered the washing need when there was no home bath.

> Lever Brothers had portable baths. They used to put them up in school playgrounds. I saw them down Kelvinhaugh way. A big canvas kind of tent erection. The children came out of school, went in there for their bath and came out at the other end. That went on for quite a long time.

That was the accommodation in the tenement house and the use made of it, with the excursion to the baths for those past the size for a tubbing in the tin bath.

There was sturdy furniture and essential utensils on the household scene too, with chiffonières, what-nots, lobby coat-stands and

the wide chest of drawers for laying out suits and dresses, where
the family didn't rise to a wardrobe. These along with built-in beds
and dressers, with washing-boards, carpet-beaters, toasting forks,
bolt-irons, tattie-champers and spirtles, were standard equipment,
however many rooms forbye the kitchen. Only in bric-a-brac
did imagination and personal taste have free rein. There were
tea caddies, presents from everywhere, fairings, dresser-plates,
crotcheted anti-macassars and cushions. And there would be a
picture or two, a wee bit silver and a favourite text.

> We'd a row of green and blue and yellow majolica jars along the kitchen
> shelf for sugar, flour and meal . . . and my granny had wally dugs.

That granny also had an épèrgne and an upmarket wally close with
olive-green tiles and a mahogany banister. And at that dizzy height
of social prestige we can leave the surroundings of home and take a
look at life within.

Affectionately recalled Edwardian and Victorian gew-gaws,
bring smiles to elderly faces. But more sharply and thoughtfully
remembered are the mothers and fathers, the grannies and the
neighbours who peopled the tenements when many of those
buildings were only quarter of a century old.

> Although in the Italian family the mother had a strong influence in the
> home in general the father was always the real boss. What the man said
> 'went'.

That was Mr. Mario Servadei's recollection of the division of
power. But another rememberer, of different root-stock, saw it
differently.

> My mother would always have *said* my father was head of the house, but
> for most of the families I ever knew that was just a myth. It was Mother
> ruled the roost . . . no doubt about that. No doubt at all. Mothers ruled
> O.K. Is that no' the way they paint it on the walls nowadays?

Mothers are best remembered for uttering precepts, cautions and
bon mots, pronouncing rules, moulding morals and dispensing
justice; for small thrifts and for their own constant busyness. That
last she urged on all her offspring. Lily Balarsky recalls a saying of
her mother's.

It was Yiddish and it came out like 'geret and geton'. It means just what it sounds like, 'get up and get on' with it. But it's Yiddish right-enough and she meant it.

Most mothers had taboos on certain words, quite outwith your actual swear words.

I never heard a swear-word in our house. That would've prostrated my Ma. But forbye them, she didn't like 'pal' or 'shut up' . . . and just about worst of all she couldnae thole 'bored' . . .

which sentiment meant much the same as 'gerup and geton'.

And there were hospitality rites that mothers followed rigorously . . . not only to have the kettle on the boil for tea and buns on the plate . . .

One of my mother's wee things, she always put a coal on the fire when someone called . . . for a kind of welcome. 'make yourself comfortable, hen', it meant. She did that whether the fire was needin' built up or no'.

If you'd eighteen shillings a week or less coming in, 'waste' was as bad a word, as much of a blasphemy, as 'pal' or 'bored'. Thrift was the eleventh commandment and if a Glasgow mother at the turn of the century had had the rearing of Moses it would have been higher on the list than some of the others.

When you were parin' potatoes my Ma used to say that if they werenae the exact same shape when you'd done then you'd taken off too thick a peelin'

And the whole population, it seemed, saved string.

We'd always to take the knots out of string then tie it in a wee bow. Ma used to scrape the butter paper like daft too. Mind you, I still do that. But you never see string now and there's no' a lot you can do wi' used sellotape.

But string was the thing.

Never a bit of string got thrown away in our house. It got all unfankled, tied round your finger and put away in the tin with Queen Victoria on it. My mother scraped egg shells too, to get out the last of the white.

There were limits to frugality though, even with eggs. Jimmy Dewar's mother was not interested in the treasures he brought home from the burnside at Auldhouse, would-be countrywoman though she was.

> I found duck eggs there once and brought them home, very pleased with myself that we'd get them for our tea. But she'd have none of that. 'Duck eggs from the Auld Burn . . . no thank you!'

Home baking was another economic skill in a day when 'bought' cakes were a mark of decadence as bad as 'bought' jam.

> My mother baked a lot on the girdle and the flat plate that hooked on in front of the fire for bannocks or oatcakes.

The same mother had other frugal ways.

> She'd done mill'nry and ever'thing . . . bought a hat shape and trimmed it up the way she wanted.

'Turning' collars and cuffs to revive shirts was also a chore in careful homes, although some 'turners' were more dedicated and ambitious than others. The mother-figures in Mrs. Bunty Angles' life were her grandmother and her aunt.

> They turned all our clothes. My aunt would even turn a jacket or coat . . . unpick it all and make it up the other way round. She even made a suit for my uncle by taking an older one to pieces for a pattern to cut the new one from. And then she turned the old one and so she got two new suits.

Mealtime in most homes, when the day's doings were gone over and the projects for the next day were vetted by a vigilant mother, was the scene of much upbringing. Clipings by neighbours or siblings, for cheek, misdemeanours or small deceits, might merit a cuff round the ears or an angry scolding. Mario Servadei never forgets a Tuscany raging he once had for a minor act of vandalism.

> I had a new penknife and I cut a tiny wee square of wood from the edge of the polished banister and by jove I didn't half get a hammering for that.

And along with the tea-time boiled eggs and jam-pieces, there
was a stream of things to heed about proper conduct . . . carrying
Mrs. Scobie's shopping, or Mrs. Kelly's ash-can, not speaking till
you were spoken to, giving up your seat in the tramcar . . . and all
the multifarious conditioning that would surely someday produce
the true lady or gentleman.

Then there were Grandmothers. Apart from the Babushkas left
behind in Russia or the Nonnas in Italy, grandmothers were, for the
most part, either in situ or just round the corner. Paternal grannies*
(the ones you *can* shove off the 'bus) were less in evidence.

> My father's mother wasn't there as often, but then she lived with her
> daughter's family and she mostly had to do with them.

But the *mammies'* mammies were often just another pair of hands
knitting, cooking, cuffing, alternately with mothers'. And grannies
were often the occupiers of the kitchen bed.

> I always got to sleep in the inshot bed wi' my granny on a Friday
> night and she used to give me a scone and syrup when she got up
> in the morning. She knitted all the time for us, my granny did . . .
> and she learnt me all the wee sayings about 'putting your hand to the
> plough' and 'Oh what a tangled web we weave . . .' and about 'two
> blacks not makin' a white'.

That grandmother was a home fitment, but there was another one
perhaps even more firmly rooted.

> My granny kep' her winding-sheet under the bed.

However thirled to a particular house a family may have been,
the day could come when there had to be a flitting. Lily Balarsky
came to Glasgow from Cumnock.

> There was no Jewish community there, so we moved to Glasgow to
> get mixing with our own people. I remember arriving along with the
> furniture at the close in Stockwell Street near the old Metropole. We

---

*Ref. the immortal 'pome' . . .
  'You canny shove yer granny aff the 'bus,
  No, you canny shove yer granny
  (for she's your mammy's mammy),
  No, you canny shove yer granny aff the 'bus'.

went up to a house with a big-big hall, a huge kitchen and a room that was always called the Big Room. There was a bedroom too and we'd two concealed beds. No bathroom. Six of us were brought up there.

Eileen Reilly recalls the day when her parents had at last saved enough to bribe their way into a proper house, from their lodgings.

It was in Tollcross Road and we'd to take it furnished. That just meant a table and chairs. I was still at the stage of being carried and I was taken into this new house. It was evening and the gas was lit (I can still smell the smell of these mantles). Anyway there was a rocking chair and my father just plonked me into it, thinking it would be a great experience, but I was terrified when this thing *moved* in the half-dark with me sitting in it.

Sometimes the flitting was a team effort.

If it was maybe just round the corner you hired a horse and cart. Big flitting-vans were for 'bought' houses. (Unlike cakes or jam, 'bought' houses were infinitely desirable . . . an unlikely dream for most worthies of tenement land). Well, you'd this horse and cart, and all the neighbours helped. A flitting was rare if it was good weather. And you got tea and buns after. Or maybe fish suppers.

Neighbours, of course, were almost part of the extended family.

If you were wee and doing something wrong, the slap you got was just as likely to come from Mrs. Ferrie across the landing as from your Ma.

There were bonuses as well as clouts.

I didn't like my mother's soup, but I would take Mrs. Grove's soup from up the stair. And Arthur Grove wouldn't take his mother's tart or dumplings, so he got those from my mother.

Mrs. Duffy's tarts and Mrs. Grove's soup being interchangeable was no more odd than an Eve's pudding swopped for a special brew of coffee or the potato scones and marmalade that changed hands up and down the closes.

It's hard to see in the lonely, dreary close-entries of the 1990s, rushed through by hard-pressed couples dashing out to work, the scoured and prim places that were once the pride of each clachan of neighbours in the tenements of long ago.

We'd all to take our turn of washing the close, and Mistress Rodden up
the stair always done kinda daisy-chains up ours wi' her pipe-clay . . .
nothin' as common as zig-zags or squiggles. Lovely, they were.

It was squiggles though, in Pollokshaws.

. . . wee pipe-clay squiggles all up the edges.

But daisies or squiggles, the pipe-clay had its snags if the sweep
of the artist's hand ranged too near the centre of the passage-
way.

It got all tramped through on to your good congoleum or your rugs.

Sometimes it was the footsteps that strayed on to the pipe-clay.

The women up our close worked hard and I suppose so did the men at
their jobs. But no matter how short the money was for the wives, there
was always enough for the men to get their drink on a Saturday . . . and
maybe more'n one. We'd two in our close; real respectable men all week
. . . then stotious at the week-end, staggering up the stair singin'.

And Jack Roche remembers Dougie up their close who was musical
too.

He was a big teuchter that played the pipes, and when he'd had a dram
you used to get the heedrum-hodrums all night from his chanter.

There were other intriguing characters who made up the cast of the
long-running soap operas of the tenements.

I mind we'd an old couple above us. The wife called her man 'auld
Brodie' and he called her 'auld Biddy'.

And Peggy Carson recalls others.

When you talk about flitting what comes to my mind is no' *flitting* but
fletting. We'd four spinster ladies next door us. Quite perjink they were
. . . wore hats and gloves and everything, but we used to see them
flettin' their tea. D'you know what that is? It's pourin' it into your
saucer to drink. My mother gave us a roastin' for laughing at them.
She made excuses . . . said it was because they were 'country'.

Cosy warrens of neighbourliness, warmth and polished brass
. . . or were they?

Och, it all sounds that couthy and good when you look back . . .
close-knit communities . . . you see it all rosy. But a lot of it was
cold and uncomfortable with long working days, or worse, times
that th'was no work at all . . . frightening when you didn't have
much money. Th'was quite a lot of illnesses too, chests an'that . . .
T.B. . . . and no' much colour. Your granny was aye in black. I never
mind her any other way. And she wouldnae be out of her forties when
I knew her. Th'was bad smells too and a lot of drunkenness. A thing
I couldnae thole was comin' in from the school and wet clo'es hangin'
over the table from the pulley, slappin' your face and puttin' a damp
kind of smell over your teas. Blankets was the worst.

But the rosy haze persists, and whether it covers darker or more
sinister truths, for most of the children who ventured out from
them, the tenements are remembered as nourishing wombs that
delivered them safe and strong into the demanding life of their
city. The endless round of chores to make it so, and the sharing
out of those, will keep for another chapter.

4

Blue Sparks in the Night

Ask a Glasgow ancient about the streets of his childhood and he'll give you buskers and beggers, horses, theatre-queues and vendors, push-barrows, polis-men and pick-pockets. But above, beyond and before every other sight and sound, he'll tell you about the tramcar.

By the 1840s the early waves of immigrants to Glasgow from the countryside were dying out and it had become something of a puzzle to many a Glasgow working man (whose crofting or shepherding grandsires had thought nothing of a ten or twelve mile tramp over the hills and glens of the north-west) how he was to cover the mile or so from his tenement home to the factory where he earned his weekly living. Maybe the sight of his betters bowling genteelly along the wide city streets in carriages, to business-type occupations a lot less fatiguing, gave him a simmering staw at having to tramp the pavements to his own home on Shank's pony after the sweat of ten or more hours ill-paid labour . . . a staw that prompted action in high places. Whether there was a philanthropic move to see your ordinary bunnet-and-breeks man supplied with wheels like his master, or just money-in-it for a sharp entrepreneur, public transport, run privately, came to Glasgow streets and bridges long before the earliest recollections for these pages. First there were the little one-horse two-wheel 'noddie' 'buses for hire in the city centre; and then, by mid-19th century, longer-distance omnibuses that clip-clopped their way to suburbs like Partick and Dennistoun.

In the public mind 'bus and tram are seen so much as two distinct and separate inventions, that only a solitary 88-year-old thought to mention that the tram arrived on the scene simply as an improved 'bus.

My faither used to tell us how the first horse-buses were that slow and shoogly when he was a boy that they put down the tram-lines so's they'd be quicker and more comf'table. The rails was new but they just kinda called the buses 'tramcars'.

All the same, whether bus and tram were separate brainwaves or a progression one on the other, it was the tramcar that caught the public imagination and has lingered in Glasgow as the focus of its most nostalgic folk history . . . from the horse-drawn primitive to streamlined Empire Exhibition model and beyond.

Few now have firsthand memories of horse-powered trams but one sharp 91-year-old who spent his youth in Tollcross could just recall their last days at the end of last century.

They were dark, dirty wee things, but what I mind best was being surprised how the horses could keep going right, between the rails, and no' pull the car out the grooves. And they were just one deck of course.

But then the 'electric' came and Glasgow's love affair with its tramcars really began.

Oh aye, I got taken on one for my sixth or seventh birthday, I don't just mind which. But och, it was like the Space Age in the electric double-decker.

It was a real Glasgow thing the open-top tramcar. When you were wee you always had to go upstairs . . . summer or winter, cold or hot. And if it rained, even quite hard, well you'd always your brolly.

And the daintiest of 1991 ladies smiles at the vision . . .

Och, we were tough, were we not just tough?

By now it was the Corporation who ran the tramway services and it did its meagre best to meet the weather hazards.

On wet days right-enough, they put straw on the top deck floor.

At first the bird's-eye view of Glasgow going about its business was novelty enough, but gradually knacks of swinging aboard by the brass pole, swaying with the lurch and well-balanced strap-hanging, created a tram riding expertise as skilled in its way as those of the gentry lightly flicking a rein and prancing proudly along in its carriages. The man-in-the-street soon knew all there was to know about getting the best out of his own transport system.

At the place where yon trolley-bit joined the top deck there used to be a light when it was dark . . . a very bright light, maybe about ten inches high, and you always tried to sit ahead of that, because if you sat behind it the glare on your eyes was terrible. So it was always up the stair and out to the front.

Perhaps city streets were brighter than early fading sepia photographs suggest. Maybe the ladies did rejoice in purples and scarlets, and gay flowered hats and the men sport dashing waistcoats, but there in no doubt that the arrival of the trams, boldly banded in greens and yellows, reds and blues, according to route, brought new colour to its streets. Mrs. Lily Joseph still sees her local ones as if it was only yesterday they had trundled the rails across the Stockwell and Jamaica Bridges and out to the east end.

> Different colours for different places, yes yes. A yellow one went along Norfolk Street to Bridgeton Cross from Paisley Road and the other way was the white one from Mosspark to the University.

Mrs. Mysie Kyle is something of a tram colour historian, chanting the routes like a spelling list.

> The red car went from Millerston round by Giffnock to the Rouken Glen and back out to Bishopbriggs. The other way it was up Parliamentary Road by Monkland Street. I knew all the trams . . . the red to Riddrie, the yellow one along Nelson Street, white from Dumbreck to the University.

And with the 'blue' to the Normal School, the 'green' to the east end, the yellow along Allison Street, folk made their colour-coded way from the city-centre grid to all points of the compass.

There were even pioneers who went further afield, in *alien* trams. Miss Janet Kay explored the Lanarkshire version.

> We used to visit 'family' out in Stonehouse and I remember during a train strike we'd to take a Glasgow tram to Cambuslang, get the Lanarkshire tram to Hamilton, change there for one to Lanark and walk the rest of the road to Stonehouse. Same coming back, the other way round.

You could get a cheap family outing too, by tramcar. Struan Yule remembers one favourite trip with his grandfather.

> It was the yellow tram that came our way and went on out to Riddrie, and Grandad used to take me and my brother on that, and then on a kind of safari along footpaths to find the place where William Wallace was betrayed to the English by Sir John Menteith. There was a well and a farmhouse and my grandad was sure it was the very place where Wallace was taken. I can see him yet knocking on the door to ask, and not getting a very certain answer.

And Jimmy Dewar recalls days out to the far end of Barrhead with his mother.

We got off there and walked up by Crosstobs, through a gate up to the Gleniffer Braes for a picnic. Mother was a great one for the fresh air up the braes. But there was another real bargain of a trip when we were wee. You could go anywhere on a children's penny ticket right through the summer . . . from terminus to terminus . . . say from Renfrew to Auchenshuggle . . . or was it maybe Airdrie? Anyway, it was halfway across Scotland that, for a penny! We used to go to Renfrew Ferry and there was a café there that we got ginger beer and watched the ships going up and down.

Nearer home, city centre weans packed the red 'caurs' bound for Rouken Glen and it was claimed that they brought fifteen thousand people to the park every bright summer week-end and made the terminus there as busy as Glasgow Cross on a Saturday.

The system brought with it other interesting fixtures besides rails and overhead cables.

The bundy clocks . . . d'you mind the bundy clocks? I liked it when I was wee and the driver timed in at the bundy at the side of the street.

If a driver wasn't up to time there it was perhaps because there were queues further back along the route at the tram stops.

They were quite neat, fancy wee things, the tram stops. Half green and half red, and they kind of bulged into rims at the bottom. Some just said TRAM STOP in white lettering, other ones had FARE STAGE or CARS STOP HERE IF REQUIRED. I's'pose they could just go scooshing past those ones if there was no one waiting to get on or off.

When dozens of cars were shuttling and plying in procession between termini in all directions it was inevitable that there were mishaps. Mrs. Agnes Grove remembers . . .

Sometimes in frosty weather the trams used to jump the points and the driver had to take them back a bit and try again. They'd long metal cleek things to shift the points, that they kept in the driver's wee cubby at the front end of the car.

Mrs. Mysie Kyle too recalls the hazard of bad weather.

I remember the winter of 1939/40 when the snow was deep and they'd to keep the tramlines clear and cut paths out to the rails from the tram stops.

And John Adamson . . .

> I've always mind of one stormy winter, maybe in the 'twenties, seeing a tramcar blown over on its side on yon chuckie track alongside the Mosspark Boulevard.

Jimmy Dewar recalls a type of mishap that was recurrent at his local terminus.

> After I saw it the first time I was always a bit scared when the trams came up past the Vicky Infirmary, because at the monument yonder where the rails stopped short a tram would overshoot sometimes and get de-railed. Then a trailer had to come out from the depot to drag it back again.

But if all was well at the terminus and the driver and conductor had a tasty ham or cheese piece, they sometimes farmed out one of their duties to eager volunteers.

> I remember the trams came down Sinclair Drive and they'd to change the trolley round there, so you used to wait for them and get them to let you pull the trolley off the cable, walk round and hitch it back on again the other way. That was a great thing to get to do. It was a single bar trolley and you pulled it down on a spring. If th'were nice drivers they let you do that.

Those favoured boys, though, wouldn't be the ones caught taking free hurls hanging on to the brass platform-pole when the conductor was aloft punching his tickets.

> Yous could get yersel' a mile or two through the toon for nothin' that way . . . jumpin' on two or three different cars until yous got chased or clouted by one of the conductors.

But conductors and clippies weren't always simply chasers, clouters or handers-out of coveted chores. They were legendary for repartee and apochryphal stories. Eileen Reilly remembers.

> There was a conductor who did our route and in those days they called out the name of each fare stage (y'know, the stop where the fare went up by a ha'penny). They'd shout Sauchiehall Street! Argyle Street! Cook Street! . . . Well, on our route he used to shout out 'Gor-bals . . . Wee Jerusalem!

The last night of the trams in Glasgow is talked of with all the enthusiasm of the last night of the proms, with overtones of *Rule Britannia* and *Land of Hope and Glory*.

It was sad. I was in Argyle Street when the last one went along to Auchenshuggle. I was near greetin'. Maybe I *was* greetin'.

Bundies, wee red boxes for uncollected fares, the clatter of the destination blind being changed at the terminus, the rhythmic sideways sway of the conductor swinging over seat backs for the turn-round, the touches of stained glass at window tops, the slow death of the colour swathes to the uniform green and yellow of the 'new' trams, . . . the clippies, the blue sparks in the night, the ping of the ticket punch, the platform bell and the big brass driver's handle . . . There's not a rememberer but mourns them all.

Next to their beloved tramcars, ripe Glasgow people best remember the horses that clopped the streets of an older day . . . from high-stepping aristocrats and spanking trap ponies to weary little nags that pulled slow cadging-carts along the gutter.

The first city suburbs rose as fine honey-stoned, ashlar mansions and villas, within a lunch-time's drive away from the professional and merchant classes' places of business. Pollokshields, Newlands, Hillhead and the far reaches of Great Western Road became the places for solid citizens to be, and it was to and from the gracious avenues of des. res. there, that carriages rolled four times a day, horses and vehicles gleaming, like Porsche or B.M.W. every inch the status symbol of their day.

When my Ma was fourteen she came from near Oban to go into service as a housemaid in a big place in Pollokshields. Th'was a cook forbye, and a woman for the rough work. And th'was a coachman that did the garden and kept the carriage nice, and groomed the horses . . . rubbed up the leather and brasses an' that. He took his gentleman (that was a lawyer, I think) into his office in the town, then went back for him, dinner and teatime. My mother married the coachman and they took a wee grocery after that, but he used to tell me about the kind of procession of carriages that went in and out, all competin' wi' each other to be the best turn-out. I think he always wished he was still a coachman.

Mrs. Millicent Davies remembers a house in Roman Road, Bearsden . . . with *two* horses.

> The man who built the Highland Railway lived there and they kept a carriage and pair.

For those minor gentry who fancied something more of the 'country' life there were villages like Busby and Milngavie where they could live and be driven to the local railway station to catch the business train.

> The office-boys took the early train, then the clerks a wee bit after that. And then there was a later train for the gents from the big villas who were the bosses. They came in their carriages and stepped up into the late train from wee boxes the guard or the coachman put down for them.

So it was all very spick and span and 'white glove', but Mrs. Nell Dinsmor remembers another inevitable side of the carriage-and-pair days and what it was like to live next-door to where the sweating horses came home at night.

> See that wall down there? Well, beside it yonder was the dung midden for the horses that were kept in the stable there.

But it wasn't only fine carriage horses that were loved and cosseted by their owners and grooms. The plain cuddies who were partners with their masters in earning a family living were cherished with perhaps even greater affection . . . by Ann Hutchison for one, looking back to faraway childhood.

> When I was wee in Pollokshaws there was lots of horses and carts. My Daddy had a lovely horse. We used to stable her at Brown and Adams works and then down beside the chapel. He'd a real nice cart too. Nancy was an awful nice horse. We loved her and d'you know this? On Saturday mornings Nancy used to come right down the hill and up the front steps of the house (it was a main door house) to get a treacle piece . . . right up the steps! Just herself!. Fancy her comin' down all that way from the chapel for that treacle piece. And she brought the cart with her! My Daddy would come following her, but away behind. She got oats an' that every day right-enough, but she liked her treacle piece.

Even when the Dobbins weren't petted, home-stabled members of the family, just the memory of them raising sparks on the streets of the city of their youth brings a smile to all who speak about them. Coal carts, delivery carts, builders' carts and their horses were all part of the passing show, steamy, sometimes scruffy and overworked, sometimes proud and easy, always passing steadily on their way. But it's the vending carts, stopping and starting, progressing only a few yards at a time, that became real friends . . . the Betsys, the Dapples, the Daisies. Struan Yule recalls their like.

> When I was young in Dennistoun, the streets were alive with carts and vendors and I remember one pony-drawn float that went up and down the different streets with a husband and wife selling fruit. Sometimes a tenement window, maybe three floors up would be thrown open and a housewife would call down for the man to bring up potatoes, apples, pears or whatever. It was the husband did the calling of the wares too. 'Fine Can-ary bi-na-nas the day, shill'n the duzz-in'

There was another hawker that sold tripe from barrels draped with white towels and, if you could tell the difference between tripe and towels, and were interested, then the cry,

> 'Bags, sheepsh' bags, sheepsh' bags' . . .

would have you hurrying down for a yard or so for your tea. And maybe you would wait on the soor-dook cart to get some of that to slake down the tripe, as someone else recalls.

> There was a soor-dook cart went round the streets near us. My mother loved soor-dook and she used to send us out to get it to drink fresh with the wee globs of butter floating in it. You took out a jug to the wee tap at the back of the cart. It was great . . . cool and fresh . . . funny that, soor-dook being fresh . . . but it was.

Other nights it was fish for tea.

> There was Ovens the fish man came to the Wellmeadow with his cart and his handbell. We bought fish off him.

No mention of whether it was whiting or cod, but elsewhere, down Cathcart Road, the soor-dook went with salted herrings.

> Fridays we'd salted herrin's off of Haddie Joe's cart. That made you thirsty and you waited wi' your can for the soor-dook man to come along.

If the soor–dook cart failed you, there were other ways of cooling down, that Mrs. Lily Joseph remembers from a lifetime ago in the Gorbals.

> When you were wee you used to see water-carts spreading water over the streets. There was a barrel on them with a pipe at the back and the water came out that stroup. Sometimes they stopped it when you went by but if you were cheeky and shouted a wee rhyme at the man . . .
>   'Mind oot, mind oot
>   Here comes the water scoot',
> then he'd put it on that-heavy you got all wet. Did that for fun, so he did.

The real kings among the horses were the big draught-horses. Mrs. Agnes Grove and others remember them trudging up the High Street, but those whose beat was nearer the city centre are the ones best recalled.

> I remember the draught-horses pulling carts up West Nile Street. Part of that street was wooden causeys at one time . . . very quiet . . . but at the time I remember it was the ordinary cobbles with two smooth tracks for the cart wheels to run up. The boys that waited in the street to help with the horses used to put on a kind of galoshes over their feet to run out to lead them up or push them.

To most, the sight of the plunging horses was of passing if awe-inspiring interest . . . a bonus to the day. But there was one child who made formal visits, on purpose to see them . . . and even took calling gifts.

> I always loved horses and used to like to go and watch the trace-horses in West Nile Street. I loved the scene there as a little girl. There would be three or four of them at the foot of the hill, and wee boys sitting on the kerb. Then a heavy load on a cart would come along and one, or maybe two would run out and hitch the nice big fresh horse on to the front. The original horse would still be in the shafts. I used to fancy that when he felt the new horse taking the weight to tow him he would just say 'Right chap, it's your turn, you get on with it'. And the boy would lead them up between the two smooth tracks to the top of the hill. They'd get unhitched there and the boy would lead the trace-horse down by the gutter and take his place in the queue of wee lads to lead

the next load up. It was like The Grand Old Duke of York, or maybe pilots on the river. These boys were very popular, a great street sight. And y'know they used to be given their own party at Christmas.

A little yearly largesse perhaps on an otherwise sparse livelihood. This affection for horses was no childhood whim of the small visitor, for she goes on,

> . . . even when I was older I never went into town without going round to see my horses, and I never went without sugar lumps. I *knew* the horses . . . intimately! There was one that had been through the First War and got wounded. He'd a great long scar along his side . . . about ten inches. A real old war-horse. And he knew *me*. I took toffees for the boys too.

Those recalled wooden causeys had been laid to keep horses from slipping, but the idea didn't take on and was never widespread. Instead there were private do-gooders known in their communities for being ready for emergencies. Mrs. Mysie Kyle's mother was one of those up Garngad Hill.

> In those days they didn't salt or grit the streets. But because my parents had their factory, their lemonade and toffee to make, my mother had a fire going summer and winter, and she used to save all her ashes to put out on the street for the horses when the frost came and it was slippy.

But wooden cobbles, ashes or careful driving couldn't always prevent accident and one of the real street spectacles of the days of the horse was 'the fallen horse'.

> There was this sort of uneven clatter told you a horse was down and was thrashing about trying to get up. It used to get all wild-eyed and sweaty . . . all trim'ly y'know.

And when that happened, in Garngad at least, they knew where to call for help, and ashes were soon being rushed out from the lemonade factory.

> My father would always be right out there with the fire ashes when a horse went down, they threw the ashes all round it, then took the belly-band off, took the horse out the trams and pulled them away. There was always a big crowd and they got them yelling as loud as they could to give the horse a right good fright and made it scramble up on its

feet by getting a grip on the ashes. You couldnae let it lie there you see. My father used to say if it wasn't up in ten minutes it was done for.

Others used sacks instead of ashes, and drummed some passing boy into service to sit on the horse's head, the most frequently remembered procedure for pacifying animals and getting them to their feet without frenzy. One such passing boy was Mr. Jack Roche now aged eighty-nine.

I mind once in Monteith Row a horse'd slipped and fell, coupin' the cab on its side . . . and here a gent grabs me and makes me sit on the beast's heid while they unhitched it. Me, I was terrified, but I done it and after it was up and slitherin' into its trams, he gie'd me a florin . . . a florin! After that I'd of sat on a tiger's heid, nae bother.

There's more to Glasgow street scenes remembered than tram-cars and horses, but for the time being we'll run the 'caurs' into the depot and see the horses into their stabling for a rest and maybe a check-up on their street-worn shoes.

The Cartcraigs Co-operative stables were just down the Barrhead Road from the Round Toll, with the smiddy beside them. It was a great thing when we were young to go down at tea-time and see the horses getting led in there.

Another such sanctuary was at Muirend.

Long before there was the Toledo cinema there was the old Bogton farmhouse that's fields went away up to Netherlee thonder. The cows came in mornin' and night for milkin'. There was horses too. Some were just for people learnin' to ride and they'd other ones for pulling the milk floats.

With all but the late-night trams in the depots and the horses bedded down for the night we can close the book for a moment on city streets and open it in a later chapter to look at their landmarks and some of the citizens who knew them.

5

Hets and Peevers and Kick the Can

There's a deep-rooted belief among those who played their games eighty or more years ago in nearly empty streets and wide back-courts, that today's young have neither the gift for play nor the imagination, the adventure and the fun they themselves had in their green years. They've gone soft, say the elderly, with television 'pap' and 'little ponies' sporting fluorescent hair.

Perhaps tight budgets, and the environment of their echoing closes and tightly defined territories shaped and refined their games in older days. But it may not be so different now. Perhaps imagination is still stimulated and skills are still honed, although by other surroundings and a kind of sophisticated gear unknown in the past.

These pages though, are not about the precocious weans of today who can slot in videos, operate computers, flicking the right switches before they can handle a knife and fork. They are about how their grannies and grandpas jumped and chanted and spun their peeries long long ago.

There's a hint of the part played by environment and the 'available', in an observant memory of Jenny Logan's.

> When I was very small we lived in Dennistoun and I played peever there . . . and ball beds. But then we moved out to the suburbs where the pavements were just rough ash . . . the playground was too, so you couldn't draw chalk-beds for those games. I missed my peever and ball-beds.

Another who had to adapt to new ways was Jimmy Dewar.

When I left Battlefield for Pollokshaws I found everything was different
. . . different ways of playing things, they talked different, different
words and accents. Some of them were a bit rougher maybe. But it
was good. It was lively and there was lots to do . . . places to go . . .
more countryside.

To Ann Hutchison, Pollokshaws was not new territory to explore,
but her home stamping-ground from birth.

There was nowhere like it. We'd skipping and peever and ball and that.
And everyb'dy was close. If your mother was out, or if she was ill, you
just went next door and played there.

One of her neighbours had a wryer idea of the closeness . . .

. . . an' if you were cheeky or wild or that, someb'dy else's Ma went
her dinger at you and handed you a clout you wouldnae forget in a
hurry. And in them days you didnae go whining and cliping, for fear
of getting a harder one at home.

That was maybe a wee digression from pragmatic choices of
what to play at next. So back to the lively kee-hoys and crazes
among the tenements and let the Jennies and Jimmies get on with
their new customs in suburbia.

There may have been recurring patterns in the play but the young
did not detect them themselves. Struan Yule . . .

. . . your playing went by seasons . . . just crazes that came up, you
never knew how . . . one day it was Moshie, then the next you were
into a fortnight of Kick-the-Can.

But apart from those games with rules, there was what you might
call just 'play' . . . opportunist ploys dependent on passing traffic
and people or on a serendipitous find. Even the weather, wet or
dry.

You could easy play on the streets then. There wasn't that much
traffic. They were cleaner too, the streets . . . wi' the men hosin'
them down in the middle of the night. And th'was horse-drawn
watering-carts too when it was hot weather, and us boys used to
follow them wi' bare feet. They'd sprinkler-bars at the back and you
used to could dance your way along behind, gettin' your feet nice'n
cool.

If, on the other hand, there was rain instead of sun, you just literally changed your tack.

> We used to make paper boats and race them down the gutter after a good plump of rain.

Rain provided entertainment for Alex Donnelly too.

> My father had his wee pipe–clay work up a kind of close, and on wet days we used to get wee bits of kind of dry clay, go up t'the landing above the street and sprinkle it on the top of umbrellas to dissolve and run down.

Just such a vantage point above passers-by provided diversion for another rememberer too.

> There were men from a pipe-band came down the street sometimes when we were wee, and I remember crouching on the high shed roof above them and dropping wee stones picked out the rough-cast, down into their busbies.

Alex Donnelly had another perch too.

> Sometimes we used to climb on the railings outside the pub to listen to the men singing.

But when he's asked, 'Was your father a singer, is that where you get your music?'

> Naw, naw. Never heard him singing but in the pub.

There were back–court romps and illicit hurls on tramcar platforms or the backs of carts. These were common to all areas where there were streets, back–greens or tram routes. But there were also venue features of particular districts that held fascination for playing. Lily Balarsky ran her tigs as one of a long line of weans who for centuries have pranced about on Glasgow Green.

> We used to play round yon nice fountain near the gate opposite the law–courts . . . played tig and release and all that.

Another rememberer risked life and limb, or a good head-bashing on a small rail-line near his home.

I was one of the last that used to play on the lime buggies that ran to kilns up our way, and then down again. Then the lime-pits was done and the buggies stopped, so th'was no more of that. But th'was coal-trucks too that we played on, that ran to the station. You'd to mind out for the *man* though. If you got caught he'd gie you a cuff, or maybe threaten to get the polis. They werenae safe them buggies. The man was quite right.

Do they still make fires on cold days, and bake potatoes in the embers, then bite in to savour the faint electric shock on their tongues from the charred skins? Or have the satisfying dangers of that been abolished along with the sensible taking-over of bonfires and squibs by the Establishment?

A less hazardous but equally interesting way to pass the time was occasionally offered to lucky small boys with a providential find almost on their own doorstep. One, living next door to the local synagogue, had the joy, after there had been a party there, of draining the lemonade bottles from the crate put out for collection the morning after.

More structured games to be played properly, required a *group* of youngsters and also counting-out preliminaries. 'Azeentie-teentie' had several versions depending on whether you learned one of the bawdy or one of the genteel rhymes.

> Azeentie-teentie figgary fell
> Ell dell dominell
> Urky purky taury rope
> An tan toosie Jock
> You . . . are . . . out!

That was alright. That was 'nice'. But the street-wise had another version that began . . .

> Azeentie-teentie haligolum
> Pitchin' totties up the lum . . .

No one cared to finish that, for fear of what rhymed with 'lum', but there was a local variation chanted out happily, that was peculiar to the area round Todd Street.

> Azeentie-teentie haligolum
> The cat went out to get some fun
> It got some fun in Toddy's grun'
> Azeentie-teentie haligolum.

Another incomprehensible ditty, reeled off to find a 'het' is recalled by Eileen Reilly.

> Chinese government, black man's *daugh*-ter
> Tra la la it's a very fine day
> The wind blows high, down from the sky
> And out goes Biddy with a big black eye . . .

. . . and the players circled round the counter-out, whose eyes were shut until, on the last word, she pointed to the Molly or the Biddy who was to be 'het'. Peggy Carson recalls another . . .

> . . . in the days when little Black Sambo was your friend and not your racial thing, there was Eenie-meenie-manny-mo. And I mind of Eevy-neevy-nick-nack.

Whatever the rhyme, the object was to find the one that would be catcher chaser or seeker. Simple 'het' games depended on nothing but three or four children at a loose end. There was Leave-O with chaser and chased, and a den that no self-respecting catcher 'mooched' for fear of the mocking chant . . . 'You're moochin' the den, you big fat hen!' And played universally among the closes was Robinson Crusoe. Bunty Angles and Eileen Reilly speak for over forty rememberers.

> Oh, you played Robinson Crusoe up and down all the closes, with the one that was 'het' away hiding somewhere in one of them. It was really scarey.
> It was eerie when you played near tea-time in winter . . . the calling up and down the closes in the gaslight. The one that was 'het' ran away into an entry (maybe up to the stair-heid or down to the dunny) with the rest shouting
> Robinson Crusoe, give us a call,
> Give us an answer or naethin' at all!
> He would answer in a wee squeaky voice or a gruff-gruff one and they'd to try and guess where he was and catch him before he ran back to the den.

For the girls there were 'statues', douce and lady-like for some, flamboyant and dramatic for the actresses among them. It was served by a low wall or, even better, the school-shed bench.

> Maybe five or six stood on the shed seat and the one that was 'het' gave her hand to each of the others and whirled them one by one down to the floor. They'd to stand stock still in whatever position they landed. Then she chose the best statue for the next whirler. If you moved or giggled you didn't get a shot at being 'het'.

Then there were roaming chains with sturdy leaders dislocating their shoulders to yank screaming enders off their feet. And there were all the versions of what one octogenarian called 'Hiding'-seek. Hiding-seek, Kee-hoy or High-spy . . . whatever they called it, if there was a tin can to be found, there was a new dimension that turned it all into High-spy-kick-the-can.

> I suppose right enough it was really *I*-spy, but in Glasgow we all called it *High*-spy. You done it just the same, except the first back to the den kicked the can, and got being the next 'het'.
>
> Th'were other games that you used *things* in . . . balls like. You stotted them against the wall and done wee complicated things between each stot, clapping your hands or twirling round. That was clappie or twirlie. Then you lifted your leg over it. Y'did all these things till you fumbled the ball. Then if you were just by yourself you began again, if not then it was someb'dy else's turn. Th'were wee rhymes too, to keep up the beat. I was stotting balls in the thirties and th'was one went . . .
>> Who's that walking down the street?
>> Miss-is Simpson on her feet.
>> She's been marr-ied twice't be-fore
>> Now she's chapping on *Ed-ward*'s door.

Skipping ropes in their season rocked and cawed and snaked under twinkling feet, to a dozen jingles.

> There was one . . . you skipped a few yourself, then you chanted,
>> 'I call in my sis-ter Ka-ty'
> and she'd to jink under the rope and in to jump along with you.

Eileen Reilly remembers 'French' ropes.

> You'd two enders with two ropes and you cawed them opposite ways. That was tricky. And then 'Belgium ropes' (sic). In Belgium ropes you

cawed at three-times the speed, so you'd to stay up in the air over the third caw. If you got a smack with the ropes in that, you got *some* weal!

It was your mother's old clo'es line you played with and if it wasn't heavy enough you'd to pleat three lengths together. Och, and your modesty went when you played ropes. You wrapped your skirt round your thighs and pulled your knickers over the top.

Peggy Carson . . .

Swinging the rope in a low snake was called 'wavy', and it was just for weans. 'High-low water' was kid stuff too! *It* was lifting the rope up a wee bit at a time, to jump over . . . not cawing or anything. You could make it a bit better by turning your wilkies over it, or doing a cart-wheel.

And peevers. Only the deprived small girls who had migrated to ash pavements and fancy houses in the suburbs, were non-peeverers. Lily Balarsky is sure that all the rest had peevers of some kind even if they were only boot-polish tins.

We'd all our peevers. Mine was always a nice piece of granite. See, we lived near the Clyde and there was always big piles of chips or stones on the quayside, ballast most likely, from the boats. You got good peevers there. And these piles y'know, we used to run up and down them . . . did that a lot . . . ran up and slid down. Ruined your shoes. And we used to get chased by the watchman. I s'pose that made it more fun.

If there wasn't a quorum for anything but *solo* peever your determined player, tired of that, might use her chalk to decorate her peerie, and then flex her whip for action.

You used different colours of chalk, and you made a design on the top so's when you whipped it and the peerie spun, you got a swirl of colour. Then you could wet your finger to rub it off and do a different pattern.

To some street-wise children tops were for weans, like 'high–low water' and 'wavy', for one of the deadliest put-downs they threw at timid players in other games was,

'Stick Bubbly . . . away an' spin yer peerie'.

I mind getting tormented like that by bigger ones when I was doing my peerie. But I just took my wee whip across their legs and it wasnae me that was bubbly then.

There must have been unisex city clachans where hoops and cleeks were for everyone and sang across the paving-stones for boys and girls alike . . . but that wasn't everywhere.

Up our street they were for the boys just. Th'was only one girl that ran wi' a gird. We thought she was a daft tomboy, and just got on wi' stotting our balls.

If the girls in *his* street sniffed at cleeking the hoops, Jack Roche didn't even notice.

Oh aye, we'd all our gir's. Nob'dy had a bike and the gir' was the next best to that . . . took you everywhere . . . miles it took you. It was wild. Great.
  If your gir' got broken or the wee ring came off, you'd to get it sorted at the smiddy. First time I went there I was frightened when the water fizzed on the red hot.

Come the summer children craiked at mothers and grannies for new marble bags, had a few practice-shots on the kitchen floor ready for real contests, and then went out to skech their bools or cley dawds across the pavement. Whatever Mario Servadei's forebears called them in Italy, he was sufficiently integrated to have 'jauries'.

Oh yes, I'd jauries all right . . . and glassies and steelies. And we'd all plunkers to flick at the marbles in a circle, a kind of kitty of them you'd to knock out for keepers.

That was 'Ringie' to some, and a form of 'Moshie' to others.

But the quickest way home from school was playing your ordinary jauries straight along the gutter. Y'know I'd a big tragedy once. There was a hole in my marble bag.

Bogies now . . . there was thrill. Even if earlier traffic wasn't the hazard it is in the 1990s when it would be unthinkable to hurl yourself down the likes of Hill Street, Millbrae or Battlefield Road on a bogie, it was nevertheless a perilous undertaking, and many a small boy scraped his boots to death, braking at the end of a one-in-eight gradient.

It was lethal, that game. And another risk was that Sergeant McTavish would chase you, and that would be the ba' on the slates . . . till the next time. Bogies was great!

So was doormats. Oh, there's hang-gliding and water ski-ing and all-your-orders now, but there were risks to be run in 1905 or 1906 riding down Whitehill Street on a foot-scraper. It's Miss Jenny Logan who remembers it now, but it was really all Tom McCulloch's fault!

He was my friend and he brought out one of these old wire mats. He had it on a string and I'd to sit on it while he pulled me down that hill. I'd on a little pink dress with white silk spots, and it was all into holes at the back with the dragging wire. My mother wasn't very pleased to say the least, and I never did that again.

Another who wasn't content with tame girlie ploys was Christina Rodger in Govan.

The men coming out the docks and the yard used to call me Tomboy Rodger. I played all the wild games with the boys, footb'll and kick-the-can . . . all that.

And who would deny her her fling . . . for there were harder times coming.

My mother died when I was thirteen and my father was an invalid that could just sit in his chair and tell me how to do things. I'd to leave the school to keep things going at home. So I was a wee housewife at thirteen. Not a schoolgirl any more.

And sadly not a tomboy either.

Let's close these pages on that glimpse of football, for Kirsty's gone home to her household chores, and most others to do their stint at coal-humphing and the brasses. She won't often be back out to play, but we can look forward in another chapter to a few more gegs and pastimes that the less trauchled of her playmates were still able to enjoy. And we can perhaps recall there an indoor game or two that even she can join in, between seeing to her scrubbing and cooking and clawting out the clinkers from her range fire.

6

Did you Ever Hear of a Tuppenny Hing?

Walk up Sauchiehall Street three Saturdays in a row and the buskers will have changed as many times. Break dancers will have given way to a twanging guitar or a couple of oboe students from the music college. But there's a whole tribe of more durable, kenspeckle characters remembered as having livened the streets of Glasgow in an older day . . . some busking like the tall paper-tearer outside the Cosmo Cinema or the grey-haired fiddler in Union Street, like the cloggie-dancers entertaining theatre queues. Some were simply familiar figures like the Clincher or the 'legless' beggar on Jamaica Bridge with those limbs akimbo'd out of sight under him, like the flower-seller outside the Georgic Tearoom, or Miss Cranston sweeping into one of her establishments. Those were uniques . . . recognisable, even nameable, people whose faces still linger in minds after well over half a century. But there were others, faceless as individuals perhaps, nevertheless remembered and regarded with affection as groups. Some gave the citizen a sense of security, or kept his streets clean and decent, some made him laugh or treated him to a song-for-a-penny, some by garb and habit gave a personality to Glasgow, peculiarly its own. Peggy Carson and Jimmy Dewar have clear memories of some of them.

> Remember the lamplighters tramping round with their poles? I mind the wee clatter when the glass flap went up and let the end of it through . . . then the 'plop' when the light came up and the wee tinkle of the flap going down again. We used to swing on the crossbars and it was a game to see how far you could dreep forward like the long-jump they do in the Olympics.

I liked the lamplighters, and one of my favourite poems at school
was,

My tea is nearly ready,
And the sun has left the sky,
It's time to take the windie,
To see Leerie going by.

That was Edinburgh right enough. But I remember them, all eerie in
the dark Glasgow closes. The men had wee ladders to get up to the gas
brackets in there. They lit them some different way from the pole they
used in the street.

And an eavesdropper chimes in . . .

Oh-here, I thought the wee ladder was for to change a mantle or
that, but I mind yon greenish kind of light falling all round the
lamp-post.

The policeman and the postman lit up dark corners too.

They had lamps. They would be oil I think at the time I'm talking about, but quite bright and they shone them into doorways. The postman had a smaller, flatter lamp but oil too, I suppose.

Little Jenny Logan's mother knew the worth of another civic servant and had firm strictures for her daughter about the crossing sweeper.

When I was small and going down Whitehill Street to Duke Street for messages, there were several streets that ran across those two and Mother used to warn me not to dirty my boots but cross where the sweepers kept the junctions clear of mud and droppings that made the rest of the streets dirty and muddy.

Then with a shake of her nonagenarian head she muses,

Crossing sweepers just kind of died out . . .

. . . slipping away unnoticed like old red telephone boxes now in the 1990s, and Scots pound notes.

By the end of the Second War 'shovellers' too were a dying breed, although they had been as regular a part of the scene as the official crossing sweepers. On very busy streets horse-droppings would be ground in by trundling cartwheels and Clydesdale hooves, but at quieter stretches they were prized by dung entrepreneurs as a saleable commodity in posh suburbs with gardens and scooped up while they were still steaming and pungent. One thing sure, the drivers felt no social responsibility.

You took not a blind bit of notice if your pony did it when you were on your way to the school in the trap in the mornings. Just left it for the rain or the boys with spades. They sold it round the doors out in the posh districts.

Another part of the army of cleansers was the whole battalion of stairwomen. Thorough or slittery, they clattered their buckets up and down wally closes whose tenants were above that sort of thing themselves, but who inspected their Glasgow-Style close-tiles when the women had finished and before they handed over their coppers. Unless the job was pre-paid.

Annie was our stairwoman. She was as thin as a twig and she'd a big feather hat that wafted and waved about as she scrubbed . . . and she wore men's boots. My mother sometimes left Annie's money in the pail of water at the door ready for her, if she was going out. I suppose she and others like her thought they were quite charitable to be employing these women.

Such ladies thought quite kindly too of those they called 'shawlies', and while they may not have wanted to *be* one themselves, there's no denying that they looked on these women, their babies held firm in their tartan plaids, with sentimental affection and some respect, as a colourful feature of the city's streets. Words like 'sensible' 'warm', 'a great support for the baby', (who was slung securely in the inner fold and happed close to her like a papoose) are trotted out in patronising admiration by those whose nurses or little housemaids wheeled out *their* weans to the park in handsome baby-carriages.

> I remember my mother, who was quite an elegant lady and very conscious of her social position, being dumbfounded by a query, quite innocent, from her washing-woman as she was hanging up a travelling-rug to dry. 'Was this Patricia's and Thomas's shawl when they were wee?' Mother afternoon-tea'd out on that one for many a long year.

There were shawlie-women to be seen wherever wage pokes did not allow the buying of coats or costumes. Mrs. Mysie Kyle recalls them firmly rooted in an area not far from her old home.

> Garngad Road was the home of the shawlie-women. I've heard folk say that they often went barefoot. But I don't remember that . . . and there wouldn't have been any need for it, because there were all those sugar-bags they could wrap round their feet, or they could wear slippers.

And what self-respecting woman would go barefoot if she could sally out in a pair of Tate and Lyle's designer swaddlings?

Sometimes the shawlies did venture out of their own haunts and into those of suburban folk. They came with sheets looped into bags, to buy the ladies' old clothes for a few coppers.

> I remember Mamma standing at the door of our house in Newlands haggling with an old clothes' wife over what the woman would give her for things she had no intention of ever wearing again. And the worst of it is, I thought at the time she was quite right . . . very thrifty, a good bargainer.

It's difficult to know what those good women would actually do
with the big-brimmed hats and feather-boas, or the waisted jackets
and hobble skirts . . . more suitable braws surely for the Sunday
noon promenades for which they had first been bought in the years
of Miss Alison Dow's childhood.

> I can only just remember. I must have been about four . . . before the
> First War, and it would've been Great Western Road on a Sunday after
> church, walking along with my parents. Mamma pushed my sister in
> a high pram. You met a lot of people doing that Sunday stroll there,
> with the men lifting their hats (I'm sure some were tall hats) and the
> ladies kind of dipping their parasols. The young men like my uncles
> had boaters. Then we used to go to my Grandma's for Sunday dinner. I
> don't remember much about my Grandpa except that he'd a silky beard
> I used to stroke, and a wee silver tube of water under his lapel for the
> flower he always had in his button-hole.

On weekdays Mammas surrendered their prams to their Nannies
and the afternoon baby walk was another familiar west-end scene.

> We lived out Sauchiehall Street and I can just about recall my Nana
> taking me with her when she pushed the big wicker pram with my
> wee brother, in the green bit in front of the crescents. Then she used
> to sit with other Nannies while we played. I do remember I'd a sailor
> suit with a big round hat and an elastic under my chin. I used to get
> a row for sucking that elastic and making my chin sore. I didn't like
> my Nana much. She used to push me by the shoulder and she sucked
> peppermints.

Social walking was a feature of bygone week-ends for all ages.
Peggy Carson and a dozen others recall their own versions of those
outings, the sight they presented, the people they met . . . or tried
to meet.

> Th'were a lot of places where people just walked, on Sunday
> afternoons. Th'were the family stretches of road, and then the young
> folks had theirs . . . I'm sayin' 'just walkin'' but it wasnae only that wi'
> the youngsters . . . och aye, th'was Victoria Road . . . Great Western
> Road . . . Alexandra Parade . . . even the Art Galleries was a great place
> for girls and fellas walkin', seein' if y'could get off . . . gettin' a 'lumber'
> . . . or gettin' a 'click' some of them used to call it. Didnae matter what
> you *called* it but. It was the same thing. I did it myself . . . Glasgow

Road or, if it was wet, the Art Galleries. But I got quite a likin' for pictures while I was at it there, and that never left me.

So the human scene in Glasgow shifts and changes and the tide of familiar figures ebbs and flows with day and night and changing season. But what of the landmarks? Each rememberer for these chapters has his or her own private trove of recollected places, some still there, others long gone. They lay to the north and south, the east and west and in the heart of the city itself. To the north young Janet Kay once walked by Glasgow's ancient stream.

> I used to walk along what had been the banks of the Molendinar to get to the Cathedral. Y'know they knocked down the old buildings in the Ladywell (och, that was sinful!). But when they did it, a part of the burn that hadn't been seen for ages, was exposed. Later on they covered it with a pipe and now I think you can maybe see a wee bit somewhere the other side of Duke Street.

And she has an odd little minding of the River Clyde too.

> When I was at Strathclyde school the river was very low at one period for some reason, from the weir to the part further up-country . . . just a mud hole really. And all the boys went out at playtime into it. What a glaury mess . . . paddling in the mud. And oh the stories that went about! You know, someone had found a diamond dagger or a Roman tool. Nothing of the kind, of course.

From the east end of the city comes a second-hand memory passed on to his grandson, the late Tom Watson, by Walter Freer the man they called Mr. Glasgow when he had the letting of its Burgh Halls early in the century . . . a memory of Freer's that puts the Great Eastern and the Portugal Street 'models' up there with the Hiltons and the Holiday Inns of the world.

> Did you ever hear of a Tuppenny Hing? It's hard to credit, but it seems when my grandfather was young, a down-and-out could go to some miserable dark cellar where there were ropes slung across, and for tuppence he could 'hing' over it with the rope under his oxters so he could get a sleep without lying on a filthy floor among others who paid nothing or maybe just a penny.

Jack Roche had heard of the 'hing' too and thought it had a later refinement.

Like what you do on the footb'll terracing I s'pose.

Such social recollections of a rougher Glasgow belong not to the fine displays at Kelvingrove or other conventional museums but in the startling exhibitions of ordinary life housed in the People's Palace.

That east end building is a monument to Glasgow's industrial past and those scantly-paid men and women who slaved to make it great and its merchants wealthy.

When I was a teacher in a Maryhill school nearly fifty years ago we'd always the yearly concert in the Burgh Hall. There were big stained-glass windows all round there, showing the different work the Maryhill folk did . . . there was boat-building, blacksmithing, railway work, glass-blowing and other crafts. I think they're maybe in the People's Palace now.

For over ninety years the Palace has been a Mecca for family outings, perhaps they go to reassure themselves that the history of ordinary citizens is no less colourful or important than that of the Tobacco Lords or Merchant Princes.

It wasn't all-that old when I used to go there with my father. We saw all about what the old working-class life had been like and went to the concerts in the Winter Garden . . . and then tea, I remember. He used to say the big glass hall was built like a ship, but I couldn't see that, unless it was upside down.

From over in the west-end of the city come memories that seem to hark back to a more rural past.

I was born in 1900 wi' the century, and reared in Byres Road. My granny used to say th'was cow-sheds there in the old days. Other folk said that was rubbish, that 'Byres' was a man's name. But y'know there was the Cow Loan and the Goose-dubs in the centre of Glasgow; so why no' there on the outskirts? I think I believe my granny.

Some of the recollections of places to the south of the river belong to a pastoral age too . . . like one of Mrs. Nell Dinsmor's.

There was a thatched cottage near us and when I was wee there was a fire there and it was gutted. My father took me in his arms up to see it and watch the fire brigade . . . but so's I wasn't in the way of the sparks.

And there's a picture of craftsmen at work near the village of Pollokshaws.

> There were still weavers in the weavers' cottages beyond the Wellmeadow laundry when I was young . . . old-old cottages they were.

Nearby too, was the aptly-named Picken's orchard.

> . . . opposite the Pollok Park gate. Lovely red apples you got there for a penny.

Unlike other less worthy small boys who knew the place, the speaker virtuously denies ever 'scrumping' them.

> I remember the day old Mr. Picken sold up. I've still got leek-onions in my garden that I got that day, the kind with wee bulbs at the top of the stem. I can still see him standing there telling us to take what we wanted of his raspberry canes or his Egyptian onions, and tears in his eyes.

And no suggestion that the tears were other than those of genuine grief.

The Rodger sisters remember the landmarks and sights of their days in Govan.

> We were brought up there under the big shipyard cran. D'you remember the hooters and the men streaming in and out Stephen's Yard with their piece-boxes? Stephen started with whalers out off the north-east coast somewhere y'know.

Another tale of Govan tells of the origin of the sheep's head carried on the pole in the Govan Fair procession.

> Seems some local minister quarrelled with a young man that was courting the manse maid-servant. Didn't think he was suitable (or maybe he didn't want to lose a good worker) anyway, he wouldn't let the boy come courting. The chap killed one of the minister's best glebe sheep to pay him back. He got the girl in the end and that's why the sheep's head got put on the pole to celebrate.

A happier recollection is cherished of a café at Spiersbridge.

> I minda Capaldi's place opposite the Rouken Glen yonder. It was a big hut sorta place wi' a verandah and fadin' blue paintwork, if I mind

right. And th'was rickety tables where you could sit and lick your slider or poky hat. Or if you were posh, take it from a dish wi' a wee flat wooden spoon. Och aye, and did you ever have a raspberry McCallum?

The city's Tolls and Crosses hold special myths and memories of their own, and the demolition of at least one of those quarters is cursed as desecration. Miss Janet Kay is as outraged about Charing Cross as she was about the destruction in the Ladywell.

Charing Cross! I'll never forgive them for what they did to Charing Cross. Scandalous. It was a landmark. It was *beautiful* . . . And what is it now? Nothing! With a silly half bridge going nowhere.

But then it's maybe a wee while since she's been there to see how 'them' have begun to expiate their sins at Charing Cross. But the same lady knows her Crosses.

Bridgeton Umbrella. D'you know the Bridgeton Umbrella at the Cross? I remember unemployed men . . .

(Sadly so do folk sixty years younger, but those Janet Kay recalls were the workers of the thirties) . . .

. . . standing at the Cross in their bunnets and mufflers. Once when I was very wee I was told that some workmen came along with a ladder, to fix the four-face clock there. The men in the bunnets gave them a hand to sklim up and then went back to the chat or their pitch'n'toss and paid no more heed. Well that night the clock didnae strike, and–here the innards had been stolen. There was just the face left.

The memories move south. John Adamson, knocking out his pipe on what passes for the heart-warming range of his youth, tells of a more ancient legend about a pub near Shawlands Cross, up from Crossmyloof.

Ever since I was wee (and I don't know how long before that) above the doors of that pub at the corner of Langside Avenue there's been a hand with a cross on it. They say that it was at that spot that Mary, Queen of Scots handled her crucifix before the battle of Langside, and swore to fight her enemies 'by the cross on my loof' (hand) . . . It's s'posed to be that that's what gave Crossmyloof its name.

Across the road stood another Shawlands feature of past days.

Th'was a fountain opposite Marlborough House and I mind my mother always telling me no' to drink out the iron cup that used to hang over it on a chain. If you were awful thirsty she said, you'd to hold your finger across between the rim and your lip and drink over that.

A mile south along the road, the Round Toll-house at Pollokshaws is now no more than a clinical, council-used cleaned-up relic of its heyday, isolated on a busy roundabout.

But when I was young it had a lovely rockery in the garden and there was a date-stone lying at the side of the house . . . from the seventeen hundreds sometime. I was upset when that stone disappeared. The lady who lived there when I was small kept hens that scratched about the yard.

Another house recalled from the same early century period is Old Mains House, Giffnock. Miss Jenny and Miss Mabel Logan speak of it.

Old Mains House is mentioned in one of John Galt's books and John Watson who lived there when we were young restored one of the rooms as it would have been in John Galt's time two hundred years ago.

Let's take the route back to town through the old tunnel under the Clyde to another Cross. Miss Christina Ronnie remembers making that journey.

We lived just a stone's throw from the old tunnel with the round buildings at each end . . . where the flowers were a year or two ago (the Garden Festival). We used to walk through to shop at Anderston Cross. Took you out just down from Argyle Street.

There was early car traffic too, from one rotunda to another and Ninette McDonald recalls being part of that.

I went to Park School in town and if I was a bit late I was driven through the tunnel for a short cut.

But, of course it's from the old heart of the city where the pulse beats faster that the most colourful traditions linger . . . not only from living memory, but from the days when sheep grazed the Green, women tubbed their linen and city soldiers drilled there.

> You can still see the place at Glasgow Green where Bonnie Prince Charlie reviewed his troops. I'm quite interested in that because my own family was divided over the Forty-five, or so they say. And do you remember the story about him demanding boots for his army and being fobbed off with a whole consignment of boots . . . all for one foot.

That's one tale, but someone else was 'no sure about that story'

> There was many a one at that time just had two boots with never a difference between right and left anyway . . . so even if it's true maybe it wouldnae've mattered.

Long before Bonnie Prince Charlie inspected his army there, or the Regent Moray raised his standard for the tramp to Langside, the Green was called the Bishop's forest. It was overgrown, wooded scrubland for the exclusive use of the cathedral community and its guests. Over the centuries it has known additions and subtractions until the days when Janet Kay was taken there as a child . . .

> . . . to see the big Doulton fountain and hear the public speakers ranting on about Temperance or Religion or maybe Politics . . . rare speakers some of them, mind. Or so my father used to say. I used to get taken too, to see what I called 'the iron men'. They're not there now, though I'm not sure where they were then. It was just a railing with a man's head at the top of each post.*

Not far from where young Janet saw her 'iron men', Peggy Carson witnessed a sight that must surely have been one of the last of its kind on the Clyde.

> Would be in the early thirties that I saw a sailing-ship coming in at the Broomielaw . . . a sailing ship! My father said it was bringing in paper. I've never forgot that ship . . .

*Elspeth King, Glasgow's Depute keeper of local History writes:
   The 'Iron Men' were the main support posts of the cast iron railings between Glasgow Green and Monteith Row . . .
and adds that they were stripped out for melting down in the Second War.

And she recalls visits he made with her to the Tent Hall in a street to the east of that brave sight on the river, and things he pointed out to her on the way.

> He used to take me on a Sunday morning to see the free breakfast getting served to the poor and the wee bit entertainment they got along with it. On our road there in the Saltmarket opposite the Briggait, he used to point out the medallion things carved high on the tenements. And-here just recently I saw they were still there . . . all cleaned up with a rose in the middle of one, then a thistle and a daffodil and a shamrock in the others. 'Look up,' my father always used to say, 'Look up, and you'll see things'.

Or 'Look around' he might as easily have said, as another father did in the twenties when he walked across George Square daily to his work.

> He was a great one for giving you wee ways of remembering things . . . like the statues in the Square. It's been seventy years and I can still reel them off.
> 'Poets Campbell, Burns and Scott
> Victoria, Albert, Peel and Watt
> Oswald, Glasgow's first M.P.
> Corunna Moore and Cambell C.
> Gladstone's stony face of flint
> Graham who ran the Royal Mint.'

As a last call for this chapter, it's maybe fitting to make a visit with the late Mr. Tom Watson to the old Tolbooth at the very heart of Glasgow.

> My grandfather told me that because Cameron of Locheil talked Bonnie Prince Charlie out of ransacking Glasgow for not supporting him, the city fathers gave the Camerons the right to have the Tolbooth steeple bells rung for them whenever they visited Glsagow in the future. Still got that right.

But a new age was dawning from that of Tom Watson's grandfather, and there are memories of new toys on Glasgow thoroughfares. Robert Ford remembers . . .

> The first car ever I saw was an Arrol-Johnston '18.

And out in Giffnock Mr. Robert Anderson of Eastwoodhill was driving another from the same stable, an Arrol-Johnston six-seater. There was awe at first then, in no time at all, his neighbours were totting up their savings and following his lead, and soon after an alarmed local authority felt forced to impose a ten-mile-an-hour speed limit through the suburb, and the revolution from cartwheels to Dunlops was underway.

7

Paddys and Biddys

Perhaps life became too earnest when youngsters went to the Big School, too fast moving and with too many different teachers, for the now elderly to be able to pin down as great a number of recollections as they had of younger days. But most of those were vivid and mostly, if not universally, appreciative.

One rememberer recalls doing Latin translation for a redoubtable Classics lady in Hutchesons' Grammar School.

> I got a bit fanciful with the meanings and she just looked at me as she handed back my exercise. 'Isobel Horn, words fail me!'

But they didn't often fail the same sturdy lady with her high bun of hair and trailing gown, and many a Hutchie 'bug' remembers wincing as she boomed out warnings at marching lines winding up the stairs, and yet learning to appreciate her continuing interest in them, long after schooldays. 'Puella stupida!' was a favourite verdict on a struggling pupil.

> That voice, my, my, that voice! She was a one-off . . . unique.

In her turn Janet Kay left Strathclyde Elementary for John Street Higher Grade.

> That was a great school with Mr. Paterson and Miss Fish . . .

and as she passed out with some distinction from their hands, Jimmy Dewar was starting at Shawlands Academy. There's no doubt that, from its first days, Shawlands Academy was a centre of academic excellence, though his account of his homework there does not conjure up a sense of high expectations from teachers or visions of lamp-light slavery to be ready for next day.

> I mostly walked from Pollokshaws Round Toll to Shawlands Cross, but sometimes I took a pennyworth home in the tram. We used to do

our homework on the tram . . . up the stairs and out in the wee front
compartment with the sliding door.

Not a very heavy burden of prep, if it could be accomplished in
the five stops between the Cross and the Round Toll. Perhaps
the sketchy attention to homework was because there was, on
the whole, less awe of teachers in the secondary than in the

elementary school. Older pupils were shrewder too in assessing them as people, and how far they could be pushed. Some, like Mysie Kyle simply sized them up physically.

> I remember the headmaster at Whitehill School was called 'Spondy'
> . . . Spondy Smith . . . because he'd big feet (that was a sort of Latin
> nickname meaning 'bear's feet').

A door or two along from Spondy's room in the same school reigned Paddy McGlynn remembered by Struan Yule.

> All the men teachers were Paddys and the women were Biddys. Any-
> way we used to do all sorts of things with ink. When we were starting
> a test maybe one boy would put up his hand and say that he'd no ink.
> Paddy would say, 'Follow me, boy'. This was to go and get ink.
> Another boy and then another would join in and there would be a trail
> of maybe a dozen trudging along after Paddy to get their inkwell filled.

Shrewder teachers brought the ink to the room.

> There was this big-big jar of ink wi' the wee spout, kept by the jannie,
> and if you were top of the class you got taking it round on a Friday
> to fill the inkwells.

Some waited eagerly for the full well and dropped in a wee lump of calcium carbide to make the ink fizz; others doused bullets of blotting paper and flicked them silently about the room with rulers. And Paddy McGlynn suffered another indignity . . . not with ink though.

> He used to report on Schools football for the Evening Times and sat up
> late writing his column. Sometimes next day he'd nod off and let his
> bald head drop forward. We used to pick wee crumbs off our rubbers
> and flick them at his head to waken him up.

The teachers themselves, mind you, weren't above a little back-sliding.

> I went to Sir John Stirling Maxwell school. I was never any other-
> where in Glasgow for I was away a few years with a sister in Pitlochry
> after my mother died. I remember two teachers at Sir John's when I
> was pretty-up in the school. They were in love, I think, and instead
> of teaching the children they were too busy talking and kissing at the
> partition door.

Whether such evidence of an amorous liaison would have stood up
in court that's how it was seen and rumoured in the playground at
the 'Shaws.

But like their elementary counterparts, the Paddys and the
Biddys did try to engage their charges in more cultural pursuits,
like music and poetry.

> We'd one called McIntyre at Whitehill who taught us singing. He
> told us about projecting the voice and getting the consonants right.
> A lot paid no attention of course but he was quite easy-osey.
> 'Please yourselves,' says-he. 'It cost me twenty-five guineas in
> Milan to learn to do this properly, and here you are getting it
> for *nothing*'. I quite liked the singing myself though, and I went
> into the school choir . . . sang 'Who's dat a-calling?' in the City
> Hall.

As for poetry . . . there were negatives as well as positives to
Eileen Reilly's recollections of verse-speaking and its enunciation.

> Sometimes we wrote poetry. I wrote one on 'Autumn' and I was very
> proud of it.
>> Autumn is a lady who paints the leaves all brown,
>> She sends them flying in the air to fall upon the groun,

> Singing softly to the roses, she sends them all to sleep,
> She wants us all to love her and mem'ries of her keep.

The priest was in the school that day and I was taken by the teacher to
say it aloud to him. They both smiled but I knew fine why, because
I wasn't stupid . . . It was because I'd written 'groun' for groun*d*,
because that was the way I said it.

Perhaps this carelessness with consonants was repeated at home
because we hear next of young Miss Duffy being sent for
corrective treatment.

An elocution teacher came to school to take pupils privately, for a small
fee. My parents did everything possible for me so I was sent to the
elocution. We started by saying familiar words like GIRL. Now here
was me thinking I was Glasgow through and through, but I'd been
reared by Irish parents and I said Geu'l. The teacher looked shocked at
me, 'You can't birl your Rs'. So there was I *branded* as one who couldn't
birl her Rs . . . as well as put a D on her groun'! I felt different, inferior.
And there was worse, because when I spent the summers in Ireland I
was odd man out there too, being *Scottish*. Never mind, I liked the
elocution and some of the poems we got to say. But not them all.
There was one called 'Mother' . . . kind of sickening really.

> O Mother my love if you give me your hand,
> And go where I ask you to wander,
> I will lead you away to a beautiful land,
> The dreamland that's waiting out yonder . . .
> . . . and I'll rock you asleep on a silver dew stream,
> And sing you to sleep when you're weary,
> And no one shall know of our beautiful dream,
> But you and your own little dearie.

Oh no! that was awful, but I liked one about Kew Gardens.

> Go down to Kew in lilac time,
> In lilac time, in lilac time.
> Go down to Kew in lilac time,
> It isn't far from London.
> And you shall wander hand-in-hand,
> With love in summer's wonderland.
> Go down to Kew in lilac time,
> It isn't far from London.

I liked the rhythms of that.

Schooldays passed eventually and the future beckoned. For
most, in early decades, it was the real and earnest world of waged

work. For others, more fortunate there were further studies ahead.
For a very few it was possible to combine the two. Struan Yule had
joined the editorial side of things in *The Glasgow Herald*, on the
Stock Market and Business page.

> Since my work then was at night I could go to University classes
> during the day . . . burned the candle at both ends.

Another student career of those days, not entirely conventional,
was that of Miss Jenny Logan.

> It was during the First War so a lot of young men were away and
> university taboos on women eased a bit. Before that most women
> who studied at all were at the Normal School (for teacher training)
> or at Queen Margaret College. So I was in one of the first real mixed
> classes at university.

At that time and for thirty more years the University of
Strathclyde was still the 'Tech'.

> When I went there first we heard a lot about the founder John
> Anderson. They called him Jolly Jack Phosphorus . . . some said
> because he was a chemist, others that he'd a fiery temper.

Not everyone enjoyed further education.

> I went to university, Gilmorehill, but I didn't like it much. I did get
> a First Class Honours degree in Modern Languages . . . but a bonnie
> lot of good it did me. I taught for a time in a small private school for
> girls . . . not very well known. It didn't survive.

Nor, as a reluctant teacher, did that rememberer. Perhaps her first
choice would have been music but that didn't seem to the family
'safe' and she was denied it.

> I think I was allergic to education . . . unless it was something I really
> wanted to do.

At either of those degree-course establishments the young spent
three or more years . . . long enough to enjoy the traditional
college life-style. Others equally qualified, but for whom the need
was more pressing to put in their pennyworth to the household
kitty, took shorter courses or went to evening classes.

I went to night school in the twenties to learn book-keeping. You got
your first year free. But I kept on going until I was twenty-one.

I'd to take a job whenever I left school. But I'd an uncle helped me to
go to classes and I learned a lot there about business. Later I was able to
set up as a kind of agent for ironmongery an' that. Did very well really
but that was thanks to my uncle. And he wasn't all that well-off.

It's a hundred and twenty years since Glasgow School Boards
had all its youngsters compulsorily with a Paddy or Biddy. In the
1960s, and retired after a long career of teaching in city schools,
Jenny Logan continued to put the experience of those years to
use delving into the educational archives in the basement of the
City Chambers. This was in preparation for celebrations at the
centenary of official schooling. Maybe she discovered that here,
and there and elsewhere in Scotland, a child slipped through the
net and did not enjoy his or her full entitlement of sand trays and
subtraction, books and beltings. Take young Alex Donnelly born
in Calton thirty years after that Education Act.

My father was killed at the Dardenelles when I was thirteen. There
were five younger than me so I just had to leave the school.

But if that seems like the end of education for Master Donnelly,
tune in to other chapters and follow his appetite for self-
improvement.

Another of the same breed was Mr. Robert Ford, who started
life in Portpatrick.

I'd three miles to walk to the school. I was wee for my age so I didnae
go till I was seven. They weren't so partic'lar in those days. Then
the Great War came and with me being twelve and about two years
behind, and my father having the croft, I just left the school to work
with him. Anybody that could work the land was just let work. So I'd
just the five years at school.

Like Alex Donnelly he refused to leave it at that.

Later on I went to night-school and was taken on by a joiner. I learned
that trade and studied geometry and other subjects till I was over thirty.
But I'd always missed out on English so I took an interest myself in
poetry, wrote some and read some and learned quite a lot by heart

. . . Cocker and Service and Scott and, of course Burns . . . going to Burns' Suppers with James Currie and so on, y'know . . .

Robert Ford had done it the hard way but as he sits now going over some of his own verses, reminiscing in the suburban home built fair and square with his own skilled hands . . . and declaiming without a note over a hundred lines of William Landles' narrative poem 'Herod and John' it can only be said that Portpatrick's loss was Glasgow's gain and that his self-acquired education has served him as well as most who had twice as long at school.

8

Nellie Kelly Smoked a Pipe

They talk a lot these days about modern work expertise and the sophisticated high-tech education required to master it. But looking across the whole range of waged occupations of eighty and ninety years ago, remembered here, one gets the feeling that the young of the 1990s might easily find the skills of their 'simple' forebears quite beyond them.

Before describing their own life-work many rememberers recalled that of parents and grandparents, often hard darg unbuffered by Health Insurance . . . no work, no money.

Perhaps the earliest livelihood spoken of, was that earned by Mrs. Agnes Grove's great-grandfather who kept a pub in the Cubie Street area about the time that George IV and William IV were on the throne in the 1820s and 1830s. But it's the work of her own father that she recalls as an everyday part of her own early life.

He was a tailor and cutter. He'd been at the Buchanan Institute near the Glasgow Green when he was young. It was for fatherless boys and they were taught trades there. It was the tailoring for him. His mother would be working, so he had all his meals there too. I remember him working at home . . . in the Room . . . legs crossed on the table. Said that's how he was bow-legged. But all tailors sewed like that, to keep their materials up beside them. When he was making a suit I had to pick up all the clippings . . . that was called 'the woollen' and my mother sold it at the rag store for a few pence.

Her grandmother was in textiles too, working a Jacquard loom in Templeton's.

Aye, the Doges' Palace* y'know. And she used to take me up by Parkhead and Tollcross, and through the windows you could see in the single-ends some of the handloom weavers doing piecework with home looms . . . eighty years ago, easy.

That was weaving on quite a heavy-weight scale, but Mrs. Millicent Davis's grandfather worked with finer materials.

He was a silk merchant trading a lot in the Far East. There was a man he dealt with in Prestwick (it was quite a remote village in my grandparents' time). He was called Rab and he was one of the last of a colony of handloom silk weavers. Rab was very old at the end of last century so he must have been working in early Victorian times. I still have some of his silk . . .

*The architects of Templeton's carpet factory, built in 1889 to replace the original mill, designed it as a replica of the Doges' Palace in Venice.

. . . a hundred years old now, a prized possession reverently handled and shown off.

Dr. Ellis Barnett cherishes memories of his father Bernard, another of those young Jewish men of the early century whose sufferings in Lithuania drove him to 'get on a boat' to look for better things elsewhere. After some years learning his trade in South Africa, 'elsewhere' became the Glasgow Gorbals where he set up as a shoemaker in Crown Street and quickly endeared himself to the community.

> It was a tough place then with youngsters roaming wild and breaking windows. Instead of chasing them my father started what he called the 'Gorbals Pals Club' with about four hundred in it. He had membership cards for them and gave every one a Saturday penny every week . . . ticked their cards to stop them coming twice.

The shop was a kind of Lost Property depot too.

> If a child got lost in the Gorbals he always knew how to get to my father's shop and his mother would find him there.

Small wonder his clientele, when they were solvent, bought their shoes from him.

> He'd once a man just out of jail coming in for shoes when he hadn't even a pair of socks on his feet. He bought the shoes and got the socks free.

Even when he prospered, Bernard's tastes remained simple.

> He'd a small office and when a wealthy acquaintance asked why he didn't get himself a big place like the man's own, he had a typical reply. 'Friend,' he said. 'One day you and I will both be in a smaller place than this. It'll be a shock for you. But not for me.'

Another, feeling his way in a new culture was Mrs. Lily Joseph's father from Russia. He found work close to where the immigrant community had settled.

> Came here in 1897 and got his first job where a lot of foreigners worked, at a tobacco factory near the Saltmarket Bridge.

Perhaps one of his workmates was Lily Balarsky's mother, a lady

with drive and the adaptability to leave lack of opportunity behind
and turn her hand to anything in her adopted country.

> They were ready to try whatever turned up and when she first came
> to Glasgow she worked, like a lot of Jewish folk, rolling cigarettes at
> a factory not far from where they lived.

Her father was flexible too and had several strings to his bow.

> He was a jack-of-two-or-three trades. He mainly sold drapery from a
> suitcase . . . all over Scotland. Then he'd a wee sideline with a friend
> in Oxford Street who was very good at repairing watches my father
> collected on his rounds. And another line was selling lengths of tartan
> cloth that a friend wove. I went with him to Invergordon to sell bits
> and pieces and the tartan to English sailors. We went out to a navy ship
> in a wee ferry. And at home I used to run to Oxford Street to deliver
> and collect the watches.

Millicent Davis's other grandfather worked on a grander engineering scale than watchmaking.

> He built the big crane at Govan. It was a landmark, the biggest in the
> world at one time.

And perhaps even grander than that, must have been the proud
task of Mr. Rodger, the skilled operator who worked it.

> My father driv the big Govan crane . . . for years. Then one day he
> took a shock up there on it and he never worked again. I was just
> young then.

What Ann Hutchison's father driv was his beloved horse,
Nancy, and his pride was in the quality of his firewood.

> He'd a real nice cart with his logs and briquettes and sticks. It was never
> rubbish wood my Daddy sold . . . never yon dry rot stuff . . . not at
> all! He used to take his cart to Port Glasgow and bring back pine logs.
> Oh, what a lovely smell! We'd all to help chop it into wedges then bag
> it to sell for about a shilling a bag.

There are niceties in every job and Mr. Hutchison observed his
own tight code of behaviour.

> He never-ever shouted from his cart, my Daddy, not like some.
> Never. He'd his regulars every week that he went round just.

Two who would have approved of his fine wood were Struan Yule's father and grandfather.

Everything to do with wood my grandfather did. Early on he was a brewers' cooper, then a joiner, cabinet-maker and funeral undertaker. My father was a cabinet-maker too.

Alex Donnelly's recollections of his father's trade give a real glimpse into a couthy old Scottish world, long long gone and scarcely remembered now. He too was a skilled craftsman . . . his medium not wood but clay.

Aye, my father had a wee clay-pipe work in the Gallowgate. I used to play guns wi' the moulds there. They'd to serve seven year to be a right pipe-maker. They got the clay fae Cornwall, steeped the big block in a byne of water to soften it. Then they cut off a slobbery dod and divided it up into bits like a bunch of bananas. They pushed each one into a half mould wi' the name DONNELLY engraved on it and got a needle thing to make the bore in the stem. The women trimmed the mould and put the extra back into the clay. No waste see. Then they touched it up all neat and put the two sides together and polished it. Each worker had her own number on wee cubes of clay and she put them beside her finished pipe . . . piece-work see. Men got the pipes free in the pubs wi' their pints. Other places it was a ha' penny or a penny. Forbye the pipes, they made pipe-clay squares for doin' the closes . . . farthing a square . . . In Ireland later, when I was busking, you often seen a couple there havin' puff about of the one clay, by their turf fire. No' many women in Glasgow smoked the pipe but. No' when I was young.

An eavesdropper knew one though . . .

. . . old Nellie Kelly that worked for us did.

Real Glasgow that, clay-pipes and pipe-clay. So too were the toffee 'balls' and the 'ginger' made at the factory run by Mysie Kyle's father and destined for sale at the city's oldest building.

When my father had the lemonade and toffee-making place he supplied Mistress Haddow in the wee shop in Provand's Lordship. The bottles went in wooden crates on the horse-lorry. For making the toffee he'd a hook on the wall and he took the hot toffee with flour on his hand and pulled and stretched it till it was golden, then he mixed it with the dark stuff, rolled it out so it was striped, and then cut it up.

Poles apart from that old Glasgow, and seemingly bizarre in the midst of city life, except perhaps as a lingering echo of a more rural town of 17th century cottages and grazings, is the home Christina Ronnie and her sister Mary Brisbane remember from their youth. Mrs. Ronnie first . . .

I was born in a two-room and kitchen tenement in McLean Street, Plantation, out Govan Road. My mother was a farmer there with cows and chickens and there were horses in the stable there. Th'was a big backcourt for all the houses and the cows were in a cobbled pend. She used to take them up Craigwell Street Wee-Brae to the grazing in a field over Ibrox way. I never heard of any other farm like that. The byre was in the back too and th'was a dung midden. My mother worked hard, milking the cows and that, and in the dairy she had, on the front street. I still have her milking-stool and the wee tub she had for making butter. And I always mind when she worked wi' the cows she wore what was called a 'shorgun'. It came to just below the waist and th'was wide petticoats under that, and a sacking apron. My father was an invalid so we depended on her wi' the farm and the dairy. She sold her own butter and eggs and milk there . . . and baking. She needed us too. 'Chrissie,' she'd say before school in the morning, 'churnin' the night, mind. Hurry home.' The churning with the first plunger-churn we had was like doin' washing the old way . . . plunge and twist, plunge and twist. Then we got a barrel one, with a handle to caw. All I got for doing that was a drink of buttermilk wi' the wee pearls of butter left in it. No pay. It was hard.

A man who by then was devoting his working energies to making life more than bare survival for such families was a neighbour of Mrs. Dinsmor's family in Barrhead.

My father was friendly with Jimmy Maxton, and my mother with his sister, Annie. (Jimmy was a widower and Annie brought up young Jimmy that I played with.) Many's the time I was in that house. He was a gentle, nice man Jimmy Maxton and he worked hard. There's a Maxton garden now in Barrhead that was put there by his friends in the House of Commons, even in other parties. Churchill put to it too. He was that popular. The M.P. for Bridgeton he was, I.L.P.

But friendship can be stretched too far for a strict mother to thole.

For a while my father took us to the I.L.P. Sunday school. Not for long though. My mother was a Quaker and saw to it that we went to the right Sunday School.

Apart from Millicent Davis's family, who had a three-generation connection with Fairfield's, there wasn't much dynastic continuity in the work of most rememberers. A few skills descended to a son or daughter but, as technical progress made their crafts redundant, seldom further. Of those few the young Rodgers of McLean Street had little alternative at first to carrying on at least part of their mother's work. Mary, now Mrs. Brisbane, remembers her share in that.

After my mother died we gave up the cows, but we kept on the chickens and the dairy. We bought in butter and milk for that. Folk used to come in for one egg, a pennyworth of milk, a wee loaf and a penny packet of tea. Dockers just got twelve shillings a week then . . . before 1920. My oldest sister did the shop but I used to go out at six o'clock in the morning before school wi' the milk in cans, a whole row of them clattering on my arm . . . two-pint, one-pint and half-a-pint. I'd to chap all the doors up the closes, up four stairs, then collect the emptied cans on the way down again. Cream too . . . just a gill people would get.

All the Rodger brothers went off to sea.

They went as 'dunkey' men, that was ships' greasers. So th'was just the girls left at home. It was hard times. Nothing coming in but from the dairy. The area got to be rundown and rough-spoken. But we never-ever swore or anything. My mother wouldn't't've had that at all. I was behind yon counter from ten-year-old and full-time at fourteen. We'd the big ten-gallon cans to scour and scald, and when the boats came in up the Clyde at night we'd to open up and sell them bread and milk and that. Later the factor gave us a better shop across the road.

When their mother died Chrissie took over the house and the nursing of their father.

May was young at the school at first, and my other sister Effie done the shop. (Mind I had delivered the early morning milk for a while . . . got exemption from the school till half-past nine for that) but I was fourteen now and I was to be in charge of the house, and nursing my father for the next five years till he died. I'd to bath him every Sunday.

Income was low and state help non-existent, and when the girls were finally left alone it was big decision time for Chrissie.

I couldnae think to stay in the house and I wasnae one for the shop so I decided that it would be a help if I went into service. Effie and May didnae like it, but I went temporary to my first place, that was to a part of the family that Angus Ogilvie's of now. I went to Gryffe Castle, Bridge of Weir . . . done the kitchen work and the cooking there. Then I went back to the Domestic Registry for another place. A lady looking for someone interviewed me there for a scullery maid rising to cooking. Her place was at Comlongen Castle near Dumfries. I said 'Aye' I would dae't. She pushed a shilling across the table. 'What's that for?' says-I. She said it was my word that I would come, and her word that she would have me.

So Christina Rodger was 'arled' to Comlongen Castle and into a long life of Service. We can't follow her here through the list of her fortunes and misfortunes, colleagues, employers and kitchens: the skinning of game, the plucking of fowl, the burnishing of copper, the high life of the London Season in Park Lane, the romance begun when she was in 'Dunragit Big Hoose'. There's a novel in there somewhere, but not for these pages and we must leave her, earning her monthly two pounds and sending home the precious share of it to make things easier in McLean Street.

The old building there . . . everything's away now, nothing left.

Except the recipe for the dairy's dumpling, of which a delectable slice was carried home by the compiler of these notes after her meeting with Mrs. Brisbane.

Agnes Grove was another who followed family footsteps, though not at first.

I went to the paper-bag-making near Glassford Street when I left school. You done all the folding and pasting and you got fivepence for a thousand bags. You'd to get quick at it or starve! But then I went into Templeton's . . . not the big building at first, but the shed at the back. Ocht, but Templeton's was better'n the paper pokes. It was treadle looms and we wove the chenille to be wound round big drums to go and be made into carpets.

'Chenille' was for the French 'caterpillar' and described the hairy surface produced by the loom on one side of the fabric which, bonded to a jute backing, James Templeton had long before realised would make a sturdy carpet.

At the looms you worked from a chart card that told you how many shots to do in this or that colour, twelve shuttle shots to the inch. I always wanted to see the finished article, but you never did. The backing was done at a factory in West Street. You got five shillings a week for the fortnight you learned, and when you got your own loom you'd to pay back that ten shillings before you got any more pay. That was all early in the century. Templeton's did the carpet for the White House Oval Room y'know, and for the *Queen Mary*.

After a variety of schoolboy jobs Jimmy Dewar went to sea. His father had been a sea-travelling salesman, but Jimmy was a bona fide sailor.

Magical life it was. Before that I was in a stevedore's office, but all I could think of were the wonderful ships coming in from Hong Kong, Malaya, Yokohama. So I joined a ship and started off to sea . . . all over the world, into all the ports. I loved it.

While this son of Glasgow was off on his travels the Servadei family arrived.

It was mostly ice-cream, that Italians went into . . . don't know why really. Very few of them made it in Italy. But it was an opening here. That and fish and chips. Don't get them in Italy either. Hairdressing was another thing. My father had trained as a hairdresser in Genoa and when he came here before the First War he worked at that for an uncle. Then he set up on his own and when I grew up I went in with him.

Angelo Lamarra settled for the ice-cream . . . at first in the way most familiar of all to four generations of young Scotland.

I went out at first pushing an ice-cream barrow in Falkirk . . . STOP

ME AND BUY ONE y'know . . . all round the streets. Then we came to Glasgow and I worked in a café in Parliamentary Road, purely a café . . . the real thing y'know, marble tables with iron legs. I served over the counter too.

Then he graduated to that other matchless skill of the true Glasgow Italian.

. . . a fish 'n chip shop at 794 Garscube Road. My brother and I tried our own shop for a while, but that was a flop and we went to work for the Castelvecchis in Paisley . . . the thirties . . . an awful bad time for drunks coming in to pick fights, much worse than later. Then the war came and I was interned. But I was engaged to be married by then and my young lady worked awful hard . . . took on a café and had it paid off by the time I came back. Then we'd another place, rough with street fights outside . . . maybe I'm easy scared but I didn't like that. Then when this place here, 'The Trees', came on the market we took a big breath and bought it. No trouble here, never-ever, and we're busy. D'you know I'm so happy here I wish I could live to be a million.

Like Mrs. Grove, Bunty Angles had a go at something else before settling to her real career.

I was in a sweetie shop, but I only lasted a week because the woman kept asking if I was eating the sweeties or touching the money. My grandmother wasn't going to have that, so I left. After that it was fashion shops. Wallace's in Maryhill first, learning to serve and to poke the money into yon wee cups, twist them and scoosh them up to the cashier. I was in Dresses at Wallace's. Then I went to Colthart's in Queen Street. I became a buyer there . . . used to go to London to see the Collections and choose what would sell in Glasgow. I'd always to be well-dressed, and that was nice . . . no overalls or anything.

Lily Balarsky was at the creative end of the same business, inheriting her skills and economies from her mother, who'd had to build and furbish home and family from nothing bar the candlesticks from Lithuania.

She never wasted a scrap of material, made all sorts of things with her cuttings. Sewed all our clothes so we'd always nice things to wear. I became a dressmaker too, I was apprenticed to the Barbacks' establishment at Eglinton Toll . . . three sisters had it. Miriam became very well known. They did beautiful work . . . very strict taskmasters, but good teachers. It was first class training. From there I went as an alteration hand to the Morrisons' Group, and I did dress-making from home.

In her young days Mrs. Mysie Kyle's was the skilled hand that added the finishing touches . . . the crown of glory to an Angles' London gown or a Balarsky original.

I learned to be a milliner at Daly's when I left school. Very posh. I got seven shillings a week there. That would be the twenties. Sometimes it was re-blocking and trimming customers' hats, sometimes making them up new. We all sat round four big tables to work and, later, when I was 'head of the table' I got thirty shillings or two pounds. Sometimes you were sent downstairs to serve. That was a wee change, but lots of ladies came in just to try on hats and the manager didn't like you not getting sales. I gave up that work when I got married. You had to. Didn't keep married women on.

Earlier than that, Lily Joseph was in 'eggs'.

When I left school my third sister's husband was in the egg business. I had been to college to learn the shorthand and typing, but when he opened his place in Adelphi Street we all went into the eggs. My mother too. And we sold a home-made drink too that was awful good. He was a marvel my third sister's husband. He was well-off but he shared . . . good to us all.

Ann Hutchison was thirled to the house.

. . . but my sisters had jobs in Pollokshaws, one at the weavin' and one at the pottery. I think it was in Cogan Street. You used to could see the wet clay runnin' out at the back . . . awful messy. Th'were a funny thing though. Some of the pottery pieces had MADE IN IRELAND on the bottom. Maybe they sold better for bein' a bit kinda foreign.

Perhaps in another context the Shanks' Patents referred to by Nell Dinsmor could be loosely, and doubly, called 'pottery' too.

Barrhead was always famous for that. I knew a man in the Company and when he went on holiday he was more interested in the cludgies than the fancy places or the sight-seeing.

Robert Ford, having left school after only his five years there, to work on his father's seven-acre croft at Portpatrick, nevertheless struck out independently into his own line of work, his own further education and finally into successful business for himself.

After my father's place I was waged on to a farm and got about fifteen pounds at the end of six months. This was at the end of the First War. You worked wi' your bare feet all the time except maybe for the very hard winter. Your feet got tough like that . . . leathery. Saved your boots. Anyway, fifteen pounds for six months of working, five in the morning to eight at night. The cows were to milk night and morning. D'you know it was 1931 before ever I saw a milk bottle? My parents lived very sparse and whatever else was spent, fifty pounds was always kept for funerals.

Small wonder he lost the notion for farming and went to learn the joinery.

It was mostly horse-carriages and wheels I started on, but by the time my four years was up nob'dy wanted horse-carriages. So I went to night school to learn about building and do maths.

'Nob'dy' might want horse-carriages but tramcars were in their prime.

I came to Glasgow for work and went to Coplaw Street tram depot.

That was 1929, and I was working closing up the open-end trams . . . glassing them in. Took eighteen months to do them all, then we were paid off. It was bad times, 1930, to get a job, so I started up my own wee business in Kinning Park . . . rented the old byre the Rodgers sisters had given up. After that I was in Plantation there for thirty-eight years. Wheelbarrows was my main line at first . . . my speciality. There was hods for builders, and bakers' trays too, for Peacock's and Ross's Dairies and Price Brothers. Then th'was the wee war ladders as well.

And three entire houses built with his own skeely hands and the mathematics knack he had learned at the night-school long ago. The vandalism of the sixties, and unsympathetic officialdom, finally drove him to retirement, to the books and poetry he had come to with such pleasure, long after his brief schooldays.

It wasn't only Robert Ford's glassed-in tramcars that took people to their work, there were the trains remembered by Jack Roche.

Most folk out Calton way worked in the tobacco or one of the mills there, but a lot of Bridgeton people had jobs at Clydebank . . . Singer's or John Brown's. I worked for a while as a guard on the trains going that way. Th'was what was cried the 'First Brig'ton' and the 'Second Brig'ton' . . . one early in the morning and one later.

Perhaps those who worked so far from home had fewer perks than the locals who could walk home from work in Clydebank.

Th'was a thing they used to say . . . that Clydebank did a roaring trade in the fallin's off of the yard lorries. Aye, that nearly the whole of Clydebank was furnish'd, court'sy John Brown . . . first class fittin's and furniture . . . carpets even.

Those living too far to make such 'economies' possible, *and* the virtuous, were indignant.

. . . mind a lot were real cocky about their pilfers, blowed about them . . . right gallus.

Not all recollected skills were manual. Miss Isobel Horn and Struan Yule were wordsmiths in their working life.

I was desperate to get into journalism, but the nearest I could get at first

was writing advertising copy for Copland and Lye. Then I got a chance
to go on the Women's Rural Institute Magazine. That was great . . .
did some of the editorials and went out interviewing and reporting on
branch meetings. Did that for seven years, then had to do war work.
Eventually I got back and became the editor. I travelled a lot then to all
the country places. I visited the Castle of Mey once. The Institute had
sewn a boudoir set for the Queen Mother . . . a couch coverlet and a
cushion and a hot bottle cover. Then she invited the Caithness branch
to the castle to see them in place.

More mundanely there was the matter of the cleekit gloves . . .
just as knacky but more down-to-earth.

We answered queries too and I remember one about these 'cleekit'
gloves. Have you ever heard of cleekit work? It was quite a *man*'s
craft.

And here the long arm (or deft hand) of coincidence brings the
quirk of the same incident being related quite separately by two
people now living sixty miles apart. The cleekit gloves query had
been from Millicent Davis.

I once saw a pair of these gloves in a craft shop. They were a dreadful
colour and I didn't buy them. But I was always sorry after. I knew
cleekit work when I saw it, but I didn't know how it was done. I wrote
to The Scottish Field and got a few replies. 'My father (or grandfather
or the grieve) made them', sort of answer. But they didn't know how.
Later I got a little piece done by a lady in Canada and I tried it myself
with an old hook like a thorn, but not properly. Then someone said I
should write to Miss Horn of the W.R.I. magazine. She put my letter
into the next issue and I got a lot of information from all over.

And Isobel Horn . . .

Later we gave a copy of the directions free to anyone who would make
gloves for our Conference sales table. Oh, it was an interesting life on
the magazine.

Many another Dennistoun man was a 'killer' in the meat market,
earning big money, but from school there, Struan Yule set his
sights on *The Glasgow Herald* . . . preferably the Editor's chair
and as soon as possible.

I applied by letter and there was a wee delay in getting a reply, so I thought my letter had got lost in the post and I went to see them. Said I was interested in a job on the editorial side.

'Oh!' says the man, 'everyone starts here on the post desk.'

'Well,' says I, 'as long as it's not for too long.'

In spite of his nerve he was appointed and after his obligatory stint with the letters, spent the whole of his working life there in the Business Section.

We'll look elsewhere at another side of Alex Donnelly's career on Glasgow's entertainment scene in his fiddling days, but he earned a more prosaic bawbee in a variety of other lines.

When my father got killed in the First War the clay-pipe factory got sold off and I left the school at thirteen and went to the Co-op as a message-boy at five shillings a week . . . carried the basket on my head on a wee round cushion like a black puddin'. After that I worked in The Castle pub in Calton, then in Rowan's boiler shop, screwin' rods for big-big forty-ton ships' boilers.

All the while, of course, practising the music, against hard times.

I used to knock the gas mantles off wi' my bow, so when I met this fella that was sellin' an old tin saxophone I bought it and learned that . . . and then a mandolin. I earned a bit extra that way. You just did ever'thing you could. Eventually me and my wife took a newsagent's shop in Oatlands and another in Eglinton Street. Ocht aye, you'd to turn your hand to anything.

Not many could turn theirs to such a plethora of skills though.

And that 'turning the hand to anything' says it for all of them really . . . the cooks, the dressmakers, the restaurateurs and the milliners, the joiners, the pipe-makers and the scribes. None made fortunes. None claimed brilliance. But all unconsciously radiated a sort of sensible Glasgow pride in their own crafts well done.

9

Tea and a Hot Co-op Pie

Family outings in Edwardian times, sometimes by the whole tribe, sometimes by only assorted members, came in a variety of forms, depending on weather, pocket, season or what parents thought was for the ultimate health and welfare of their offspring.

The most sedate came under the heading of Visiting, a much less casual activity than the mug-in-the-hand or barbecue of the 1990s. There would be the prim walk to the host house, the handing over of the small present or the bunch of flowers. Then, once embraced by Auntie and patted on the head by Uncle, the Visit was in progress. The visit could be 'from' as well as 'to', but the niceties, although reversed, were the same. Miss Ann Hutchison remembers both coming and going for high tea.

> Oh, we went visiting right-enough, We'd an Aunt McKenzie in Tassie Street that we went to reg'lar. And we *had* visitors. We'd my Daddy's brother and his wife every second Sunday for their tea.

There would be 'knife and fork'.

> And there would be baking on the range for that visit.

After the meal of cold ham or fish or ham-and-eggs, plain bread and butter, tea-bread and cake, there often came the formal entertainment. Jean Paterson was one performer.

> You'd always to do your 'turn'. Stand up in front of everyone in the room and say a poem or maybe do your newest piece on the piano . . . your Farmyard Tunes or Joys for Ever.

Week-end visiting was a multicultural activity. Certainly the immigrant communities used it to keep in touch with their own roots. Mario Servadei recalls . . .

316

Our family life was very Italian I suppose. You integrated right-
enough during the week, but Saturday and Sunday you kept close
to relatives on a visiting basis. It was just visiting. They're still done,
Italian things, but not so much now. Some have even given up the 'i'
at the end of their names . . . maybe a Rossi becoming Ross. And yet
even after a generation or so, a bit of you still feels Italian. Maybe that
visiting helped you to feel part of Italy.

And Mrs. Lily Joseph looks back to immigrant days in her circle.

> The Jewish community kept close for support and because of language and religion and all the customs. We did a lot of visiting, informal get-togethers, sometimes in houses but other times in the synagogue. We'd sing songs, tell real stories about the Jewish past . . . say poems maybe.

Perhaps a foretaste of the casual culture that was coming can be detected in a memory of Nell Dinsmor's. Or maybe it looked casual because it concerned the breaking-out of one of a protected and confined species, the dutiful daughter-at-home.

> I had this aunt, the unmarried one at home. She would be s'posed to be shopping in Shawlands, but-here instead she'd take the blue Renfrew Ferry tram to her sister's in Barrhead to get tea and a hot Co-op pie. She wouldn't tell at home but she'd kind of rebelled a wee bit.

Then for most youngsters there were parties, both given and gone to. There they ate their buns and their Playmate biscuits over a crumb sheet sensibly tacked to the floor over a prized carpet and they learned the repertoire of singing games for socially correct tots. These were the activities that came before the sophisticated kissing games that were heady stuff for teenagers.

> Och, you didnae call them 'teenagers' then. Anyway early-on you played 'Here we go gathering nuts in May', 'The Farmer's in the Dell' 'Musical Chairs', 'Water Water Wallflower' or 'Broken Bridges'. Later it was 'Postman's Knock', 'Winkie', 'Cushiony' and 'The Grand Old Duke of York' . . . you did kissing at them.

There were times when parties were illicit excursions, even if entirely innocent once in progress. Mrs. Jean Walker has a tale of her mother as a determined gate-crasher . . . not *into* the party but out of her own home to get to it.

> My grandmother was dead so my mother was brought up by a housekeeper around the Gorbals somewhere. One time she was invited to a Jewish girl's party and the housekeeper said 'no' she couldn't go. But this Jewish girl was her friend, so she just turned her pinafore to the clean side and went.

There were other parent-figures too who didn't always give their blessing to parties . . . not birthday parties anyway. Mrs. Agnes Grove's father was suspicious of *motive* and said so bluntly to a mother who lived to rue the fact that she hadn't heard of crumb drugget.

> My father didn't believe in birthday parties. 'Present parties' he called them. If you're to give a party, give a party just. So maybe at Hallowe'en my mother'd make champit tatties with trinkets in. But not after once when the tatties got tramped into the carpet. After that it was dumplings and sing-songs and dookin' for apples . . . or treacle scones hanging from the pulley that you'd to catch in your mouth, with your hands behind your back. That was messy too mind, but only on your face.

It was a very rare house in which there was an easy, hand-in-pocket supply of money; and bought treats were seldom enough to be real occasions. For the Hutchison brood the briquette-and-sticks business yielded an annual season of two outings.

> Every year my Daddy treated us to two things, the pantomime and the Kelvin Hall carnival. That cost a bit too much money, but he always did it, and we got our teas as well.

Alongside the carnival was the circus, favoured by some over the push-penny and the roundabouts.

> I liked the circus righ'enough an' Dave Willis at the pantomine (sic). He was awful good. D'you mind his wee Injun song?
>   All dress'd up in m'Injun fea-thers
>   Listen to the talkin' Injun ble-thers
>   Me an' my squaw an' my wee papoose
>   My wigwam's better'n a cooncil hoose.

Two outings seemed to be the done thing in the Festive Season.

> We always used to go to two pantomimes . . . Tommy Lorne at The Royal, and George West at The Princess's. There was always thirteen letters in the name of The Princess's pantomime. They weren't your traditional Cinderella or Mother Goose or that. There was the likes of 'Tammytoorytap' then later, after I was grown up th'was 'The Tintock Cup'. One year my father must've taken a notion to one

of the Principal Boys and got me to write for a signed photo. It
didn't go on *my* wall with my film stars. It disappeared into *his*
desk.

That was the panto scene with the gorgeous Harry Gordon,
the lancer-prancing Dave Willis of the cherry nose and wee
moustache, Tommy Lorne with his lugubrious gawkiness, and
all the rest with their 'feeds' and leggy Principal Boys.

But the spectacle that took the breath away more than any
of those was surely Hengler's circus, for it is recalled by
almost every rememberer who had a Glasgow childhood in its
heyday. Mrs. Mysie Kyle has nothing to say of pantomimes or
carnivals . . .

> No, we didn't get taken to pictures or theatres but we did to go to
> Hengler's Circus . . . oh my, Hengler's circus!

There was more to this performance than traditional circus acts.
Music-hall type turns were inserted here and there throughout the
programme.

> I mind of someone singing 'On Mother Kelly's Doorstep' and doing
> some kind of parody on that. And th'was other song and dancing acts.
> I mind too, at the hall where Hengler's was held, that at other times
> you got to watch lantern slides for a penny on Saturday afternoons.

Mrs. Bunty Angles went to the circus performances when they
took place near St. George's Cross.

> There was always Doodles the Clown at Hengler's. He was good was
> Doodles . . . clever clown. Everybody loved Doodles.

For some the animals were the real stuff of the circus.

> It was the lions and the lion-tamer that I remember. I was taken every
> year by an uncle, with my wee sister. There was a cage dropped round
> the arena with the lions and this lion-tamer in it, in his riding breeches
> and white polo neck. He'd a long-handled whip that he cracked, and
> the first time he did it one year, my wee sister thought he was whipping
> the lions and she screamed so much I'd to take her outside till the next
> act came on.
>   The horses were good. There was a thing about one being able to
> distinguish colours by name. The man used to say 'I'm putting the

blue cloth at this side . . .' and 'I'm putting the red cloth at the other side'. Then he would get the horse to bring him the one he asked for. He would try and cheat the horse and change them over, but the horse never got confused. I thought it was magic.

But lions, clowns, magic . . . whatever else, the most vivid, marvellous memory of all is of the climax to the performance. Bunty Angles has it spotlit and sharp from her pre-First War childhood.

It was the Indian shooting the rapids scene. There would be a beam of light picking out the Chief Brave that stood away up high above the arena. The floor went down then the water rushed into some kind of circular tank and the Indians and horses were in and across it yowling and doing their war cries.

Miss Isobel Horn speaks for a whole generation.

The water scene at the end . . . great stuff! Dramatic and wild!

And there's an intangible something that always brings Hengler's rushing back to Struan Yule.

When I smell oranges, the circus always comes to mind. People ate oranges at shows because they made less noise than sweetie papers.

That then, was Hengler's circus; but the aroma of oranges, and the sweetie papers they replaced, also hung about the venue of another well-loved social and moral institution that was part of the fabric of life in former days. While the Band of Hope may not have been founded principally for entertainment its young adherents certainly look back on the malarky rather than the precepts of the Friday night out. Struan Yule was no better than the rest.

We always bought toffees on Band of Hope night. The toffees were good but as well as that you could stick the papers on each other's noses.

At the swarry you got a bag of buns and an orange. Th'was always oranges at the Band of Hope. I always think on the two together, the oranges and the Band of Hope.

And the wicked Struan Yule again . . .

The Reverend James Muir B.D. was the boss of our Band of Hope.
When we'd lantern slides that moved along in strips of four pictures
(Y'know the sort of thing . . . poor wee waif with the drunken father)
well, the minister sat down at the front and clicked his fingers for the
change of picture. In no time at all everyone cottoned on and we'd all
be clicking away to hurry them on and get to the tea or the oranges.

All the same they signed the pledges and learned the slogans that
have stuck in the mind for seventy and eighty years. 'Strong drink
is a mocker' 'Think . . . not drink!' and they can still chant even
their own wee rhymes that parodied yet echoed official policy.

Look on spirits as your foe
Make your answer ever 'No'!
See the drunkards o'er the edge
Keep yer heid and sign the pledge.

When the winter was past and the time for the singing of birds
was come, it was the great outdoors that beckoned, and families
put panto and circus into moth balls until next December and took
to the highways and byways for their outings. Mary Brisbane was
a sprig of a robust family of walkers.

People just did walk in those days . . . that was before the First War.
I'd an uncle used to walk from Glasgow to Greenock and back. Reg'lar.
Thought nothing of it.

Mysie Kyle's father took his young ones on instructive folklore
expeditions from their home near the Bell o' the Brae at the top of
the High Street, where William Wallace faced up to the English.

He came at them over the wooden Stockwell Bridge and won. My
father was keen on Wallace, for we used to go walks out to Wallace's
Well at Robroyston where he's supposed to've been hiding in a nearby
house when he was given away to the English and taken to London to
be hung, drawn and quartered.

They had another lesson, this time in Covenanting history, at the
Martyrs' Monument and Well, near the canal.

That's where the Covenanters Nisbet, Lawson and Wood got put to
death. It's all away now. There's just a memorial slab at the Martyr's
Church.

Another grisly Glasgow incident has come down through the annals of Janet Kay's family as having been the cause and scene of an unofficial outing of her grandfather's as a youngster.

> He went to see the last public hanging in Glasgow when he was a boy.
> It was yon Doctor Pritchard who poisoned his wife. He was hanged
> outside the Glasgow Law-courts and my grandfather and his pals were
> in the crowd. Nob'dy at home knew where they were.

There's no word of what retribution followed that little adventure but it surely can't have been worse warning than the sight of what society did to bigger-time sinners.

There are not so many now who can remember the very early Glasgow Exhibitions as pictured for a previous volume of memories. But the one in 1938 is as clear to Janet Kay as if fifty-odd years and a Garden Festival had never been.

> What a thing! It was great the Empire Exhibition so it was. Tait's
> Tower. I remember going up it in a hoist, then walking down. It
> was a long walk down. And yon coloured fountains all lit up at night.
> My!

It's not the mighty Palaces of Art and Engineering, the Empire Pavilions or the erudite historical displays that Struan Yule recalls.

> I remember the Laughing Sailor, a sort of dummy that laughed all the
> time . . . just shook with mirth. And I remember seeing Sir Thomas
> Lithgow there, very trim in his bowler hat.

He doesn't say why these two should come into his mind together unless ship-builder and laughing mariner had the sea to connect them. Also dressed in a sailor suit, was the Stratosphere Girl, spotlit and visible from all over the Exhibition, performing acrobatics on her swaying pole . . . a favourite memory tinged with sadness over her death not long after 1938 in a fall from her dangerous perch. There are other memories too . . . the 'automatic' chippery where, for tuppence, a poke of vinegared chips came scooshing at you down a chute . . . the Scenic Railway and the wee buggies that shunted you round from place to place when you'd paid your shilling at the Exhibition turnstile.

Away now from officially organised fun, Agnes Grove recalls
early family picnics . . .

> . . . along the canal banks. Must've walked miles out to what's
> Easterhouse now, with the baby in the pushchair. Instead of taking
> them to the pictures or that, I had a table-cloth and a kettle with a
> cap to its stroup, sangwidges and cakes and a primus stove . . . aye,
> away along the canal.

When the Grove family had served its apprenticeship as
well-organised local picnickers, they became flabbergastingly
ambitious.

> We went cycling as a family. It all started when Pop bought a tandem.
> Agnes (my daughter Agnes) shared the tandem with him and he got
> a seat fixed to the back of my bike for young Arthur. We'd a tent of
> course and Pop made a side-car for the tandem and put the tent and
> pots and pans in it.

With this Heath Robinson outfit they were off.

> We'd maybe go to Burntisland and stay overnight at Kincardine on the
> way . . . put up the tent for the night or the week-end. We were a sight
> to behold! Then we'd drum up.

The screw-top stroup and the old primus were still in service.

> Drumming up was just brewing up, with the water that we'd carried
> in the kettle. And we used to meet up with other regulars . . . there
> was Grandpa Grove and his friends Mr. Caldwell and Mr. Johnston
> and other folks. Some called the whole bunch the O.M.C.C. . . . the
> Old Men's Cycling Club. But it wasn't really a club. It was just us.

Burntisland wasn't the only destination. There was the west to
be explored as well.

> Sometimes we cycled to Saltcoats from Alexandra Parade. Och, it
> was maybe good for our lungs and heart . . . but it fairly told on
> our legs. Mind you, Grandpa Grove went on at the cycling till he
> was over seventy.

And that in a day when seventy really was three-score-years-and-
ten and more than that said to be 'labour-and-sorrow'. Mrs. Duffy-
next-door looked after the family dog during these excursions and

he had to be restrained from over enthusiastic welcome when they arrived home.

> He would have knocked us down the stair. We were carrying the tandem and the bikes up to the lobby. They were kept there. Three stairs up mind.

Outings there were a-plenty, forbye parties, pantomines and picnics. There were 'the pictures' and to a more 'artistic' extent the theatre. But since the whole culture of Glasgow as Cinema and Repertory city is a subject in itself, it's perhaps best to hang 'outings' on the hook and reminisce about more formal entertainment and maybe 'the dancin' in another chapter.

10

When Buttons were for Sewing On

There's a myth that the housewife of the 1990s has it easy . . . that because washing and ironing, heating, cooking and polishing are done by flicking switches, shaking clothes into shape, opening packets and dipping the family silver into magic liquids, she lives the life of Reilly. She is, it's true, familiar with a plethora of knobs and shortcuts, but on the whole they serve only to release her to do a dozen things her granny never did. There's her share of the working week in office, classroom or shop. There are the committees for the relief of a long list of ills unnamed in older times but that can now be cured or alleviated . . . and the miles she runs up on the car dial to shop for elderly relatives.

All the same she might find her weekly round a dawdle compared with the hassle of rearing six or seven children on a single income, in two rooms if she was lucky, and three if she was bien. Beyond three, she'd probably have had a maid, but still a multitude of other chores to do. All this is a touch simplistic perhaps, for there were cushioned women then, as there are those hard-pressed now, whose lives are the drearier for seeing their sisters with every buyable gadget under the sun. But we are reminiscing here and those who offer their recollections are looking back on years when every hour of the day was given over to putting the clan out clean, well-fed and clothed, and making a tight budget stretch around its weekly needs. Maybe rose-coloured spectacles were issued with clean semmits, for no shiftless, lazy mothers are remembered here. One and all they are recalled as skilled economists and managers. There must have been aimiable sluts, but there was a tightness, a keeping-up with the Tamsons, about tenement life that made it difficult to neglect duty altogether.

> There was a right rammy if the stair didnae get done, and Mistress Whoever got a roasting off the rest up the close.

Today's house-person can choose whether to wash on Friday, do the brasses Monday or Wednesday . . . or even whether to clean the front doorstep at all. There was no such flexi-time or eesie-ose in the rigid order of the closes.

> Yous had your day for this and your day for that. And yous had to stick to them, or else there'd be murder . . . ever'thing out of kilter . . . big rammies.

Of all the rituals brought to mind by those who knew that life in the early century, those to do with the week's laundry are best remembered. Jimmy Dewar was part of that.

> We'd one day a week in the wash-house. It was my job to do the fire under the boiler . . . lit about six in the morning. Then my mother went down. There was a big-big tub and a wooden paddle and the Fell's Naphtha soap. The whites got boiled and stirred, then a wee bit Dolly blue, twice through the wringer and out on the line. When it was just about coming on dry you took it to an old lady along the street who took in mangling and did a load for about tuppence. Sometimes I got to caw the handle. That was a kind of treat.

The wash-house ritual was the same for most, though some like Agnes Grove's mother, before the turn of the century, favoured Reckitt's blue over Dolly and a big spirtle instead of the paddle, and maybe A.1. powder rather than Fell's Naphtha.

> We'd a dumper too, like a big zinc bell on a pole, and you dumped your clo'es with that . . . got up a rare sapple. Then it was all sined a couple of times and your blankets or sheets or that, went to the mangle-wife for flattening and folding. You couldn't iron them if they were too big, y'see. The mangle was the thing, so the laundry didn't get put away all bumphlie.

Indeed Eileen Duffy's mother went into a wee business enterprise with her mangle.

But it was heavy work . . . she couldn't manage, so she didn't keep it long.

Perhaps she hadn't quite the guile that shrewder manglers had, who conned youngsters into believing that it was a big treat to get turning the handle. Agnes Grove was one such willing dupe.

I used to get working the mangle. It had a long wide linen strip you put your clo'es on, and the whole thing went through rollers two or three times as you cawed.

Another who invested in a mangle was a granny in Main Street Bridgeton.

> She did a lot of wee things to get a bit of extra money. She made
> toffee and she did mending and stitching for ladies. She got hold of a
> second-hand mangle and got tuppence-a-pair of sheets doing that . . .
> went out cleaning twice't a week too, and she liked that.

Sometimes a hard-pressed woman went on a wash-house night-
shift.

> Mrs. Corrigan up our close done her washing at night. She was out
> working to some woman and couldnae do it in the day. I used to watch
> her from the window working with candles lit and the steam comin'
> out the door across the kin'a whippering light of the candle.

There were few tenement blocks without a wash-house neatly
tucked into the corner of the back-court. However weel-kent
to those who used it, what it *was* wasn't clear to everyone.
Mrs. Mysie Kyle recalls . . .

> I remember reading about a delegation of Russian visitors to Glasgow
> who went home and wrote up articles about the Glasgow tenements
> with wee-wee houses built in behind them.

Maybe they saw them as Granny or 'Babushka' annexes, or just
for the tenements' overspill.

> Yes, they thought, what with the fires and chimneys, the windows and
> the door, and likely a pram sitting outside, it must've been a house.
> (The prams were for carting the washing, of course.)

Everyone had big washings to do, but the young housewives
Christina and her sister Mary, struggling at Maclean Street, had
more than their fair share.

> There was always some of our brothers coming home from sea.
> Not to help . . . oh no! They didn't know the dairy work or that.
> They just brought more work with them because we'd their bags
> to sort out and their washing to do. We did that in the wash-
> house out the back, where the byre and the stable was. Chrissie and
> I.

If the wash-house facilities were't up to scratch or if you fancied
wash-day as more of a social occasion, you could go to the steamie.
The Hutchison clothes went to the Pollokshaws steamie.

My sister used to go at six o'clock in the morning and if I was on my holiday from school I went with her. Th'was wee kind of places each. At the side of your sink was your own wee boiler 't you could boil up your things yourself. An'en you took them out and into the big tub and let the water run on them . . . then into your wee tub and you did your wash wi' a board. Yon 'Steamie' on the T.V. was just th'exact real thing . . . awful good! Then you sined the clo'es. (Mind you can go dressed to the steamie now, it's all just machines, but you couldnae then. It was big wellies and a rubber apron, for you got soaked.)

The chummy time of chat with other perspiring women came when you were waiting for the next stage.

What they called a spin drier . . . no' a machine, just a big drum that a man pulled the lever and the brake, and the water came scooshing out. You werenae allowed to touch it. Just the man did that.

A few more bits of local clash and 'the man' was finished.

Then you pulled out a rack from a kin'a cupboard wi' hot pipes running along it, put your clo'es over that and pushed it into the heat again. That was extra mind. But it was all just coppers.

For a likely lad there was another copper or two to be had on steamie day.

My mother-in-law used to do her washing at the one off the Garscube Road, and my husband when he was wee got thruppence for carrying the basket of washing on his head to the steamie and back.

Wash-house or steamie, A.1. or soft soap, one thing was for sure a 'nice washing' got gold stars, and a 'gey grey' one was the kiss of death to respectability.
Then there was the ironing.

It seemed to go on for days. All the petticoats and sheets, the table-cloths and the other clothes. I got doing the hankies sometimes. At first it was flat irons that sat at the front of the range fire . . . different sizes. Later we'd a bolt-iron. You heated the bolt then slid it in through a hole in the back . . . put it in and out with a cleek that had a wee hook on the end.

The next advance on the bolt iron was the smart new gas iron favoured in Janet Kay's home . . . hazardous but trendy.

> We'd a gas point for the gas ring on the range and we could take it off and just push the rubber tube on to the iron instead.

The bodies that had to go into these sappled, sined and flat-ironed sarks and petties, had to be scoured themselves into the cleanliness that was next to godliness. Much has been related elsewhere of Friday bath night, so a reminder of such scenes is enough to bring back a passing picture here.

> Friday nights . . . oh aye . . . your hair 'looked', then your tubbing in front of the range in the zinc bath that was kep' hung up behind the toilet door. Sometimes when I was bigger we went to the public baths and got a good steep. After wir bath, if it was the zinc, all the six of us sat in a row along the kitchen bed . . . a' shinin' in wir nightgowns, and got a cup i' cocoa.

Even when those angelic young were up and had flown the nest they sometimes came home for a scrub. Mrs. Mysie Kyle did.

> When I got married we'd no hot water, just a toilet. We went to my mother for baths. Other folk went to Townhead baths and for a shilling you got your bath and a towel.

Zinc tubbing or shilling steep over, attention could be turned to surroundings. Priority was what was going to meet the visitor first or the beady eye of other women in the close, however intimate.

> Twice in the week you did the stairs. The factor got the upper part of the walls white-washed, that was his job. But then you took a bit of pipe-clay (whitening y'know). You champed it up then put it in the water. When it dissolved you white-washed down the whole stair. Some folk just drew designs down the edge instead. Neighbours could be quite sniffy if it wasn't done right.

So could grandmothers.

> There was always the stair to do. It was a wally close ours . . . nice green and brown tiles, and my grandmother inspected to see you'd no wee splashes on the tiles from your pipe-clay. Yes she did. She inspected that.

They could have done with Bunty Angles' granny and her eagle eye in the Andersons' close.

We'd an old woman washed our stair . . . slittered the water all over the place . . . left the close swimming. My father used to call her Mrs. Noah.

The pipe-clay, universally employed as it was to create a trig ambience, had its drawbacks.

There were thirty-six weans up our close all tramping whitening on to their lobby rugs.

The blame for that misfortune might have been laid firmly at the Calton door of Alex Donnelly's father.

In his wee pipe work he made the pipe-clay for the closes, farthing a square.

The state of the brasses was another touchstone for a family's reputation. Outside first.

The door handle and the name-plate and letter-box got brassoed every day and the wee knobs on the bannister that stopped you sliding down.

Granny was on hand to examine those too, and woe betide the slattern who left grey-green smudges round the brass bosses or the post-box. There were some households whose outside-the-front-door duties did not stop at pipe-clay and brasses . . . those who added to their labours the scouring of the stairhead cludgie.

We were in a single-end off of Argyle Street when I was young, and it was my job to clean the cludgie when it came our turn. We shared with the Boyles and the Shaughnessys. I hated that, but it had had to get done twice't a week . . . scrubbed and done wi' Jeyes' Fluid.

Scrubbing was a skill learned young and skinny, when you'd to do almost a limbo dance to get into the places where oose or even the scandal of actual *dirt* might lurk. That granny again, saw to it that her dark corners were clean as a whistle.

She was sixty when I was born and came to live with her . . . well-on to be bringing up a wee one. But she was strict and I had my chores. One was to take everything out from under the Room bed and get in on my hands and knees to scrub the floor. Then you'd to let it dry before the boxes went back.

That press bed space was virtually a bedroom too.

> I slept in there with a shelf above my head and another one above
> my feet for all my clothes. The bed was quite high . . . just a feather
> mattress on top of slats of wood. My grandmother stretched over and
> made the bed with a walking-stick. Oh, she was quick and nimble
> with that stick! And when she turned the mattress she fairly made the
> feathers fly.

Mrs. Dewar of Cartvale Road was another stickler for below-bed
perfection.

> Except for under the rugs and mats that would have slipped, she
> polished all the lino . . . Mansion polish . . . even under the bed
> . . . had to be shining. Spotless, the lino floors were, but awful
> cold.

Whether lino was cold or not, Peggy Carson's mother tossed her
head at the sight of a *carpet* arriving at a neighbour's door.

> When her man won a wee bit money she put down this carpet in her
> kitchen. Ma thought she'd just got above hersel' . . . lazy too, that only
> the surround had to be scrubbed.

While mothers took their smeddum out on the floors, the young
had their tasks.

> I'd to lift all the rugs and take them out to beat on the clothes line down
> the green. Had to do it before 12 noon on a Saturday. There was some
> bye-law or other said that.

No doubt he did that at his busy mother's bidding, but for
the independent young Rodgers in Govan the chores were self
inflicted.

> All the lino'd to be done ev'ry morning. And then it was all white
> wood in our kitchen . . . chairs, dresser, table, shelves, everything
> . . . even the top of the coal bunker. So that had to be scrubbed.

You can't get much spicker or spanner than scrub your coal
bunker. But this, after all, was 'farm' forbye city tenement and
when the scrubbers got round to the press in the corner they often
found reward.

We'd a particular hen in the yard and when the window was opened this hen used to flap up from outside, jump into the sink and then down to the press door that was always a crack open. We'd a piece of woollen cloth there for her and she used to go in on to that and lay an egg. Then she would walk across the floor, out the front door and down the back close to the rest of the hens.

Best recollected of all the home scenes of eighty and ninety years ago, are those surrounding the range. The elderly who basked in its warmth as youngsters and waited for what it delivered to them of soups and scones, look back with nostalgia. Mothers who were slaves to such fires blessed the day it was hacked out of the wall in favour of a prissy turn-off gas cooker. Janet Kay's memories take her round her granny's kitchen before coming to rest on the range.

There was the dresser with cupboards above, then round to a single window with a black sink under it . . . and then the kitchen press for dishes and food. Then there was the range. My granny's range was very old . . . no polished trims and just the black kerb. In our own house the hearth was white enamel with flowers and there was a polished towel-rail right across the top. My granny's had no shiny bits.

But the Hutchisons' 'shiny bits' were their pride and joy. Ann Hutchison . . .

My, our range was beautiful! My Daddy kept it lovely. That was always his job. You know the steel bit at the front? Daddy had it beautiful. Did it with emery. And he'd the doors an' that black-leaded. We heated all our water on that range. The kettles were on the boil all the time.

Jimmy Dewar recalls the emery-and-zebo treatment.

I loved that range. I did the emery paper all round the steel bits. I'd be maybe ten or eleven. Mother did the black-leading, and buffing with a velvet pad. The range had a black fender with wee low lumpy pillars at the corners. Mother baked cakes in the oven and oatcakes on the big girdle on the top. She'd a gas ring too that was hinged to lift out the way when she was using the top of the range.

A dozing eavesdropper suddenly open his eyes to recall theirs . . .

. . . had burnished steel that you did with a wee pad with two rings
on it for your fingers and close metal coils for the rubbing. There was
a wee shelf in front of the fire ribs with a grid you could pull up and
slip your oatcakes in to dry out.

Your mother might be from Tuscany but, once a Glasgow
housewife, she had to master her range . . . and her Scottish
weans. Mario Servadei's mother did both.

We'd all our household chores. Yes the boys in Italian families had
to take their share. I'd the brasses to do and the range . . . the Zebo
and the steel bits. And I'd to chop up the sticks on freezing cold
mornings.

The range in Mrs. Mysie Kyle's early married home had the usual
steel rims but was unique in another way.

Y'know someone had *painted* that range, and they'd done a good job
on it, so it wasn't nearly the work. I never had to black-lead that grate
all the time I was there . . . just emery the edges.

Girdle scones and stews, dumplings and oven baking came out
of Glasgow's ranges in a steady stream. Only a prodigal woman
admitted to using 'bought cakes' and maybe only a hard-pressed
one had to resort to cooking what she called 'buff'.

Our charlady used to tell us about cooking buff. It was the lungs of
an animal. 'You just hook the thrapple over the edge of the pot,' she
used to say, 'and the rest of it gets boiled. Then it gets cut up and eaten.
Fair fills them a' up'.

Coal for the range, kept in the kitchen bunker, was a big item
on a tight budget, but there were what some called 'savers' and
others 'briquettes' and there were other fly wee ways of making
the coal spin out. There were fire-bricks you could put at each side
or maybe an iron nest in the middle, to take up space. And there
were also local resources.

That same charwoman that cooked the buff lived in Kinning Park,
beside a big ash-covered area of waste ground, and she said people
used to send their children out after dark with buckets to bring back
cinders for the range.

Wherever the fuel came from, there was a set pattern for the fire chore.

> You put on your dust cap and your thibbet apron, picked out the big cinders, cleeked the ashes forward and put them in a baikie to take down the back. Then you made the fire.

Ranges were treated with, if not always *loving* care, at least with respect by most folk, for they could be stubborn. But there were the cavaliers.

> People used to put their chimneys on fire . . . to save the sweep. Put the whole close in danger that.

There was another feature of houses around 1905 that might have sent the close up in flames.

> It was gas light we had, you turned up the screw and put a taper to it . . . just the naked flame.

In Janet Kay's home the arrangements were not so primitive.

> Oh yes, gas lights. They had swan neck fitments, wide brackets and glass bowls, and mantles that you lit with a taper. Veritas mantles . . . a wee white net thing with a pipe-clay ring round it. I can smell them yet. You'd to kind of 'prove' the mantles with a taper to get the waxiness off them.

Even safer, if less mellow, illumination was on the way.

> I remember when we got the electric. The factor lived in our street so maybe that's why we got it so early in the twenties. They only laid quite a small cable in Cartvale Road because they thought it was a flash in the pan and not very many would want the electric. It cost seven pounds to wire the whole house and put up the fittings.

As well as those old glowing ranges that were at the very heart of home and memory, there was another set-piece that took a worthy woman hours of work to have to her satisfaction.

> My granny slept in the kitchen. The bed was in the wall on bierers, a frame of slats laid on wooden legs that held up the mattress. You took them with you when you flitted mind. Then th'was a front board and over that hung the bed poinds. That was crocheted lace points

on a white insertion, a kind of valance really. Then th'was always a white-white bedspread. Later when you got coloured spreads you'd still always a white one for when the doctor came. Then th'were pillow shams with nothing in them. They'd goffered frills that my mother stood for hours with a goffering iron to get the rucks just right. It was like Marcel waving, so it was (D'you mind of Marcel waving for your hair?) Your wall bed *had* to be just so, because your friends and neighbours came right into the kitchen. I remember too that Granny had a weaver's kist beside her bed that she used for blankets. Th'was a wee drawer in it too where the weaver had kept his bobbins. I used to sit on that kist.

The polished black kettle with the marble in it against 'furring', the glowing range, the brasses and the cludgie, the weekly bath, the hair hunt, these were Friday night operations in most families, but in Jewish households, like Mrs. Lily Joseph's, Thursday was the big night.

We'd a samovar for making our tea . . . a brass samovar my parents had brought with them when they came from Russia. It got polished with the other brasses on a Thursday night. And I can always remember the six silver dish-covers all shined up. The range got done and all the dishes ready. We'd different dishes for different things. We were very Orthodox and at Passover you'd a different set altogether for everything. Anyway, it had all to be ready for Friday, the very special Friday dinner. By the Friday at one o'clock everything was done and we'd a non-Jewish fireboy in to get the range going for us. We got home early from school on winter Fridays to be ready before dark.

Come the Friday night all was ready.

Never less than twelve of us sat down at the big kitchen table and we'd always strangers sat down with us. There'd be two or three soups, chicken maybe, or broth or cabbage. We weren't flush with money but never short. Mother was a great cook, learned it from their housekeeper back in Russia. We'd all the Orthodox rituals like in the Bible, the candles and all that, and the right things that were read and said.

So tenement families, whether Glasgow-born for generations or immigrants from less hospitable places, learned to hone their household skills and economies early. Perhaps the first sign of

becoming part of the more effete, upwardly mobile society was
to acquire a maid.

> I was a lazy wee snob. I hated Molly's half-day, because I'd to lay the
> table, go to the kitchen with dirty plates or whatever . . . and then
> *wash-up*. Then the war came and put the kybosh on the maids. They
> all went home and into war work. That was as big a shock to me at
> twelve, as the British Expeditionary Forces going to France.

> Oh yes, I had a maid. I had a wee brass bell at the tea-table to summon
> Agnes in her afternoon pinny, cuffs and black dress. She'd fetch and
> carry between kitchen and table, then take her own through there by
> herself. And of course she'd always a lot of housework while I was
> maybe out in the town. Terrible when you think on it now.

There's a thowlessness about families being waited on hand and
foot that does seem objectionable in the 1990s . . . almost feudal.
But one who did the running after, and answered the table bell or
the front door, sees another side to it all.

> I left home at sixteen and into service and y'know, when th'was a lot
> of unemployment and you'd a house burstin' wi' weans and mibbe two
> or three wi' T.B., then a place in a nice house, wi' a garden p'raps, your
> ain warm room, good meals and your keep, wi' a wee bit money in
> your pocket on your half day . . . plus something to send home, it
> didnae seem that bad . . . and you often got quite nice clo'es off of
> the mistress. Eighteen shillings a month I got in the early 1920s.

However much maids or mothers or tenement children had to do
to keep families clean, warm, fed and solvent, few could have had
the additional duties that fell to the household in McLean Street.

> With my father being an invalid and Maw gone and the shop and the
> farm there . . . we'd a lot of chores, scrubbing and washing and ironing
> . . . *and* the cows, the chickens and the dairy.

And that wasn't all.

> The boys got off with it away at sea. When I was young one of them
> left me with his doos. And I got what-for if anything went wrong with
> one of them, I can tell you.

Sometimes there was even a little veterinary work.

> When a hen got the croup . . . you should've heard a hen wi' the croup,

going ooo–ooo–ooo! What a noise! I used to say to Papa (always called him Papa, Mother was Maw) 'Papa, that hen's got the croup'. And he would lift her in a bag and I would make wee balls of fresh butter and roll it in pepper. Then Papa would open the beak and put about six of these down the hen's thrapple. That seemed to work great.

All that then, was the domestic way of it, in the days when coal had to be dragged up three stairs, washday started at six in the morning, and buttons were for sewing on, and not just pressing to magic housework away.

11

Annaker's Sausages are the Best

Since an ancient pedlar first laid out his wares one fine day on a grass track verge and, for the good weather and honest prices, called the pitch a 'fair', bartering, comparing and selecting have added up to shopping as one of man's favourite activities. For these pages there was no exhaustive list of where this or that emporium was sited, just a random mulling over of recollected counters and encounters. And yet there emerged memories of almost the entire range of household and personal merchandise . . . from clothing to china, butcher to bakery, furniture to fish, ironmongery, the gamut of grocery to haberdashery, tobacco and flowers. And best remembered of all, the joys of cheuch-jean, sherbet-dab and buttermilk dainty.

Take the big stores first. Upmarket, downmarket, between market, each had its own specialty, each its own circle of customers, and only in a determined hunt for something elusive did the clientèle of one overlap another.

> Oh there was nothing like Sauchiehall Street for elegant ladies, maybe up to about the 1930s! They'd their choice of a dozen or more big shops. They all sold everything in the way of clothes, but had their own different specialties too. Daly's was very chic for gowns and beautiful coats. Copland's was school things and gloves . . . for the gloves you leant your elbow on a wee cushion, hand straight up, and the assistant drew them on finger by finger.

Gracious days indeed with the only sounds the low hum of discreet conversation between assistant and shopper or the soft 'woosh' of money being conveyed by tube to the counting-house.

That used to intrigue me when the money was sent up yon tube-thing for change, screwed into a wee container.

One who operated that mechanism, no doubt in all the dignity of black jacket and striped trouser, remembers a less formal use for the tube and claims to have caused pandemonium in the cash-office by putting a live mouse he had caught into the tube and sending it off.

Pettigrew's had its following too.

They'd lovely material and good quality school clothes, and they'd a small orchestra in the tea-room too. Henderson's was just general . . . nice though. There was Forsyths' too and the likes of Rowan's and

Fraser's, and Simpson, Hunter and Young in Buchanan Street. Some preferred it down there, but for a real afternoon out I liked Sauchiehall Street.

At a time when Glasgow to outsiders was 'shipyards and slums', discerning local women were well aware that it was also a fine shopping centre, second to none, and certainly not to its rival in the east.

> I can remember my mother meeting an Edinburgh lady on holiday and–here this lady asked her if she never came to Edinburgh to shop! Go to Edinburgh to shop? With Sauchiehall Street and Buchanan Street on her doorstep. Edinburgh . . . sight-see maybe. Shopping . . . never!

There were those passing mentions of Buchanan Street and some loyalists would have gone no further than the majestic stairway, galleries and stately ambience of Wylie and Lochhead; the refinement of Macdonald's, sober, tailored Rowan's; even the more popular bustle of Fraser's and Wyllie Hill's. But it is the big-store names in Sauchiehall Street that trip most readily off elderly Glasgow tongues. Mrs. Millicent Davis, now of Dunblane, is quite adamant that things have not improved.

> I like to remember Glasgow as it was in the days before the demise of Pettigrew and Stephen's, Copland and Lye and Daly's. There's nothing comparable now. I remember Daly's with the real Willow Tearoom. It was just delightful.

Occasionally, perhaps with a friend who was a Pettigrew's devotee, or in the days when she went where she was taken, as a child . . .

> I used to go for tea at Pettigrew's. It was decorated in pale grey and their china was *gorgeous* . . . grey lattice designs with pink flowers.

And people used to beat a pathway to the Aladdin's basement at Trèron et Cie (where someone claims to have once had Mr. Cie* pointed out to her!)

*et cie – and Company

It was the china . . . oh my, that china! A whole hall of it there
was. It was a good shop all over, but it was best known for all
the different makes of china . . . the Spode and the Doulton and
the Wedgwood, and just the old 'Blue Dawn' and Meekin's using-
wally.

The dainty Trèron tearoom upstairs is recalled as another feature.

There was a quartet played music and they'd always posies of flowers
and silver cake-stands on the table. Once I remember we must have
been sitting there near closing time and the waitress (y'know, in nice
black dress and white pinny and cap) came over and was going to take
away the flowers.
    But Mamma said 'Excuse me, but could you leave the flowers till
we're finished please. We're enjoying them so much'. and so we
were.

Come August though, when it was down-to-earth shopping for
the winter under-duds and working gear, good, plain, middle-
priced Paisley's in Jamaica Street was the place.

Paisley's was all kinds of uniforms and work clothes like overalls and
boiler-suits . . . and maids' wrappers and pinnies, and of course for
your combinations and liberty bodices.

An elderly lady still smarts at what she sees as her family's
chauvinistic excursions to Paisley's.

I got taken for my Chilprufe combinations and pinafores. It wasn't so
much the pinafores but I couldnae thole the combies . . . or the ribbed
stockings held up on yon suspenders that buttoned on to your liberties.
I'm sayin' *held up* but they crinkled round your knees and you'd a big
gape at the back you'd to keep hitching up. But my brother! Oh, he
got his kilt and all his orders, silver button jacket, tartan socks . . .
standing there quite jokoh in his Balmoral with the red toorie . . .
and a dirk for his sock. He got a *dirk* . . . and I got combies! That was
Paisley's.

And it still rankles after eighty years. Furniture stores too had their
social layers, from the sedate exclusiveness of Gardner's and Wylie
and Lochhead to the more modest 'Bows-of-the-High-Street' and
Wyllie Hill's and even a turn-of-the century one opposite Boot's
Corner, that Jack Roche remembers.

An uncle of mine used to work at that Glasgow Bedding and Bedstead
Centre on the same side as the Hielan'man's Umbrella. That would've
been eighty years ago and I remember seeing women working at the
mattresses.

Those were the places that the discerning, quality-rather-than-
bargain folk spent their solid budgets and where the polished
brass facings to their deep window-sills were unhooked at night
and taken inside for safe-keeping. Most families being 'wage'
rather than 'salary' earning, couldn't always afford the economics
of the 'good thing' that would last for years, and found that other
emporia (or even the Barras) suited their purses better.

Th'was Dallas's and the Colosseum and Arnott Simpson's, quite good
serviceable clo'es you got there, but not the kind of cut and quality of
the other places. I went there a lot for clo'es and at the Colosseum you
could get a three-course lunch and a cup of tea for 1/9. That would be
the late twenties. They were good for towels and sheets and things.
Bow's and the 'Poly' were good bargain places too. And sometimes,
maybe before the First War, my mother went to the Bonanza in George
Square if things were a bit tight for my father.

They knew their stores, those thrifty ladies, and their stores knew
them.

They're great nowadays for their 'market research', but in the big
stores, where I worked long before it was heard of, we knew fine
what it was all about.

And the long-retired employee of one such store shakes a knowing
head over modern arty lay-outs and packaged, untouchable stock.

It's a mistake . . . your wee Glasgow body likes a good rummage.

Many a good rake in the likes of Dallas's is remembered by those
with quite slender purses. But there were other well-doing folk
even harder put to it to present a bien appearance, even if they
weren't all as badly off as those who resorted to the pawn-shop.

When you were skint your father's Sunday clo'es went into the pawn,
but that was quite good forbye the wee bit money, because when you'd
no cupboards or wardrobes your things got hung up and looked after
till you wanted them the next Sunday.

The Hutchison family were not pawners but still hard-put-to-it to present the bien appearance they managed to keep up.

My Daddy had a big family to manage, and my Mother dead. When we were nearly grown-up we got half-a-crown a week . . . and that was for everything. You'd to buy all your clo'es out of that. My sister Jeanie didn't get much either to keep the house and see to the five boys. She really brought us all up. We didn't go up the town often, except if you'd something big you needed.

For Mrs. Chrissie Ronnie too, a trip into the town was a rare treat.

I was away in service and I wasn't home often, but when I was, I used to go in to look at the windows or, say, buy a vest. That would maybe be 1s.11½d. And if you'd only 1s.11d well, you didnae get it. My wages then, in the early twenties, were never over £2 a month.

Sometimes a visit to town was for service rather than goods. Joe

Harper lifting his head from a game of Senior Citizen dominoes, recalls Boot's Corner as it used to be.

> Th'was this big tobacconist's long ago (I'm talking maybe 1908 or 1909) and you could see from the top of the tram SMOKE HOWELL'S TOBACCOS on its shop blind. Then above that th'was Cherry's Shaving Parlour and brush-up place with an advertisement black painted on the wall for THE MOST HYGIENIC HAIR BRUSHING MACHINE IN GLASGOW. You could get your boots polished there an' all. All that was below a hotel on the next storey . . . maybe the old Adelphi . . . or maybe it had some other name before that.

Those blind and wall-stencilled adverts were an extension of the centuries-old hanging signs.

> The shops used to all have signs set up to hang outside them. I s'pose originally for them that couldnae read . . . but I'm talking maybe seventy-eighty year ago. Usually they were on hinges or wee rings and you could hear them creakin' in the wind. There would be a big haddie or-that outside the fishmonger . . . and mortars and pestles at the chemist. And I mind a lum hat outside a gents' shop . . . and the barber's pole, of course . . . and was there no' a yellow and green cow at the Buttercup or some other dairy?

Jack Roche recalls a sign on the southside, or at least hearing about it.

> My grandpa used to talk about a pub sign in Strathbungo that was a cut-out head of Robert Burns . . . no' very like him, he said (how he could tell that I don't know). But there was quite a lot of Burns connections in that area wi' Burns' daughter by Anna Park livin' there. She's buried out at Pollokshaws. Her son was brought up there and he wrote poems too.

That southside pub brings us away from the city where the department stores, however grand or modest, were for all-day excursions, with tea and a slice of Craig's fruit loaf or Fuller's walnut cake thrown in. From such establishments a face or figure may sometimes be remembered . . . a Tartar at the Outsize Dresses or a wing-collared shop-walker pacing a stately beat among the counters. But the warmest and most human memories are not those of the big stores, they're rather of the corner shops where Maggie Brodie or Charlie Nolan cut your ham to your precise thickness, or trusted you with half-a-pound of cheese till pay-poke day, and where the surroundings were as familiar as your own front room.

> I mind a nice grocer's in Dennistoun . . . wi' all wee polished drawers for lentils or peas or that, and the names of what was in them on the outside, under kind of crystal handles. Th'was sacks of grain and potatoes, big brass scales and a marble counter . . . and celluloid black and white price tickets stuck in the cheeses. Th'was big black, what they called 'Japan', tins for different teas, and a biscuit rack with big containers that had hinged lids to get at the biscuits, it was always loose biscuits then.

And at the East Kilbride Dairy in the early thirties you got red pencil-sharpeners with Youma bread, from Miss King.

> . . . remember Youma bread? Yon were nice pencil-sharpeners, and in the chemist you got a board game with toothpaste . . . that was the Ivory Castle game, all about Giant Decay, for good children that brushed their teeth.

Not that your actual *shop* was always the place to go for messages. Jimmy Dewar remembers the buying and selling that went on out at Hogganfield.

> There was an interesting small holding there, maybe about five or six acres. Pinkerton's Rhubarb Farm. I used to see all the work people out in the summer picking rhubarb . . . famous place was Pinkerton's. Next door to the grocers I worked for at Battlefield was a fruit and veg shop owned by a Mrs. Pinkerton. I wondered if she belonged to that same family.

Jewish children often had interesting and exotic errands.

> I can remember when we lived in Stockwell Street I used to go with my mother to buy fish at the Clydeside, where the *Carrick* sailing-ship was for a long time. Often on a Friday they'd sell you a big parcel of fish . . . cod mostly. She'd cook it in milk and it was delicious. You got those cheap parcels of fish at the fish market too.

There were Jewish shops too, and Lily Balarsky remembers those.

They were mostly just across the bridge. I remember some of the old Jewish shopkeepers . . . yes . . . with long beards. Mr. Greenberg had a delicatessen and Mother used to send me for messages and of course she hadn't learned to speak English properly. There was a grain, a pin-head oatmeal that she used as a base for soup, but she didn't know the English name for it and she would send me across the Stockwell Bridge to this man's place for a pound of 'hoberni gropen' . . . it's groats really. That's the Yiddish name, and I was all embarrassed and crying at having to go. Says-I, wailing, 'But I need to know the right name'. And she says 'you just go and ask for "hoberni gropen", *he'll* know'. And right-enough the man knew fine what I wanted.

Sometimes the fish too was from Mr. Greenberg rather than the Clyde quay.

He'd big barrels of salt herrings outside the door, real salt herring. And he used to lift it out dripping on to the scales, then into a newspaper. There were a lot of 'deli' and fruit shops there in the Gorbals, and Jewish butchers where you got wurst and so on. The meat was kosher, butchered on the same principle as the 'halal' . . . the traditional religious customs from the hot climate in the Middle East. Still done of course, but if I'm a bit nostalgic it's because my memories are warm of that time, and you've got to say it the way it was. Otherwise there's no real truth.

Vivid pictures from seventy or more years ago can be dredged up even from something as insubstantial as remembered smell. Mr. Edward Aldington sees a Tollcross dairy.

I used to be sent from Mount Vernon to a dairy in Tollcross for butter. You stepped down into the shop and it had a rough slabbed floor with barrels and with cans of milk on it. And there was always this slightly *sour* smell hanging about. I've always remembered that.

Sometimes a rememberer himself was part of the mellow scene in an old shop . . . like the late Mr. James McClelland.

I was a grocery boy my first job. In the east end. I took the deliveries of course, but there were other things you'd to do. I did the sawdust . . . wetting it to sweep up, then put fresh stuff down. I can still smell that new sawdust and the potatoes I unloaded into a big open-fronted bunker. Another job was shovelling them out into quarter stones.

Maybe seventy years from now people will yearn when they remember the obstinate set of supermarket trolley wheels, or the thrill of lifting down a packet of biscuits from among a thousand others tasting much the same, or even the plastic spacemen they got free with their cornflakes. Maybe there'll be the same nostalgic sparkle for the slimy feel of pre-packed bacon as lights up elderly faces now when the bakers or butchers of their greenstick years are recalled.

> I used to get sent to this butcher in Crosshill. There was a shelf for all the hams . . . Belfast, Wiltshire, Ayrshire. You chose what you wanted, then I always remember a wee thing he did. He always took his knife up the cutting end of the roll of bacon as if he was brushing up the fibres or the grain or something. We bought cuts for soup too or maybe a sheep's head. Shops were open till all hours then and the only light in that butcher's was gas . . . jets all round the shop. No mantles, just raw sort of spade-shaped flames. I think they were called butterfly or fish-tail jets. And then of course there was always water trickling down the windows to help keep things fresh.
>
> I used to put my tongue to the window for a wee drink, thinking the water was outside.

The Dewars' butcher was quite a novelty in her day, for she was what old gravestones call a 'relict'.

> We'd this lady butcher. Her husband had been killed in the First War, maybe about 1915. She carried on the shop. What a talker! You went in for three quarters of mince . . . took you about an hour. That was Maggie Graham. There was another butcher that sold mince at sixpence a pound. My mother thought it was rubbish at sixpence instead of maybe ninepence at Maggie Graham's.

Sometimes a shop was one of a small chain around the city's outskirts. Peggy Carson recalls a well-known name that has long passed into proverb.

> We used to talk about someb'dy's house being like Annacker's midden. Annacker had butcher's shops . . . made sausages . . . so I s'pose his bins at the back would be messy. Mind, I used to wonder if his name really was Annacker right-enough, or if he just called himself that and it was really *a knacker's* midden . . . but that's just my own wee idea.

But Mrs. Bunty Angles shakes her head at such blasphemy and rummages for a photograph.

> No, no. Here's a picture of the shop with his name quite clear at the top. See . . . William Annacker. There was rivalry y'know, between Annacker's sausages and Waddell's of Napiershall Street, and there was a wee rhyme.
>> Annacker's sausages are the best
>> In your belly they do rest
>> Waddell's sausages are the wurst
>> In your belly they do burst.

McGonagall rather than Tennyson, but the message is clear. Peggy Carson has the last word though on her suspicions of the old name.

> Could've been just a made-up shop name. There are no Annackers in the 'phone book now, sure there aren't?

There was the Co-op too. The Co. did well for those who were loyal to it and cocked a snook at those who looked down on it.

> My mother was black-affronted once when someone saw only half of the back door of Cooper's van outside our house . . . didn't see the 'er's . . . and said to her, 'didn't know you dealt with the Co-op, Mistress Hunter'.

But Lily Balarsky's mother took a different view.

> Great thing the Co-op. My mother shopped there a lot. I can remember her number even yet . . . 23930. You used to get stamps you saved up and got your 'divvy' every year. It was great for working people. My mother once got a holiday through the Co-op.

Co-op numbers are branded into many an elderly Glasgow mind . . . 63450, 4075, 63785 . . . a dozen rememberers rattled them off. Mrs. Nell Dinsmor recalls her mother's Co-op days at Barrhead.

> 4114 was her number. Och, the Co. was an institution . . . in the middle of Barrhead. That was the big Co-op for all over . . . the whole kaboodle, the bakery and the big-big laundry. The bakery was a marvellous place. Before the New Year your mother mixed her Ne'erday bun and I got to carry it to the bakehouse to get it baked there for thruppence or sixpence, depending on the size. And they'd

horse-drawn vans that went round selling. On Fridays the specialty was meat pies. The steam fairly came fleeing out the van because all the stuff was put in hot. Another specialty was what we called Cat's Faces. a sort of cookie in stuck-together sections with sugar on the top. That was a real treat.

The lady who was mortified at the idea of taking her custom to the Co. had an altogether more remote relationship with her grocer.

It was Cooper's of Howard Street we dealt with. They phoned for the order, then the groceries would be delivered in a big square coffee-coloured van the next day. Sometimes you paid by post, but sometimes you went into town to pay the account. I remember the lovely smells of coffee and ham. It was quite a dark shop I remember, but kind of 'classy'. Not so posh though as Manuel and Webster's. My friend went there, but I was like my mother, just a wee bit too thrifty for that.

Morning shopping was for groceries, but when you'd had your dinner (in early-century Glasgow almost invariably at midday) there was other local shopping to be done. There might be darning needles, buttons, hair ribbons, or wool for the interminable knitting of socks and stockings. There was a wee draper-cum-shoe shop in the Carsons' street before the First War.

It was an old lady had it, a wee lady *overflowing* with fat. She'd black woollen stockings and flat, strap-and-button shoes. One side the shop was yarns and knitting pins, stockings and corsets, on the other side she sold laces and speckled sandshoes along wi' the boots and shoes. For them you sat with your feet on a sloping box and if it was button boots she tweaked them through wi' a wee button-hook. It just twinkled up the row of buttons.

After all the worthy purchases your mother made when you were young if you were lucky and there was a copper or two left you had your own precious income to lay out on luxuries.

Friday night was Band of Hope night and you'd your penny to spend. It was the done thing on your way there to go into Birrell's and buy Russian toffees.

Ogo-pogo eyes were the great thing wi' us. You sooked them fae one colour to another, yellow, pink, blue, green . . . maybe five or

six different colours. You'd to keep takin' them out your mouth . . .
to make sure you werenae missing a colour.

Soor plooms, spearmint chews, X.L. chewing gum, aniseed balls,
midget gems . . . all had their following, but Jack Roche preferred
quality to quantity.

My favourite was yon FIVE BOYS chocolate, with the row of wee
boys' faces on the front. The first one was crying and miserable, then
each one after that was a bit more cheerful. What were the words under
them . . . DESPERATION, PACIFICATION, EXPECTATION,
ACCLAMATION, REALISATION.

It's sherbet dabs I mind of the best. You licked the sherbet off a wee flat
stick or sooked it through a liquorice tube. We'd cinammon sticks that
we chewed and we made sugarollie water. You just shook your hard
liquorice in a bottle of water. It was s'posed to go darker and better if
you did it under the bed.

Mary Rodger was a sugarollie-water-maker.

If you'd a ha'penny you bought liquorice, long ropes of it. You could
eat it or make sugarollie water. Or you maybe bought caramels. I was
awful fond of caramels.

Her sister Chrissie preferred tiger nuts.

You got an awful lot for a ha'penny and chewed them. They were
like wee hard raisins.

All these would be bought in small shops around the home streets
of their customers, but north of the city there was a Mecca for
connoiseurs from all airts, like the Morton family.

There was Skene's shop up Alexandra Parade at Castle Street where
the white tram and the red tram stopped. There were queues there on a
Saturday night for their sweeties. Skene's was a famous sweetie shop.

Of course there were always expansive souls who preferred
fleeting pleasure to the long investment in sucking or chewing.

The first time I'd real money in my pocket I went in and had a peach
melba. What an extravagance! But it was good.

Ice-cream fanciers had almost the whole Italian immigrant

population of the city providing for their samplings and comparisons, and rememberers are still fiercely certain that their own local 'Tally' had the secret of the perfect recipe. 'Tally'? Perhaps there are still Italians who bridle at that term, but the genial restaurateur reminiscing for this book is not one of them.

> Used to it. In the old days they didn't like it. But it's just a sort of term of affection now. I think 'Paki' will get to be like that too, that's the way most people use it . . . kind of friendly. And when the Pakistanis get to know the Glasgow folk better, the feeling of being offended'll pass. I hope so. They're nice people.

The final forlorn word on sweets and similar treats must go to Robert Ford who is one of the few not to have a list of old-time favourites.

> Got no pennies, nothing like that. You didn't get much sweeties.

Later years have been kinder to Mr. Robert Ford than they were to the young Bobby and he can now enjoy (the better perhaps for sparse times in childhood) the pleasures of the purchase that other rememberers knew in the days of seventy, eighty, ninety years ago when they bartered with Mr. Greenberg or Mr. Cie.

12

Ladies from Hell

The wars of this century have been its marking years, chaptering the lives of those who endured them, who went into them from one life-style and with one set of expectations and emerged into a world changed for them out of all recognition.

There are fewer and fewer now who have memories of the First War, but such recollections are sharp, tender, brave and full of pain. Those who have them, seem to look back with awe, marvelling that they lived through such a holocaust and sometimes even smiled.

First though, there is a single, second-hand memory of a much older war, that Millicent Davis has carried with her over all the conflicts of her own lifetime.

> My father was born in the 1870s and he used to tell us that as a small boy he had been taught to do the proper military salute by a retired soldier who'd been young at Waterloo.

Earlier wars than that of 1914 were fought by officer-younger-sons and the 'rough soldiery', and scarcely touched the lives of ordinary men and women. So the echoes of romance and adventure that went with the tale of her father's salute perhaps gave a deceptive thrill to the young Millicent when she heard her father say in the early days of 1914, that he was sure there was going to be a war. But reality was a dark shadow in the wings, and war was scarely declared before young men, who should have been tradesmen, clerks and students, were off to the strange dance of death . . . a brutish life they had never dreamed of leading.

> We were on a painting holiday in Dunning in August 1914 and whenever we came home Herbert, my older brother, joined up . . .

354

couldn't wait. I've still got his sketch of Dunning Square from that holiday. He went to the Cameron Highlanders.

For all the rumours and certainties that war was coming, the country was caught unawares.

Some of them had no uniforms at first. Britain didn't seem to be prepared. A lot of them just drilled with sticks. I remember seeing that.

It was worth a chuckle in the Second War that the Home Guard was armed with wooden poles, but those men of the First were soldiers no more than a month from the trenches.

Life at home became grey with restriction and shortage and gloomy folk complained at first, but gradually common gumption and imagination, and the shameful realisation of what was happening in France spurred civilians into action. For the playing with poles had soon turned into this bloodiest of wars and stupefying casualty lists began to appear in daily newspapers. Those who had waved off their lads with jingoistic cheering, glorying in their handsome courage, were sobered now and threw themselves into making the best of trifling difficulties at home. As apprentice by apprentice, office boy by office boy, the young disappeared to France, or to sea, older men doubled their workloads by day, and by night rolled up their sleeves to other tasks.

I remember a rough area near us you'd've thought was good for nothing, but it was marked off into allotments for growing vegetables. A lot of business men came off the train with their high bowlers and brollies, got home and changed, and away down to dig and weed their wee patches and try to grow bigger turnips than anyone else.

Older women made small thrifts, boasting of what would have shamed them before. Janet Kay remembers her mother.

She used to cut bits out of the tail of my father's shirt to make new collars and cuffs . . . got quite expert at that.

Younger women hitched up their skirt hemlines to a more practical level, to pour into factories . . . and some found unexpected perks there to help eke out wartime household

furbishings. Agnes Grove's mother worked at Templeton's carpet
factory.

> They used to make chenille for carpets and if there was a wee bit
> mistake you could get the strips cheap. My mother would get maybe
> four and make curtains wi' that . . . for next-to-nothing.

That bargain was too good to be longlasting and those who found
it first were the lucky ones.

> When the bosses discovered a woman could *do* things with the likes of
> these strips they started to charge more.

The chenille-making gradually wound down and eventually
stopped altogether for the duration of the war. Looms that had
proudly woven carpet for the White House Oval Office went over
to more mundane warps and woofs.

> Y'see the looms got put to making army blankets instead, until after
> the war when they went back to the chenille again.

Lack of chenille and other fancies were the least of the shortages,
and basic household supplies were at first scarce and then
rationed.

> We went to stay with friends at a farm in Auchterarder during the
> war, and they gave us . . . *butter*! We hardly ever had butter at home
> because the small ration you could get wasn't very nice . . . wasn't
> worth buying. We were better with marg really. There was a kind of
> art about the way you used your wee lump of ration when you did take
> it. You all had different ways of eating it. My sister ate all hers on the
> first slice of bread. I eked it out all through the meal, and my brother
> kept his to have on the last slice. Showed up our personalities really.

For most families there could be a wee glut of at least one of the
rationed foods . . . a modest black market or sly offering from
under the counter. Bosom friendship with a grocer was suddenly
a great asset, or some tit-for-tat arrangement that allowed the
exchange of half-a-dozen oranges for a pound of sugar concluded
by grave business men with more in their Gladstone bags than
insurance or stockbroking documents. Sometimes it was a case
of the early bird . . . Lily Joseph's father was one who knew a fat
worm when he saw it.

He knew the right people. He used to go to the butcher at six o'clock in the morning and get a wee bit of whatever was going. And he gave them some of what he had. It was a tight community, they helped each other.

Sometimes the extra was legitimate and smiled on by authority. The making of Mrs. Mysie Kyle's family lemonade was rated as essential.

Sugar was rationed of course, but we got an allowance for making the lemonade, we got enough even for the house, so we didn't need to take up our ordinary ration. But we got a wee bit extra butter instead, because some people couldn't afford theirs.

Some who were too prodigal with their tea-sugar early in the week, were resourceful enough to find a substitute by the end.

We put toffee balls in our tea if we'd no sugar. You could stir it about a bit, then take it out to keep for the next time.

But long before rationing was biting and queues were long, before the chenille-making stopped or the first carrot-fronds poked up on the allotments, it was apparent that the war that was to have been 'over by Christmas' was only just starting and that civilians would have to find a use in the war effort for whatever talents they could dredge up.

In school we were put to knitting for the troops . . . socks, scarves, balaclava helmets and so on, because it was miserable and cold in the trenches. And we'd to buy things and write wee letters to put in the parcels with the woollies. I can remember putting in boracic powder . . . for the soldiers' feet.

At the receiving end of the parcels one nonagenarrian recalls getting candles and matches sent.

You put the flame up and down the pleats of your kilt for to kill the lice. The sight of us in kilts was s'posed to make Jerry feart . . . the 'Ladies from Hell' they called us. But it wasn't very practical, the kilt . . . not in the muddy hell of Flanders.

Some troops who had been cheered by the messages in their parcels made contact with the writers on their leaves.

> There was a Private Turnbull came to see me twice. He got the V.C. later so he was a star and I was the talk of the class because I knew him.

Another star of the '14–18 War who was right at the other end of the command chain from the good private, caused Bunty Angles to commit the only school misdeameanour she can recall. There were visits round the country of certain big-wigs to rally people from despondency and urge their support for the troops when things at the front were going badly and casualty lists were long.

> The only time I plunked the school was to see Earl Haig going along Great Western Road. We went out at lunchtime and saw him passing along in his big car . . . quite quickly . . . but we did get a glimpse of him. Then we didn't bother to go back to school.

The money for the comforts parcels came from selling home-made toffee or soft goods or paper flowers, from fund-raising concerts and flag days.

> Right through the war I collected on flag-days. The first one I remember was for 'gallant little Montenegro'. I don't know what was happening in 'gallant little Montenegro' but I rattled my can all the same. Then there was 'poor Belgium' and the Red Cross. There was no half-measures with me. I was out standing at Cessnock subway before breakfast to get workers coming off their shifts.

'Poor Belgium' had much need of the rattled can for the refugees pouring across its borders after the German invasion, and of the services put at their disposal on their arrival in Scotland. Miss Jenny Logan remembers the quota of them that came to Glasgow, terrified that they'd find it savage and primitive and not a lot better than staying at home under harsh occupation might have been. A warm welcome at Central Station with hot food and brisk organisation to find them comfortable billets surprised and reassured them.

> Quite a lot were put into the Mansion House at Rouken Glen. Our uncle had a lot to do with the whole arrangement because he was

the City Collector. And his wife had been at school in France, so she was fluent in French and interpreted for them. Later for all that she was presented with a signed photo of the King of the Belgians.

As well as the worthy works of comfort and mercy, with knitting-pins and flag-days and the relief of the refugees, there were other skills to offer. Musicians of varying talent dusted down instruments, gargled their throats and set out to entertain low-spirited civilians or the troops themselves . . . to relieve the boredom of waiting for action or cheer convalescent invalids to whom the high adventure had brought broken bodies and haunted minds. Alan Dale's father was one of those who took their music to wherever there was need and ran their own risks in the doing.

He was a turn in a touring circus at that time . . . a trapeze artist for a bit . . . and a clown. But he played the saxophone as well. In the First War he went round with a group entertaining the troops . . . went to Ireland and so on. One night they missed the ferry from Belfast, and-here that boat was sunk and people lost on its way across.

There were long days for the convalescent sick and wounded sent home from the front and these little groups of 'Good Companions' tried to lighten the gloom.

My brother was in a wartime hospital in Edinburgh at one stage, ill with trench fever. We were all quite a musical family, and we went as a group to this school in Edinburgh that was the hospital. We entertained the troops there non-stop for a whole day in the main hall. I would be about fourteen. I remember handing out programmes my father had done in his nice script. I sang too. I sang 'The Green Trees Whispered Sweet and Low', and then pantomime songs. My mother and my brother, Harold, played some of my father's musical arrangements. He'd studied music at Leipzig and taught us all.

That was one of the last happy events for the family. Having survived spells of trench fighting throughout the war, since the instant enlisting in August 1914 when he was just eighteen, and come through the dread trench fever, Herbert was killed three weeks before the armistice.

For that was the reality of the war . . . not the sturdy support going on at home, however useful, but the blood-soaked glaur of trench warfare, and the slaughter of a generation there, or in the icy bleakness of winter at sea. And young men could be lost in other ways than by death.

My brother took a kind of depression at the front . . . sort of shell-shock. He'd been the kind and affectionate one of all my brothers, clever too, and humorous. Very steady. But he just stopped writing home altogether . . . lost touch. He got through the last months like a kind of zombie, then when it was over he just went wandering and it was a long time before he eventually came home. Never made anything of life after that. It broke my mother's heart.

And one who didn't come home to the Rodger family at all . . .

. . . my brother was at sea. He jumped ship and had the Navy police after him, so he just disappeared altogether.

There were other old friends who were casualties of war too. Mysie Kyle's family lost their horse to army service.

Big Prince used to draw the lemonade lorry and was stabled at home so he was a great favourite. Well, my father was up at Saracen Street with him one day and these men just came up and said, 'We need your horse' and without a by-your-leave or anything they just led him out the trams and took him away . . . to the war. My father'd to come back home that day for the old horse, Donald, to take him up to Saracen Street and put him in the trams instead. We never saw Prince again. He was killed in France. I was young in the First War, six when it started. There was Prince, and then my uncle was wounded and missing, so I was frightened of the Germans.

There were other horses than Prince called from the pleasant plod of peacetime to the screaming shells of France. Hard times for dobbins. But one not very gruntled Tommy in France saw the conscripted horses as having more comfort and consideration than himself and his mates. Trucks were lined up to take animals and men to the front and large notices posted in French by the allied soldiers making the behind-the-lines arrangements. The Tommies made for the trucks, each vehicle allocated to thirty men, passing the ones to which only five horses were headed. 'Och here,' remarked the private climbing into his cramped quarters, 'I wish't I was a chevvocks and no' a hom' . . . and the old soldier remembers and chuckles.

Mrs. Agnes Grove's husband too saw life at the front with the horses.

He was a lead horse-driver with a six-horse vehicle taking ammunition to the front. Sometimes when he arrived they'd cheer him because they were right out of ammunition. One time the Germans were firing and he got wounded . . . lost part of his leg with shrapnel . . . affected him on that side all his life after.

Having lost Prince, and seen tears for the missing uncle, young Mysie had more trauma to bear.

My brother was taken to the army after that, near the end of the war, and he took yon terrible 'flu that killed so many people. He developed T.B. and was in a sanitorium in the Ochil Hills for a long time.

Bert Paterson was another who left the front with a shattered leg that still troubles him sorely at ninety-two.

I mind how the nurses looked when I came wounded out the trenches . . . looked like angels, in white dresses and white pinnies and caps . . . and crisp kind of cuffs up to their elbows. I can still see that picture after seventy year. And mind a lot of them girls had been lady kind of lassies that couldnae move for their hobble skirts a few years afore. My leg still plays up but I was one of the lucky ones 't got back at all.

Nine million young men on both sides were not so fortunate . . . ten times the entire population of the city of Glasgow were killed in the 1914–18 War . . . every death an individual tragedy.

My younger brother was about eighteen and on embarkation leave when word came that my older brother had been killed. It came in an orange envelope from the War Office. I remember Mamma taking in the telegram and my father taking it from her to open. Oh, the tears of that day! I adored that brother. He was only twenty-two.

The elderly voice, remembering, has no detachment in it that this was over seventy years, another war and long years of marriage ago.

Three weeks after that death came the cease-fire, and for some it was bunnets in the air and dancing in the streets. Agnes Grove was in the streets.

Do I remember the Armistice? oh aye . . . easy! I was working in Templeton's. We all just stopped our looms and got ready to walk out. The tenter says, 'Here, you cannae d'that till we've seen the boss'. The Boss said 'yes' but we'd've been away anyway . . . into the town, all shouting and singing. What a carry-on! Then we got an extra five shillings in our pay that week.

Janet Kay was a little younger, but her recollections of the day, the scenes of relief, and rejoicing, and the players, are just as vivid.

I was in Miss Cay's class at the school (the others used to say she was my granny because of the name). She'd maybe be about thirty-two or three then. She was lovely. I can remember she wore nice coat-frocks. She was like that the day of the Armistice. Well anyway the jannie chapped on the door with the big brass handles (the last jannie had got killed in the war). 'Miss Cay' says this new one, 'can I speak to you?' She went out, and came back into the room, crying. She says 'It's peace'. We'd all to go out to the gallery above the hall that was down below in the dunny, (where you usually marched-in to someone thumping out 'The Flowers of Edinburgh' or that, on an old piano). The headmaster talked to us, we sang 'O God of Bethel' and repeated the Lord's Prayer. I've always had a lump in my throat singing that, since then. Then we got sent home.

For some, the day of the Armistice was not much different from any other and work went doggedly on . . . but it's a day remembered for all that. Robert Ford was still in Portpatrick.

I was labouring on the land at the time the war ended. We could hear the church bells ringing that day, three miles away, but we were in the field gathering up potatoes, and we just went on digging.

That November day held one of Struan Yule's early memories . . .

. . . of seeing a woman across the street struggling to put out a big flag from her window . . . almost falling out. I remember asking my mother what she was doing. And-here it was the end of the war . . . the Armistice.

Peggy Carson danced in an arm-linked trio across Jamaica Bridge, Millicent Davis went from terminus to terminus through the town on the open top of a yellow tram, to see the revellers. Jack Roche went into church. But for many others, it was a day of tears and sorrow.

> My mother and her family weren't throwing their hats in the air. They'd lost their brother and there wasn't much to rejoice about. They were very subdued. My father'd been killed on the Somme and when the Armistice came, my mother just went into the Room with her lips all tight, and shut the door. I was about ten and I didn't know what to say to her. I still had a black ribbon in my dress.

As the surviving men came home and people shook themselves down into routines of living again after the war, the pattern of its results began to show more clearly.

> Almost all the boys in my age-group were lost. It was like nearly a whole generation gone . . . killed in the trenches or drowned. And that left almost a whole generation of women with no chance of marriage. All those good lives wasted . . . and no children to follow them.

Isobel Horn's family was evidence of that.

> My mother was the only one of five sisters to marry. So there was I, living beside a whole household of quite young spinster aunts.

Local War Memorial lists revealed another appalling result of the war and the system of forming comrade-squads from the same places, towns and shires. Robert Ford speaks for his neighbourhood.

> Just about all the boys from our village died, in actions where they were alongside each other. There's about a hundred names on the memorial. Later they put men into regiments and other services, more kind of at random, so they wouldn't be fighting together and all get wiped out.

In the later aftermath, Glasgow, like other places, was too busy licking its own wounds to notice that over in Germany insidious problems were sowing the dragons' teeth of war for the children whom that culled First War generation *had* been able to produce.

One of our professors at the university told us about being in Germany in the inflation period . . . when people were trundling handcarts of money to pay their bills, or suitcases of it to do their shopping.

Jack Roche saw it all in hindsight.

The Armistice of 1918 was just the first half over, of one big-big war. It was just, what you would say? . . . a kind of deadly interval.

13

Epifania was our Big Thing

Festivals are, by their very nature, occasions that don't change much and are for the most part still celebrated . . . if not always with the same awestruck understanding and belief, at least with delight in the secular trimmings and social round. Take Christmas. There's a kind of rosy glow over memories of what they were like in young days when everything was new, exciting and full of promise. There is no talk though of expensive toys or of the expectation that wants would be automatically met.

> I always wanted a bicycle, but I never got that . . . got old ones that other people had done with, but never a shiny new one of my own. And football boots . . . I never got them either. I wanted them badly, but it was always just someone's old ones that were always too big or too small and gave you blisters . . . or they'd maybe a nail in them. So I couldn't play proper school footb'll . . . just in the street or a bare patch of grass beside the burn. But I did get one thing I wanted. I got a Meccano set one Christmas . . . the basic set that my uncles added to for me.

Little Mary Rodger got cinders in her stocking for luck. Just how lucky was she in her finds as she delved past the clinkers?

> No' a right stocking . . . more a wee sort of bag . . . with an apple a wee poke of sweeties and the cinders. But the best was the tuppence you got at the bottom . . . you fairly scattered the rest to get at that.

No Barbie dolls, computers or high-tech everything for the likes of the McLean Street Rodgers. Bunty Angles fared rather better at her grandmother's home.

> Oh I always got a stocking. They filled it with a tangerine, an apple, some sweeties and chocolate and a sixpence. And I remember once,

because it was my favourite tea, my uncle, for fun, putting some ham and an egg in my stocking.

. . . hopefully hard-boiled!

And I always got a small present as well.

Mysie Kyle's memories are more of the season's socialising than its loot.

We went down to Blochairn Church for the service and for the Christmas Eve 'swarry' in the big hall. You got a bag of buns and a cup of tea. Then New Year's Day it was the Sunday School prize-giving. You got your prize, and an orange going out at the door.

Eighty years ago Christmas was certainly not the extravagant thrash it is now, nor even the most widely celebrated day in the Christian calendar, and many Reformed Kirk folk looking back, recall more excitement at New Year, which held none of the dubious hang-overs from midwinter pagan festivals.

We didnae do much at Christmas forbye we got wee bits of presents and stockings. There was no work holiday for your father and we never-ever had a tree or that.

But New Year . . . ah New Year was different!

Come Ne'erday my mother went daft. It was a room and kitchen and ever'thing got cleaned for dear life, brasses polished, curtains washed, range cleaned (never mind it was scoured and blackleaded every week anyway) the flues were done . . . even the ceiling got white-washed . . . kitchen table scrubbed (again!). You'd of thought black shame on yoursel's if you went dirty into the New Year. It was all ready the night before really . . . for Hogmanay.

There must have been Edwardian women who slittered cloths over kitchen tables from time to time, who let their brasses turn dingy or left rims of grease round their jaw-boxes, but none of them were the mothers of any of the loyal offspring who remembered for these pages.

Mamma scoured every corner for Hogmanay and put clean sheets and poinds on the beds, to go spotless into the New Year. The table would be set too because your first visitors would arrive at midnight. Us young ones would be in nightdresses or pyjamas, but you got to taste the shortbread or blackbun and the ginger wine . . . Crabbe's . . . no' very nice really, but you sat there mim as a pussy cat and sipped it. Most of the visiting was done the next day, you *had* callers and you *went* visiting . . . in your Sunday braws. You took ginger wine with you or a wedge of your own black bun.

In some homes there was the annual skiddle of brewing their own wine.

It was my Da made the ginger in our house . . . got a wee bottle of essence and brown sugar, fairly fancied himself at that job. It wasnae the ginger he fancied *himself* though.

Italian winter solstice celebrations were even later than 1st January, as Mr. Mario Servadei remembers.

Italian families when I was young didn't hold Christmas as such . . . not very much. Not on 25th December. And New Year wasn't anything special either. We looked more to what we called Epifania on 6th January.

Epifania (Epiphany) celebrated the visit of the Wise men to the stable with their gifts.

Epifania was our big thing when the immigrants came here at first. Now of course Italians have taken up with the Scottish ways . . . did that quite early on. I remember that because my father always had to first foot the people up the stair.

Later in the year, Easter celebrations were a poor shadow of what they had been in the homeland.

It's always an important festival in the church in Italy but when the Italians came here they lost the Easter procession and all the Saints' days processions too. Maybe if the Italians hadn't scattered all through Britain when they came, but kept together in a 'quarter' like the ones that emigrated to New York they'd have kept up the old customs the way they do there.

And Mario Servadei senses another difference in the fates of immigrants to the two countries.

Then they became American almost at once. Maybe because America was a hotch-potch of nationalities already, trying to weld themselves together into one; while here, Italians were foreigners among the British. When my cousin over there talks of 'my country' he means America. When I talk about 'my country' I mean Italy . . . though maybe I would call myself Scots-Italian.

Before there ever were great Christian festivals to celebrate, Jewish people were holding the selfsame feasts and rituals they enjoy today . . . highlighting the turning seasons with gatherings and rejoicings hallowed since the days of Abraham. They seem perhaps less splendid now than they did when Lily Balarsky was a child.

Chanukah was always a great festival with us. It's all about the story of the oil in the Temple lasting for eight days . . . a miracle . . . the Miracle of Lights. I remember the Chanukah candles burning brightly and vividly when I was small. The family takes it in turn that week to light the candles. I was one of the young ones so I'd to wait until late in the week. When I was very wee my father guided my hand. Then the fifth night we got what Jews call 'Chanukah gelt'. . . wee presents of money your parents and friends gave you. There were parties too with latkas and doughnuts and songs . . . 'Moaz Tsur' and a Yiddish song telling the Chanukah tale, 'Little lights, you have stories to tell'. It's still a great festival, but oh! I loved it when it was all new and magic to me.

Apart from comparatively recently relaxing into festivity at Christmas time, and marking Easter by the rolling of eggs to celebrate the rolling away of Christ's tombstone, the Presbyterian and other reformed Kirks in Scotland have never been greatly 'into' festivals. Their people can only envy the pleasure and hospitality of the Muslims at Eid-ul-Fitr after the fasting month, the Hindus' Diwali and the long and hearty Chinese New Year . . . and the all-through-the-year celebrations punctuating Jewish life.

In the spring of the Jewish calendar year comes the ancient Feast of the Passover.

We didn't go much to parties but we did a lot of visiting among our own people, all together in the community around Saltmarket, the

Briggait and the Gorbals. Passover was a big thing in our family . . .
with as many as you could seat, no matter the size of the house. Then
when everyone was gathered my father would tell the story of the
Passover from the Haggada. In those days the preparations weren't
all commercialised the way they are now. There wasn't the money.
But, mind you, maybe we'd more the spirit of it all. Like you do
at Christmas, I suppose, you lose a wee bit of what it's really all
about, under all the trimmings. There's wee practical things too,
about modern life . . . your expensive carpet gets awful messed up
with unleavened bread . . . it was easier in the old days to sweep the
crumbs off the lino.

Ah, who was it said with feeling. 'They're weel-aff that's no' weel-
aff'. Even weekly Friday night Shabbos celebrations (touched on
in another chapter) are not quite what they were in days when
entertainment was not so suffocatingly available at the touch of a
button.

Jewish Friday nights used to be so special . . . much more sacred than
now. Your mother had had a hard week, washing and cleaning and
often helping in some wee family business. But on a Friday night
she sat down with us all. It was nice that, in the candle-light . . . all
the polishing and cleaning done on the Thursday. I still have the old
candlesticks that came with my mother from Lithuania.

The big day for the Jewish male is neither weekly nor annual.
It is, as it always has been, the once-in-a-life-time, ever to be
remembered day of his Bar Mitzvah, celebrated at puberty. Here
too, there's the shaking of an older head over the altered emphasis
on the customs surrounding it.

When I was young Bar Mitzvahs were quite simple . . . very serious
but simple . . . the most important occasion in a boy's life. My
husband Solomon Balarsky is over eighty now and when he had his
he went to the synagogue in the Gorbals, read his piece and his father
gave him *a whole sixpence*, and he thought that was a very good gift.
Just the same as now he'd to learn the Hebrew rhythm and chanting
of the Torah (that's part of the Pentateuch . . . first five books of the
Bible). It was the most important part of the Bar Mitzvah, still is, but
there's a lot of expensive presents now that maybe a boy thinks about
more than the meaning of the whole thing.

Not all ritual observances were conventionally religious. Mrs. Lily Joseph recalls her father's pride in his weekly occasion.

> He became a mason, got initiated in 1902 at Bath Street. Only one of all my brothers did it later, they were the only ones in the whole family. Oh, my father was like Beau Brummel when he went to his meeting . . . all dressed up. He'd a best suit made to measure specially. Th'were lots of tailors near where we lived in the Gorbals. And he'd this private drawer where he kept all his Masonic accoutrements. These things were very very secret and nob'dy else got to open that drawer.

Drama, theatre and the good life woven together. That was what Masonic secrets looked like to the uninitiated.

It's small wonder Glaswegians of past times whooped it up at New Year or saved up hard for the July Fair on Glasgow Green (or if they were bien and very lucky, for a trip down the Clyde) for they had precious few of the structured and ancient ceremonies that immigrant minorities enjoyed and still keep now. There were commemorations though, very stiff and British . . . very worthy, but recalled in elderly days with pleasure. Janet Kay was an ardent member of the Red Cross.

> It was a big event every year on the Sunday nearest to Florence Nightingale's birthday (this would be about twenty years or less after her death) we'd this big-big assembly of nurses, hundreds and hundreds parading to Glasgow Cathedral. I remember once, and the place packed with nurses, the organ broke down and we'd to sing to a wee piano in yon great big building . . . couldnae hear it at all. But the good thing was . . . just *being* there.

Red Cross marches seem kind of tame beside Eid-ul-Fitr and Chanukah, but the Calvinists among us acknowledge that the old Kirk didn't leave us much of a legacy of merrymaking festivals and that we have to content ourselves with having pulled Christmas back out of the gloom to rejoice over its essential meaning, smothering our Yuletide trees with tinsel, and our friends with Magi gifts.

14

A Nice Pannyma

Funny i'nt it, how you take a wee case and go and stay in someb'dy else's house. I wonder who ever thought holidays up.

In ancient days from season to season kings moved about their realms from one residence to another so that they could collect taxes and so that their subjects in each area took it in turns to supply the court with goods and services during the time it was held on their doorsteps. The Prince Regent's time was long after that, so maybe he was really the one who, with his sea dips at Brighton, began the whole idea of holidays. Queen Victoria was partial to them of course, and the layers of folk up there beside her had, for decades past, changed houses for 'the season'. But it was when a web of railway lines and 'bus services was spun across the country that the notion percolated down to the plebs and they began to explore the possibilities of transplanting their families to live for a week or two away from their natural city habitat.

'Transplant' was certainly the word for the operation, whatever the destination, be it seaside, country, or in rare cases, overseas. The whole project had to be planned like a military operation. There was no lifting the boot of the car, throwing in a case filled with easy-care fabrics and casual jeans . . . and setting off in tops and trainers, and hatless (unless for a kiss-me-quick or Spanish sombrero).

Oh no. It was a serious matter was the annual holiday. Take the Clyde coast brigade and the Lockie family's drill.

My first recollection of holidays would be about 1905 and going to Lochranza. I enjoyed myself when I got there, but my best memories

are of getting ready to go, and the cabby coming to collect you for
your month away. You'd to take everything, all your linen . . .
for beds, table and towels, cutlery too . . . and the cat, always the
cat . . . the whole jing-bang. We'd a big Saratoga trunk with a
convex lid, a compartment for hats and a long place for umbrellas
and parasols. As well's that, you'd your hat-box and the hamper
of clothes that you closed up with a rod that went through two
loops.

That was the flitting ready and the family assembled in gloves, hats
and best coats, waiting for the cart. When the man came he heaved
the luggage first on to his back and then up to the front of the cab.
Then there was one last ritual before the big 'Gee-up!'

I'd always a wee bag with loaf sugar in it to give to the horse . . . held
it out on the palm of my hand the way my father showed me.

Then it was up and into the cab.

Now whenever I smell leather . . . I'm right back in that cab. Smells
take you back, don't they? (you don't get it with plastic though).
Anyway then we were off clip-clopping to the Broomielaw for the
boat. Did that for years.

The getting-there was much the same for the Logan family except
that they were setting off for the train, but dressed again in the good
Sunday braws for the travelling. At the end of the train journey a
waggon met them at the station to take them the five or six miles
to the rooms where 'attendance' awaited them . . . for a month.

The hamper was lifted up to the front beside the driver and we sat down,
two at each side at the back, the wee ones up on knees.

After a lifetime since these days, Miss Mabel and Miss Jenny Logan
can list their holiday places over the years without faltering . . .
Oban, Drummore, Cairnryan, then Elie and Port Logan and the
rest.

Or if it was Skipness, the horse and trap came to the pier instead of the
station, to take us to the holiday house. We'd always a long holiday,
because our father was a teacher.

Lily Balarsky's family, after the settling-in years as immigrants,
was established enough to have their holiday from the close in

Stockwell Street . . . a trip 'doon the watter' was skittles compared to the rigours of the journey from Lithuania and certainly didn't daunt her parents. Even so, it was a more complicated expedition than for Gentile families.

> It was always the Clyde coast. We took a room or two and did for ourselves . . . we couldn't have taken rooms-with-attendance, because of our food laws. So it was a big thing taking all your dishes and utensils, we wouldn't have used other peoples . . . that's just our way of life. The food was different from theirs too because the van would come from Glasgow to the Jewish holiday-makers down the Clyde with our kind of meat and bread. *We* had great holidays . . . but not the mothers. It was hard for them.

With Janet Kay it was Rothesay.

> Oh yes, Ro'say . . . a fortnight in May. I got off school for being a wee bit delicate. I was top of the class too, . . . a right wee genius. In the Elementary anyway. (It was a different matter in the Secondary!). But whatever it was, I got off the school to go to Ro'say in May. We went Third Class to Wemyss bay and then 'Cabin' to Bute. Just my mother and me; my father came at weekends. When I was very wee he didn't get paid holidays at Singers where he worked, and I'll never forget the day my mother told me 'Your father's got put on the *staff*' . . .

as distinct from the practical work force. . .

> . . .so now he'll get two weeks *paid* holidays.

'Rooms-with-attendance' was certainly the preferred way to take your holiday. It was a cut above just taking a room. You'd still your accommodation and brought in your own food, but the landlady cooked it for you. Part of the gamble was whether or not your hostess 'spoiled good butcher meat' or 'washed the lettuce right'. Another that she might be a dark presence keeping a baleful eye on her premises. All the same, rooms-with-attendance was the thing for most families, until at least the thirties.

When holiday-makers and hampers were reunited and mother had spent a tantalisingly slow hour or more, unpacking, with the young hopping from one foot to the other waiting for the sandshoes or the bathing-costume to appear, the holiday was 'on'.

My big sister had a striped bathing dress that I envied. I always wish't I looked like our Lizzie. When I look back on thon costume it was loose, no waist, hung from shoulders that buttoned together the front to the back. And it was long. But it was above her knees and that was s'posed to be daring. My Ma and Pa argy-bargy'd about that. But what I liked was it had her initials on the chest! Oh, Lizzie was something! And here's me in just my baggy cotton costume. Och, but I wish't I was Lizzie.

It might be that what came out of the trunk first, was the beach dress as opposed to *un*dress.

Me and my sister would be at the Punching Judy (sic) or playing buckets and spades on the sand and we'd have on long cotton pinafores and big straw hats (I'm talking around 1910). My father had a blue suit and a yellow panama hat, and I can see my mother yet in a deck chair wearing a great big hat with flowers and quite a heavy coat in what she'd've called 'covert' coating.

Janet Kay had one holiday outfit that remained indelibly stamped on her embarrassed mind.

We went to the entertainers, and-here it was Charlie Kemble this night. He used to pick out people in the audience and make up songs about them as he went along. Well! he pointed at me and began to sing that I was . . .
  'Sitting pretty
  With my Daddy and my Mammy
  With a wee red coat and a wee white tammy.
Well! I was absolutely mortified . . . didn't know where to put myself . . . just wanted to cry. But my mother nudged me quite chuffed. 'Listen, it's you he's singing about. It's great.' But I didn't think it was great. *I was insulted.* There was the Palace pictures too, at Ro'say. I was never allowed to go to the Saturday matinées anywhere else. It s'posed to be rough . . . and I was delicate and precious.

Another who was mortified at certain holiday visions was Peggy Carson.

My father insisted on wearing his shirt and braces *and* a knotted handkerchief on his head. He was a bald a bit and the hankie was to keep it from burning. I hated that. Thought it looked silly. 'Never heed, Hen,' I mind him sayin', 'you wouldnae want your Da to get

sunstroke'. Other men wore what my mother called 'a nice pannyma'. Come to think on it, hats were quite a thing wi' my parents. My father used to begin all his stories about his young days, 'When I was a lad in a doo-lander . . .'

Some destinations depended on strategically placed grannies or other kin. And sometimes without them there would have been no holiday at all. Ann Hutchison and her family relied on their auntie at Irvine.

She'd her own house so we didn't go with a big hamper. Anyway we hadnae that much to put in a big hamper. She'd a beautiful garden with apple trees, so we played there and we paddled down at the shore.

Another granny had a house at Millport, and her daughter at least, among all the remembered mothers, was not slavishly thirled to the change of sink.

We went there a lot, whole family loved the sea. My mother once sailed with her father and brother in a sailing-boat from Gourock round the Cock of Arran.

It was boats with Richard Fram too . . . and a built-in grandfather at Dunoon. He spent hours watching the procession of steamers that plied the Clyde.

. . . used to see the yellow and black steamer funnels on the boats from Gourock . . . and the red and blue from Glasgow, and I think red, blue and white from Craigendoran. When the steamers came in they would disgorge their passengers and there would be horse-drawn carriages for the posh people, and then a bit lower down the scale men with handcarts to take hampers and trunks to the boarding-houses. And there would be wee boys . . . 'Can I carry your bag Mister?'

That service wasn't too popular with everyone, as Jack Roche recalls.

The right porters didnae like that mind . . . losin' their trade to the wee boys; because the porters was licen'd and had their badges.

Richard Fram enjoyed the puffers too. They were the sturdy little work-horses of the river, supplying the small holiday towns beading the shores of the Firth.

As well as the steamer pier at Dunoon there was a wee stone one, called the 'coal' pier. It was for the puffers that came in every day with their loads of coal and building material. Great wee boats with just a skipper and mate and maybe an engineer (like in Para Handy). The puffers got unloaded by a big arm with a bucket that would swing over a cart on the wee quay. They were called puffers because they worked like railway engines and the smoke came out in puffs. The islands further north depended on them for sugar and paraffin and all that sort of thing.

Young Richard's grandfather had a few other pleasures up his sleeve to share with his visitor, forbye pointing out funnels and puffs of smoke.

He'd built a twelve-foot rowing boat that he told me he'd made for £1 per foot of length. Cost him £16 altogether with the rowlocks and foot spars. Sounds cheap but that would be several weeks' wages for a working man then. And he made a spear-fishing box one summer with a glass panel to see through at the stern. I would hang over with my spear made out of a broom handle and a toasting fork. We caught flounders like that and we never came home without a 'fry'. Oh, I liked Dunoon.

Small wonder with so ingenious a grandfather at hand. Mrs. Millicent Davis was fascinated, if not by all the craft that rocked or plunged on the Clyde, at least by certain particular ones. Her father was a design engineer at Fairfields.'

When we were very small and on holiday at Kilcreggan, *The Empress of Canada* was on her trials. We put up an old tablecloth to fly like a flag when she went past, and they used to give us a peep on the *Empress's* hooter as they came level . . . I think my father must've put them up to it.

Some day, in their turn, the young of present-day back-pack-safaris to India, Africa and Bangkok and their exotic explorations of little-known corners of Europe, will look back too. But however exciting their recollections as they sit in the Eventide homes of the 2050s, those memories will lack the common strands that bind todays octogenarians, with their shared memories of going down the Clyde. Of all the rememberers for these pages, only one had never holidayed there . . . Rothesay, Dunoon, Helensburgh,

Innellan, Troon, Prestwick, Ayr, Kilcreggan, Strone, Tighna-
bruaich, and a dozen other villages each had its devotees, seeing
them still in sharp bright pictures, and knowing smells and
sensations even now, that have remained with them for a lifetime.

> When I close my eyes I can still feel the sting of salt water, and the
> rubbing down wi' a rough towel my Ma had special for the bathing.

> With me it was the Arran chip-van that come round at night, and
> you went out for your poke of chips. And there was Woolley's shop
> at Brodick that I couldn't understand when I was wee. 'Woolies' to
> me should've had big gold letters on red, and sold everything at
> Thruppence and Sixpence.

But recollections, however sharp they seem in memory, can trick
us in our westering years . . .

> I remember above the pier at Dunoon was a statue of Flora Macdonald,
> y'know, the one that helped Bonnie Prince Charlie to escape after
> Culloden. Well, this statue was known locally as Highland Mary, I
> don't know why.

Ah well, perhaps good rememberer, that was because the statue *is*
of Highland Mary, the Argyll lass who loved Robert Burns too
well. A fine woman Flora Macdonald, but not monumented at
Dunoon!

Even those loyal to the Costa Clyde though, spread their wings
from time to time and tasted the delights of other parts.

> Sometimes we went to St. Monance in Fife for a change, wi' its red tiles
> and crowsteps and the big model fishing boat that hung in the kirk.
> Nearly every family in the village had to do wi' the fishing. And you
> used to hear the Salvation Army band in the streets wi' their instruments
> and their streaming ribbons. It was 'dry' then, was St. Monance, and the
> men used to complain and take the 'bus to Anstruther on a Friday night
> to get what they called 'a wee bit petrol for wir engines'.

But it seems ironical that it was those who had been of struggling
immigrant stock who had the more far-travelled and adventurous
holidays. Eileen Reilly, for one, went further than St. Monance.

> I used to be left for the summer at a house in Magherafelt in Ireland
> that had belonged to my great-grandmother. By my time it was her

daughter, my grandmother's sister, that was there. Quite a character she was. She'd worked as a cook in a big house in America, then developed arthritis . . . quite crippled she was . . . and had to come home to Ireland. She walked with crutches so she'd closed off the top storey of her cottage . . . just lived downstairs. So there she was, after the big glitzy, mod-con houses in America, back to the turf fire, oil lamps and the open grate with a swee to cook at. She'd a dog and hens and sometimes if she'd a wee weakly chick that was 'awfie no' weel', she'd a box at the fire to nurse it in, wrapped round in woolly things till it recovered. And, crutches and all, and old-old really . . . she was great with the turf fire.

Not just with the likes of soups and stews but fancies as well.

She used to make a lemon meringue pie. She'd rake the glowing peats apart and lower her big black pot down into it, with the lemon pie inside, as if it was an oven. Then she put the lid on and piled the red-hot turf all round it and over the lid. Can you imagine what it was like to a city child to see this delicious thing coming out of that kind of pot-oven?

The old lady had a way, too, with other children than her own Glasgow visitor.

She was marvellous. All the Catholic and Protestant children that didn't mix much elsewhere came to her house to play with me . . . didn't matter what they were.

Young Eileen with her summer playmates learned early the origin of the milk that just *arrived* on the cart at home in Glasgow . . . and of real water that didn't simply trickle from a tap into the tenement kitchen jaw-box.

I went to a neighbour's farm with a long-handled can every morning for the fresh milk. And there was no running water at the cottage, so I got to fill buckets from a spring-well beside the house.

There were Magherafelt picnics and berry-gathering excursions with pony and trap . . . raspberries and brambles.

That was with the Cuddons. They were a great big family and they'd a hedge I always remember. It was all topiary work, and one of the things was an old man sitting in a chair smoking his pipe . . . all hedge! I thought it was marvellous.

There was a gauntlet to be run though, before she reached the Cuddons'.

> The thing they had that I didn't like was the geese they kept near the front door, that kept running at your legs. I was frightened of them. But oh, I loved those cottage holidays.

And then it was back from paradise to Duke Street.

Another who recalls more distant holidays, to keep in touch with family roots, was Mario Servadei.

> I'd still grandparents in Italy in the thirties, and I remember two holidays there when I was young. But that was a big thing. Travelling abroad wasn't ordinary like it is now. Families like ours had to save for about twenty years to get back to see their folks in Italy. One of the times I stayed there when I was a wee boy was for several months, so I got to know my grandparents quite well. It was a very simple wee country village and that was different for me from the likes of Glasgow.

Not every remembered break, wherever it was, was a two-or-more week idyll of uninterrupted bliss, certainly not in the unchancy days of the First War. Mrs. Mysie Kyle recalls a blighted holiday in 1918.

> We always used to go on holiday with my granny. She was very strict my granny, nippy y'know. We went with her because my mother couldn't get away. The last time was in 1918 at Bridge of Weir. My auntie was with us that year and while we were away she heard that her husband had got wounded and was missing at the front. We came home. We couldn't do anything about it. But everybody just wanted home.

Some holidays were short, not because of bad news, but because funds themselves were short.

> We just always had a coupla days . . . a week-end like . . . out at an old cottage wi' an outside lavvy, at the Mearns. There was this old body . . . she'd a kinda clapped-out face and shuffled about in her baffies . . . well she let out rooms at so-much a night. The cottage is no' there now, and Mearns is just Glasgow. But it was a long way out then.

Shorter even than that tantalising glimpse of the country, was what Lily Joseph's family, still with its fortune to make as immigrants, called a holiday, early in the century. And it's maybe fitting to close the chapter down the Clyde with Mrs. Joseph's memory of the Glasgow Fair.

A holiday? We'd a holiday every year . . . just the Monday . . . Fair Monday. You left early with all your food and there was this public-house in Rothesay Gallowgate, that allowed children and gave you a private room. You could go in there at dinnertime and have your food there. Then th'was the entertainers or just walks and a wee look at the shops. At teatime we'd have a picnic at the Skeoch Woods. It was always sunshine in those days.

15
Clydebank was just Rubble

The 'deadly interval' between the wars that Mr. Jack Roche looked
back on in an earlier chapter was over. Scarcely believing it to be
possible, people still weary from 1918, and still mourning young
men (many of whom would still have been only in their thirties
had they lived) came to the autumn of 1939 sliding into conflict yet
again. But a lot of things had happened in the intervening years.
Aircraft, and methods of flying them, were more sophisticated,
and R.A.F. men were fighting this time from home bases,
returning night by night from war to home communities, their
losses countable from below as they flew back in from sorties. And
civilians themselves faced the chance of death from air raid. Radio
too was less primitive. The 'wireless' was a fact of life in every
living-room, reporting hour by hour on victory or defeat, and the
newsreel film a feature in every cinema programme. There was
therefore much more overlapping of fighting and home fronts,
much more general public involvement, so that memories of this
Second War do not belong exclusively to a band of veterans set
apart by years of sickening trench warfare that nobody else could
begin to comprehend.

This is a book of memories of Glasgow people, not just of city
life, and between 1939 and 1945 young Glasgow was abroad in
Europe, Africa, South-East Asia, Canada or at British bases far
from home. And so the recollections from those years tell how
city folk fared in far-flung places during an experience most would
have been glad to forego, but which nevertheless in some measure
enriched and matured their lives.

In spite of the Royal Navy being the Senior Service, it's 'army,
navy and air force' or 'soldiers, sailors and airmen' that is the order

of words that rattles most easily off the tongue. So let's start with an army rememberer.

> I'd never been out the country when I joined the army in the first week of September 1939 and between then and 1945 I was in France, wounded a bit at Dunkirk, went to the North African desert, Italy then Germany. I was that glad to get home I thought I would never-ever want to go abroad again.

There's surely evidence that Home Life, not Truth is the first casualty of war, and it was certainly so with the young Balarskys, now thoroughly absorbed in British life.

> My husband was called up to the army and was away abroad for four years. I was at home with a wee son, so he was five before his father came back and we were able to have our daughter. Five years is a long time between children but that was the war for you. My husband was with the Intelligence and worked a lot behind enemy lines and doing de-coding.

Conscripted men came in all shapes and sizes, and lack of soldierly bearing was no indication of potential.

> When we were in the army training camp we'd a wee skinny Glasgow chap . . . wee runty sorta fella. And-here he used to sit on his bunk doing crochet . . . crochet! But when it came time in the fighting, losh me, but he was a demon! Won a Military Medal. I always mind Ernie now when I meet the wee kinda man I used to think a bit Jessie.

But another rememberer was advised in so-many words to stick to the 'Jessie' side of war.

> I was in the Royal Engineers and thought I wanted into a fighting unit. I told the old colonel and he just walked up and down with me and said,
>   'Just you content yourself where you are. I saw men killed all round me in the last war and it wasn't nice.'
>   I must've been daft, I think, to want the fighting. Anyway I stayed where I was.

Another development in this war was the service of the mass of women who offered themselves or were called up. Some who volunteered muddied the waters a little at home in their eagerness to join up. Mrs. Helen Thomson's mother, for one, did not know a volunteer from a pressed 'man'.

> I was working in the bank and reserved at first. Then when we were de-reserved I joined up and told my mother I was called up. I went to Newbattle Abbey for three weeks of showering and de-lousing and so on, and a bit of initial training. From there I was sent with two others for N.C.O. training.

She puts that selection down to being able to do joined-up writing and having 'maybe a wee bit initiative'. First it was one stripe, then three, as a sergeant. But it was her later commissioned rank of Second Lieutenant that she describes as . . .

> . . . the lowest of the low. My first posting from officer-training at O.C.T.U. was to one of two big houses commandeered for A.T.S. girls in Morningside, Edinburgh. I looked after their pay there.

Her mother never did come to grips with what was officially 'what' in military terms and was again duped over her daughter's next display of patriotic fervour.

> I got the chance to go abroad. I'd two years still to do, but to go abroad I'd to sign on for five years So again, I didn't tell my mother that . . .; just said I was posted. Anyway I was sent to Cairo as a quarter-mistress at a big barracks beside the Nile. The girls in the barracks were mess workers, typists and so on. I saw to them, as well as looking after all the stocks and the native workers in the kitchens.

On the personal side Cairo was great.

> About ten men to every woman! A lot of the men were invalided back there from the desert. And we were well-looked after by servants in their jellabas, white loose gowns y'know. And A.T.S. officers were automatically made members of the pukka Gazira Club. There was tennis and swimming and riding there, and good food.

Less salubrious postings followed, including six months back home at Moreton-in-Marsh, with merciless weather and even rebellion to cope with.

> Conditions in the ice and snow with no coal were frightful. The girls staged a sit-down strike that I'd to sort out. Didn't blame them really.

It was hardly the Indian Mutiny but it added to the general gloom, and was followed by worse.

> The thaw came. Everything flooded and we'd to move about the camp from Nissen hut to Nissen hut in a small boat. I finished my service days there on that kind of sour note.

An army man with memories of another flooding was Alan Dale.

> Once we'd to pitch our tents on a sea of mud at Taranto in Italy, where there'd just been an outbreak of some plague. Then suddenly, from trying to cope with that, we were sent off with just blankets, rifles and bandoliers of ammunition into Greece. There was fighting there at the end of the war between the Greek forces and the Eoka groups that were trying to get Greece into the Eastern bloc. It was dreadful. People at home didn't realise. There were academics and artists being killed off and there were bodies in the streets as we went about. I was eighteen months in Greece, latterly in Macedonia helping the Greek army to deal with raids from Bulgaria and Yugoslavia taking children away over the border to bring up as communists. It was all very sad. The guerilla troops had been on our side earlier in the war. It was said they'd got financed in those days by the British dropping gold sovereigns into their patches of territory. It was all very confusing and puzzling.

Mr. Hamish Thomson wasn't a bit puzzled fifty-odd years ago, certainly not at the beginning of the war, or even before that. He knew exactly why he chose to volunteer for the R.A.F. early in 1939. He presents himself as something of an anti-hero.

> I knew I would have to go to the war if it came and I fancied the air force. There was the flying of course, but really because if I was going to be killed, I wanted it to be quick. As well as that, I thought it would be more comfortable to go out on raids or fights or whatever, and be back to Britain each night . . . not be slogging it out abroad in trenches with the army.

It was certainly home bases for the first month or two.

> I trained at Prestwick as a Gunner/Wireless Operator, then in Wales on Hawker Hinds, wee bi-planes with open cockpits that you hung out of, y'know. After that it was Fairy Battles and Wellingtons.

But that was the end of home comforts for many a long day.

> One day someone came in . . . 'Anyone here train on Fairy Battles?' I was daft enough to say 'yes', and that was it. Off to France. Dunkirk was still on and the Germans were on their way to Paris. Three of us went to No. 12 Squadron, and we had just five operational flights, dive-bombing bridges and road junctions. Then on the 13th June we were strafing troops and we were hit. We went on fire and crash-landed. The pilot had his hands burned badly. We ran a bit from the plane as it was exploding . . . nowhere to go really. Then two Germans on a motor-bike and side-car came along and, brave men, we just put our hands up . . . 'Come and get us' sort of thing. So the five of us just went off on the bike and side-car. That was that. I hardly saw the war at all.

Maybe not. Nevertheless there were forced marches, hunger, cold and prison camps for long years after that. But these belong with other tales of confinement later in the chapter. Meanwhile we leave young Hamish, scarcely twenty and a prisoner-of-war, and take a glance at Mario Servadei's service days. There were ironic quirks of fate in war when you were of immigrant stock.

> In the First War Italians went into an Italian contingent of the British army. But it was different in the Second War. My father'd been an interpreter doing liaison work between the British and Italian governments during the First War and when the next one came he wasn't interned. But my older brother was taken away as an enemy alien and sent to the Isle of Man. Yet later on I served in the R.A.F. That was war for you. Funny things happened.

Funny things happened in the navy too, or at least little twists of circumstance. Richard Fram's days on his grandfather's rowing-boat, and watching liners come and go on the Clyde, were long past by the time war came.

> The *Empress of Britain* had always been a ship that I remembered and admired. Big liners like that had to anchor at the Tail-of-the Bank and passengers got ferried from there. She was a real beauty.

Then in the war I was a Radio Officer at sea and I had the sad experience of receiving her distress signals when she was attacked by a German raider, and sinking. Couldn't help thinking of the way I'd last seen her at the Tail-of-the-Bank with the sun on her funnels.

Another who went to sea was Jimmy Dewar . . .

I got my call-up papers for the Royal Navy, but I had already been at sea before the War as an apprentice. So I hurried up and joined the Seamen's Union and got taken on the *Arundel Castle* at £6/10s a month. I was away on her with a shipload of troops while the R.N. was still chasing me up. I was with her for quite a long time around the Middle East, Suez and Africa. After that I was on a couple of Atlantic tramps doing convoys. We were in action in 1942 on the *Cape Race* off Iceland. The ship alongside was blown up and we were torpedoed. We thought. We put the two life-boats over and pulled away, and sat out there to watch the *Cape Race* sinking. But she didn't. Nothing happened. She sat there all innocent and empty like the *Marie Celeste*, or what was it . . . 'idle like a painted ship upon a painted sea', because there was a treacly sort of swell all round her. The captain decided the explosion had been from the other ship and that we'd better get back aboard. When we joined the convoy again we just muttered that our problem had been 'bad coal, bad coal'. Didn't want to admit the truth.

There wasn't bad coal or any other kind of smokescreen fibbery needed shortly afterwards when they really *were* followed by a submarine, and torpedoed properly.

. . . into the boats again and this time for about twenty minutes we did watch the *Cape Race* tip up vertically, with all the timber cargo sliding off the deck. Then she sank, bubble, bubble, bubble! We were left to wait until a corvette, *H.M.S. Dianthus*, picked us up. She was already full of U-boat prisoners and Greek survivors from another ship. I found a place beside a funnel and sat there for five days in scarcely any clothes and no shoes, until we got to Liverpool. I got a pair of sandshoes off the Red Cross there and then came home on four weeks 'torpedo' leave.

He had a graphic picture of his next ship.

She'd a wee thin funnel so we called her 'Willie Woodbine'.

Willie Woodbine shifted her cargo and sank not long after the War with the loss of all hands, but by that time Jimmy Dewar, by now an officer, was sailing the oceans in yet another ship, crossing and re-crossing the date line, the Equator and finally the Pacific.

> We'd a broken-down chronometer on that ship and I navigated with an alarm clock that I'd bought at the pawnbroker's in Pollokshaws.

If war changed life dramatically for those who were in the services, there were altered routines on the home front too, and from the outset more profound shifts of civilian activity and energy than in any previous war. Maids departed, and women who had depended on them while they window-shopped in the city or took tea at Miss Cranston's, rolled up their own sleeves and did, not only their own cooking, but marathons of fry-ups in city service canteens as well. Middle-aged men who had dozed over their evening papers or tended their roses, dug up their plots and planted vegetables, and trained as fire-fighters, Home Guards or Air Raid Wardens.

> I can always mind my old navy blue tin hat wi' the W on it, and the stirrup pump and the bucket of sand in the lobby.

Even before the war a number of Glasgow homes had welcomed the sad little trickle of child refugees coming out of Europe. Millicent Davis recalls how richly repaid her family felt later for having opened their hearts to Dorothea from Czechoslovakia.

> Sometime in the thirties there was a movement to bring young Jews out of dangerous situations in Europe . . . looking for offers of homes. There was a man on television recently that had to do with getting them out. A fourteen-year-old girl called Dorothea came to us. Her mother died in Auschwitz and she never knew what happened to her father. 'Dorry' we called her and she really became part of the family . . . like a young sister to us. She's still in Scotland and we keep in touch.

That was one life-changing commitment. Others took on jobs they would never have dreamed of doing in the ordinary plod of their lives. In the Kyles' case it was that kind of upturn for both husband and wife, and the wider family slotted in to make it possible.

My husband had gone into the Police Reserve . . .

(. . . which considering a youthful contretemps over a game of football in the street was all the more praiseworthy . . .)

> So he was called up to the Police and had to leave his work. I took it over and went round all the wee Glasgow shops, the way he'd done, selling Carter's Medical Supplies, castor oil and cough mixture and aspirins, that sort of thing y'know. That was my war work.

Their daughter was sent to school in town and her two grandfathers collected her day about.

> So that was their war work.

Another who served in the police force was Miss Isobel Horn.

> I had to be in something, but my father had just died and I thought it would be best if I could volunteer for something that would keep me at home, so I went full-time into the police as a driver . . .

There was Red Cross and W.V.R., pig-food collecting and firewatching. And there was make-do-and-mending: Bunty Angles' aunt turned her own profession to the war effort and made good use of whatever was to hand.

> My dressmaker aunt taught make-do-and-mend classes all through the war. Showed folk how to make skirts out of trousers or coats, and children's clothes from adults'.

The weirder the transformation the prouder the transformer.

> My dad's plus-fours made matching skirts for me and my twin sister, one from each leg. They were thon scratchy stuff and we hated them, but Mother thought hersel' a rare wee genius and showed them to everybody.

Another whose peacetime skills led naturally to his war work and maybe gave him, quite literally, a step-up in the doing, was Robert Ford.

> I had been making wooden barrows for an ironmonger and when the war was coming I got an order from him for twelve thousand wee ladders. Quite rough work. One of these went into every tenement in

Glasgow so people could get up on to roofs through ceiling hatches in case of fire-bombs. I just made them of small trees, eleven or twelve foot long. Cut up the centre, half on each side, and spars between.

All those war efforts were made against a background of increasing complications in just living. Helen Smith had young children to cope with.

Th'was your gas masks of course. You'd aye to have them wi' you at the beginning of the war. You'd Mickey Mouse yins for weans and a big bag-thing you'd to put your baby right inside. We didnae need any of them in the end though, thank goodness. And everb'dy minds of ration books, but d'you mind B.U.s and Points? B.U.s was Bread Units for yon grey kinda bread, and Points was for things that wasnae actu'lly rationed but just short. And mind the queues?

And her neighbour in the lounge minds fine.

Aye, for fish or oranges, and maybe cake from under the counter. But what I was mindin' while you was speakin', Nellie, was yon sticky net you pasted over your windows for 'blast' and the strips of black paper down the sides so's there wasnae chinks in the black-out. Havin' chinks was near as bad as bein' a burglar up our street. And mind how you always took a coupla eggs or a wee bit butter or that, when you went visiting.

There was another tiresome irritation in the black-out. Signposts and station names had been removed and only known landmarks guided travellers.

There were no lights at all when you were going home and you'd to count your stops on the train or the tram or that. That was all to bamboozle enemy parachutists startin' an invasion.

In the event the Glasgow area had just the one deliberate parachutist. Mrs. Jean Walker speaks of him.

My father was an officer in the army but working with the Home Guard. When Hess landed on the farm at Eaglesham they 'phoned my father to ask what to do with him. Then later when Hess was taken to Buchanan Castle my father went out with another officer to interview him before he was taken south. So he'd that conversation with Hess that he always remembered.

If there was only one parachutist there were other less welcome droppings. The blitz came late to Glasgow and for a brief spell. But it was a reign of terror while it lasted. Of course there had been extensive precautions since Day One.

> In our church th'was stretchers and Red Cross people at each door, every service, and the stained glass windows was a' boarded up. The closes were made safer wi' props and big sand-baggy walls at the close-mouth. Made them into kinda shelters.

Ann Hutchison's family used their close when the sirens went.

> I remember running to the shelter in air raids and jumpin' up and down waitin' for my Daddy. He always seemed to be in the bathroom. The close was all propped up with iron railing kinda things to be stronger. And you'd take your wee bag of money or valuables with you. That wouldnae be much mind.

Most households if they hadn't closes or Anderson shelters had 'safe' places earmarked in their houses and stocked for emergency.

> I was a young mother in the Second War and we had a mattress under the stairs. I put my baby in his Moses' basket there and sat beside him all night through the blitz of 1941. Those were bad nights, my husband was in the yard at Fairfield's, then one night a landmine came down by parachute and was tangled on the big crane so that it just dangled there. An incendiary bomb hit the Old South Church in Bearsden too, and it was burned down.
> I was lying under our big heavy dining-room table when the bombs fell beside us. What a dunt when one landed at our back, then about five more fell one after the other.

Hamish Thomson was a prisoner-of-war by that time but his home took the second of those dunts.

> I heard snatches about the bombing in our area from other prisoners coming in, but didn't really know about it till I came home. What a mess of destruction, with the house wall all propped up waiting for repairs.

All bad enough. But it was Greenock and Clydebank and Govan that took the real devastation, almost obliteration, of those nights. Miss Janet Kay's father worked at Singer's.

> My father walked into Clydebank after the first morning of the blitz there. He met women coming out of Clydebank in their nightdresses, some pushing prams with children and a few belongings. And one of their own men had gone home to find his house and his wife and his children gone. Clydebank was just rubble. But mind you, Singer's had trestle tables out and every employee got his wages that Friday.

Miss Isobel Horn was a canteen van driver at that time.

> I used to drive down to what was left of Clydebank to the docks, taking huge containers of soup and sandwiches to set up a stall.

Mrs. Mary Brisbane lived near the Govan docks.

> One night of the bombing I had my wee son of five wrapped in a blanket in the close. There was a three-storey block of tenement houses across the road from us. There was a direct hit on it and people got thrown down into the dunnies below . a lot killed. What a noise there was with the bombs and the rat-tat-tat of ack-ack guns. All our own windows were out and th'was soot and plaster everywhere.

While the armies fought and the air force flew; while grey ships ploughed grey seas and people huddled in shelters, there was a great body of men on both sides . . . prisoners-of-war who spent much of the war champing at the bit, frustrated at being on the sidelines and watching the years of their youth slip past. Let's pick up Hamish Thomson again trundling off on a German motorbike to his monastic sentence. So many things happened that the first few days after that were hazy and confused. Apprehension there must have been, of what was to come, and concern at what the word 'missing' would mean to the family at home. But on that matter there was a providential encounter.

> We were taken somewhere near Paris and we met this girl Bessie Myers who was an ambulance driver and had strayed behind enemy lines. She took our names and addresses in a notebook in case she got back home, and a few weeks later she did go back to Britain and contacted our parents.

If that first stage was hazy, the next one was brutally clear, when the captives were taken on a long week's forced trek to Belgium with other prisoners.

> We'd no rations at all, no food, no water. But as we passed through places, villagers came alongside and gave us bread. Some of us were nearly collapsing from de-hydration.

From Belgium they were transported in railway cattle-trucks to Poland.

> On that train we'd no rations either, but one fellow had got hold . . . somehow or other . . . of a bucket of raw potatoes in water and we survived on that. We were crammed together in that truck, standing . . . couldn't move.

In Poland they registered officially as prisoners-of-war.

> I suppose I must have been about the first R.A.F.V.R. to be captured. Wasn't a great honour that was it? First to be caught! For our rations in Poland we'd roasted acorn coffee for breakfast, watery soup, maybe sauerkraut or potato for lunch, and at night a small loaf among five of us.

After Poland there was Lubeck in Germany, a more comfortable camp with stoves and wooden huts.

> I was one of a group that was caught pinching a better stove from an empty hut . . . got three days' bread and water for that . . . literally bread and water.

Those dreams of commuting home to Britain between sorties, must have seemed very far away, as 1941 slipped into 1942 and 1943. There was Czechoslovakia and the famous Stalagluft 3.

> That's where the big Wooden Horse escape was from, out of the officers section. We used to see them doing their jumping, but we didn't know what it was all about. They got out through the tunnel they'd opened under the vaultinghorse. There was a book about it by one of the ones that got away . . . and then a film.

Lithuania came next . . . and then it was 1945.

The war was nearly over and there was pretty well chaos. We were sent off roaming around in cattle trucks. Nobody knew where to go. Then after a week in a big barn somewhere a guard told us just to go, because the S.S. was coming. So we wandered off . . . just like that! There was no great dramatic liberation. We met Germans in one village and an officer wished us luck! We met Americans newly into Europe who'd never seen uniforms like ours . . . nearly shot us as Germans. From there we reached Salzburg, Brussels and home. One thing I always remember. When we got back I could have listened to girls' voices for ever. That was my war.

He makes light of hard times and talks of another local man with more startling memories of being a prisoner in Japanese hands and working in a mine at Hiroshima when the atomic bomb hit the city.

He was put to clearing up there after the bomb. That must have been a terrible thing to survive and remember.

Sitting like a bright-eyed sparrow in her suburban nest there's a dainty little lady touching ninety (and preferring to remain anonymous) whom it's hard to see as a detainee of war. It wasn't quite like that but, trapped in Persia with her engineer husband when 1939 came, she spent the years of the Second War there 'doing her bit' as energetically as she had sold flags for 'gallant little Montenegro' in the First.

I had been in a dramatic society in Abadan, putting on plays or pantomimes in peacetime. Well, when the British occupied Abadan the General asked us to entertain the troops. I sang things from musical comedies and songs with my banjo and then I did my whistling solos to my own piano arrangements. I was what they called a 'siffleuse'. We went on tour . . . oh but it was rough tough travelling . . . to Basra, Kirkuk, Mosul and Baghdad and into Syria. The young King of Iraq was there one time when I was singing. It was all hard work. I once played till my fingers were raw. It was very professional really . . . great memories.

It's difficult to imagine a less likely siffleuse-banjo player, but these's a twinkle in the eyes that says it was all a bit of a lark, that it entertained lonely soldiers, and that if you had to be exiled anyway, it was best to accept it with devil-may-care gusto.

Back at their ex-patriate homes between theatrical tours, company wives were asked to do another little service for the army authorities, a service that came to nothing . . . absolutely nothing.

There was a general shortage of meat, and trial packs of dried mince (a bit like grapenuts) were sent to the wives to experiment with.

Ali, the cook, had never heard of grapenuts . . .

Food de-hydrated like that mince, if it was good y'see, could be very useful to help move army food supplies easily. Anyway, I was up early and left my package in the pantry. When I came in later I didn't see it so I asked Ali, four foot-nothing and temperamental, where he'd put it.

'Memsahib, I plant it . . . plenty flowers . . . plenty 'sturtium. Come.'

And he took me to the garden and sure enough there were drills and drills planted out neatly with mince.

'That's meat you've planted, Ali.'

He looked pityingly for what the sun had done to me.

'Oh, Memsahib, too many hot season.' He shook his head.

'These *seeds* for the garden.'

But when Memsahib and her husband finally came home it was neither nasturtium or sprouting mince that the homesick couple gloried in.

It was the Scottish gardens along the shore with wee rows of green cabbages that we saw through our binoculars as we came up the Clyde . . . then we knew we were home.

Mr. Angelo Lamarra had a strange war for a Stenh'smuir supporter, born here and on sunny terms with all his Glasgow café customers.

The very day the Italians came into the war in 1940 we'd a brick through the café window. It was shattering in more ways than one. We'd been brought up friends with everyone, and-here all of a sudden we were enemies. I was alone in the café when that brick came through the window and I was trembling. Two men came in and looked at me. I was quite fair, so one of them says, he says, 'He's no' a Tally.' And they went away. The police came and just stood around watching for any more trouble. Gangs of lads were just roaming around looking for Italian cafés. Anyway, that very night my brother and I were arrested. They had our names from the 'Casa', the Italian club. It was s'posed to be

Fascist, but it wasnae Fascist at all. We were all Scottish really, just getting together with each other. Italians are like that. Besides we'd registered for the British army ten days before. Och, it was all a right mix-up. One of the friends I've played golf with for years was in the Italian army.

They were sorted out in Edinburgh. 'Just moved about like chessmen y'know' then taken south to the docks for shipping out to Canada as internees.

We saw two ships at the dock. They filled up the *Arandora Star* first. (It was torpedoed and went down with all of them.) Then we were put on the *Ettrick Star* and zig-zagged across the Atlantic to the St. Lawrence. We were put on an island near Montreal. Didn't see a woman all the time we were there, except someone had binoculars and you could see girls walking across the bridge that way. We wore sort of blue uniforms with red stripes up the trousers and a red circle on your back.

But it's a small world even in war.

The Canadian guards pushed us around a bit . . . thought we were Germans. Then one of them shouted,
   'Anyone here speak English?'
   'Aye of course we do, half of us are from Glasgow.'
   'You're kidding' says this big Canadian. 'I was born at Parkhead!'
After that we were well-treated all the years we were there. We came back to the Isle of Man before the end of the war, then did a bit of what they called 'work of national importance'. Then it was home and back to the café again. Wasn't bad my internment, just kind of silly and sad. But that's war!

Jimmy Dewar shared the deck of his rescue ship with German prisoners and Greek survivors from another ship.

The Greeks were always at daggers drawn with the Germans, but we found the Jerries O.K. We played cards with them and they talked about how sure they were to win the war . . . sink everything and have their armies all over. We listened, but just went on dealing the cards.

He doesn't mention though, whether the Germans were as 'model' at sea as Helen Thomson saw them with the female eye on land.

I was in a camp for a while alongside a German P.O.W. compound. Never saw anything so neat and tidy and well-looked after . . . everything ticketty-boo y'know. Quite outshone the British section or any other camp I ever saw.

But in the end maybe the slappier-happier allied ways fired their energies better for the final outcome. And while no victory ever prevents people being displaced, lost, or even massacred to tidy them out of the way, the Glasgow war wanderers who remembered for these pages, finally took up their blessedly humdrum lives again. They melted back into grey suits and family life so that younger generations can scarcely imagine them as quarter-mistresses, fighter-pilots or grim-faced men with bayonets and machine-guns, or see genial Stop-Me-and-Buy-One ice-cream men as dangerous enemy aliens.

16

There was None of this Sex or that in Those Days

The years when little boys pull their jerseys over their hands to avoid the contamination of actually taking little girls' hands in school circle games, are soon over. They pass quickly into the 'looking over' stage . . . days when egos are easily bruised and hearts broken. Norma Morton remembers their bitter sweetness . . . with a twinkle in her eye.

> I thought I was lovely when I was at school. Here's me wi' my forty-two inch bust and my long hair that I used to throw over my shoulder all the time and toss my head . . . kind of flirty . . . y'know the way. But here I knew that I wasnae really lovely . . . just fat . . . fat! I used to think I'd be thin when I grew up right, because grown-ups didn't eat sweets.

With families of nine and ten you might think there was little need for sex education, that regular arrivals of midwives and clash in the close would have told them all they needed to know. But it wasn't invariably so. Mrs. Chrissie Ronnie remembers.

> My mother was too busy with the farm and shop, and the family of course, to tell me anything about life. But I always remember just before she died, when I was thirteen coming up fourteen, she told me I shouldn't play so much with the boys. Then she lifted my arm and stretched it out.
>   'Chrissie, see how long your arm is there? Well, never let the boys past your finger tips!'
>   They wouldnae like that nowadays, would they?

And her sister too, one of the twelve Rodgers, looks back on primmer days.

Some say 'good old days', some say 'bad old days', I don' know. There was none of this sex or that, and if you were seen going in or out a pub in those days with a man . . . well! Nowadays they're *floating* in and out.

There's ample evidence that it *was* a more innocent day . . . polite too. One rememberer recalls hearing of a girl having a young woman pointed out to her in company as being lesbian, and then in later conversation with the young lady in question . . .

. . . asking, friendly-like, 'And whit-part of Lesbia d'you come fae?'

Alas for such naiveté.

There were mating rites of course, the stalking and the chase. One gentleman was not prepared to kiss and tell.

We went to the pictures right-enough when we were coortin' (winchin' we called it, no 'coortin'). Forbye that it's a secret.

But Mrs. Agnes Grove was more forthcoming, and looks back nearly eighty years to how it was in her day.

Th'were places you walked on Saturday and Sunday looking for a chap. We walked up and down at the canal where the locks were . . . some girls did it at Alexandra Parade. Boys did the same . . . 'looking for a lumber' they called it. And they used to sit on the canal wall too, the boys and girls.

Jack Roche and his peers had another beat.

You could meet wi' clicks at the Park bandstand. You kinda walked about outside the railing lookin' each other up and down. When you were serious wi' one you took her inside . . . *and paid*. That was dead serious.

In Italian circles Mario Servadei recalls, there was a touch more formality.

Y'know folk talk about arranged marriages? Italians didn't exactly arrange them, when I was young, but when you visited other families on Sundays they maybe put you in the way of each other if they thought it was suitable. Maybe left the young folks in a room with a gramophone or that. . . and waited to see if a date came out of that. And of course there was always the dancing on a Thursday night at

Green's Ballroom. That was the night all the Italians went . . . just a thing that happened. About the actual weddings . . . well, in Italy there'd have been dowries . . . specially southern Italy, but that didn't last beyond the first generation here.

In Jewish circles between the wars it wasn't pounding the clicking beat, or Green's dancing that brought the young together; it was the Jewish Institute in South Portland Street, a social rendez-vous for the immigrant community.

My husband Solly was a staunch member of the Institute and I met him there. When we were getting married he was offered the use of a room. So the canopy (you know how we're married under a canopy with flowers up the corner poles) well, it was brought from the synagogue, and we'd the breaking of the glass and all the symbols for long and happy married life. After the wedding Mrs. Geneen, who was a great caterer, did the purvey. She was a real benefactor to couples who hadn't a lot of money . . . didn't take much at all. It's all big presents now y'know, videos and dishwashers . . . but not then. Somebody would play an instrument or sing and entertain at these old traditional weddings.

Sometimes it was at work that people took a fancy to each other. Mrs. Grove found her partner that way.

I met my husband at the Templeton's factory. He was a tenter. Tenters kept an eye on the looms, hooked up your pieces and watched in case things went wrong. He came into the factory to help get the looms back to doing the chenille, after they'd been put to making the army blankets in the First War.

And another claimed that her work romance had a touch of *The People's Friend* about it.

I worked in a big store when I was young, right after the First War, about 1919. I thought I was a bit of a catch wi' my hair up an' my nice blouses. And so must've Alec in Gents' Suits. He kep' asking me out. He was quite pan-loaf spoken, y'know . . . dark wavy hair and a wee moustache (wee moustaches was just comin' in). Anyway when Bert the doorman seen him chattin' me up, he says, 'You mind what you're doin' wi' that Alec. He's maybe a heid-bummer in Gents, but I wouldnae trust him wi' a window dummy.' Bert was just a wee nyaff and I didnae pay any heed. But I didnae marry Alec. It was him really

was the wee nyaff. I got wed in the end to Bert. It was just a poke of
sweeties and the pictures when we went out. Bert did me fine though,
for forty-two year.

She could count her honest-woman anniversaries, but another
rememberer wasn't so sure . . .

. . . married eleven years. Or d'you count the common-law years afore
we got wed?

So for some those days were maybe not so innocent, but Peggy
Carson recalls one relationship that clearly was.

I went to see a weddin' once at a chapel in the east end and th'was some
women standin' watchin' the bride go in.
   'She's no' expectin' y'ken.'
   'No' expectin'. That's posh for you, sure it is.'

A virtuous ceremony like that must surely have been preceded by
a douce courtship, like the wooing and winning of Mary Rodger.

There was no what you'd call 'courting' done with Mr. Brisbane. He
lived just over the road from us. It was just 'hello' and that. And then
he began to come about the house and do this and that to help us. It
was just every second Sunday or Monday after seven o'clock we went
for walk, and maybe very occasionally the pictures. I was in service for
a wee while and he came to see me there. We were married in the wee
church up in Scotland Street. I was in a blue dress with a blue hat and
my going-away coat was blue with braid round it and a very pale blue
cloche hat. We just had our tea at home and then our honeymoon in
Ireland. I was married fifty-seven years.

Mrs. Mysie Kyle also favoured blue for her wedding outfit, perhaps
surprisingly not *navy* blue with a white trimmed pill-box.

My brother was a great one for the football and I met my husband
when he came up with his Boys' Brigade footballers to Blochairn
Church. They trained in our cellar. It was a big cellar. Anyway
when the teams were playing near-at-hand I took out the oranges at
half-time and met him like that. He used to come to the Bible Class
too. We'd a quiet wedding at the manse and I wore a blue frock with
a bolero, and a hat I made myself that had roses on it the same as my
bouquet.

They went to Girvan for the week-end, but Mr. Kyle was too far-ben with the B.B. to make it more.

> We came home and took the B.B. to camp at Tighnabruaich. Yes, the honeymoon was the B.B. camp, but we enjoyed it fine. We'd our holidays for years at the camp after that.

Ann Hutchison viewed her sister's Pollokshaws courtship with interest.

> When Jeanie had her boyfriend they used to sit in the hut where my Daddy kept the wood for his cart. Jeannie always sawed up that wood and chopped the sticks. No pictures for them. They just lit the lamp in that hut and sat splitting the wood . . . done their courting over them sticks. She worked hard, Jeanie. And then there was the bobby going round on his beat. When he seen the lamp lit he would come in the hut for his cup of tea from the wee stove.

Like those others, Mrs. Bunty Angles' wedding to her baker-suitor, John, was an all-Glasgow affair. He was a City Bakeries man, and there was a new C.B. restaurant in Partick.

> It was in Byres Road . . . Peel House it was, and big Willie Urie says to John, 'How about getting married in our new hall. Give it a nice opening.' So we did. It was lovely. I wore a white lace dress gored with georgette, 'bought'. And I'd a wee cap and veil with a cluster of bride's blossom at my ears.

She wasn't so pleased though, with her going-away hat.

> It was to go with my outfit and it was orange and brown pan velvet . . . My, it was big! Great big brim. If ever you saw anything ridiculous it was that hat. A daft thing to go in the train to Stonehaven with.

Not all courtships were boy-and-girl next-street or neighbourhood affairs. Robert Ford went a-wooing in Kilmarnock where a chance introduction had brought him an embarrassment of riches in the bevy of seven bonnie sisters from among whom he found his wife. 'Spoilt for choice he was,' she claims. There was maybe a near miss though.

> He'd an old highland girl friend, Flora, who was a very good dancer and very keen on it, and I've said to him many a time, 'You know if you could've danced as well as that Angus that did get her, he wouldn't have had a look-in with Flora.'

So maybe young Mr. Ford did better to occupy himself making
his hods and bakers' trays than pay for ten lessons at McEwans'
Dancing and end up with the wrong wife . . .

Kilmarnock in earlier days was a fair stretch to go a-wooing, but
some relationships were conducted at even greater distances. This
one began quite conventionally in Glasgow.

> I met my husband at The Plaza in 1926. I was at a friend's twenty-first
> birthday party. John was home on leave from British petroleum in
> Persia and he'd been persuaded to come to this party. That's how we
> met and all his leave we were very chummy.

There was no rush though.

> I was courted from Persia really. I met him in 1926 and he was home
> again to get married in 1935. Nine years . . . no hurry. I was very
> busy with other interesting things to do. We went to Persia after the
> wedding.

Angelo Lamarra's romance looked like following good Italian-
Glasgow traditions, but the war and separation tested it.

> My wife had come over from Italy when she was twelve to help in the
> family shop when her older brothers were away at the First War. She
> still speaks with an accent. It's nice that. I admired her for a long time at
> the Italian Club, but then we met properly. We played tennis and went
> to films, and we danced at the Locarno and the Albert. 1/6 at the Plaza
> too, in an afternoon. Louis Freeman's band. For the pictures we went
> to the La Scala . . . wee cups of tea in the side seats, y'know.

(A well integrated Italian-Scot, Angelo Lamarra, to refer to *the* La
Scala!)

> But then I was interned in Canada for the war. Interrupted everything.
> But she worked hard at home and had a wee business ready for us. We
> kept writing and I came out the camp in April and we got married in
> the July. Didn't waste any more time. She and I get on great. We've
> one wee argument every day . . . over nothing. If we don't have that
> I start worrying.

Perhaps, although it's related at second-hand, we should end the
chapter with the most exotic, and eventually doomed, romance,
that of the wooing and marriage of Mr. Alan Dale's father.

Short-lived it may have been, but there is no doubt that he was head-over-heels in love.

> My father was born in 1873. He ran away to sea at twelve on a ship called *Gipsy Maid*. He worked in America for a year or two and then he was back to sea. On one voyage he met a girl from a circus and the only way he could stay with her was to join the circus. She was with a trapeze family so he learned to be a trapeze artist too. He was very young and off they went round the world with Talbot-Cook's circus. They'd a daughter, a trapeze artist too . . . my half-sister. That first wife died of blackwater fever in Sumatra.

Wooings, weddings and honeymoons, romance. And reality. For it wasn't every woman who found her honeymoon on the highlight of her life and Mrs. Norma Morton remembers a fellow-patient in hospital, disgruntled at the prospect of going home.

> 'I don't want to go home. I want to stay here,' she says. 'The food's good and it's clean. It's been better'n my honeymoon I tell you that.'

17
D'you Mind the Penny Geggie?

Whatever their deprivations Glasgow people have always had a reputation for enjoying themselves. And never more than in the Edwardian and later days covered by this book, coming as they did close on the heels of Victorian Presbyterian times when public entertainment was a decidedly suspect frivolity. Of course there was great theatre and music-hall last century, but it was not wholly approved by Kirk and Session who witheringly minuted such ongoings as 'theatricals'.

But the hoi-poloi liked its theatricals, as it later loved its 'pictures' in the days when Glasgow became Cinema City with over a hundred picture-houses. The taste for performance showed itself early in life and even organisations dedicated to moral uplift had begun to grasp the revolutionary notion that fun and games could go quite sinlessly with precept.

> I used to be in the church kinderspiel. That would be before the First War. Kinderspiels were wee kind of children's musicals.
> We used to go to the Rechabite kinderspiels in Dennistoun. I loved that but I was too shy to actually be in one.

Not so other stage-struck tots.

> I was an angel in the kinderspiel and I mind Miss Duckett at the piano with her long-long earrings that used to jingle when she plonked out the tunes. She'd a long neck and a red nose, but she could fairly bash out the songs.

Mrs. Lily Balarsky was fascinated by theatre long before she was old enough to have a ticket and sit on a plush seat. It was her *elbows* that sat on the velvet.

You know about 'hings'? Well, when we were young and living in Stockwell Street people had wee cushions at their windows to lean on when they hung out to have a chat or just watch the passing show. We'd an orange-box to stand on and look across into the dressing-rooms of the old Metropole Theatre. It was great . . . very glamorous to see the show-biz folk getting changed and the girls sharing a wee puff. That shocked me, it was so wicked. We saw them pulling up their tights too. That was good for a giggle.

Sometimes the thrill of living so close to the Metropole was almost heart-stopping.

We used to stand in the lane at the stage-door and see them *in the flesh* coming in. There was a Jewish performer . . . what was his name? Yes, Ike Freeman, he was good, and there was G.H. Elliot, the Chocolate-Coloured Coon. He was lovely at the stage-door. We just stood there and got a wee pat on the head.

The day did come when Lily was actually *inside*.

My older brother got a wee job with the ice-cream and sweetie tray. We thought we were practically *in* the profession. I remember getting in at the back to watch Gertie Gitana shimmying around the stage and singing . . .
   'How do you feel when you marry your ideal?
   Ever so goosey, goosey, goosey . . . gooo-sey.'
And the audience all joined in.

Many a later theatre or cinema-goer served an apprenticeship at what they called the Penny Geggie.

D'you mind of Penny Geggies? Och, I fair loved the Penny Geggie. It was a wee kinda portable magic-lantern that came round the schools or the street, and you got in for a ha'penny.

If the likes of the Geggie was no longer a Victorian sin, Isobel Horn made a moral lapse out of its arrival at her local school.

I wasn't at school yet, but this man they called 'French Geggie' was coming with his show to the playground. I wanted to go and it was arranged that the maid at my friend Jean's house would take us. So I got my penny. But-here Lizzie couldn't take us and we just went ourselves. I knew I shouldn't but I did. Well, when we got to the playground it was all over and the Geggie barrow covered up. So the bold Jean led

me astray a bit more and we went to Clements' shop on the main road
and *spent* the penny. Mrs. Clement was a wee fat lady in a black dress.
Anyway, did I not get lalldie when they found out at home?

Another glimpse of the show and its admission charge . . .

. . . A Geggie-man hurled his cart, and a monkey with it, round near
us, and you paid a bottle to see his moving-picture show . . . great!

The Penny Geggie stuck to streets and playgrounds, but buskers
penetrated the closes into back courts and were a source, not only
of entertainment, but also of inspiration to imitate.

We'd great people coming round. There was a hurdy-gurdy man and
there was one lot always started off with 'I'll sing a hymn to Mary'.
Then if it wasn't a very Catholic tenement they went on to 'The Old
Rugged Cross'. There was a coloured man too, came to Parson Street
(there weren't many coloured folk around at that time so he was quite
exotic) he used to come with a horn gramophone on a pram, and you
threw your pennies out the window. He looked quite poor but they
said he left a lot of money.

Alex Donnelly was on the receiving end of the pennies for a time.

Things were bad in the slump. We'd no work. Even my fiddle was in
the pawn. I got together with a friend that was a good singer and got
the lend of wee Willie Spraggan's fiddle and went busking. We went to
Paisley first where nob'dy knew us. We didn't make much, but enough
to get my fiddle out the pawn. I went on my own after that and did
better. Eventually I went all over Ireland . . . knew the purser on the
Irish boat and got over for five shillings. Played for the passengers on
the way over. When I got a job back in Glasgow again I chummed up
wi' an accordionist and we went out on Saturday afternoons to make
a bit extra.

There's scarcely a rememberer of tenement days who didn't
emulate the buskers and hold their own back-green concerts. Eileen
Reilly was prominent (in a refined way) in their troupe.

Great these concerts were. I couldn't sing so I used to say poetry. Mind
you, my father had taught me how to whistle. But my mother was
indignant. It was not ladylike to whistle and the idea of me doing
it in public had her speechless. There's a saying 'The two things
God hates most are a crowing cock and a whistling hen.' So God

and my mother had the same idea. Anyway, the kids from the other closes would come to your concert and pay a penny. There'd be your singers and reciters and some that did their dancing-class dances.

Such concerts were often charitable efforts . . .

. . . maybe for a book or a game for someone in hospital. That was very unselfish because it was usually the fever, and everything got burned so you couldn't get a shot of it after.

At our concerts they paid at the close-mooth, then came through and sat on the ground. I always mind one hefty wench Bridie Cooney, covered and jinglin' wi' medals doin' Irish dancin'. Light as a feather too, she was.

Down on the back-greens after dark, other unwitting, in-house entertainment was provided by the midgey-men on their rounds.

I used to watch them from the window if I couldnae sleep. They came round with lamps on their heids for the dark and made a right racket clattering the bins. And woe betid you if it had of been your job to bring in the clo'es line that day, for the midgeys wi' baskets on their back, would just take their knife and slash the rope to get by . . . they'd of got their throat strangled if they'd walked into it. We'd midgey-rakers too, lookin' for treasures.

Not a fat living in days when every ha'penny was looked at twice and every article used till it was worthless, then fliped and used again.

Then it was on to the Big-Time . . . real, paying shows, although some future stars had got their start right there in the back-courts.

Some of your back-green singers went on to be proper music-hall turns (maybe no' always that proper), and some got started in wee local shows. Will Fyffe, Harry Lauder and Harry Gordon did their early stand-up comic turns in these wee Glasgow halls.

And then there were the 'filums'. Nothing about those very early shows, the bioscope and the quick 'shorts' suggested the popular rage that cinemas would shortly become.

Film came in as a novelty with a hand-cranked projector. Sometimes it was just a wee extra at the circus.

Alan Dale (later Glasgow cinema manager) had that straight from the clown's mouth, so to speak.

> I know that because my father was in the circus then, at the turn of the century. After the trapeze thing he clowned with his saxophone. He was the one who told me that they used to put up a screen for a short film as one of the items on the programme.

From being a 'flash-in-the-pan' novelty 'the pictures' soon became a part of everyday life and certain names and cinemas began to be household words, certainly in the Roche home.

> When I was very wee th'was the Electric Theatre in Argyle Street (no' the Eglinton Electreum. That was Eglinton Street) and th'were the Panopticon in the Trongate . . . used to be the Britannia Music Hall. I always remember seein' Stan Laurel in his first film there.

Some recall those two halls with affection, others with shocked awe.

> I always remember my brother taking me there. My, it was a wild place! It was yon German one, Marlene Dietrich. In this film she'd gone into the water and all her clothes were sticking to her. I was very embarrassed.

But Glasgow flocked to see Marlene and her like, skuddy or not. And by the 'twenties picture-houses were mushrooming . . . fancy sophisticated palaces in the city, a plethora of back-street bug-houses, and small cinemas between the two.

> A lot of early cinemas were just built in back-courts of tenements and came through to the front on to the street. They said the City Fathers approved of this because the pictures should be where the people were. There was an idea that when the cinema came there was less drunkenness.

Some of those were the kind that Mr. Bill Bain recalls.

> When I was wee there was a picture house that I thought was called the Matinee. It was really the Crownie. It was bench seats and they used to grab you under the oxters and shift you along to get more in. You tried to spread your bottom out to get more space. There was another place called the B. B. Wellington Palace and you got in for a penny on

Saturday afternoons. The manager there was a big-big giant and he'd a long pole he poked you with to close up in the queue.

In the cinema's heydey there were eleven big cinemas in the city centre square mile, with outwardly radiating circles to the furthest suburbs. In Shawlands three miles out, an inner suburb no more than a mile long and a furlong wide, there were seven. Ann Hutchison remembers them all.

Sometimes I went to the Wee Pollok beside the river. Then Mr. Noble had his place that was a mixture of music-hall turns and wee films. Wasn't really his. He just looked after it. There was a wee toty hall between Shawlands Cross and Minard Road. No' many people mind of it. And th'was the Camphill behind the Marlborough. The big ones was the Waverley, the Embassy (it was newer) and the Elephant. D'you mind the wee lit-up elephant outside that used to toss up his trunk wi' the wee umbrella on the top:

I used to go a lot to the pictures in Shawlands . . . Jeanette MacDonald in her crinolines and Nelson Eddy and Rudolph Valentino. It was historical films in old-fashioned clo'es that I liked the best.

But they weren't everyone's favourite. Some who had a surfeit of those costume dramas moaned at the prospect of more.

Och, no' another of them filums where the guy writes wi' a feather! I like Westerns.

That cinema heydey is long gone now, but memories of it linger with the likes of Lily Joseph.

I liked the pictures in the days of Douglas Fairbanks and Mary Pickford, Gloria Swanson . . . good clean pictures. I went regular. But it must be ten years now since I saw a film, except on the television and they're not always very nice.

Some, like Janet Kay, thought they were a cut above the cinema and preferred the genteel ambience of the theatre, though they defected occasionally.

Oh yes, for Spencer Tracy. *Anything* with Spencer Tracy. But mostly it was theatre. My friend and I thought we were a bit superior going to the Brandon Thomas rep. and the opera. Mind you it was just the gods. We would be earning about eighteen shillings a week at the time. You knew everybody in the gods . . . not their names right-enough, but you spoke to them week by week.

There were audience skills and techniques early learned by theatre-goers. You didn't just shuffle in, show your ticket and sit quietly down. Oh dear no!

When it was the opera you'd been standing in the queue eating your sandwich. Then the doors opened and you went belting up the stair, because it was 1/6d 'early doors' and 2/3d 'ordinary doors'. 'Early doors' you got your choice of seats. When they played the National Anthem at the beginning you could always tell the regulars because they sat down at the beginning of the last line to get their bottoms on the bench first . . . the rest had to wiggle theirs in between as best they could. It was hot too. You sat fair steamin' up there in the gods.

When the Brandon Thomas Players folded, the two drama addicts graduated to permanent weekly seats for his successor, Wilson Barratt . . .

. . . and you went dressed with your best coat and hat, and your handbag under your arm. You wouldn't have *insulted* Wilson Barrett or Richard Matthews by going casual. You'd your tea at the interval too. Oh, we werenae-half ladies by then! The company had Kitty de Legh and Phyllis Barker, George Larchet and Simon Lack (when he was still just Alex McAlpine from Tollcross). I had a real crush on Wilson Barrett. Oh my, they were terr-ific, wonderful!

Lily Balarsky had graduated from her 'peeping teenie' days across to the Metropole, and become an enthusiast for the drama too.

Early in the century there was a group of Yiddish players used to go round . . . travelling players performing Jewish plays, mostly Yiddish. They came to the Princess's Theatre and the immigrants flocked to see them. They didn't get paid much and they'd to rely on Jewish families to give them hospitality. Dalnikoffs, the leather merchants, were one family that was specially good at giving them lodgings. Later there were the Avrom Greenbaum Players. They didn't just stick to Jewish plays, but a lot of them were.

Not everyone had the money to be regulars at theatre or cinema and when hard times came even those who had managed an

occasional night out had empty pockets. But sometimes help was
at hand.

> During the General Strike in 1926 there were special free concerts for
> the workers. My father was a railwayman on strike and I went with
> him to one of these in a hall somewhere. I always remember a man
> singing 'Rocked in the Cradle of the Deep'.

Cheek by jowl with the eleven big cinemas and nine theatres in
that central Glasgow mile, there were ten dance halls, for Glasgow
was one of the hoppingest, skippingest, Palais Gliding cities in
Europe between the wars. Indeed it claims that, for its dance-halls
and other entertainments 95% of all Americans on leave in Britain
in the Second War came at some time to Glasgow. Young Glasgow
was serious about its dancing.

> When I was young, coming up a bit, we used to go to McEwan's
> Dancing Class in Pollokshields Burgh Hall, so when you went to the
> Plaza, you could do it.

Bunty Angles studied the steps and picked them up as she went
along. She too favoured the Plaza, though not always.

> On Saturday nights I went to the dancing. You were working late in
> the shop so you went straight there . . . had your dancing shoes at
> work with you, and something for your tea. Or maybe John, my
> young man, would bring them when he came to meet me. There
> was the Plaza for big nights out and tea-dances in the afternoon, if
> John's shifts fitted in.

Tuesday afternoon being what they called in Glasgow 'the half-
shut-day' for big stores, shop workers trooped to the afternoon
Plaza.

> An' if your fella wasnae off-shift you just danced wi' your China.

That wasn't for Bunty Angles though.

> The Plaza was nice with the coloured fountains and wee tables. John
> and I liked it there. But we went to the F. and F. Palais in Partick too,
> and Green's Playhouse, the Locarno, and the Albert in thingummy
> street. It was the Lancers and the Charleston then with your legs all
> kicking and twisting from the knees. Later it was foxtrots and waltzes.
> I loved the dancing.

Providing some of the music for the dancing craze was that resilient Victorian, Alan Dale's father. From runaway sailor to trapeze-man to clown, he turned to straight music with his saxophone.

He got a band together and played for gigs and for the dancing. Must've been quite old then, but the bands began to go out and, in the end, he and my mother just ran a boarding-house for actors and music-hall people.

Alex Donnelly, now ninety, still plays a lively fiddle, saxophone and keyboard, up in his own eyrie in a high-rise flat, but in his day he too played for the 'jigging'.

Sometimes you got dressed up wi' your bow tie an'that, when it was a late-night dance or a wedding at the Marlborough or the Grosvenor. You just took every job you could get.

There was music in the parks too, at the bandstands where the young hovered looking for their clicks. Struan Yule's local bandstand was in Alexandra Park.

May to September the bands played there. The notices said WEDNESDAYS and FRIDAYS, D.V. and W.P. There were Dixie Minstrels too and a troupe called 'Song Salad'.

The young still dance and listen to their music, watch their drama. To an older generation their pleasures are almost incomprehensible . . . to those reared on neat little shoe-bags, formal steps and small courtesies, their dancing seems wild and disjointed, their music raucous. But it is *theirs*, and half-a-century from now, they will surely look back as we do, with tenderness and laughter at the seriousness with which they took the entertainment of their youth.

18
Tennis Bats and Golf Sticks

We promised young Christina in an earlier chapter that while there would be precious few more tomboy games in the street, there would surely be a diversion or two in and around the house for a thirteen-year-old with a tribe of brothers and sisters to 'mother'. Roaming far from home was over but you could still do your five-stones.

> Aye, I'd run for miles with my gir' in my young days, but then, after, it was things like chuckies. I mind being in Craigton Cemetery one day with Chrissie . . . down to see our mother's grave . . . and–here, we saw the place where they did the grave-stones.
> 'Come on' says I. 'See if he'll make us chuckies'.
> 'I'm no' going to make you chuckies,' says he.
> 'Well that's tellin' me straight,' says I.
> 'If I mak' you chuckies, that wee lass there'll want chuckies, and then you'll go and tell some others and I'll have a queue at my door for chuckies'.
> He didn't know Chrissie was my sister. So we didnae get the nice marble chuckies . . . just had to play with wee stones.

Chuckies were versatile, you could carry them in your pocket, play them indoors or out and there was no particular shape they had to conform to. Everyone had them. But some better than others.

> You could just play wi' wee stones, but I had awful nice chuckies. They were an inch square maybe, and corri-gated. Four of them, a white, a brown, a green and a red, and you'd your jaurie on the floor. You'd to throw them up and before they came down, pick up the jaurie and see how many of your chuckies you could catch.

Children of an earlier age were more familiar with what might lurk in their hair . . . even in heads where the pigtails were excruciatingly tight, pulled back so hard that the temples rose in itchy lumps. So the rhyme that went with some games of five-stones was not the insult it might seem in the 1990s.

> See the wee beasts in your heid
> See the tate in mine
> See the wee beasts in your heid
> See there's nane in mine!

That last line came from Jack Roche with the triumphant shout that meant carpet or pavement was clear of chuckies. Even at ninety-odd, Mrs. Agnes Grove can think wistfully of her set of stones.

> I wasn't good at them mind. They used to fall off my hand. But I often wish I'd kept my chuckies. They were nice.

Playing shops was another indoor/outdoor pastime and especially engrossing when like Miss Isobel Horn, you stocked your own store.

> I used to sit on the back step and champ down wee bits of sandstone into smithereens or powder. If the stone was white that would be sugar or sugar lumps, or maybe cheese. If it was red, that might be mince. I liked 'shops'.

Then there were the collections. You might be in a room-and-kitchen or a single-end . . .

> . . . but there was aye room for your scraps, losh me, aye! Or maybe later your foreign stamps. I kept my scraps in a Coronation tin . . . George the Fifth it would be. Was that about 1911? I'd angels and fancy ladies, and some big baskets of flowers that you could change for a whole-lot of wee scraps from other people . . . enough to cover yours to make the bargain fair.

For boys one of the favourite collections was of cigarette cards.

> D'you minda cigarette cards eh? 'Hey Mister, gaunnie gie's your cigarette photie?' You used to watch for men takin' out their fags . . . workmen an' that. I'd a lot of sets, battles and footballers and inventions. And one time th'was wee silk flags and wild flowers . . . Kensitas that was. They were nice.

There were young capitalists of course, who collected money, as entrepreneurs with small businesses in lemonade bottles, or as fire-goys to Jewish neighbours. And, like John Adamson, they often banked their takings.

I loved my Golliwog bank. You're no' allowed to say that now, but if you knew how much I liked that nigger-bank you'd know it was a love-name. He was metal and he'd a red enamel jersey, and he had a bent arm wi' an open hand you put your penny in. Then you pushed down a wee stubby lever behind his shoulder and the hand came up to his big open mouth so's the penny got swallowed. There was a grating on the bottom you unscrewed to get at your money.

But however much the bank, any bank . . . was loved, there was no showing him off.

You werenae allowed to bring it out in front of your aunts or uncles or visitors for fear they would think you were cadging for money.

Stamps and chess and dominoes were for the patient and painstaking and in the 'teen years of the century and again in the thirties, there was another craze that delighted those who could wait for results.

I once had a goldfish that died and we'd a lovely funeral and everything for him. But-here I was awful upset and it was my granny said I should make a coalie-plant in the bowl. You put in bits of coal in the bottom and then you sprinkled on the top some wee bits of chemicals that she sent me to Ogg's the chemist for. After a few days it grew lovely fl'rescent mould in all different colours and patterns. I wish't I could get that recipe again. It was beautiful.

So, wet days and winter nights, there was plenty to do indoors. They played houses and hospitals, schools and shops and concerts. They made makeshift cots and prams and chairs for the dolls that were their babies and patients, pupils, customers and audiences. Alison Dow had two particular dolls.

One was just stuffed and had a cloth face and I played with her all the time. She wasn't bonnie but I loved her. The other was beautiful. She had a china face, nice yellow hair and jointed legs. She'd a green velvet coat with fur trims and a fur hat. I only played with her when we'd visitors or on Sundays . . . or sometimes I got to bring her out when we were playing houses and we needed her to be the minister's wife.

Most dolls had names but Peggy Carson's was a modern mystery-miss from overseas.

I'd a doll that came from my auntie in America. That would be about 1920. She'd an Eton crop and long-long legs. (No' my auntie . . . the doll!) She'd a blue wardrobe with hangers and a whole-lot of clothes in it. She was different from other dolls. But, funny thing, I never had a name for her.

There were other little mothers who had to do without real dolls and adapt dish-mops, dressing them up with handkerchiefs and copying-ink faces. Some few like the little Rodgers had no dolls.

Och no! We'd no toys at all. We certainly hadn't a doll in the house. No money for that sort of thing.

They did have hens in the back court that others might have envied. They had a real house too, and a real shop out-front. But there the play was all too earnest.

You see, at thirteen, I was in the house . . . and my sister, at a wee bit older, ran the shop.

They don't do too much learning by rote nowadays, not even much learning of poetry to recite for a sweetie or a gold star on a Friday afternoon. But maybe it was that old abandoned practice that spawned all the counting-out rhymes we've looked at elsewhere, or that gave birth to singing games, maybe even produced the chants for being as rude as they dared in Edwardian times when they hurled insults at offending peers.

Singing games could be played in street, playground or backyard (or at parties if the family finances ran to 'sangwidges', reading-sweeties, jellies and iced gems). Of some of the games only the jingles are remembered now, What was this for . . . ball . . . skipping?

Hey, gee-up my cuddy
My cuddy ower the dyke
And if you touch my cuddy
My cuddy'll gie you a bite.

Or this obscure story?

> My mither mendit my auld breeks
> And wow! They were a-diddy-o
> She sent me to get Mally shod
> At Robbie Tamson's smiddy-o
> The smiddy staun's ayont the burn
> That wimples through the clachan
> There's ne'er a time that I pass by
> But whit I fa' to lachin'-o

They may not know what that meant but, to a man or woman, they can tell you how to play Bee-Baw-Babbity, Water Water Wallflower and Queen Mary.

> Water water wallflower, growing up so high
> We are all maidens and we must all die
> Excepting Carrie Grossmith, the youngest of us all
> She can dance, and she can sing, and she can knock us all down.
> Fie, fie, fie-fie shame, turn your face to the wall again.

> Queen, Mary, Queen Mary, my age is sixteen
> My father's a farmer in yonder green
> He's plenty of money to dress me in silk
> But there's nae bonnie laddie will tak' me awa'

More of a street game, since it called for outdoor space, was Eely Ally-o

> There's a big ship sailing through the Eely Ally-o
> The Eely Ally-o, the Eely Ally-o
> There's a big ship sailing through the Eely Ally-o
> On the nine-*teenth*-of-De*cem*-ber.
> You played that all joined in a line behind a leader wi' her's arm makin' an arch against the wall. Then the rest went under till you were in a tight curl, then you'd unwind . . . singin' away all the time.

'Singing-games' . . . the very words conjure up a picture of merry innocence . . . a romp of little girls in crisp pinafores, woollen stockings and tammies, or small boys in button-bunnets, playing happily like sanitised children in a pantomime with never a sour note. The truth is, of course, that they rejoiced in rude little rhymes, sang corrupted versions of their 'nice' songs and threw

venomous insults at each other with even more enthusiasm. One
just had to trill two parody-lines of a popular classic to have a sarky
reply from another to match it.

> La Donna mobile
> My legs are wobb–ely . . .
> No bloomin' wo–ender
> Look what they're u–ender!

There were sniggers too about the luckless Mrs. McGuire, who
apparently didn't know where to put herself, as the saying goes.

> Mrs. McGuire sat on the fire
> The fire was too hot, she sat on a pot
> The pot was too wide, so she sat on the Clyde
> And a' the wee fishes ran up her backside.
>
> Th'were all sorts of wee rude things you could say too . . . Not bad
> things really, but your mother didn't like to hear you say 'Christopher
> Columbus!' . . . near swearing she thought that was.

She might have been a deal more horrified if she had heard her
offspring giving lip to the guardian of the law himself. It was no
doubt lucky for them that he kept his cliping for more serious or
dangerous offences.

> When I lived in Cumberland Street, it was teeming wi' lads. We played
> ever'thing right enough but specially footb'll. Then we'd get chased by
> big Rab the policeman . . . and we'd make faces and yell things at him.
> 'Yous are awful cheeky gettin'. I'll tell your Ma's'
> But he might just give you a skelp on the bahoochie and tell you no'to
> play footb'll in the street. He never did tell your Ma . . . just gave you
> lalldy again the next time. Then till he was round the corner you just
> played keepie-uppie in a close.

If Rab the Cumberland Street policeman didn't clipe, other
malicious peers did. But not without retribution. Jack Roche
wished a vicious fate on his enemy, that had been common
currency to almost all rememberers.

> Tell-tale tit, your tongue shall be slit
> And all the doggies in the town will get a little bit.

And there was slander on the clipe's family too.

Tell-tale tit, your Mammy cannae knit
Your Da, he cannae go to bed
Wi'oot a dummy-tit.

More deadly still in any controversy (though it took Peggy Carson
a while to know what it meant) was the put-down . . .

Your Mammy couldnae run a menauge!*

Actually, since Mammy was no doubt running a family of seven
or eight, managing a capricious range and stretching a thin wage
to gossamer, running a menauge would have been child's play.
Peggy had another wee puzzle when she was only a Mixed
Infant and telling a tall story. Then her granny was in for it
too.

'Och, your Granny's mutch!' someone'd say.
But-here my granny *did* wear a mutch and I didnae know what that had
to do wi' me telling a wee fib.

Squabbling, name-calling, sworn best-friendships, feuds and
mild vendettas kaleidoscoped and slotted in and out of the
bosom-partnerships of childhood . . . but always within a loose
grouping in their own stamping grounds, but as they left peever
and cigarettes cards behind, they began to sample the activities that
would engross some of them in adult life, and to stretch their wings
into other districts.

When we were in the big school we used to go swimming . . . in your
one-piece costume down to your knees . . . went to the baths down
the Green. You took your chittering bites for after, too. A biscuit or
maybe a slice of soft toast from breakfast time. I still like a bit of soft
toast so I do.

Mr. Jimmy Dewar went to the Pollokshaws baths.

You used to go past the steamie women doing their washing, along
the corridor with the smell of chlorine wafting towards you and the
moving green reflections on the water as you got near the pond . . .

---

* A 'menauge' was an arrangement in which a group pooled a sum from each week's
pay, one among them in turn getting the total pooled.

Sometimes if you were swimming in a school gala you got taken through the steamie and down the stair to a kind of basement to get a mug of Bovril.

And a chuckling eavesdropper adds a memory that has stayed with him for over sixty years.

I mind wandering by mistake into the Turkish bath place, and–here th'was a lot of fat, bare women with towels round their heads sittin' in clouds of steam. That was a sight I tell you!

And what about this for sheer whole-heartedness in learning to swim?

I was well up before I learned and this fella in the pub, he says to me he says, 'You cannae swim! Away t'the chemist and buy a pair o' water-wings' So I gets my Captain Webb's Wings and goes to the Greenhead baths. I learned quite quick and later I was in the Scottish championships . . . breast stroke. I still swim . . . 9 o'clock every Sunday morning.

But at ninety Alex Donnelly does confess to being taken by car.

Swimming was all-the-year-round of course, but when the summer came it might be 'anyone for tennis?'

There was an old empty house, a ha'pennyworth on the green tram from us, and it had a kind of rough tennis-court. We used to take wir bats and play there. The lines was all gone so th'was a right lot of squabbling. It was good but, that tennis.

Golf too had its learner devotees . . . on a better site certainly than the run-down tennis-court, but hampered a little in the matter of equipment.

We'd a set of golf sticks in our house and I'd two brothers and two friends. When it was quiet the greenie at the Corporation golf course used to let us in on the one ticket because there was just the one set of sticks in the old bag. That was dandy.

Miss Isobel Horn's early days as a golfer started more conventionally at a bona fide club.

What was Radleigh School later on, was once the Williamwood Ladies' Golf Clubhouse and my friend Keith Ramage and I got joining as junior members. We couldn't have been more than eight. We must have been like two wee rabbits scuttling about the course.

When ponds were 'bearing', skating with blades that they clamped on to their shoes was a favourite ploy. So was cycling . . . in earnest, on organised excursions . . . and rambling. They all had their enthusiasts.

> I was in a cycling club . . . be about 1912. I can remember going out in my white stockings, a wide frilly cotton dress and even a hat . . . a flowery straw hat that you let down your back when you were on the bike. It was that silly really, the white . . . because you always came home with oil on your stockings or on your dress.

Even for those who couldn't rise to a fifth of a set of golf sticks or a tennis bat and certainly not a bike, there was always the likes of the plain running that set Bobby Ford up for a long-term interest.

> There wasn't much 'playing' for me when I was wee. There was too much work on the croft. But I did exercises to make me grow . . . I was very small. And I did a lot of running. Twice I won the quarter mile at the county sports, and then in Glasgow I was always in a club. The Coplawhill Running Club met at the park in Elmvale Street. Best wee park in Glasgow.

But above and beyond them all there was what, to a man, they all called 'footb'll'. They followed their teams, of course, and chanted their rhymes . . .

> Jock McGraw, he never saw
> Where Alan Morton pit the ba' . . .

and others less polite. They played their own games in back-courts, school yards, parks . . . and on the street with bundled jackets for goal-posts. The street could be a hazardous pitch, not so much for the threat of carts or carriages, but because of vigilant and over zealous policemen. Mrs. Mysie Kyle is still indignant on her husband's behalf, indignant enough to keep a treasured document safe in a plastic folder.

> I kept it from 1923. It's from the City Police Department charging him and two other boys with playing football in Wishart Street . . . 'to the obstruction and annoyance of the lieges' whoever they may be! The penalty was to be a twenty shilling fine or *ten days in jail*. That would've been Barlinnie. Just for kicking a wee rubber ball about! The policeman used to have his cup of tea at the Necropolis gate-house and he came out and chased them down the road into the arms of another policeman.

A slip-up over the date of the alleged felony happily saved the boys from either the then huge fine of twenty shillings or the ten days in Barlinnie. But after seventy years his wife is still in shock.

Twenty shillings . . . ten days in jail!

So we'll leave 'playing', with the ninety-four-year-old yearning for her chuckies and another, not much younger, wishing she had the coalie-plant recipe. The years were passing for those youngsters of the early century and beyond, and as the finish of little Christina Rodgers' palmy days brought a previous chapter to an end, we'll let one of Jack Roche's memories draw this one to a close. He was done now with pulling his sleeve over his fist if the teacher made him join hands with a girl in a circle-game . . . he was almost ready to look at them in a new light.

In the school we'd a wee rhyme we tormented the girls with . . .
   Doh Ray Mi, when I was wee
   I used to pare the tatties-o
   Now I am big, and I can dig
   And I can kiss the lassies-o.

And that was them, readier than they knew, for the next of the Seven Ages of Man, and the ongoings they would store up as memories of their courting days.

19
I was a Shabbos Goy

It was all very much you didn't do this and you didn't do that on Sundays. Oh no! You did nothing on the Sabbath. It was the day of rest.

Or was it? For all that resting and refraining, it seems that what they did do occupied every hour and minute of the day.

You didn't play or read ordinary books or anything on Sunday. It was taken up with church and Sunday School and Boy's Brigade, and walking to the services at Langside Hill. That was from the Round Toll at Pollokshaws to the church at the Battlefield monument. That church's just a shell now, but I've an old photo of it and the place beside it where the house stood that they called Queen Mary's cottage. That's where she got resting at the time of the Battle of Langside.

If you did those two miles back and forward two or three times a Sunday, there wouldn't be much leisure left to chafe at the long hours hanging on your hands. In the opposite direction to the one the Dewars took, trooped the Hutchison clan. Ann Hutchison remembers . . .

On Sundays we walked from Pleasance Street away up to Eastwood Church. That was quite far when you were wee. You'd always your best clo'es on . . . your good dress or coat. After the church th'was the Sunday School in the hall beside the cemetery.

Whether or not that was regarded or feared as an intimation of mortality she doesn't add, but goes on . . .

That was what we called the Morning Meeting. I got a prize there . . . a Bible. We'd wee texts to learn from cards, but I don't think I ever got a prize for that. It would've been the good attendance wi' me, not the texts.

One of the kenspeckle worthies around Pollokshaws that she might have passed on her way to Eastwood Church was the 'rival' Secession minister recalled by her neighbour.

> He was a figure that fascinated me because of his clothes. He wore a big Father Brown hat with a brim and a sort of frock coat like Chairman Mao.

For many others, like Mysie Kyle, morning kirk was far from being the only diet of worship.

> We'd two lots of Sunday School as well, one at eleven before the church and another at five o'clock . . . and the evening service. We went to them all. There was nothing else to do.

Janet Kay recalls precisely where she sat in their church, over seventy years ago.

> I went to the two o'clock service with my mother and father . . . sat between them. He was a deacon. We sat in Gallery-pew number 116 I remember.

The journey to church wasn't always as sedate as the procession of Dewars and Hutchisons at Pollokshaws . . . not even for adults. Jimmy Dewar's granny (who must have been born in the middle of last century) had a special dispensation for her Sunday cantrips. She lived with a son a mile or two and several hills away from her kirk, and there was nothing in the Shorter Catechism to answer a little personal moral problem she had.

> My uncle used to take her in his motor-bike sidecar. She was worried about the propriety of that and asked the minister if it was quite decent. Dr. Chisholm just laughed and told her 'of course' and then she was quite happy.

But the Catechism did answer many religious queries. And however imperfectly it was understood by the young of the flock, like the Struan Yule of tender years, in later days the 'jargon' had shaken itself down into comprehensible and wise counsel.

> I remember doing the Catechism. It was difficult then, but I've always been grateful for it as a man.

John Adamson looks back too and considers the delayed-action value of the rote question-and-answer that seemed so pointless at the time.

> Oh aye. In my day it was the Catechism and all that. 'What's Man's chief end? and so on. Then you answered, 'To glorify God and enjoy Him for ever'. Didn't know what it meant then, but funny . . . it's like the Psalms you learned, you find them quite a lot coming into your mind when you're grown-up . . . and all of a sudden you know fine what they mean.

So there was, in those remembered years, a general mood of strictness and convention. Yet here and there were some who were not quite so thirled to jot and tittle of the Law and the Prophets. The Lockie family were allowed one or two not particularly religious pursuits on the Sabbath. Maybe *ever* so slightly Bohemian were the Lockies . . . but only after the correct observances had been made.

> I went to Sunday School of course, in my Sunday best . . . always dressed. I find it difficult at eighty-nine to change from the wee gracious nice ways that used to be normal. Anyway, after the Church and Sunday School we did other things. Our family being musical and 'arty' we had music . . . not just hymns . . . and did a bit of sketching and watercolour painting. We were a bit kind of liberal, I suppose.

Even in earlier twentieth century days than the eighties and nineties, there was a small Muslim population in Glasgow for whom Friday, not Sunday, was Prayers day. Indeed there's an old jingle to remind of the various holy days observed by different religious groups in the city.

> Christians worship God on Sunday,
> Grecian zealots hallow Monday,
> Assyrians Wednesday revere,
> Egyptians, Thursday . . . Friday, Turks.
> On Saturday no Hebrew works.

That last was true of the Balarsky family certainly, and Mrs. Lily Balarsky has warm memories of the Jewish Shabbos.

In winter on Friday we used to get out of school a wee bit early to get
home in time to do all the traditional things. We were sent to Callender's
big bakehouse in Hospital Street, where the night before we would've
put in the Shabbos dinner for cooking in the enormous oven there.
That dinner was the 'cholent'. It was a traditional kind of hot-pot.
Abie Callender had come from Poland as a boy and he'd worked his
way up to having this bakehouse. The whole family worked in it and
delivered bread, schaltz herring and wurst in an ancient van to Jewish
families all over Glasgow. There was a non-Jewish driver of course
(had to be to work on the Shabbos) but he'd picked up quite a bit of
Yiddish during his deliveries because a lot of Jewish people then had
very little English.

Carrying the cholent home was forbidden manual labour so that job was done by a willing non-Jewish neighbour, with the little Lily running alongside sniffing like a Bisto kid. Another friend pressed into service between Friday and Saturday dusk would be a 'Shabbos goy' who would see to the cleaning out and lighting of the Jewish household fire. Jimmy Dewar was a 'goy boy' in his young days.

> When I was a message-boy at week-ends I often went in to do the fire in Jewish households. Sometimes I got a penny or tuppence . . . maybe ev'n more. The Shapiros were a nice family like that.

That 'cholent' would be a sociable meal eaten round the Shabbos goy's fire. But it wasn't always hot-pot that was on the menu. Sometimes it was a tender treat supplied by someone called the Hen Lady.

> It was the Bensons in the Gorbals who supplied poultry specially for Jewish households. Mrs. Benson was a widow and we called her the Hen Lady. Her son and daughter bought hens from the farms round Glasgow and took them to the Jewish slaughter-house . . . the shacht, off Norfolk Street. Then she would come round her customers. In our close it was my mother's house she came to, and we used to pull the other bells to tell everyone that the Hen Lady was there. She weighed them out using your mother's bags of sugar and packets of tea as weights.

She went away after this communal marketing and left the women to their tea and strudel and a good blether.

When the hen-killing Bensons graduated to having a shop in Crown Street, a move vividly recalled by Mrs. Balarsky, the bell-ringing became only a memory, but the cosy chat flitted to the Gorbals.

> I used to get sent to the shop. There was live poultry in cages all round and you queued for your hen and listened to the Yiddish gossip. They used to singe the feathers off at a gas jet that was lit all the time . . . and I remember getting told to mind that I had the giblets safe in my newspaper parcel of hen.

So much for Jewish cultural rituals. But there were Christian customs too, though then as now, not all branches of the church had the same emphases, but Sabbath-day food is remembered by all denominations as 'special' after the mince and turnips and tapioca of the workaday week. Mario Servadei recalls the Italian Catholic Sunday with the social obligations and good eating that were slotted in and around church attendance . . . and shatters a little illusion.

> There was church, always church. Then after that the Italians visited relatives . . . had a special meal . . . maybe chicken, which was quite a treat in those days. Not so much pasta. Italians don't eat as much pasta as people think.

And Peggy Carson . . .

> We'd maybe just sausages or stew through the week but there was always a wee bit roast beef for your Sunday dinner, and then we went to my granny's for tea and always had an iced cake wi' a base of jam and pastry . . . an Albert cake. I cannae think on my granny wi'out seeing that Albert cake.

On the lively Christian wing were the Missioners whose meetings were a bright haven for the hard-worked farm family from Govan.

> We didn't have special clothes for Sunday. There was never enough for that for all of us. So we didn't always get to the church. But we did go to the Paddy Black Mission. We sang choruses there. Y'know the sort of thing, 'I will make you fishers of men' and 'He did not come to judge the world'. And there was 'I'm H.A.P.P.Y.' I always mind those and I still hum them to myself after seventy-five years.

They were H.A.P.P.Y. at a mission in Springburn too.

> Th'was a tram conductor and his wife ran a mission here. 'Seth and Beth' we used to call them. I don't think that was really their names, but the second name was Sykes right-enough. I liked the mission and bawling out the choruses to the piano.

On the other hand, there were grave worshippers with no piano, but who sat under a precentor with his choir and tuning-fork. They were sticklers for what was 'fitting' and would have thought it blasphemy to use the actual words of the Psalmist in their midweek practices. To skirt this problem they resorted to metrical psalm 'ditties' not to confuse worship with rehearsal, which was no doubt as po-faced a performance as that on the Sabbath.

> O mother dear, John Laurie's lum
> When shall it sweepit be?
> For a' the soot right doon it's come
> And spoilt my Granny's tea.

There's a niggling thought that David himself might just have taken a wee staw at such parody. There were other inhibitions too at choir practices.

> The beadle that was the grave-digger as well, sang in the choir with my uncle and he used to say, 'you cannae ask folk how they're keepin' for fear they think you're lookin' to a fee for turnin' ower their grave sods'.

There's a persistent notion of more modern times that for the whole sixty-odd years of the Victorian age, man lost his sense of humour and the absurd, under the impact of a few Sabbatarians. But healthy people are seldom so brainwashed that wit and laughter die on the tongue. In those sober days they were simply enjoyed around moral matters, or rose from the observances themselves. There's many a quiet chuckle among those who remember how much fun came from church life itself.

> I remember in the Sunday School the class being told the story of Mary and Joseph going on the journey into Egypt from Bethlehem. Then they'd to draw a picture of the story. One wee girl had the three of them, Mary on the donkey, Joseph leading it, and a little chap walking alongside carrying a suitcase with the initials J.C. on it.

And Mr. Alistair Cook recalls a generous mite he once put into the Sunday School collecting bag.

> I put in an I.O.U. for a million pounds. I put in a button too and the next week the Superintendent stood up with a dead serious face. 'Thanks very much,' he says, 'to the generous boy or girl who put in such a handsome offering last Sunday'.

He laughs at the recollection and adds . . .

> I'm still trying to pay off that debt in the same church.

A more seriously intended I.O.U. heard about by Jack Roche, was once put on to the plate by a farmer on Glasgow's rural fringe.

> This old boy put in an I.O.U. for a whole pig. My grandpa came from the country and he said it wasnae all that unusual for farmers to promise a bit of money after the next market day. But a pig! He said as well that it was a recognised thing in his old kirk that if the collection was small they just gave it to the beadle . . . a perk like.

A head appears from behind the wing of an armchair in the retirement-complex lounge.

> My father used to tell a story about a minister he knew, scolding his congregation for just putting five-and-tenpence in the plate the week before. 'Heaven's a long ways away,' says-he. 'You'll no' get there for five-and-tenpence'.

It's hard to visualise a Sunday School nativity play ending in chaos.

> I mind hearing about a wee chap that was the Innkeeper. Right wee caution he must've been. Maybe he just forgot his bit or maybe it was just devilment, but when Joseph asked if th' was' any room at the inn' he threw a spanner in the rest of the play when he says, 'Oh aye, plenty room!'

Although most people found humour, warmth and friendship in their kirks and congregations, and in the organisations that kept them together during the week, there were places where pleasure was hard to find.

> After a nice minister that encouraged social things we got one that wouldn't let you do anything . . . not even a Sale of Work, never mind a social . . . no making money and friends at the same time for him! And he put down the football team. He was a right hell-and-thunder man.

Mysie Kyle voted on him with her feet and took her custom to Montrose Street Congregational Church where her young man was a leader in the Boys' Brigade. The B.B. still inspires the loyalty of the very elderly who joined it when it was still a young organisation, and many a man sitting in an Eventide home sports the anchor badge in his lapel even now.

> My father was connected with the Woodside Mission when William Smith started the Boys' Brigade. It was a rare thing for boys. I think it was the B.B. that gave me a bit of discipline.

. . . or perhaps the mother that saw to the white trimmings and sent him off to its meetings. Not long after him, another rememberer was sprucing himself up for B.B. night.

> I was in the B.B. in its quite early days. It was started about 1883 and I would be in it twenty years after that, wi' my wee pill-box, my belt and haversack and a dummy rifle for drill. Later it was my suit and a Glengarry . . . just your Sunday suit, no' a uniform. But you'd to have a straight shed in your hair and it all sleeked back.

Their sisters weren't far behind them.

> I was in the Girls' Guildry, the Glasgow 29th. We wore a white blouse and a blue skirt, and a red sash with pom-poms at the end. We'd round felt hats too.

Peggy Carson was a Brigade lass too.

> We did crafts and things, and bar-bell exercises like yon . . . what d'you cry them . . . majorettes is it?

Many a mother who ran a tight family ship and sent her young out to the uniformed organisations hailed the Band of Hope too, as a power for good, *and* took the pledge herself.

> I was a Little White Ribboner of the British Women's Temperance Association. The 'ribbon' was a wee brooch in the form of a bow. There was a lot of public drunkenness when I was young and some women lived a life of hell with men that drank their wages and came in at the end of the week with nothing. Some of the women went to the Works gate to wait for their men.

Mrs. Agnes Grove's family favoured another temperance organisation, The Order of Rechabites.

> I went to that as a juvenile. You paid three ha'pence a week, a penny for funeral benefit and a ha'penny for the doctor . . . a kind of wee insurance. If you brought in four members you got a badge with 'Faith, Hope, Truth and Love' on it and round the edge 'We drink no wine'.

Wine or not, they could kick up their heels with the best and while mothers were knitting tea-cosies for bazaars, and fathers organising the juveniles as Sons of Rechab . . .

. . . we'd rare dances once a month at the Rechabites' Good Templars' Lodge.

As well as the week-night meetings connected with church life there were Saturday activities for the likes of Jimmy Dewar, provided by well-meaning philanthropists.

There was a Peacock's bakery and rooms in Shawlands and we used to have tea and buns there after a sort of mission youth meeting in the Waverley cinema . . . paid for by the Jam man at Carluke who was far-ben with the evangelicals.

On summer Saturdays there were Sunday School picnics. In a more sophisticated age when the young are as familiar as their elders with half-a-dozen different international cuisines, it's difficult to imagine the thrill of counting off the days until *the trip* . . . of seeing your pinafore starched, of putting a new string on your tinnie and blanco-ing your san'shoes till they were powdery and stiff.

We used to get the tram, a special tram for the trip. and go to Spiersbridge. There was the burn and a field behind the tea-room. And there was a big corrugated barn we went into if it rained.

From the Paddy Black Mission the young Rodgers went to their trip on a coal lorry.

The horses got all decorated and the lorries scrubbed. You just stood up there, holding on to each other and the horses gallopin' away . . . your tins dangling . . . away ready for your races . . . See when you think on it . . . running races for prizes, knockin' your breath out for a wee bun!

Not all Sunday School trips were smiled on by kirky parents. Jimmy Dewar had just a single experience of one of those.

There was a Socialist Sunday School in Pollokshaws, connected someway with the Co-op. My friend Charlie Brown (that lived in one of the single-ends with wooden stairs and landing, and an old well outside at the back), anyway Charlie went to the Socialist Sunday School. My mother didn't like that connection at all. I went with him to a picnic at Saltcoats . . . oh you carried on at a church trip, but that one was a lot wilder. Charlie Brown was clever . . . became a doctor.

Perhaps it's because the old kirks don't mean so much to even the earnest young of the 1990s, the ones who still 'do justice, love mercy and walk humbly' but *without* their God, that old antagonisms are fading between the two largest denominations. Of course there are still the diehards, those who hold fiercely to their own certainties; but few youngsters confront each other now with the old provocative question 'A Billy or a Dan or an old tin can?' to pick a fight with the opposition. Perhaps because there are more agnostic 'old tin cans'.

> I'm a Roman Catholic but I used to like to see the Orange Walk when I was young . . . the drums and whistles y'know? I remember once making my father's hair stand on end by coming in saying how I'd watched it and *waved*.

Eileen Reilly too, found denominational edges blurred on a small embarrassing adventure she once had.

> I went with a friend to a Catholic teachers' meeting in the City Chambers. We went up the marble staircase and 'mingled', eating the nice wee sandwiches and sipping the sherry . . . ever so genteel. Then I caught sight of this man in lace frills and cuffs and black breeches, and I knew it was the Moderator of the Church of Scotland Assembly! and that we must be at a Protestant church reception. We slunk back down the staircase past the flunkies and hot-footed it to the City *Hall* for the right meeting . . . no sherry and nibbles there though.

Perhaps we should close the door on religious affiliations with that ecumenical jaunt, and end with the last few lines from a poem by Struan Yule who, in spite of pinging ink wads at the Whitehill Paddies of his youth, grew up quite literate and took to composing verse. In writing of deep denominational division in time past, he finishes . . .

> But now today's Geneva gown
> At ease with priestly stole, kneels down
> To thank the Lord who made this town
> The Dear Green Place
> That flourishes, to wear the crown
> Of civic grace.

Glossary

Airts	Directions	*Brae*	Hill
All-his-orders	Bits and pieces	*Braw*	Fine
An' all	Too	*Braws*	Best clothes
Argy-bargy	Argue	*Breeks*	Trousers
Arle	Contract by coin	*Breenge*	Barge
A.R.P.	Air raid Precautions	*Bridie*	Meat turnover
Ashet	Serving plate	*Bruit*	To noise or gossip
A.T.S	Auxiliary Territorial Service	*Bumflie/ Bumphlie*	Rumpled, bulky
Aye	Yes, always	*Bundy*	Time-clock
Ayont	Beyond	*Bunnet*	Cap
		Burn	Stream
		Byne/boyne	Basin
Bahoochie	Backside		
Baikie	Ash-can	*Cadge*	Beg, carry
Ba' on the slates	Game over	*Cadger*	Carter
		Cairt	Cart
Barras	Barrow market	*Calm-sough*	Sense of peace
Bawbee	Halfpenny	*Camsteerie*	Unruly
B.E.F.	British Expeditionary Force	*Canoodle*	Cuddle
		Cantankers	Surly grumbles
Belt	Punishment by strap	*Cantrips*	Ongoings
Bethankit	Grace	*Caun'le*	Candle
Biddy	Lady teacher	*Caur*	Car, tram
Bien	Well-off	*Causeys*	Cobbles
Bierers	Bedstead slats	*Caution*	Winning child
Billy	Protestant	*Caw*	Turn (handle, rope etc)
Birl	Twirl	*Chaff*	Chat-up, tease
Blae	Blue with cold	*Champ*	Strain, mash
Blether	To talk nonsense	*Chanter*	Finger part of bagpipes
Bogie	Plank on wheels	*Chantie*	Chamber-pot
Bonnie fechter	Brave warrior	*Chap*	Knock
Bool	Marble	*Chawner*	Prattle

443

Cheeper	Kiss	*Darg*	Day's work, laborious task
Chenille	Cloth with velvety nap (Fr. caterpillar)	*Dawd*	Lump, clod
Cheuch-jean	Twist of toffee	*Dawdle*	Linger
China	Girl-friend	*Deave*	Deafen
Chink	Gap	*Doo*	Pigeon
Chitter	Shiver	*Dook*	Immerse
Chuck	Food	*Doo-lander*	Flat cap
Chuckie	Small stone, pebble	*Doss*	Sleep
Clachan	Village	*Douce*	Quiet, modest, prim
Cladding	Clothing	*Dreep*	Drop from fingertips
Claiy	Clay	*Dreich*	Dreary
Clarty	Dirty	*Driv*	Drove
Clash	Gossip	*Drouthy*	Thirsty
Clawt	Fire rake	*Dry*	Unlicensed for sale of alcohol
Cleek	Hooked rod		
Cleekit	Hooked	*Duds*	Clothes
Cley dod	Clay marble	*Dunkey-man*	Ship's greaser
Click	New girl/boyfriend	*Dunny*	Well, basement, back-close, cellar
Clinker/ *Clinkers*	Stoney cinder, slatey coal	*Dunt*	Blow or knock
Clipe/clype	Tell-tale	*Dyke*	Wall, fence
Clippie	Bus or tram conductor		
Clootie	Cloth	*Easy-osie/* *Eechy-ochy*	Lackadaisical, half-hearted
Clout/cloot	Cuff		
Cludgey/(-ie)	W.C.		
Cock-a-snook	Defy	*Fankle*	Mix-up, tangle
Cocky	Saucy, pert	*Fash*	Agitate, worry
Coofy	Simple	*Far-ben*	Well-in, committed
Coont	Count	*Farden*	Farthing
Coort	Court	*Feart*	Afraid
Coup	Spill	*Fender*	Kerb
Couthy	Comfortable	*Flet*	Pour tea into saucer
Covert	Fine material	*Flit*	Move house
Crabby	Ill-tempered	*Flummox*	Bewilder
Craik	Whine for	*Fly*	Shrewd
Cran	Crane	*Flype*	Turn inside-out
Cratur	Creature, whisky	*Flyte*	Scold
Creeshed	Hit or thrashed	*Foozled*	Bamboozled
Cry	Call, name	*Forby/Forbye*	As well, also
Cubby	Small cupoard		
Cuddy	Horse	*Gallus*	Cocky
		Galluses	Braces
Dan	Roman Catholic	*Galravaitch*	Gad-about

Galumphing	Romping, barging	*Hippins*	Nappies
Gammy	Disabled	*Hullarackit*	Noisy
Gaunie	Will you please	*Humph*	Carry bulky object
Gawp	Stare	*Hurdies*	Upper legs and
Geggie	Magic lantern		buttocks
Genteel	Refined	*Hurdy-gurdy*	Barrel-organ
Gey	Very	*Hurl*	Wheel
Ghoulie	Ghostly	*Hurlie*	Bed on wheels
Gie	Give		
Gin	If	*Jannie*	Janitor
Ginger	Any kind of aerated	*Jaurie*	Stone marble
	water	*Jaw*	Pour out
Gir'/Gird	Hoop	*Jaw-box*	Sink
Girn	Whine	*Jiggin'*	Dancing
Gizinties	Arithmetic	*Jing-bang*	Whole thing
Glaur	Mud	*Jink*	Dodge
Glebe	Manse land	*Jokoh*	Unperturbed
Glob	Globule	*Jotters*	The 'sack', dismissal
Glunchy	Glum	*Jouk/jook*	Dodge
Going-your-	Going-at-it		
dinger	hard	*Kee-hoy*	Hide-and-seek
Gomeril	Blockhead	*Keepie-uppie*	Keeping ball in the air
Goy	Non-Jew	*Ken*	Know
Greet	Cry, weep	*Kenspeckle*	Well-known by sight
Grieve	Farm foreman	*Ken't*	Known
Grue	Shudder	*Kidding*	Teasing
		Kilter	Order
Haddie	Haddock	*Kist*	Chest
Hame	Home	*Kybosh*	Put a halt to
Hap	Wrap		
Haud	Hold	*Laching*	Laughing
Hauf	Half	*Lalldy*	Scolding, punishment
Hearken	Listen (to lessons)	*Leathering*	Beating
Heed	Pay attention	*Loof*	Hand
Heedrum-	Bagpipe music	*Lug*	Ear
hodrums		*Luggie*	Small pail or basket
Hooshie baw	Hush-a-bye	*Lum*	Chimney
Heid-bummer	Boss	*Lumber*	Boy/girlfriend
Heidie	Headmaster		
Hen	Pet name for female	*McCallum*	Ice-cream with
Het	'It' in a game		raspberry sauce
Hidlin's	Secretly	*Majolica*	Green/blue/fawn
High-falutin'	Pretentious		pottery
Hing	Hang (at window)	*Malarky*	Mischief

Mask	Infuse	*Pooch*	Pouch, pocket
Mealie-puddin'	Oatmeal and suet in	*Potottie*	Potato
	skin	*Press*	Shallow cupboard
Midden	Rubbish tip	*Proddy*	Protestant
Midgie/Midgy	Dustbin	*Pulley*	Drying rack on pulley-
Mind	Remember		wheels
Mooch	Scrounge, loiter, prowl		
Moshie	Game with marbles	*Qually*	Qualifying examination
			at 12 years old
Naething	Nothing		
Nane	None	*Rammy*	Row
Nyaff	Insignificant person	*Readin'*	Conversation lozenges
		sweeties	
O.C.T.U.	Officer-Cadet Training	*Redd*	Refurbish
	Unit	*Relict*	Widow
Oose	Greasy, fluffy dust	*Roastin'*	Fierce telling-off
Out-of-kilter	Disordered	*Runty*	Worthless
Oxter	Armpit		
		Sapple	Soapsuds
Paddy	Male teacher	*Scart*	Scratch
Palmy	A blow on the hand	*Scoosh*	Chute of water
Pan-loaf	Posh	*Scuddy*	Naked
Pare	Peel	*Scullery*	Kitchen
Pawn	Ornamental frill,	*Semmit*	Vest
	pelmet	*Shabbos*	Sabbath
Peelly-wally	Pallid	*Shacht*	Slaughterhouse
Peenie	Pinafore	*Shammy*	Chamois
Peerie	Spinning top	*Shed*	Hair parting
Peever	Hopscotch stone	*Shoogly*	Shaky
Penny-jo	Streetwalker	*Shorgun*	Short gown
Perjinkety	Fussy	*Shot*	Turn
Piece	Jam or butter sandwich	*Sine, syne*	Rinse
Pinkie	Small finger	*Single-end*	One-room house
Pinnie, peenie	Pinafore	*Skaffy*	Scavenger
Pinsil	Pencil	*Skech*	Knockout
Pirn	Bobbin	*Skeely*	Skilful
Plowter	Flounder	*Skeff*	Chamfer
Plunker	Big marble	*Skelp*	Slap
Poentry	Poetry (pure Glasgow)	*Skiddle*	Play about with water
Poind/pon'/	Lace point, bed trim	*Skint*	Hard up
pawn		*Skite*	Slip, slide
Poke	Paper bag	*Skivvy*	Overworked kitchen-
Poke-shakin's	Leftovers		maid
Pokey-hat	Ice-cream cone	*Sklim*	Climb

Skuddy	Naked	*Thirled*	Tied
Slider	Ice-cream wafer	*Thole*	Endure
Slitter	Messy work/worker	*Thon, thonder*	Yon, yonder
Smeddum	Vigour, mettle	*Thrapple*	Throat
Snash	Cheek, insolence	*Tim*	Empty
Sod	Turf, clod	*Tocher*	Dowry
Sonsy	Plump	*Toff*	Person considered
Sook	Suck		upper class
Soor	Sour	*Toty*	Tiny
Soor-dook	Buttermilk	*Trams*	Horse shafts
Spirtle	Stirring-rod	*Treckle*	Treacle
Staw	Aversion, grudge	*Trim'ly*	Trembling
Stays	Corsets	*Tumphie*	Childish adult, petty
Steamie	Public wash-house		person, cry baby
Steep	Soak	*Turn-your-*	Somersault
Stint	Period of work	*wilkies*	
Stookie	Stiff		
Stot	Bounce	*Under-duds*	Underwear
Stotious	Very drunk	*Unfankled*	Unravelled
Stramash	Uproar		
Stroup	Spout	*Wally*	Earthenware
Sugarollie	Liquorice	*Wally close*	Ceramic-tiled close
Swank	Show-off	*Wean*	Small child
Swarry	Soirée	*Weel-aff*	Rich, all right
Swop	Exchange	*Wee Murray*	Small bottle of ale
Syne	Since	*What-for*	Scolding, punishment
		Wheech	Whip
Tak' tent	Pay attention	*Wheeching*	Rushing
Tate	Small amount	*Wilkies (to*	Somersault
Tattie, tottie	Potato	*turn the ...)*	
Taury	Tarry	*Winching*	Courting (wenching)
Teabread	Scones and buns	*Windie*	Window
Tenter	Loom attendant	*Wir*	Our
Teuchter	Highlander		
Thibbet	Coarse material	*Yirdfast*	Stuck fast (as boulder
	(orig. from Tibet)		in clay soil)